THE COMPLETE BOOK OF THE DEVIL'S DISCIPLES

OTHER BOOKS BY LEONARD R. N. ASHLEY

The Complete Book of Devils and Demons
The Complete Book of Magic and Withcraft
The Complete Book of Superstition, Prophecy, and Luck
What's in a Name?
Elizabethan Popular Culture
Colley Cibber
George Peele: The Man and His Work
Ripley's "Believe It Or Not" Book of the Military
Authorship and Evidence in Renaissance Drama
The Air Defence of North America (NORAD)
Nineteenth-Century British Drama
Mirrors for Man: 26 Plays of World Drama
The History of the Short Story
Other People's Lives
Tales of Mystery and Melodrama

editor

Phantasms of the Living
Reliques of Irish Poetry
The Ballad Poetry of Ireland
Shakespeare's Jest Book
Soohrab and Rustum
A Narrative of the Life of Mrs. Charlotte Clarke

co-editor

British Short Stories: Classics and Criticism
Geolinguistic Perspectives
Language in Contemporary Society
Constructed Languages and Language Construction

The Complete Book of the
DEVIL'S DISCIPLES

XV

THE DEVIL

Leonard R.N. Ashley

BARRICADE BOOKS / NEW YORK

Published by Barricade Books Inc.
150 Fifth Avenue
New York, NY 10011

Printed in the United States of America.

Library of Congress Cataloging-in-Publication Data

Ashley, Leonard R. N.
        The complete book of the devil's disciples / Leonard R.N. Ashley.
            p.   cm.
        Includes index.
        ISBN 1-56980-087-1
        1. Demonology.   2. Witchcraft.   3. Magic.   4. Superstition.
        5. Feminism.   6. Religion.
        I. Title.
BF1531.A74   1996
133.4'2—dc20   96-24934
                                                                          CIP

Designed by Cindy LaBreacht
First printing

FOR MARK

Those who consider the Devil to be a partisan of Evil and angels to be warriors for Good accept the demagogy of the angels. Things are clearly more complicated.
— Milan Kundera
The Book of Laughter and Forgetting

Table of Contents

Read This First

Margaret Atwood has said that "popular culture is the dream of society; it does not examine itself." However, it needs to be examined, for it tells us a great deal that we need to know about ourselves. One aspect of popular culture that I have studied extensively and written about at length is the supernatural: superstition, magic, witchcraft, the occult in all its forms. The book you hold in your hand is the fourth in a series. The others are called *The Complete Book of Superstition, Prophecy and Luck*; *The Complete Book of Magic and Witchcraft*; and *The Complete Book of Devils and Demons*.

In *The Complete Book of the Devil's Disciples* I collect interesting pieces illustrative of the history of direct contact (or supposed contact) with evil forces of the supernatural in Europe, the Americas, Africa, Asia, and indeed all over the world and throughout recorded history, right up to the witches and Satanists of these last years of the second millennium since Christ came to promise us liberation from the powers of darkness.

But before Christianity there were devils and demons, and outside Christendom they still are deeply imbedded in cultures old and new. Ever since mankind changed an awareness of negative or evil forces in the universe into a conviction that there were personalities which embodied these forces, it has tried in many ways to reach and to persuade or command or placate or annul those forces. Man has tried to deal with The Devil in at least two senses of the verb. He (or especially she, for almost ineradicable sexism has consistently blamed women in their supposed weakness for dabbling in the forbidden) has ventured bravely or blindly into the unknown in search of power. Others have feared, deplored and despised this and avenged themselves upon the practitioners of black magic. The conservative have regarded all, from the necromancers and signers of pacts with The Evil One to those who deal in fortune-telling or lucky charms or channeling or table rapping, as desperately deluded or as dangerous enemies of the human race. They have attempted to eradicate them as in league with the powers of darkness. The struggle is a history written in blood and fire. It is a history with mountebanks and martyrs and almost incredible events and people. It is even involved in Green movements today.

I attempt to explain in my first book the origins and nature of superstitious thinking and in my second the application of the former to the search for power and advantage in magic and witchcraft. In the third volume I show how the concept of The Devil developed in the Judeo-Christian world and how all kinds of devils and demons populate the imagination of peoples around the globe. I trace patterns from the earliest transformation of the concepts of evil and pagan gods and goddesses into Satan, The Adversary of God, and all his fallen angels and demons "who roam through the world seeking the ruin of souls." I describe how in other cultures demons are believed to bring everything from disease to justice. I conclude with horrifying reports of alleged Satanic child abuse and other terrors of our own time.

In this companion volume to *The Complete Book of Devils and Demons* I have room for much material of value that I could not fit in the earlier book and for information on the would-be servants of evil powers in their depredations, their destruction in witch hunts, their impact on the way we look at life as reflected in literature and folklore. I have delved deep to find these facts and fancies for you.

I have cited elsewhere—it is so true!—Dr. Samuel Johnson's dictum that "a man will turn over a whole library to make one book." I have done just that to make this, as well as many another, book. I want to express my sincere thanks to all the scholars who have written before on these subjects and all the librarians at Brooklyn College and elsewhere in the United States as well as abroad, who have assisted me to find and use the treasures stored up. I cannot undertake to thank them all by name, but my gratitude is none the less. Useful references which are still in print or are reasonably accessible to modern readers I have often cited in my text; however, I emphasize that my readership is intended to be not the expert seeking bibliography (although I believe any expert will in these pages find authoritative and accurate material and indeed learn something new) but the general reader seeking pleasure as well as profit. For that reader I have adopted in this whole series as user-friendly a format and style as I can command. I am encouraged by the critics who have been so kind as to praise not only my industrious scholarship —*Publishers Weekly* greeted the first book in the series as a masterpiece of reliable and broad-based research— but to remark on how readable and entertaining, as well as educational, these books are.

But that is for you to judge, and if this volume is appreciated as much as the others before it, you may look forward, perhaps, to more in the series. If you have comments, corrections, congratulations, or criticism to offer about *The Complete Book of the Devil's Disciples*, please feel free to write to me in care of the publishers. I know from experience that it would be unwise to promise to reply to each letter, but you have my assurance that I read and carefully consider all correspondence, and if this book enjoys reprinting (as others have done) I shall have future opportunity to add what is missing or correct what is in error, thanks to the assistance of my readers. Getting things right is everybody's business. I attempt to do this in a book for people like the Salvation Army lady named Luci Swindell I heard of and who said: "My favorite thing is to learn something new while having a good time."

To each of you, I commend my newest book. I hope you will enjoy it and learn from it. I and my patient editor, Eileen Brand, have done the best we can to make the book correct and companionable. Any errors are my fault.

God bless. Blessed be.

Cena Domini, Maundy Thursday, 1996

King James VI of Scotland personally presides at the trial of Agnes Simpson and other witches at North Berwick (1590).

1

The British Isles and Ireland

WITCHCRAFT IN ENGLAND GOES BACK A THOUSAND YEARS

Actually, a lot longer, but the earliest record I can find is in *English Historical Documents I* (ed. D. Whitlock, second edition 1979). A document of A.D. 970 mentions a witch who harmed people by sticking pins in dolls. She was drowned and her son was banished from the kingdom.

SKEPTICISM ABOUT WITCHES

Not all Englishmen and women believed in women who sold their souls to The Devil, though most had some belief in folk magic and sorcery, and the early literature has some milestones in challenging the prevailing opinions about witchcraft. We can mention one example for each of the sixteenth, seventeenth, and eighteenth centuries:

Scot, Reginald, *The Discouerie of Witchcraft* (1595)
Webster, John, *Displaying of Supposed Witchcraft* (1677)
Hutchinson, Francis, *An Historical Essay Concerning Witchcraft* (1718)

EARLY ENGLAND

The shamans of the Celts, Danes, and Norse, and the traditions of the Druids and other native religions, did not disappear in a flash when St. Augustine arrived to make angels out of the Angles. Robert Henry's six-volume history of early England says that "after the Anglo-Saxons embraced the Christian religion, the clergy were commanded by the canons to preach very frequently against diviners, sorcerers, incantation, and all the filth and wicked dotages of the Gentiles."

Note that first in the list came "diviners." John of Salisbury (d. 1180), one of the most learned men of his time, identified thirteen kinds of divination. The English seemed to like all of them; and witches, wizards, and such were often called upon to foretell the future by fair means or foul. Other early witchcraft may have involved rites of the Moon Goddess or other pagan survivals and certainly involved the casting of spells, making of magic potions, and even diabolical pacts (because those had been noted in Christianity in Rome hundreds of years before Christianity was brought to the British Isles). In fact, however, any recourse to older gods would have been looked upon by most Christian clerics as intercourse with The Devil, though some pagan traditions and practices were quietly and effectively integrated with Christian ones as simply as gargoyles were put on cathedrals along with statues of the saints.

TAKING OVER THE TEMPLES

St. Bede (too often given the lower title of The Venerable) in his *Ecclesiastical History* quotes the letter that Gregory the Great wrote to the Abbot Mellitus, whom he was sending to help St. Augustine convert the English. The wise pope advised that the "idol temples of that race" be converted to Christian shrines and, "because they are in the habit of slaughtering much cattle in sacrifices to devils," new ceremonies be given by the new magical agency to converts from the old one.

> Do not let them sacrifice animals to the devil, but let them slaughter animals for their own food to the praise of God. . . . It is doubtless impossible to cut out everything at once from their stubborn minds. . . .

Keith Thomas in *Religion and the Decline of Magic* writes of "the notorious readiness of the early Christian leaders to assimilate elements of the old paganism into their own religious practice, rather than pose too direct a conflict of loyalties in the minds of the new converts." Thus did Christianity accommodate in the shift from paganism, and thus (when Christianity failed to take hold or otherwise was found wanting by some) witchcraft was facilitated in its growth as a heresy or (one might say) a religion to challenge Roman Catholicism.

An Anglo-Saxon sorcerer at work, from an
ancient MS.

SILENCING BRITISH WITCHES

It appears that in Dorset, late in the days of the Roman occupation of Britannia, the locals found a way to keep the witches from calling on their evil god or cursing other humans. The witches had their heads cut off and their lower jaws removed.

This is the explanation that archeologists offer for the tomb found containing the decapitated corpses of a number of old women. Cutting off heads is a well-known way of making sure that vampires will not reanimate, but taking away the lower jaw so that witches cannot utter their curses and spells is novel.

CELTIC METAMORPHOSES

There are stories in Celtic mythology about the power of gods and goddesses to assume both human and animal forms. The Formors, for instance, those hideous creatures that lived beneath the waves and caused drought and bad weather and many other evils, were extremely ugly, but one of their number is said to have seduced many by appearing as an extraordinarily handsome young man. The Irish war goddesses were sometimes wild women and sometimes appeared in the shape of black birds such as crows or ravens. This is probably the explanation of the unusual early Celtic coins that depict a raven sitting on the back of a horse.

Evil creatures could also be affected by certain animals (and even by the evil eye of one of their own, Balor, who had to keep his "bad" eye closed lest he destroy even his evil companions). And they could put a curse or enchantment on mere mortals, turning them into animals. In Welsh we hear in *The Tale of Culhwch and Olwen* that even a king (Twrch Trwyth) could not escape being turned into a wild boar. The children of Lit, in Irish legend (he was a sea god there, unlike the Lear of Shakespeare's play), were changed into swans by a jealous witch of a stepmother.

Some people switching from animal to human and back again, or imperfectly accomplishing that metamorphosis, may account for the Horned God of the British Isles who rules in the Old Religion before (and, some assert, after) the introduction of Christianity by St. Augustine.

All shape-changing was of The Devil and was strictly forbidden by early Christian penitentiaries. Early Christians in Britain and Ireland had no doubt that it went on and that witches could shift from old hag to seductive maiden when required. The Wife of Bath in *The Canterbury Tales* tells of a knight who married a hag who offers to become beautiful for him.

THE BANSHEE

The ghostly woman, whose horrendous wail prefigures a death, brings bad news but cannot, strictly speaking, be classified with devils and demons. The borderline between fairies and devils or between ghosts and demons is often hard to distinguish. The banshee would be grouped by the Irish with lesser sprites such as pixies and leprechauns. The English might associate it with their elves. See Karen Louise Jolly's *Popular Religion in Late Saxon England* (1995).

ANGLO-SAXON ATTITUDES

In an Anglo-Saxon homily against magic and witchcraft:

> We are ashamed to tell all the scandalous divinations that every man uses through the teaching of The Devil, either in taking a wife, or going on a journey, or in brewing, or at the invocation of something when he begins anything, or when anything is born to him. . . . Some men are so blind that they bring offerings to immoveable stones, and also to trees, and to wells, as witches advise, and

will not see how foolishly they do, or how the lifeless stone or the dumb tree may help them, or heal them. . . . Moreover, many a silly woman goes to the crossroads and draws her child through [a tunnel in] the earth, and so gives to The Devil both herself and her child.

Thomas Wright translated this Cambridge manuscript (in slightly different words) in his two-volume collection of *Essays on Subjects Connected with the Literature, Popular Superstitions, and History of England in the Middle Ages* (1846) and he also quotes (his translation) from a Latin penitential of the Middle Ages now in the British Library, which objects to the clergy (especially) doing heathen things. Condemned among others are:

> He who, deceived by the illusion of hobgoblins, believes or confesses that he goes or rides in the company of her whom the foolish peasantry call Herodias and Diana, and with immense multitude, and that he obeys her commands. . . .
> He who makes an offering to a tree, or to water, or to anything, except a church. . . .
> He who shall say any charm in the collecting of medicinal herbs, except such as the paternoster and the credo. . . .

Today the worship of The Goddess is popular both in the United Kingdom and the United States, and we still cling to Yuletide traditions of the Christmas tree, the holly and the ivy and the mistletoe of the Druids, and have superstitions about the yew, the rowan, and other trees. We still say it is unwise to bring mountain laurel flowers into the home; it brings evil. Many believe that there is a resident spirit in this or that place, a *genius loci*, or that some places are more to be avoided than others because of the spirits. Given a choice here in Brooklyn between walking through Greenwood Cemetery or Prospect Park at midnight, the majority of persons would choose the more dangerous course of action and try the park. We now, however, pride ourselves on our freedom from irrational beliefs and would think it superstitious to say even Christian prayers when collecting herbs; those we like to think of as medical, not magical. We say we reject all silly old ideas and yet will take the trouble not to walk under a ladder. A friend of mine walked around a ladder on Madison Avenue in New York and fell into a manhole, breaking a hip.

I received a lot of critical mail when I said on the *Today* show on television that another guest's rabbit's foot was useless. I added that "the rabbit had four of them, and it's dead." People wrote to let me know that rabbits' feet *work*.

We can still say with Thomas Wright, "Strange it is that so many centuries after the abolition of paganism, these superstitions, so intimately grounded upon it, should still keep their hold on people's minds so firmly. . . ."

FLYING OINTMENT

In 1595, Reginald Scot published *The Discoverie of Witchcraft*, which was way ahead of its time in its attempt to debunk superstition. King James (at the time James VI of Scotland) hated the book and had it burned. He would like to have had Scot burned, too. In his book Reginald Scot gives the recipe for flying ointment, a preparation which was supposed to empower witches to soar off to the *sabbat* on their broomsticks (or other phallic symbols). The "R" is the modern R_x of prescriptions.

> It shall not be amiss here in this place to repeat an ointment greatly to this purpose . . . .The receipt is as followeth. R. the fat of young children, and seethe it with water in a brazen vessel, reserving the thickest of that which remaineth boiled in the bottom, which they lay up and keep until occasion serveth to use it. They put hereunto *eleoselinum*, *aconitum*, *frondes populeas*, and soot. Another receipt to the same purpose. R. *sium*, *acarum vulgare*, *pentaphyllon*, the blood of a flitter-mouse, *solanum somniferum*, *et oleum*. They stamp all these together, and then they rub all parts of their bodies exceedingly, till they look red, and be very hot, so as the pores may be opened, and their flesh soluble and loose. They join herewithal either fat, or oil instead thereof, that the force of the ointment may the rather pierce inwardly, and so be more effectual. By this means in a moonlight night they seem to be carried in the air, to feasting, singing, dancing, kissing, culling and other acts of venery, with such youths as they love and desire most: for the force of their imagination is so vehement, that almost all that part of the brain, wherein the memory consisteth, is full of such conceits. And whereas they are naturally prone to believe any thing; so do they receive such impressions and steadfast imaginations into their minds, as even their spirits are altered thereby; not thinking upon any thing else, either by day or by night. And this helpeth them forward in their imaginations, that their usual food is none other commonly but beets, roots, nuts, beans, peas, etc.

FROM AN OLD ENGLISH MS :
CHARM FOR CAPTURING A SWARM OF BEES

Take some earth and throw it up with your right hand,
and so beneath your right foot, and recite,

*I catch it under my foot; I have found
  it.
Lo! earth has power over all creatures,
And against envy and against
  forgetfulness
And against the mighty tongue of
  man.*

And then, when they swarm, throw
  sand over them and recite,

*Settle, women of victory, sink to the
  ground,
Never fly wild to the wood,
Be as mindful of my advantage
As every man is of food and land.*

"THE HEATHEN WORLD HAS VANISHED"

The defeat of paganism and the capture of its places of worship were celebrated by Angus of Clonenagh about the year 800 in Old Irish verse:

*Ind Locáin gabtha
 Dessaib ocus trírib,
It Rúama co ndálaib
 Co cétaib, co mílib.*

Little [pagan] places taken over by twos and threes
are like Rome reconstituted, holy places for
[Christian] people.

*Ro milled in genntlecht
 Ciarbo lígdae lethan;
Ro lín flaith Dé Athar
 Nem, talam la trethan.*

The heathen world has vanished though once it
spread everywhere; the kingdom of God the
Father fills heaven and earth.

Then Irish monks went to the Continent to complete the conquest for
Christianity. There they found pagan superstition also.

GORDDU AND HER FRIENDS

Gorddu was a Brythonic sorcerer, a female demon. Dahut, a continental Brythonic sorcerer, this one from Brittany, caused the downfall of the kingdom by favoring her lover over her father, the king. She haunts the waves, since her father threw her into the sea. The Cannered Noz or "Washerwomen of the Night" are cursed ghosts you can hear near pools and streams at midnight. They are compelled to wash and re-wash their shrouds, trying to get them clean. Long Meg is a British giantess, a demon who can hurl huge rocks long distances. In World War I large guns were named for her just as a huge German cannon bombarding Paris was nicknamed "Big Bertha." The *Ignis Fatuus* is an Irish will-o'-the-wisp that leads travelers astray with a fairy light. The Hag is much worse, a Scottish witch, an ugly old crone in league with The Devil. She can send your soul to hell. On the Isle of Man there is the Gaistrig, a demon half human and half animal and all bad.

Demons in many strange animal shapes (some said) were the imps of the witch Elizabeth Fletcher, charged with other women living in the Forest of Knaresborough of bewitching children. The alleged witches were acquitted and their accuser, Edward Fairfax of Fewstone, was said to have acted out of "malice."

ANGLO-SAXON SUPERSTITION PRESERVED IN PLACENAMES

Placenames sometimes preserve ideas in languages that have died, but not always obviously. Among British placenames we find demons such as the *scinna* or *succa*, the *thyrs*, and elves, dragons, etc.

Shincliffe (Goblin Hill), Warwickshire

Skinburness (Demon-Haunted Fortress), Cumberland

Shacklow (Demon Mound), Debryshire

Thirlspott (Thyrs' Pit), Cumberland

Tusmore (Thyrs' Mere), Oxfordshire

Alvedon (Elf Valley), Lancashire

Eldon (Elf Hill), Derbyshire

Drakelow (Dragon Mound), Derbyshire

Drake North (Dragon Howard), Wiltshire

THE *NORTHAMPTONSHIRE* WITCHES.

Being a true and faithful ACCOUNT of the Births, Educations, Lives, and Conversations,

of

Elinor Shaw, and *Mary Phillips*, (The two notorious Witches)

That were Executed at *Northampton* on *Saturday*, March the 17th, 1705, for bewitching a Woman and two Children to Death. &c.

CONTAINING

The manner and occasion of their turning Witches, the League they made with the Devil, and the strange Discourse they had with him; As also the particulars of their amazing Pranks and remarkable Actions, both before and after their Apprehension, and how they Bewitched several Persons to Death, besides abundance of all sorts of Cattle, even to the ruin of many Families, with their full Confession to the Minister, and last Dying Speeches at the place of Execution, the like never before heard of.

Communicated in a Letter last Post, from Mr. *Ralph Davis, of Northampton*, to Mr. William Simons, Merchant in *London*,

---

Licensed according to Order.

London, Printed for F. Thorn, near Fleet-street, 1705

THE Northamptonshire Witches.

THE Birth and Education, Lives, and Conversations, of Elinor Shaw, and Mary Phillips,

&c.

Sir,

According to my Promise in my last, I have sent you here Inclosed a faithful Account of the Lives, and Conversations of the two notorious

Witches, that were Executed on the Northside of our Town on Saturday the 17th instant, and indeed considering the extraordinary methods these wicked Women used to accomplish ther Diabolical Art; I think it may merit your Reception, and the more, since I understand you have a Frind near Fleet-street, who being a Printer, may make use of it in order to oblige the Publick; which take as followeth; viz.

To proceed in order, I shall first begin with Elinor Shaw (as being the most notorious of the two) who was Born at Cotterstock, within a small Mile of Oundle in Northamptonshire, of very obscure Parents, who not willing, or at least not able to give their Daughter any manner of Education; she was left to shift for her self at the age of fourteenyears, at which time she got acquainted with a Partener in Wickedness, one Mary Phillips, Born at Oundle aforesaid, with whom she held a frindly Correspondence for several Years together, and Work'd very hard in a seeming honest way for a Livelihood; but when she arriv'd to the age of 21 she began to be a very wicked Person talk'd of not only in the Town of Cotterstock where she was Born, but at Oundle, Glapthorn, Benefield, Southwick, and several Parts adjacent, and that as well by Children of four or five Years of Age, as Persons of riper Years; so that by degrees her Name became so famous, or rather infamous, that she could hardly peep out of her Door, but the Children woud point at her in a Scoffing manner, saying, There goes a Witch, there's Nell the Strumpet, &c. which repeated Disgrace, agravated her Passion to such a degree, that she Swore she would be revenged on her Enemies, tho she pawn'd her Soul for the Purchase. To Mary Phillips her Partener in Knitting, who was as bad as her self in the Vices aforesaid she then communicated her Thoughts, relating to a Contract with the Devil. . . . In fine, as these two agreed in their Wickedness, to go Hand in Hand to the Devil together for Company; but out of a kind of Civility, he sav'd them that Trouble for he immediately waited upon 'em to obtain his Booty, on Saturday the 12th of February 1704, about 12 a Clock at Night (according to their own Confessions) appearing in the shape of a black tall Man, at whose approach they were very much startled at first, but taking Elinor Shaw by the Hand he spoke thus, says he, be not afraid for having power given me to bestow it on whom I please, I do assure you, that if you will pawn your Souls to me for only a Year and two Months, I will for all that time assist you in whatever you desire: Upon which he produced a little piece of Parchment, on which by their Consents (having prick't their Fingers ends) he wrote the Infernal Covenant in their own Blood, which they signed with their own Hands, after which he told them they were now as substantial Witches as any were in the World, and that they had power by the assistance of the Imps, that he would send them to do what Mischief they pleased.

I shall not trouble you with what is already mention'd in the Tryals of these two Persons, because it is in Print by your Friend already, but only instance what was omitted in that, as not having room here to contain it altogether; but as to their general Confessions after their Condemnations take as followeth.

The Day before they were Executed Mr. Danks the Minister visited them in Prison; in order if possible to bring them to a State of Repentance, but seeing all pious Discourse prov'd inefectual; he desired them to tell him what mischeivous Pranks they had Play'd, and what private Conference they had with the Devil, from time to time, since they had made that fatal Bargain with him: To which Elinor Shaw with the Consent of the other, told him, that the Devil in the Shape of a Tall black Man appear'd several times to them, and at every Visit would present them with new Imps, some of a Red Coulour others of a Dun and the third of a black Coulour, and that these infernal Imps did Nightly visit each of them; and that by the assistance of these Animals they often Kill'd Men, Women and Children, to the great surprise of all the Towns thereabouts; she further adding that it was all the Delight they had to be doing such wicked Actions, and that they had Kil'd by their Inchantments, and Witchcraft in the space of nine Months time 15 Children, eight Men, and six Women, tho' none was suspected of being Bewitch'd but those two Children and the Woman that they Dy'd for; and that they had Bewitch'd to Death in the same Space of Time 40 Hoggs of several poor People, besides 100 Sheep, 18 Horses, and 30 Cows, even to the utter Ruin of several Families: As to their particular Intreagues and waggish Tricks, I have not Room to enumerate they are so many, only some remarkable Feats they did in Prison, which was thus, viz. one Day Mr. Laxon and his Wife coming by the Prison, had the Curiosity to look through the Grates, and seeing of Elinor Shaw, told her, that now the Devil had left her in the Lurch as he had done the rest of his Servants; upon which the said Elinor, was observ'd to Mutter strangely to herself in an unknown Language for about two Minutes, at the end of which Mr. Laxon's Wifes Cloaths were all turn'd over her Head, Smock and all in a most strange manner, and stood so for some time at which the said Elinor having Laughed Heartily. The Keeper of the Prison, having one Day Threatned them with Irons, they by their Spells caused him to Dance almost an Hour in the Yard, to the Amazement of the Prison, nay, such Pranks, were Play'd by them during their Confinement, that no one durst give them an ill Word, insomuch that their Execution was the more hastened in the regard of their frequent Disturbances, and great Mischief they did in several places of the Town, notwithstsanding their Imprisonment:

They were so hardened in their Wickedness that they Publickly boasted that thir Master, (meaning the Devil) would not suffer them to be Executed, but on Saturday Morning being the 17th Instant they were carried to the Gallows on the North-side of the Town whither numerous Crowd's of People went to see them Die, and being come to the place of Execution, the Minister repeated his former pious Endeavours, to bring them to a sence of their Sins, but to as little purpose as before; for instead of calling on God for Mercy, nothing was heard from them but very bad language: However a little before they were ty'd up, at the request of the Minister, Elinor Shaw confessed not only the Crime for which she Dyed, but openly declared before them all how she first became a Witch, as did also Mary Phillips; and being desired to say their Prayers, they both set up a very loud Laughter, calling for the Devil to come and help them in such a Blasphemous manner, as is not fit to Mention; so that the Sherif seeing their presumptious Impenitence, caused them to be Executed with all the Expedition possible; even while they were raving, and as they liv'd the Devils true Factors, so they resolutely Dyed in his Service, to the Terror all People who were eye Witnesses of their dreadful and amazing Exits.

So that being Hang'd till they were almost Dead, the Fire was put to the Straw, Faggots, and other Combustable matter, till they were Burnt to Ashes. Thus Liv'd and thus Dyed, two of the most notorious and presumptious Witches, that ever were known in this Age.

Saducifmus Triumphatus.

Or, full and plain

EVIDENCE

Concerning

Witches and Apparitions.

In Two PARTS.

The Firft Treating of their

POSSIBILITY.

The Second of their

Real EXISTENCE.

By *Jofeph Glanvil*, late Chaplain in Ordinary to his Majefty, and Fellow of the *Royal Society*.

The Third Edition with Additions.

The Advantages whereof, above the former, the Reader may underftand out of Dr. *H. More's* Account prefix'd thereunto.

WITH

Two Authentick, but wonderful Stories of certain *Swedifh* Witches. Done into *Englifh* by *A. Horneck*, D. D.

LONDON. Printed for *A. L.* and Sold by *Roger Tuckyr*, at the Golden Leg, the corner of *Salisbury-ftreet*, in the *Strand*. MDCC.

Rev. Joseph Glanvil's *Saducismus Triumphans* was often reprinted. First published in 1681.

I am Sir,
Your humble Servant

RALPH DAVIS.
Northampton, March
18th 1705

AN EPITAPH THAT REMEMBERS SORCERY

In a rare book kindly brought to my attention by Paul Beale of Lough-borough, Ray Palmer's *The Folklore of Leicestershire and Rutland* (1985), some "wychrey" tales are told. Old Mother Cooke was hanged for witchcraft in Leicester (1596) and in 1619 there was "a spectacular trial" at the Lincoln Assizes.

Joan Flower of Langham and her two daughters, Margaret and Phillipa, were arraigned. Phillipa was said to have bewitched Thomas Simpson when he did not return her love. Margaret "entered the service of the Duke of Rutland at Bevoir Castle, where she lived in as poultry keeper and laundress, but she was dismissed for pilfering," so she cursed the family. Now this must have been the family of the sixth earl of Rutland (Francis Manners, 1578–1632) and not the sixth duke (Charles Cecil John Manners became the sixth duke in 1857), but the rest of Palmer's story seems generally accurate.

Margaret Flower was joined by three other witches (Anne Baker of Bottesford, Joan Willimott of Goadby, and Ellen Green of Stathern) who sold their souls to Satan for revenge. Palmer writes:

> . . . _____They first made a pact with Satan, pledging their souls in return for power and the aid of familiar spirits, then procured a glove belonging to Henry, the infant Lord Roos [this should be Ros]. This was rubbed by Joan Flower on the back of her familiar spirit, a cat named Rutterkin, then dipped into hot water and pricked with pins. The child died, in 1613. The same treatment was tried on the next-born, Francis, but merely caused illness, so his glove was buried in a dunghill, with the expectation that as it rotted he would decline. He died in 1620. His sister, Katharine, was also ill, but all six women were arrested at Christmas time in 1618 and taken to Lincoln Gaol to await trial. On the way or, according to another account, in the gaol, Joan Flower called for a piece of bread and butter, saying that if she was guilty God would strike her down as she ate it. She indeed fell dead after

biting it, though she may have seized the opportunity to take poison, knowing the likely fate which awaited her.

The others were all tried, and found guilty. Margaret and Phillipa Flower were [probably] hanged, though their fate cannot be verified, since records for the period at Lincoln have not survived. What happened to the others is not known. A number of contemporary publications, including a booklet and a ballad, tell the story. The monument in Bottesford Church to the sixth Earl of Ruland, who died in 1632, his two wives and children, bears an inscription, the only one in England which refers to sorcery. 'In 1608', it runs, the earl 'married Lady Cecilia Hungerford . . . by whom he had two sonnes, both which dyed in their infancy by wicked practise & sorcerye'.

THE DEATH OF MARY, QUEEN OF SCOTS

After keeping her confined for years, Elizabeth I finally signed the death warrant of her arch-rival, Mary, Queen of Scots. Later she lied and said she was tricked into signing.

Three Lincolnshire witches, with their familiars.

Mary arrived at the place of execution dressed in black, as was her custom, but threw off her outer garment and revealed a blood-red dress. She knelt. She prayed. The headsman took a chop at her but only managed to split the back of her head. Those close to this dreadful scene said they heard Mary mumble "Sweet Jesus." The headsman took a second chop and this time almost completely cut her head off. A little sawing and the head was separate from the body. He held it up for the crowd to see. The lips were still moving in prayer. But what shocked the onlookers was not all this gore. It was Mary's pet dog, whom she had carried under her skirts. It ran out from under her skirts and the superstitious thought it was a demon leaving the body.

HALF A DOZEN BRITICISMS AND STRINE EXPRESSIONS

demon uniformed policeman
devil streak of blue thread in a white ship's sail
devil's testicle mandrake root
devil's trumpet jimson weed
dickens devil
Satan's apple mandrake root

OLD VERSES INSULTING BRITISH TOWNS

Deal, Dover, and Harwich,
The Devil gave with his daughter in marriage;
And, by a codicil to his will,
He added Helvoet and The Brill.

OLD BRITISH FOLK SAYINGS

The Devil go with you and sixpence (that way you'll have money and
 company on your journey)
He married The Devil's daughter (and lives with the old folks) (he
 has a wife difficult to deal with)
**That will be when The Devil is blind (and he hasn't got sore eyes
 yet)** (that is a long way from happening)
To hold a candle to The Devil (to be polite to someone out of fear)
The Devil may dance in my pocket (I'm skint, broke)
I'm The Devil's own boy (I'm a mischievous imp)

FEARING THE SAINTS AS WELL AS THE DEVILS

William Tyndale, martyred because he translated the Bible into English in order to improve the understanding of religion, commented that his superstitious countrymen were afraid of saints, who could turn nasty, as well as of devils and demons. "We worship saints for fear," he wrote, "lest they should be displeased and angry with us, and plague or hurt us; as who is not afraid of St. Laurence? Who dare deny St. Anthony a fleece of wool for fear of his terrible fire [a disease], or lest he send the pox among our sheep?"

A HEADLINE FROM A BRITISH NEWSPAPER

"Egyptian Collectors in a Panic" (*Daily Express*, 7 April 1923). The death of Lord Carnavon, responsible for the expedition which opened the tomb of the young pharaoh Tutankhamen, and disaster striking some other associated with the expedition, made some people feel that "The Curse of King Tut" would affect them also unless they got rid of the antiquities they had that had been stolen from Egypt. "All over the country people are sending their treasures to the British Museum," the newspaper reported.

That mechanical devices or even poison gas might have been built into the tomb stretches the imagination. That King Tut could send devils and demons to execute revenge so long after his death goes beyond any credibility.

TOUCHING FOR THE KING'S EVIL

When it was believed that the monarch ruled by Divine Right and was, in effect, God's vicar on earth (a title only popes claim now), it was also believed that the mere touch of the king's hand could drive out demons of disease, especially "the king's evil" (scrofula).

John Aubrey in his seventeenth-century *Miscellanies* reports a story from Elias Ashmole that one Arise Evans (b. 1607) was cured of a "fungous Nose" by kissing the hand of Charles II.

SUPERSTITIONS OF THE SCOTTISH HIGHLANDS

These are worth a book to themselves, but we can mention the habit of using rowan to drive away evil spirits (especially when hung over a baby's cradle), the habit of leaving food out for the spirits to consume (including leaving some parts of fields to wild oats for the use of the spirits), the fear of cats (especially black ones) that might steal souls, the use of iron to ward off evil fairies, the building of bonfires and need-fires, and so on.

WITCHCRAFT NEWS FROM SCOTLAND

When King James wrote a book to answer Reginald Scot's exposé or "discovery" of witchcraft frauds, he believed he knew whereof he spoke. Like French kings (whom witches made impotent by tying knots in cords, the same way they had cursed Mohammed) and rulers everywhere, he was constantly on the lookout for witchcraft directed against himself. He took a personal interest in the trial of one Agnes Sampson, for instance, as *News from Scotland* (1591) reported:

> Within the town of Trenent, in the kingdom of Scotland, there dwelleth one David Seaton, who, being deputy bailiff in the said town, had a maid called Geillis Duncane, who used secretly to absent and lie forth of her master's house every other night. This Geillis Duncane took in hand to help all such as were troubled or grieved with any kind of sickness of infirmity, and in short space did perform many matters most miraculous; which things, for as much as she began to do them upon a sudden, having never done the like before, made her master and others to be in great admiration, and wondered thereat: by means whereof, the said David Seaton had his maid in great suspicion that she did not those things by natural and lawful ways, but rather supposed it to be done by some extraordinary and unlawful means. Whereupon, her master began to grow very inquisitive, and examined her which way and by what means she was able to perform matters of so great importance; whereat she gave him no answer. Nevertheless, her master to the intent that he might the better try and find out the truth of the same, did with the help of others torment her with the torture of the pilliwinks upon her fingers, which is a grievous torture; and binding or wrenching her head with a cord or rope, which is a most cruel torment also; yet would she not confess anything; whereupon, they suspecting that she had been marked by the devil (as commonly witches are), made diligent search about her, and found the enemy's mark to be in her fore crag, or fore part of her throat; which being found, she confessed that all her doings were done by the wicked allurements and enticements of the devil, and that

she did them by witchcraft. After this her confession, she was committed to prison, where she continued a season, where immediately she accused these persons following to be notorious witches, and caused them forthwith to be apprehended, one after another, viz. Agnes Sampson, the eldest witch of them all, dwelling in Haddington; Agnes Tompson of Edinburgh; Doctor Fian alias John Cuningham, master of the school at Saltpans in Lothian . . . .

The said Agnes Sampson was after brought again before the King's Majesty and his Council, and being examined of the meetings and detestable dealings of those witches, she confessed that upon the night of All-hallow Even last, she was accompanied, as well with the persons aforesaid, as also with a great many other witches, to the number of two hundred, and that all they together went to sea, each one in a riddle or sieve, and went into the same very substantially, with flagons of wine, making merry and drinking by the way in the same riddles or sieves, to the kirk of North Berwick in Lothian; and that after they had landed, took hands on the land, and danced this reel or short dance, singing all with one voice,

> Commer go ye before, commer go ye,
> Gif ye will not go before, commer let me.

At which time she confessed, that this Geillis Duncane did go before them, playing this reel or dance, upon a small trump, called a Jew's trump, until they entered into the kirk of North Berwick.

These confessions made the King in a wonderful admiration, and he sent for the said Geillis Duncane, who upon the like trump did play the said dance before the King's Majesty, who in respect of the strangeness of these matters, took great delight to be present at their examinations.

The said Agnes Sampson confessed that the devil, being then at North Berwick kirk attending their coming, in the habit or likeness of a man, and seeing that they tarried over long, he at their coming enjoined them all to a penance, which was, that they should kiss his buttocks, in sign of duty to him; which being put over the pulpit bare, everyone did as he had enjoined them. And having a made his ungodly exhortations, wherein he did greatly inveigh against the King of Scotland, he received their oaths for their good and true service towards him, and departed; which done, they returned to sea, and so home again. At which time, the witches demanded of the devil, 'Why he did bear such hatred to the King?' Who answered, 'By reason the King is the greatest enemy he hath in the world.' All which their confession and depositions are still extant upon record.

The said Agnes Sampson confessed before the King's Majesty sundry things, which were so miraculous and strange, as that his Majesty said 'they were all extreme liars'; whereat she answered, 'she would not wish his Majesty to suppose her words to be false, but rather to believe them, in that she would discover such matter unto him as his Majesty should not anyway doubt of.' And thereupon taking his Majesty a little aside, she declared unto him the very words which passed between the King's Majesty and his Queen at Upslo in Norway, the first night of marriage, with the answer each to other; whereat the King's Majesty wondered greatly, and swore 'by the living God, that he believed all the devils in hell could not have discovered the same,' acknowledging her words to be most true; and therefore gave the more credit to the rest that is before declared.

Touching this Agnes Sampson, she is the only woman who, by the devil's persuasion, should have intended and put in execution the King's Majesty's death in this manner. She confessed that she took a black toad, and did hang the same up by the heels three days, and collected and gathered the venom as it dropped and fell from it in an oyster shell, and kept the same venom close covered, until she should obtain any part or piece of foul linen cloth that had appertained to the King's Majesty, as shirt, handkercher, napkin or any other thing, which she practised to obtain by means of one John Kers, who being attendant in his Majesty's chamber, desired him for old acquaintance between them, to help her to one, or a piece of such a cloth as is aforesaid; which thing the said John Kers denied to help her to saying he could not help her unto it. And the said Agnes Sampson, by her depositions since her apprehension, saith, that if she had obtained any one piece of linen cloth which the King had worn and fouled, she had bewitched him to death, and put him to such extraordinary pains, as if he had been lying upon sharp thorns and ends of needles. Moreover she confessed, that at the time when his Majesty was in Denmark, she being accompanied by the parties before specially named, took a cat and christened it, and afterwards bound to each part of that cat, the chiefest part of a dead man, and several joints of his body: and that in the night following, the said cat was conveyed into the midst of the sea by all these witches, sailing in their riddles or sieves, as is aforesaid, and so left the said cat right before the town of Leith in Scotland. This done, there did arise such a tempest in the sea, as a greater hath not been seen; which tempest was the cause of the perishing of a boat or vessel coming from the town of Brunt Island to the town of Leith, wherein was sundry jewels and rich gifts, which should have been presented to the now Queen of Scotland, at her Majesty's coming to Leith. Again, it is confessed, that the said christened cat was the cause that the King's Majesty's ship, at his coming forth of Denmark, had a contrary wind to the rest of his ships then being in his company; which thing was most strange and true, as the King's Majesty acknowledgeth, for when the rest of the ships had a fair and good wind, then was the wind contrary and altogether against his Majesty; and further, the said witch declared, that his Majesty had never come safely from the sea, if his faith had not prevailed above their intentions.

Small wonder, then, if the witches on the heath in *Macbeth* appealed to King James when it was presented for his entertainment in London by the King's Men.

"THE SPEEDIEST WAY" TO KILL BY MAGIC

Here is the way Elizabethan witches attacked you by sympathetic magic (from a woman burned as a witch for confessing it, as reported in the *Wonderful Discovery of Witches in the County of Lancashire*, 1613):

R. Griffith's illustration of "The Table of the Archangel Michael" from Francis Barrett's *The Magus*.

The Speediest way to take a man's life away by witchcraft is to make a picture [figurine] of clay, like unto the shape of the person whom you mean to kill, and dry it thoroughly.

And when you would have them be ill in any one place more than another, then take a thorn or pin and prick it in that part of the picture you would so have to be ill. And when you would have any part of the body to consume away, then take that part of the picture and burn it. And so thereupon by that means the body shall die.

THE DEVIL CLAIMS HIS OWN

I went to the work of the chronicler William of Malmsbury (*c.* 1098–1143) in search of information on St. Dunstan, who was famous for besting The Devil in a business deal. St. Dunstan brewed beer. The Devil was (as is mentioned elsewhere in this present book) useful in cutting down the local competition from scrumpy, which anyone who has visited Britain's West Country knows is a fairly lethal version of cider. William was a biographer of the saint.

William also tells stories of devils and demons, as what monk of his time would not. One of his tales, retold by Roger of Wendover (d. 1236) and others (such as the *Polyolbion* of Ranulph, translated by John of Terevisa, 1326–1412, sometime vicar of Berkeley). Once a good story made an appeal it was sure to be repeated, even elaborated. Thus grew and spread the legends of The Devil and thus the basic concepts of theology were slowly altered by history or literature. Telling tales of how The Devil seized the wicked was a pious duty and a certain way to gain popular attention.

Briefly, one story William tells (*Chronicle*, II: 13,230) is of an old woman of Berkeley who sold her soul to The Devil and lived in luxury and peace until one day a raven appeared. Her time, she knew, was up, and immediately the news reached her that her eldest son and his whole family were dead. She took to her bed and, calling her family around her, told them she had been a witch for years but wanted now to keep The Devil from claiming her corpse. She made them promise to sew the body in the hide of a stag, put it in a strong stone coffin, chain the coffin with three huge chains, and pay the clergy to sing psalms for the repose of her soul for fifty nights and Mass for her for fifty days after her death. She said also that if she lay secure in the church for three days and nights it was safe to bury her on the fourth day.

She died and the heavily protected coffin was placed in the church. On the first night, while psalms were being sung, the church doors burst open, a host of demons rushed in, and some succeeded in breaking one of the chains. On the second night they similarly broke another chain. On the third night the third chain held but just before the crow of the cock signaled dawn and safety there was a shaking of the earth, the foundations of the church rocked, the bolted church door was broken open, and a demon, perhaps The Devil himself, approached the coffin and told the old witch to come with him. She replied that she could not: she was chained.

"You shall be loosed," said the evil spirit, and he broke the chain with ease, smashed the stone coffin with a blow of his hand, and dragged the old woman outside the church, where a black steed was standing, its back equipped with iron hooks. Onto the hooks the corpse of the old woman was thrown and off rode the evil spirit with her body and soul. The old woman's cries were heard for four miles in all directions, fading into silence at last.

THE MAN WHO MET HIS OWN DOUBLE IN WHITBY

From Gutch's second volume of *Folk-Lore*, this story of the North Riding of Yorkshire (included in Katherine Brigg's useful selections from her four-volume study in *British Folktales*, 1977):

> Not very many years have gone by since a man in Guisborough entering a shop in this old fishy town [Whitby] saw his own wraith standing there unoccupied. He called it a "waff." Now it is unlucky in the highest degree to meet one's own double; in fact, it is commonly regarded as a sign of early death [death soon, that is]. There is but one path of safety; you must address it boldly.
>
> The Guisborough man was well aware of this and went up without hesitation to the waff. "What's thou doing here?" he said roughly. "What's thou doing here? Thou's after no good, I'll go to bail. Get thy ways yom [home], wi' thee, get thy ways yom." Whereupon the waff slung off abashed and the evil design with which it came there was brought happily to nought.

MORE FOLKLORE OF THE NORTH OF ENGLAND

From W. Henderson's *Folklore of the Northern Counties*:

A country minister, after attending a meeting of his presbytery, had to return home alone, and very late, on a dark evening. While riding in a gloomy part of the road, his horse stumbled, and the good man was flung to the ground. A loud laugh followed, so scornful and so weird, that the minister felt no doubt of the quarter from whence it proceeded. However, with a stout heart, he remounted without delay, and continued his journey, crying out, "Ay, Satan' ye may laugh; but when I fall, I can get up again;

when *ye* fell, *ye* never rose"—on which a deep groan was heard. This was firmly believed to have been an encounter with the Evil Spirit, and a great triumph for the dauntless minister.

THE LANCASHIRE WITCHES

Their case was the largest and most sensational witchcraft prosecution in England up to the time (1612), and it was long noted in literature, starting with a report of the trial of Mother Demdike (Mrs. Elizabeth Sowthern) and nineteen others, taken from the court records by Thomas Potts and published in London in a book of 188 pages in 1613. It had everything: octogenarian crones who looked the part, sensational revelations of dark deeds (including murder by bewitchment), a plot to blow up the jail to rescue the accused, and half of the accused going to the gallows (including a boy of eleven). Two others were sentenced to a year in jail with four appearances in the pillory at market times. The convictions were based on prejudice and the alacrity with which flimsy evidence was seized upon is frightening. We mention elsewhere in this book Ainsworth's novel on the subject and for a more historically accurate report see Vera Winterbottam's *The Devil in Lancashire* (1962).

THE SPELL

Poetry (or doggerel) from the clergyman and metaphysical poet, Robert Herrick (1591–1674). An exorcism.

> Holy Water come and bring;
> Cast in Salt, for seasoning;
> Set the Brush for sprinkling;
> Meale and it now mix together;
> And a little Oyl to either;
> Give the Tapers here their light,
> Ring the *Saints-Bell* to affright
> Far from hence the evil Sprite.

JUST CHARMING!

The word used by prestidigitators—*abracadabra*—comes from an ancient charm written thus for good luck:

ABRACADABRA
BRACADABR
RACADAB
ACADA
CAD
A

Nobody knows what it means. The charm to drive off The Devil can, however, be explained: Abraxas was the name of an ancient god. This charm is written:

ABRAXAS
BRAXAS
RAXAS
AXAS
XAS
AS
S

CASPAR ✠ MELCHIOR ✠ BALTHASAR ✠

Unsatisfied to have the Magi (three astrologers who followed a star to the birthplace of Christ) go unnamed, tradition invented for them the names Caspar, Melchior, and Balthasar (and later made one of them black). In his diary the Elizabethan theatre magnate Philip Henslowe (d. 1617) noted that if you write the three names with crosses as he did, on virgin wax, and place that under your pillow, you will dream the whereabouts of any object that has been stolen. For lost objects, it does jog memory.

OTHER PROTECTIONS AGAINST EVIL

Margaret Baker's delightful *Folklore and Customs of Rural England* has this passage:

> Despite their sanctity, it was often thought wise to protect churches with charms and amulets as though they were houses or cowsheds. Rowan was built into walls, and horseshoes hung up or discreetly buried under doorsteps. The common device of the foundation sacrifice is often found round the church. The Rev. M. R. Heanley, watching some men building a churchyard wall in Hampshire, made a remark doubting its stability. 'Never fear,' replied the mason. 'He'll stand right now, for I built your shadow

into him yesterday when you wasn't looking'. . . . *The Yorkshire Herald* for 31 May 1895 reported that when the tower of Darrington church near Pontefract, Yorkshire, was damaged in a gale, under the west side of the tower, in a bed of solid rock, was found the skeleton of a man, the west wall resting on his skull. It was thought to have been there 600 years. . . .

Removing stone from ecclesiastical buildings was unwise . . . . But alabaster tombs sometimes owe their mutilated state to a general belief that scrapings from them were healing ingredients for medicines. . . .

Churchyards have always been places of presence and mystery, awe-inspiring enough to give authority to divinations practised and bargains struck within them, and often haunted. . . . A turf cut from a ghost's grave and laid under the altar for four days would effectively put an unwelcome phantom to rest. To horsewhip its grave was also helpful. . . .

Because it was thought that the first soul buried in a new graveyard was taken by The Devil, a dog was often the first to be buried there. Each new burial becomes a "watcher" until the next corpse is buried, so you don't want to be the last to be buried in a churchyard or you will be on duty for eternity. The north side of the church is the worst to be buried on, good only for "suicides, unbaptised children, or tramps." Churchyard yews must not be cut, though magic wands of yew are the best, and cypresses only encourage the ghosts to shelter under them in bad weather. Of course you want to see that witches do not steal water from the baptismal font for witchcraft nor the hands of corpses to make the Hand of Glory nor hosts for Satanism, and so forth.

You can try spells and amulets, certain flowers (red ones in rows as "soldiers" are recommended in folklore), herbs (such as parsley), trees (such as rowan), hex signs and witch balls, holy water and other blessed or powerful things, prayer, etc. Good luck!

WASHING AWAY EVIL

Water, essential to life, has naturally been associated with protection against destructive forces. Vampires and similar evil creatures cannot (folklore argues) cross over water. Holy water—the anti-witchcraft element of salt and magical incantations having added to its power—is used to drive away many evils in the Christian tradition. Witches were tested in water. Some possessed persons refuse to drink water and claim it burns them when it strikes their bodies (especially if it is holy water asperged by a priest). Jane Snejana Tempest in her doctoral dissertation on folk belief and ritual in the East Slavonic wondertale, *Water . . .* (1994), shows how in the folklore of Russia, Ukraine, and nearby places water has long been a way of getting rid of evil spirits.

THE CROSS ON A LOAF OF BREAD

We have all seen the cross on hot cross buns which come around every Easter, but it was an old English tradition to combat witchcraft's spells by making a cross on the dough before it rose when baking a loaf of bread.

The important thing was that the knife that cut the cross had to be steel, for iron and steel were thought to frighten away witches, which was why metal pieces were put under thresholds of houses.

An old poem called *The Hesperides* has this couplet about averting spells and avoiding the Evil Eye:

> Cross your dough and your despatch
> Will be better for your batch.

HOW TO COUNTERACT SPELLS

Witches can stick pins in dolls or wax figures to bring evil upon you, say some, but people also believe that you can counteract the spell by sticking pins in a bullock's or pig's heart and hanging it up inside your chimney. As the heart dries out, the witch herself will suffer. Or you can simply put some ash "keys" (which are the seeds of the tree) in your left stocking. This works quite as well (it is said) as a silver coin.

AN OINTMENT FOR THE BEWITCHED

The Mirror of Literature for March 4, 1780, a popular English journal, reported a young girl who was bewitched and vomited feathers, straw, pins, broken glass and nails from cartwheels. It helpfully offered this recipe:

> Dog's grease, well dissolved and cleaned, four ounces; bear's grease, eight ounces; capon's grease, twenty-four ounces. Three trunks of the miseltoe, of hazel while green—cut it in pieces and pound it small till it becomes moist. Bruise it together, and mix all up in a phial, and expose it to the sun for nine weeks, wherewith if you

annoint the body of the bewitched, especially the part most afflicted, they will certainly be cured.

A CHARMING PUNISHMENT

G. C. Coulton's highly regarded *Social Life in Britain from the Conquest to the Reformation* (1938) on page 505 tells that in 1382 Roger Clerk was condemned by an English court to ride through London with urinals tied to his neck. His crime? Pretending to cure illness with charms.

THE MAYPOLE

The Maypole went back to pagan ceremonies, so the Puritans of New England especially objected to it as an abomination. Like mince pies and Christmas trees, it was "of The Devil." In Britain, from which the colonists came, the Maypole was often gigantic: the church of St. Andrew Undershaft (London) was supposed to have got its name from the fact that the nearby Maypole was higher than the church steeple. It may have had phallic significance, too, of which the Puritans were aware.

HOLY WELLS

Water has always been associated with magical rites, which is why we are baptized as Christians, and holy men even in pagan times often lived near streams (thought to be the abode of water sprites, sometimes demons) or wells (some of which were thought to have miraculous curative or protective powers). Each well had its attendant spirit, good or bad. When Christianity came,

A

Compleat Hiſtory

OF

MAGICK, SORCERY,

AND

WITCHCRAFT;

CONTAINING,

I. The moſt Authentick and beſt atteſted RELATIONS of *Magicians, Sorcerers, Witches, Apparitions, Spectres, Ghoſts, Dæmons,* and other preternatural Appearances.
II. A Collection of ſeveral very ſcarce and valuable TRYALS of *Witches,* particularly that famous one, of the WITCHES of *Warboyſe.*
III. An Account of the firſt Riſe of *Magicians* and *Witches;* ſhewing the Contracts they make with the *Devil,* and what Methods they take to accompliſh their Infernal Deſigns.
IV. A full Confutation of all the Arguments that have ever been produced againſt the Belief of *Apparitions, Witches,* &c. with a Judgment concerning *Spirits,* by the late Learned Mr. *JOHN LOCKE.*

VOLUME I.

LONDON: Printed for E. Curll at the *Dial* and *Bible, J. Pemberton* at the *Buck* and *Sun* Both againſt St. *Dunſtan's* Church in *Fleet-Street ;* and *W. Taylor* at the *Ship* in *Pater-noſter-Row.* 1715. Price of the Two Volumes 5 s.

Five shillings was a large price for this two-volume history of witchcraft (1715) by Richard Boulton with material by John Locke.

saints replaced these spirits. In Cornwall and Wales, for instance, there are saints whose names are otherwise unknown to hagiography to whom wells are dedicated. Even today the decorating of holy wells is a common folk custom, as we see from little pamphlets such as Margaret Gascoigne's *Discovering English Customs and Traditions* and many more substantial volumes.

Gerald Findler in *Folk Lore of the Lake Counties* tells how "Fiends Fell" was renamed "Cross Fell" and of the christianizing of the ancient wells and the custom of the "waking of the wells" at various times and places. He regrets that "many of the thirty Holy Wells in Cumberland are now forgotten, and except for records given in books written in the early part of the eighteenth century, may be very difficult to trace."

Some water was said to have sprung miraculously out of the earth as at Holywell (Flintshire). Legend says that when St. Winefride was martyred there by Caradoc, whose sexual advances the virgin repulsed, her head rolled to a place where water instantly sprang from the earth. St. Winefride's Well, one guidebook says, "has been diverted by mining operations and is now fed from a reservoir into the original bath in the crypt of a chapel built in 1480 by the mother of Henry VII." The mother of Henry VII was the Lady Margaret Beaufort, sole heiress of the first Duke of Somerset. It was she who married Edmund Tudor (Earl of Richmond), then Sir Henry Stafford, then Thomas Stanley (Earl of Derby). St. Winefride's Well was long a place of pilgrimage and hospices for pilgrims were built at various times, last in 1870. There are other stories of other places where The Devil caused water to appear.

A

Timely Warning

To Rash and Disobedient

CHILDREN.

Being a strange and wonderful RELATION of a young Gentleman in the Parish of *Stepney* in the Suburbs of *London*, that sold himself to the Devil for 12 Years to have the Power of being revenged on his Father and Mother, and how his Time being expired, he lay in a sad and deplorable Condition to the Amazement of all Spectators.

EDINBURGH: PRINTED ANNO 1721.

A Scottish chapbook (1721) describes the fate of a Londoner who sold his soul to The Devil.

THE FORFAR BRIDLE

In the town hall of Forfar, capital of Angus in Scotland, you can see the ancient gag used on witches, much persecuted at this place in Scotland in earlier times.

WITCHES' MILL IN LANCASHIRE

At Castleton (Lancs.) there is a so-called Witches' Mill with a museum of magic and witchcraft.

FOLKLORE OF THE LAKE COUNTIES

In a book of this title Gerald Findler wrote in 1968:

> Faith in the little folk still exists in the minds of some people. Even to this day one hears of a farm girl putting a pinch of salt in the fire at churning time [which traditionally is aid to drive away evil spirits], so that the fairies may not stop the butter from coming. A rowan branch used to be placed above doorways to keep away evil spirits. The stick for stirring cream was made of rowan or mountain ash wood to counteract the bewitching of the churn. The chasing away of evil spirits was always popular. An old man residing in the village of Winton was so convinced that witches really existed that he wore a beaver hat with a hare's foot on one side and a piece of rowan bark or leaf on the other. These he believed would keep all witches away.

THE DEVIL THREW A ROCK AT A CHURCH

From Wilfred Taylor's "The South Highlands: Perth and Angus" in *The Shell Guide to Britain and Northern Ireland*:

> Over [the county of] Angus there is a lurid glow of theological memories, and near Invergowrie there is a rock in the shallows of the [river] Tay which all decent Dundee children firmly believe was thrown, somewhat inaccurately, by the Devil in a tantrum at the parish kirk in Invergowrie.

MOONRAKERS

Back in the days when the most notable industry of the West Country was smuggling and lighting false fires to wreck ships so that their cargo could be stolen, back in the days before tourist traps and holiday camps, the area was popularly believed to harbor Moonrakers. They were supposed to be able, by raking the image of the moon out of standing water, to produce the dark nights needed for their nefarious deeds.

THE DEVIL IN CORNWALL

In the bleak, moorland parish of Advent there is The Devil's Jump. It's a granite mass 50 feet high with another granite mass across the valley. Presumably there was a tale, now forgotten, about how The Devil jumped from one to the other, strewing boulders as he went.

At Cadgwith, a port in the parish of Grade (for St. Grade) there is a hole in a cliff called The Devil's Frying Pan, flooded by the sea at high tide.

The parish at the point of The Lizard is Landewednack. Nearby, on Asparagus Island, is a blow hole named The Devil's Bellows.

These placenames, however, take the name of The Devil chiefly because it is often used, as elsewhere, for any large or extraordinary toponymic feature. For the real history of The Devil in Cornwall you have to dig deeply in obscure records of the folklore. With the tales of the Phoenicians (who introduced mining), the neolithic remains of the pre-Christian holy wells, obscure saints, and the castle at Tintagel (said to be King Arthur's)—well, this is a land suitable for tales of wonder, even if The Devil seems disinclined to bother with Methodists. The granite and slate and wind and rain seem, for other denominations, however, to make a tale by the fireside just right.

The Duchy of Cornwall, cut off from the rest of Britain pretty much until well into the nineteenth century, has a history worth a whole book on pixies and The Devil and his Dandy Dogs (a version of the Wild Hunt) and witchcraft. Here two stories will suffice. The second is from personal experience, but first this story from print, from Thomas Quiller Couch in a Victorian *Notes & Queries* (XI: 397):

> One instance occurs to my memory of a poor, unhappy fellow, who pretended, in vulgar parlance, to have sold himself to the devil, and was accordingly regarded by his neighbours as a miracle of impiety. He was not, however, actively vicious, never being known to use his supernatural powers of ill-doing to the detriment of others, except, indeed (and they were the only occasions upon which he is said to have openly asked the foul fiend's assistance), when the depth of his potations had not left him enough to pay the reckoning. He was then accustomed to hold his hat up the chimney, and demand money, which was promptly showered down into it. The coin so obtained the landlord invariably refused with a shudder, and was glad to get quit of him on these terms. This compact with the spirit of evil is now but vaguely suspected as the secret of the witch's power.

My own story is that once, traveling in Cornwall with a friend named Reginald Farmer, he having been told this Victorian story by me, decided on his own to play a trick. When it came time to pay for our beer I called the bartender over and was about to pay him when Reg surprised me with one of his sleight-of-hand tricks and produced a crisp five-pound note with the remark, "The Devil will pay for us, as usual." The bartender and the usually placid pub regulars, their seats as warm as their beer, were amazed. The bartender turned to me to pay. He said he would not accept any money produced "out of the air." Reg insisted, "It's yours now. If you refuse it you will regret the decision. If you do not want it, I suggest you just leave it on the bar and give it to the first really needy person who comes along, without explanation about where you got it." I wonder how long it stayed there before someone got it. Our stately exit from the pub was impressive, in total silence. We didn't laugh until we had driven away.

We never tried it again. We didn't think we could keep straight faces a second time. Nonetheless, we may have added a footnote to the rich folklore of Cornwall, just as jokesters and journalists have made up London ghosts out of whole cloth only to see "authentic" reports appearing in print time after time thereafter.

IRELAND'S FIRST WITCHCRAFT TRIAL

Alice Kyteler was rich. She had inherited much from her first three husbands (William Outlaw, Adam le Blond, and Richard de Valle) and her fourth (John le Poer) was in failing health and likely to leave her more. Perhaps her wealth attracted the charge of witchcraft that was made against her in 1324.

It was lodged by Richard de Ledrede, Bishop of Ossory, and it made 7 indictments: that she and her son William Outlaw and others had denied God and the church; that they sacrificed cocks and other creatures to Robert "son of Artis," a minor demon; that they asked the demons to reveal the future to them; that they held *sabbats* and mocked Christian ceremonies; that they made hideous witch brews to do evil; that Alice Kyteler had poisoned her first three husbands and stolen the inheritances of all but one, William Outlaw, her son by her first husband; and that Alice Kyteler had had sexual relations with the demon Robert.

Alice Kyteler fought the bishop (who excommunicated her) in a civil court and when it looked as if he might prove successful in his prosecution she fled to England. Her son, William Outlaw, was briefly jailed but survived. Her maid, Petronilla de Meath, confessed to whatever the bishop and the torturers wanted her to say. She was burned at the stake on 3 November 1324.

THE WEXFORD FESTIVAL

In Ireland this festival continues to this day and may be recalling the *Lugnasad* of old Eire. That was a festival at which the magical powers of women were demonstrated as superior to the physical strength of men. It in its turn derived from a Greek goddess of war who somehow got to Ireland and, like many Irish goddesses, preferred to use witchcraft rather than brute strength to win ferocious battles. The Irish goddess Nemain, for instance, whose very name suggests "frenzy," was one of five war goddesses. The others were Fea (The Hateful), Badb (related to the Banshee), Macha of The Red Tresses (who garned human heads like a crop of acorns), and Morrigan (Great Queen). These sent men into battle maddened and wild.

One goddess was called Carman. Her three sons were called Calma (Valiant), Dubh (Black), and Olc (Evil). They are also given in folklore the names Dian, Dub, and Douther.

THATCHED COTTAGES

In Irish superstition, straw has protective powers. He who lives in a thatched cottage has over his head a defense against evil. This is discussed in work on Ulster folk beliefs and elsewhere.

THE FAIRY CHILD, AN IRISH BALLAD

I wrote the introduction to the facsimile reprint in 1973 of Sir Charles Gavan Duffy's anthology of *The Ballad Poetry of Ireland*. We reproduced the fortieth edition (1869) of that very popular book. In it was the ballad of *The Fairy Child* by Dr. Anster, the translator of the first part of Goethe's *Faust* (1835), with the sad tale of a changeling provided by the fairies. John Anster (1783–1867), a professor of civil law, took an interest in Irish myth and balladry. Sir Charles' note runs: "The woman, in whose character these lines are written, supposes her child stolen by a fairy. I need not mention how prevalent the superstition was among the peasantry, which attributed instances of sudden death to the agency of these spirits." The Irish woman is pleased with her golden-haired child but then—

I sat alone in my cottage,
The midnight needle plying;
I feared for my child, for the rush's light
In the socket now was dying!
There came a hand to my lonely latch,
Like the wind at midnight moaning;
I knelt to pray, but rose again,
For I heard my little boy groaning.
I crossed my brow and I crossed my breast,
But that night my child departed—
They left a weakling in his stead,
And I am broken hearted!
Oh! it cannot be my own sweet boy,
For his eyes are dim and hollow;
My little boy is gone—is gone,
And his mother soon will follow!
The dirge for the dead will be sung for me,
And the mass be chanted meetly,
And I shall sleep with my little boy,
In the moonlight churchyard sweetly.

IRISH WITCHCRAFT IN ELIZABETHAN TIMES

Elizabeth I's English invaders looked upon the "mere Irish" as barefoot barbarians and ignorant savages, but at the same time all too wise in evil magic. The English confused the folkways of the peasantry with black magic. The English soldiers were quick to denounce the Irish as devils and devil-worshippers, which helped in their own minds to excuse the atrocities committed.

Peter Sommerville-Large in *Irish Eccentrics* (1975) writes about how the English condemned the Irish for using witchcraft to control the weather (presumably only to cause trouble to the English forces). The persistent rains which make The Emerald Isle so green were said to be the work of The Devil:

Sir Geoffrey Fenton [on active service in Ireland in the 1580's] wrote how it 'maketh me to think that if God hath given Liberty to the witches of that country (which aboundeth with witches) they are all set on work to cross the service by extraordinarily unseasonable weather.' Sir George Carew blamed them for the storms in west Cork that interfered with his campaign of 1601, noting 'that the country of Beare was full of witches.'

THE SHAMROCK

St. Patrick is said to have used the shamrock to help explain The Trinity, three in one, to the Irish he was converting. A four-leaf clover, an unusual variation on the shamrock, is supposed to bring unusually good luck. An old verse runs:

> One leaf for fame,
> One leaf for wealth,
> One leaf for faithful lover.
> One leaf to bring us glorious health,
> That makes a four-leaf clover.

HOW TO AVOID BEING TRIPPED UP BY FAIRIES AND LEPRECHAUNS

The Irish traditionally knitted socks with white toes, for this purpose.

DEALING WITH THE DEVIL IN IRELAND

Stories abound about witchcraft in Ireland, malicious witches harming cattle, preventing butter from coming in the churn, stealing children, and worse. From Patrick F. Byrne's *Witchcraft in Ireland*, the buying of the sheaf:

> "Buying the sheaf," a practice in the black art, was still being carried out in 1893 in Co. Louth. The person first visited a church, with back mockingly turned to the altar as witches do, [and] muttered certain words. A sheaf of wheat was selected and shaped like the human body, the head being made like pleated straw. Into this and at the various joints pins were deeply stuck, and with horrid invocation of the devil the sheaf was buried near the home of the intended victim. As the wheat rotted, the victim sickened, expiring when it was completely decomposed. This was mentioned in a court case in Ardee in 1893.

Another story dates to 1698 in Antrim. A girl gave a begging witch bread and beer at the door and later put into her mouth a leaf of sorrel the witch had given her. She had convulsions and went into a coma and the minister was sent for and scarce had he laid his hand upon her when she was turned by the demon [possessing her] into the most dreadful shapes. She

An Irish chieftan and his entourage at an Elizabethan cookout. The English regarded the "mere Irish" as primitive as well as superstitious.   296

began first to roll herself about, then to vomit needles, pins[,] hairs, feathers, bottoms of thread, pieces of glass, window-nails, nails drawn out of a cart or coach wheel, and iron knife about a span long, eggs and fish shells, and when the witch came near the place, or looked towards the house, even though at a distance of about 200 yards from where the child was, she was in worse torment . . . .

The witch was apprehended, condemned and refused to recant. She was then strangled and burned.

THE ISLE OF MAN

The Manx are said to be haunted by the ghost of the wife of Henry, Duke of Gloucester. She wanted to know when her brother-in-law the king (Henry VI) would die and, it is said, she dealt with The Devil to find out. She was banished to the Isle of Man. It was considered a good place for her.

WITCHCRAFT IN GUERNSEY

In 1672 Lady Hatton at Castle Cornet died and people said that a witch had prophesied and perhaps caused her death. The story is told in a book by Sidney Smith and J. Stevens Cox, *The Witch's Prophecy* . . . (1981).

THE GRANDMOTHER OF ENGLISH WITCHES

History records many poor souls in England forced to confession by terrible tortures and burned as witches. Extensive documents go back to the thirteenth or fourteenth century. In our century the woman most responsible, perhaps, for the revival of witchcraft in England is Dorothy Clutterbuck. She lived in the New Forest and when Gerald Gardner, retired from the civil service in the East, returned to Britain, and moved into her area, she recruited him and inducted him into her coven. That was in 1939. In 1940 the coven, with the assistance of many other patriotic British witches, created a "cone of power" directed against Hitler's forces to prevent them from invading the British Isles. That political use of witchcraft seems to have worked. An American effort to levitate The Pentagon did not. Gardnerian witches, inspired by his life and the writings and witchcraft museum he left, may be said to be in the mainstream of modern British witchcraft. It is not Satanism but pre-Christian in inspiration.

RAISING THE DEAD

Out of the ancient fear that speaking of the dead might bring them back as ghosts, some societies forbid any mention of the departed by name. Others may drop the name but hasten to add, "May she rest in peace" or "God bless his soul," etc.

THE SHINING

It was once believed that anything shiny could fascinate and be used in magic. This is part of the reason for magical uses of bowls of water, knives, pins, mirrors, crystals, etc. Moderns have elaborated crystals into instruments of power and many attribute to them rather magical powers of healing.

SCOTLAND, CHANNEL ISLANDS

Anonymous, *News from Scotland* . . . (1591, Bodley Head Quartos 1924)
Black, George F., *A Calendar of Cases of Witchcraft in Scotland 1510–1727* (1938)
_____, *Some Unpublished Scottish Witchcraft Trials* (1941)
Bliss, Douglas Percy (ed.), *The Devil in Scotland* (1934)
Brodie-Innes, John William, *Scottish Witchcraft Trials* (1891)

Campbell, James G., *Witchcraft and Second Sight in the Highlands and Islands of Scotland* (1902)

Dalyell, Sir John Graham, *The Darker Superstitions of Scotland* (1834)

Davidson, Thomas Douglas, *Rowan Tree and Red Thread* (1949)

Harper, Charles G., *Haunted Houses* (ed. Cecil Palmer. 1924)

Keiller, Alex, *The Personnel of the Aberdeenshire Witchcraft Covens* (1922)

Pitts, John Linwood, *Witchcraft and Devil Lore in the Channel Islands* (1886)

Sharpe, Charles K., *Historical Account of the Belief in Witchcraft in Scotland* (1884)

Sinclair, George, *Satan's Invisible World Discovered* (reprinted 1871)

Wood, John Maxwell, *Witchcraft and Superstitious Record in the Southwestern District of Scotland* (1911)

WALES

Trevelyan, Marie, *Folk-Lore and Folk Stories of Wales* (1909)

IRELAND

Carleton, William, *Traits and Stories of the Irish Peasantry* (ed. D. S. O'Donoghue, 1834)

Seymour, St.-J. D., *Irish Witchcraft and Demonology* (1913)

_____ & Harry L. Neligan, *True Irish Ghost Stories* (1914)

CONVICTED BRITISH WITCHES

Jane Wenham was the last Englishwoman convicted of witchcraft (1712). The most gripping story on record, however, remains that of the first British witch conviction: Dame Alice Kyteler was tried for sorcery in Ireland in 1324, as we noted above. *The Sorcery Trial of Alice Kyteler (1324)* at long last has its well-deserved book. It is by L. S. Davidson and John O. Ward (1993).

DEMONOMANIE
DES SORCIERS

A MONSEIGNEVR M. CHRE-
stofle de Thou Cheualier Seigneur de Cœli, premier Pre-
sident en la Cour de Parlement, & Conseiller
du Roy en son priué Conseil.

PAR I. BODIN ANGEVIN.

A PARIS,

Chez Iacques du Puys Libraire Iuré, à la Samaritaine,

M. D. LXXX.

AVEC PRIVILEGE DV ROY.

Title page of *Demonomanie*, by Jean Bodin of Anjou (1580).

2
Most of Continental Europe

A BRIEF SURVEY OF CONTINENTAL WITCHCRAFT

I cannot produce "infinite riches in a little room" but perhaps *multum in parva*: some details interesting in themselves and good as far as they go. I shall feature French, German, and Italian examples, but of course I must touch on Spain of the Holy Inquisition, the Jews of the cabalistic tradition, legends of the *golem* and *dybbuk*, and even mention the gypsies in passing. I regret I do not have space again for the Basque witches mentioned all too briefly elsewhere, nor for full treatment of the Slavic traditions (rich in the lore of demon-defended places, werewolves, vampires—almost synonymous with Transylvania), but there are other sources where scholars can dig up such things. I offer here an unusually detailed look at some aspects of the witchcraft of the Far North, of Scandinavia and related places to which the German ideas on witchcraft went and mingled with the native traditions. I believe you will find that section especially stimulating and you may wish to delve deeper into Nordic folklore.

But to commence, with France. First off, her tradition is long. Corrective to the tradition of beginning the discussion of witchcraft and magic in France with "The Widow" and others who participated in the Black Mass to bind the king's mistress closer to him in the mid-seventeenth century is a learned survey of *The Practice of Witchcraft and Magic in Fact and Fiction during the French Middle Ages*, a doctoral dissertation by Joan Nancy Ricardo-Gil, 1980. The story of French witchcraft is long.

THE MOST FOOLISH DESCRIPTION OF THE *SABBAT*

Jules Michelet (*Satanism and Witchcraft*) says that on the subject of the *sabbat* "the prize and the crown of folly belong to the Dominican Michaelis— in the Gaufridi affair, 1610. His *Sabbath* is undoubtedly the most improbable of all."

It was 19 January 1611 when Sebastien Michaelis (since ranked Venerable by the church, a step on the way to canonization!) examined the nun Madeleine de la Palud (who had been seduced and had renounced "God, Father, Son, and Holy Ghost") and wrote down her wild, detailed descriptions of the witches' *sabbat*, which this pitiful woman was under the impression Gaufridi had innovated! We have, published at Aix, her accusations against and the legal process concerning the priest Louis Gaufridi, who in April 1611 confessed to two Caupchin monks that he had renounced "all good, both spiritual as well as temporal" and had joined The Devil's party. Jacques Fontaine published the sensational stories in Paris in 1611: *Discours des marques des sorciers*, with emphasis on Father Gaufridi. In 1612 Father Michaelis published in Paris: *Histoire admirable de la posession et conversion d'une penitent seduite par un magicien*, Gaufridi again.

Michaelis believed the nun when she told him that she had seen demons, that the *sabbat* was held "every day" and for the crime of the day, that the witches were required to attend under pain of punishment and that they were summoned by the sound of a horn. "Surely an excellent way of securing their own capture," snaps Michelet. The witches were taught evil (beginning with killing babies and working their way through the curriculum). Clearly academics are at work reporting all this stuff: witchcraft has required attendance at class, examinations, diplomas, degrees. Michelet speaks of the ranks:

> Those of the lowest class, novices and folk of small account, get their hand in as a beginning by killing babies. Those of the upper class, the gentlemen magicians, are assigned the part of blaspheming, defying, and insulting God. They do not condescend to the trouble of evil spells and bewitchments; these they perform by means of their valets and waiting-maids who constitute the intermediate class between the well-bred sorcerers and the clodhoppers.

Sister Madeleine had it all worked out: certain demons for certain purposes, certain saints directed by God to counter them. The medieval mind with its hierarchies and theories of order and correspondence lasted a long time; it was applied to everything. Satan (or his representative or someone pretending to be such) at the *sabbat* looks suspiciously like one of those little French kings with clothes more impressive than themselves, perched on a throne, holding a levée, receiving reports from minor officials, and dispensing their favors or their punishments according to whether or not they were pleased with their subordinates' work. After the business meeting, as it were, there was an unrestrained office party.

BISHOP ORESME

Nicole Oresme died at Lisieux, of which he was then bishop, in 1382. Will Durant in *The Reformation* (Part VI of his *History of Civilization*, 1957) called Bishop Oresme "the great antagonist of astrology" in his time, noting that astrologers who could not predict the sex of a child before it was born offered as soon as it was born to predict its whole life. Skeptical of magical claims, Bishop Oresme suggested that people were being fooled by charlatans and were ascribing to the miraculous what was simply unknown or mysterious. Like Cicero, who also wrote a *De divinatione*, the bishop denounced soothsayers, the interpreters of dreams, and the makers of horoscopes. But, Durant adds, he was himself not entirely free of the superstition of his medieval world:

> Amid his general skepticism of the occult he admitted that some events could be explained as the work of demons or angels. He accepted the notion of the "evil eye"; he thought that a criminal would darken a mirror by looking into it, and that the glance of a lynx could penetrate a wall.

And he was the first person to mention the so-called Hindu rope trick, which he was sure was a fake.

THE MADNESS AT LOUDUN

The story of the village priest and the nuns at Loudon would be one of the most important chapters in the history of demonology if any of the accusations of a pact with The Devil or the possession of the nuns by Asmodeus and other lustful demons had any truth in them whatsoever, but it was all untrue. What was true is that Father Urbain Grandier was outrageously condemned to death for witchcraft even after those who first accused him came to their senses and withdrew their charges. He was obscenely tortured and then brutally killed, burned at the stake without being strangled first (as had been promised if he "confessed"). It is, in fact, one of the most important chapters in the history of human infamy, not of the evil of The Devil but of the evil in mankind.

In 1630, Father Grandier, who for years had led a blameless life as the local priest, was accused by Trincant, the equivalent of the district attorney, of having seduced Trincant's daughter. Father Grandier took his case to the ecclesiastical authorities and the archbishop of Bordeaux exonerated him. Three years later, Soeur Jeanne des Anges and other nuns from the convent of Loudun picked up on his having been charged with a sex offense and accused Father Grandier of having put a spell on them and opened them to attack by Asmodeus and other demons who possessed them and caused them to be thrashing around, screaming imprecations and obscenities, acting lewdly.

The same year Father Grandier, on another matter entirely, crossed Cardinal Richelieu and the cardinal immediately ordered a full investigation of the charges of these hysterical nuns. The inquiry was to be conducted by a relative of Soeur Jeanne des Anges.

In November 1633, Father Grandier was imprisoned in Angers and denied the usual appeal to the Parliament of Paris. A pact with The Devil, supposedly signed by Father Grandier, was produced in evidence in 1634. This went well beyond what his original accusers wanted and they attempted to withdraw their complaint, but Father Grandier was tortured for a confession and was burned alive at the stake, to the permanent disgrace of Loudun, in April 1634.

His oppressors came to bad ends, too. Father Lactance, a Franciscan, died insane in May 1634. Tranquille, who rushed to print with his *Relation de Loudun* (1634) died insane five years later. Surin, the third man most responsible for Father Grandier's death, was insane (some say possessed) for twenty years. Cardinal Richelieu ended his days peacefully and happily.

By 1716 Aubin's *Histoire des Diables de Loudun* was popular, and in our time Aldous Huxley's novel of the same name (in English) and Ken Russell's violent motion picture have made the gruesome story world famous.

In our day a man's life can be ruined sometimes by the unsupported evidence of a woman who cries sexual assault. In those days a man's life could be lost on the word of a few nuns, driven to insanity by burdensome vows of chastity unassisted by the consolation of real religion. It was an argument that nuns perhaps ought to have gone back to earlier Christian practices of fasting, self-flagellation, blood-letting, general mortification of the body, even spiritual exercises, to take their minds off the temptations of the flesh. When women without true vocations were locked up in convents, many distortions of the mind and the spirit resulted. Father

Grandier, who happened to be one of the priests who was not having sex with nuns, was the victim of their obsessions.

DESECRATION OF THE HOST

The Black Mass involved insulting God and desecrating the Host because the consecrated wafer was, in the eyes of the faithful (and apparently of the blasphemers), the Body of Christ. Evil persons took Communion but did not swallow the Host and took it away for blasphemous acts, or they broke into the churches and stole consecrated Hosts from the ciborium in the tabernacle.

One French Satanist was accused of keeping a consecrated Host before him on his desk while he wrote vile magical texts and he (it was charged, albeit by his enemies) used to stick the Host with the point of his pen.

Diable (sculpture de la facade de N.-D. de Paris).

In Brussels in the Cathedral of St. Michael and St. Gudule a stained-glass window tells the story of an attempt to desecrate the Host. Satanists stole a host and stabbed it, but it bled so much they were detected and punished. An annual religious procession in Brussels commemorates the *Miracle du St.-Sacrement.*

How those who do not believe in Transubstantiation (that the bread and wine do not merely signify but truly become at consecration the Body and Blood of Christ) can say an effective Black Mass is unclear.

ITE, MISSA EST

Joris-Karl Huysmans' study in Satanism, *La Bas*, includes a terrifying description of a Black Mass of the sort he probably actually attended in Paris, and here is the end of it, set in "the chapel of an old Ursuline convent." We omit the "torrent of blasphemies and insults" and obscenities that preceded the consecration. (The translation is by Keene Wallis, 1958.)

> Docre contemplated the Christ surmounting the tabernacle, and with arms spread wide apart he spewed forth frightful insults, and, at the end of his forces, muttered the billingsgate of a drunken cabman. One of the choir boys [actually, acolytes] knelt before him with his back toward the altar. A shudder ran along the priest's spine. In

a solemn but jerky voice he said, "*Hoc est enim corpus meum*," then, instead of kneeling, after the consecration, before the precious Body, he faced the congregation, and appeared tumefied, haggard, dripping with sweat. He staggered between the two choir boys, who, raising the chasuble, displayed his naked belly. Docre made a few passes and the host sailed, tainted and soiled, over the steps.

Durtal felt himself shudder. A whirlwind of hysteria shook the room. While the choir boys sprinkled holy water on the pontiff's nakedness, women rushed upon the Eucharist and, groveling in front of the altar, clawed from the bread humid particles and drank and ate divine ordure.

Another woman, curled up over a crucifix, emitted a rending laugh, then cried to Docre, "Father, father!" A crone tore her hair, leapt, whirled around and around as on a pivot and fell over beside a young girl who, huddled to the wall, was writhing in convulsions, frothing at the mouth, weeping, and spitting out frightful blasphemies. And Durtal, terrified, saw through the fog and red horns of Docre['s headdress] who, seated now, frothing with rage, was chewing up sacramental wafers, taking them out of his mouth, wiping himself with them, and distributing them to the women, who ground them underfoot, howling, or fell over each other struggling to get hold of them and violate them.

The place was simply a madhouse, a monstrous pandemonium of prostitutes and maniacs. Now, while the choir boys gave themselves to the men, a little girl, who hitherto had not budged, suddenly bent over forward and howled, howled like a dog. Overcome with disgust, nearly asphyxiated, Durtal wanted to flee. He looked for Hyacinthe. She was no longer at his side. He finally caught sight of her close to the canon [Docre] and, stepping over the writhing bodies on the floor, he went to her. With quivering nostrils she was inhaling the effluvia of the [burning] perfumes and of the couples.

"The sabbatic odour!" she said to him between clenched teeth, in a strangled voice.

"Here, let's get out of this!"

They go to a room over a nearby bar and Hyacinthe says "I want you" and drags him into bed and "obscenities of whose existence he had never dreamed." Then he discovers that the bed is "strewn with fragments of hosts." Disgusted, he decides to terminate his affair with this married lady who likes Black Masses.

THE BLACK MASS EXPLAINED

Jules Michelet in his *Satanism and Witchcraft* traces the blasphemies of the Black Mass to the revolt of the peasantry against the strictures of the church and the perverse sexuality of the ritual's orgies to dreadful social conditions under which the peasants lived. Encouraged by the church to increase and multiply, the peasants could not feed the mouths they had. Forbidden by the church to marry close relatives, they were forbidden by their feudal lords to marry strangers lest they become the serf of the wife's lord. Only the eldest son inherited his father's few holdings, his power in the family, and the right to marry. Brothers and sisters mated with each other out of wedlock and the mother committed incest with the eldest son, who now exercised all his dead father's rights. In unholy unions, which Michelet finds reminiscent of "the Jews and the Greeks" of old, the Black Mass's excesses found their start. The blasphemous rituals offered psychological and physical release for the peasants, an outlet for anger and resentment, a time of festivity and feasting and sexual abandon. While the chatelaines of great castles indulged themselves in the vilest excesses that their privileged positions permitted, with slaves, gigolos, love-sick knights, and even on occasion their noble husbands, the poor in their dreary lives had the escape valve of the *sabbat*, of the Black Mass.

MARTIN D'ARLES AND PIERRE DE LANCRE

The Basque region (now in Spain and France) was one area into which the Spanish Inquisition had trouble penetrating because of the language, as we can see by histories of the Spanish Inquisition by H. C. Lea (1906), J. Plaidy (1969), and others. A cleric, Martin d'Arles, reported in his *Tractatus de superstitionibus*, published in Paris in 1517, that witches were common among the Basques. A lawyer of Basque origin (but born in Bordeaux), Pierre De Lancre (1553–1631) was sent to root them out and proudly boasted of having had 600 of them put to death. His *Tableau de l'inconstance des mauvais anges* (1612) shows him to have been a firm believer in the *sabbat*, werewolves, and magical spells.

THE AFFAIR AT LOUVIERS

Madeleine Bavent was born in Rouen in 1607 and from age nine was an orphan. She was apprenticed to a linen worker who made nuns' robes, and a Franciscan confessor to the local convent convinced the young girls who worked for the linen worker that he was taking them to *sabbats*. He had sex with all four of them.

Madeleine escaped from that situation into a worse one. She joined the local Franciscan convent, where the director was an Adamist who thought nudity was purity. Madeleine was forced, like the others, to appear nude on many occasions, even in church, and she was reprimanded for holding the altar cloth up to hide her breasts at communion. She had to fight off the director, one David, but he was an old man. Nonetheless he terrified and abused her.

His successor, one Picart, drugged her with magic potions that filled her mind with insanities, had sex with her and got her pregnant. Madeleine bore several children. No one knows what happened to them. Unwanted babies had a way of disappearing in convents. She went more or less crazy, and the nuns around her showed signs of insanity as well. They dabbled in witchcraft or thought they were doing so. Madeleine was accused of having been seen with The Devil himself. She accused her accuser of having attended a *sabbat*. The convent was in an uproar. The bishop got involved, and Picart's body was exhumed and thrown into a sewer farther away in the hope that devils would go with it. The bishop also caused Madeleine to be tortured by the nuns seeking signs of The Devil on her body and then condemned her without a trial to be immured for life. That would stop the evil in the nunnery.

It did not. The nuns went into wilder fits of possession, saw visions, got hysterical, and acted insane. They did not fool the queen's own surgeon sent from Paris (who had witnessed the shenanigans at Loudun recently and instantly realized this was a copycat performance). Nor did they fool the local Rouen magistrate whom the surgeon asked to investigate with him and who caught one of the nuns in the act of planting a talisman she was pretending to know The Devil had put in the convent garden. Yvelin, the surgeon, announced that of the fifty-two nuns six were possessed (diabolically or otherwise), seventeen more under a spell (or a delusion), and the rest were confused and irrational. They prophesied, but the prophecies did not come true. They spoke in foreign tongues, but suddenly lost their Latin and Greek when the educated man arrived from Paris. They performed feats of great strength, but these were fake. What they did most was spout obscenities. They were frauds and hysterics. The surgeon had exposed the nuns.

But that did no good. The surgeon was not believed. The clergy did not want to hear from a man of science. The surgeon was rejected as a mere barber by the so-called learned doctors of Rouen. He wrote a report no bookseller would peddle. He stood on the Pont Neuf in Paris and sold copies himself.

In Rouen, this did no good at all. Madeleine remained in a filthy *oubliette*, repeatedly attempting suicide in her despair and not succeeding, raped by her jailers, forced to confess to all sorts of crimes she had not committed, and calling in vain on both God and The Devil to release her from her pain.

She was let out of her pitch-black, rat-infested cell only to go to court on occasion when her arch-enemy, the Prebendary of Evreux, wanted to ruin one of his many enemies. Madeleine could be counted on to say that this one or that one was seen at a *sabbat*. This went on for a long time. Madeleine did a lot of damage under the prebendary's direction. This was the sort of man who held a responsible office in the church at that time and place.

Eventually the despicable convent at Louviers was closed and some small attempt was made to inspect such institutions more carefully in the future. The bones of Picart were not given to his family for proper burial but were handed over the clergy to burn them, and the third and last director of the convent, one Boulle, was burned at the stake (1647). Madeleine died in jail. Before she died a priest interviewed her in her cell in Rouen and wrote the *Histoire de Magdelaine Bavent, Religieuse de Louuviers, avec son interrogatoir*, etc. (1652). "I do not know a more important, a more terrible book, or one better deserving to be reprinted," wrote Jules Michelet. I don't believe the book has ever been reprinted. But that is the horrendous story of Madeleine Bavent.

THIRTY BASIC BOOKS ON THE HISTORY OF FRENCH SORCERY

Arnould, Arthur, *Histoire de l'inquisition*
Baissac, Jean, *Les Grand jours de la sorcellerie*
Bizouard, Joseph, *Des Rapports de l'homme avec le démon* . . . 6 vols. (1863–1864)
Bodin, Jean, *De la Démonomanie des sorcières*
Bois, Jules, *Le Satanisme et magie*
Bossard, L'Abbé, *Gilles de Rais*
Bricaud, S. J., *J.-K. Huysmans et le Satanisme*
Cauzons, Theodore de, *La Magie et la sorcellerie en France*
"Christian, Paul," *The History and Practice of Magic* (trans. J. Kirkkup & J. Shaw)

Collin de Plancy. J.-A.-S., *Dictionnaire infernal* (revised 1863)

"Corte, N.," *Satan, L'adversaire* (1956)

DeLancre, Pierre, *Du Sortilege*

Gougenot de Mosseau, H.-R., *Moeurs et practiques des démons*

Guaita, Marquis Stanlislaus de, *Essais des sciences maudites*

Huysmans, Joris-Karl, *Down There* (trans. K. Wallis)

Jacquot, F., *Défense des Templiers*

"Lecanu, L'Abbé de," *Histoire de Satan*

"Lévi, Éliphas," *The History of Magic* (trans. A. E. Waite)

_____ , *Transcendental Magic, Its Doctrine and Ritual* (trans. A. E. Waite)

Lillie, Arthur, *The Worship of Satan in Modern France*

Martin, B. J., *The Trial of The Templars*

Menant, Joachim, *Les Yezidizs . . . adorateurs du Diable*

Michelet, Jules, *Satanism and Witchcraft*

Nidier, Johan, *Formicarius*

Poitiers, Jean de, *Les Diables de Loudun*

Rémy, Nicholas, *Dæmonolatriæ libri tres*

Salverte, A.-B.-E.-J. de, *Essai sur la magie*

St.-Hebin, Alexandre, *Du Culte de Satan*

Vair, Leonard, *Trois Livres des charmes, sorceleges, ov enchantements* (trans. from Latin, Julian Baudon)

Waite, Arthur Edward, *Devil Worship in France*

Yve-Plessy, R. *Bibliographie française de la sorcellerie*

THE CURATE OF ARS

A simple priest, the *Curé d'Ars*, became St.-Jean-Baptiste Vianney, one of the most remarkable Frenchmen of the first half of the nineteenth century. He was credited with a number of miraculous cures and was pestered by demons, he said, which he called *grappins*. They would make incessant and infernal noises, banging on things to the point where he could not concentrate. They followed him from place to place; when he came to visit, he seems to have brought them with him. The priests at St.-Trivier-sur-Mignans, for instance, testified in 1826 that in the night the noise was fearful, the doors slammed throughout the presbytery, the windows rattled, the walls shook, and the priests were afraid that the building would collapse.

This is reported in the English abridgment (preface by Henry Edward, Cardinal Manning) of the Abbé Alfred Monin's two-volume French biography of the *curé* (1861).

ZANONI

A novel of this title was Lord Lytton's discussion of a magician and an occult society rather resembling the nineteenth-century Rosicrucian organization in France. It was published in 1842 and may include some personal experience of the author or reports he received from French magic contacts.

THE PRINCE OF SORCERERS

Father Louis Gaufridi of the diocese of Marsailles was called "The Prince of Sorcerers" by some, but it didn't save him from execution in 1611, as we have seen. His interrogators considered that they did get an important piece of information out of him. Under torture, he said that at the *sabbat* there is a baptism-like ceremony to bind the followers to The Devil; and that those so baptized have to swear to bring their children for a similar ceremony.

How things have changed in France since the sex and violence of Father Gaufridi's time is chronicled in P. Christiani's *Présence de Satan dans le monde moderne* (1962).

Today Father Gaufridi would be seen as a mental case, as was the unfortunate Austrian Christoph Haizmann, who died in 1700. Ida Macalpine and Richard A. Hunter deal with Haizmann in a book, the title of which telegraphs their approach: *Schizophrenia 1677* (1956).

UNPLEASANT MEDICINE

A mad, defrocked priest, the Abbé Boullan (1824–1893), who followed the insane Pierre Vintras (who thought he was the Prophet Elijah reincarnated) as head of the spurious Work of Mercy, an occult organization in France, took two common thrusts of black magic, blasphemy and reversal, to the extreme. His prescription for nuns under his care—one of whom he got pregnant (he sacrificed the baby in a Black Mass)—who were troubled by demons was to take (stolen) consecrated hosts mixed with feces. This was supposed to cure them of troubles (chiefly sexual) caused by demons.

Boullan's pupil in Satanism, Jules Bois, wrote a book about "Satanism and Magic" in a series given the English title of *The Little Religions of Paris*.

More curious facts on French Satanism in "P. L. Jacob" (Paul Lacroix)'s *Curosités infernales* (1913?) and Alphonse Gallais' *Les Mystéres de la magic . . .* (1909).

WHERE VOODOO CAME FROM

Voodoo has some claim to being one of the religions created in America. It is a peculiarly United States and black mixture of African and pagan European elements along with Christianity. Its name was said to be French. In 1460 the Holy Inquisition burned a dozen heretics and alleged devil worshippers at Arras in France. They were called *Vaudois*. We made it Voodoo, sometimes Hoodoo. Not! The word and most crucial voodoo elements came from Africa. A minor point, perhaps, but useful here to point up the fact that "facts" in the long and confused history of demonology and the occult in general are often invented or distorted and that you must be wary of errors handed along from one "expert" to another. I hope I have been guilty of perpetuating few errors in this compilation.

NINETEENTH-CENTURY SPIRITUALISM IN FRANCE

France, which was much taken with the hypnotism or "animal magnetism" of Dr. Mesmer, fell in love also with spiritualism, overcoming its aversion to American innovations for a while. Probably the most interesting of the spiritualists was the great writer Victor Hugo. Drawn to communicating with the dead as the result of a profound personal loss, as were so many people during the wars of the nineteenth and twentieth centuries, Hugo (whose adored daughter Leopoldine was drowned while still a teenager) tried to reach her on the Other Side. He claimed to have succeeded and to have heard the ghostly voices as well of French luminaries such as Joan of Arc and even English ones such as William Shakespeare.

TWENTY-FIVE MORE BOOKS ON FRENCH WITCHCRAFT

Äbischer, P., *Le Diable* (1933)
Baissac, Jules, *Satan ou le diable* (1876)
Bavent, Sister Madeleine, *Confessions of Madeleine Bavent* (trans. M. Summers, 1933)
Biurneville, M. D. & E. Teinturier, *Le Sabbat des sorciers* (1882)
Bodin, Jean, *De la Démonomanie des sorciers* (1580)
Bouget, Henri, *An Examen of Witches* (trans. M. Summers, 1929)
Calmet, Augustin, *The Phantom World* (trans. H. Christmas, 1850)
Dubal, R., *Psychanalyse du diable* (1833)
Garcon, Maurice & Jean Vinchon, *The Devil* (trans. S. Haden-Guest, 1930)

"Caufeynon" & "Jaf," *Les Messes noirs* (1905)

"Coulange, Louis," *The Life of the Devil* (trans. S. Haden-Guest, 1930)

Dintzer, Lucien, *Nicholas Rémy et son oeuvre démonologique* (1936)

Lamothe-Langon, Etienne Léon de, *Histoire de l'inquisition en France* (1829)

Lancre, Pierre De, *L'Incredulité et mécreance du sortilege* (1622)

Lassus, Jacques, *Les Incubes et les succubes* (1897)

L'Hermite, J., *Vrais et faux Possédés* (1956)

"Lévi, Éliphas," *Magical Ritual of the* Santum Regnum (trans. Wynn West-cott, not seen)

Masson, A., *La Sorcellerie et la sciences des poisons au vii siecle* (1904)

Monter, W., *Witchcraft in France and Switzerland* (1976)

Palou, Jean, *La Sorcellerie* (1957)

Scarf, J., *The Figure of Satan in the Old Testament* (1946)

Schwaeble, René, *Le Sataniste flagelle* (1912)

Williams, Thomas A., *Éliphas Lévi, Master of Occultism* (1975)

A PLEA FOR TOLERANCE IN RELIGION—-AND A REPLY

As the paper bullets of the brain (as Shakespeare would call them) flew thick and fast in the religious dissension of the Reformation and Counter-Refor-

German methods of punishing witchcraft.

mation, a small voice of tolerance was heard from Sebastien Castellio Caelius Curio in *De Hæreticis an sint persequendi?* (1544). He said that the Laws of the Old Testament (which included "Thou shalt not permit a witch to live") had been superseded by the forgiving Laws of Christ, Who called on us to love God and to love our neighbors as ourselves and to leave burning people to God. Their work had little effect. Having done away with the Holy Inquisition, people set up new thought police. Immediately Théodore de Béze answered for the strict Calvinists with *De Hæreticis a civili magistratu puniendis libellus* (A Little Book on the Duty of Civil Magistrates to Punish Heretics, 1544). The persecution of witches continued unabated and later increased considerably.

ALRAUN

In German mythology there is a minor goddess, or elf or goblin, called Alraun. The name comes from *Alraun* (German for "mandrake root"). The mandrake, resembling a human being in shape, was often used in magic and superstition said that if one pulled the root from the earth the resulting scream would drive one mad. (So mandrakes were tied to dog's tails; dogs pulled them up for their masters.) Amulets and talismans were carved from mandrake roots and much mentioned in German superstition.

CHANGES FOR BILWIS AND HIS (OR HER) FRIENDS

Bilwis was a male nature spirit who somehow changed his sex in the Middle Ages and was known throughout the German lands as a vile witch.

Drude in Austria and Germany was known in folklore as a demon who haunts the sleep of humans and casts vicious spells on them. She may derive from some Persian myth, because *druj* is a Persian demon.

Mistress of the fairies, Frau Welt, changed in German folklore from a pleasant person into a foul witch in the Middle Ages.

Holla started out as a beneficent nature goddess, protector of the home and hearth, and became queen of the witches, queen of the elves, a demon.

Mora was a demon whose reputation went from bad to worse. At first she liked changing into a butterfly or a horse and then started to be a vampire.

Die Nixen are water spirits. Sometimes they appear as beautiful women, sometimes as partly woman and partly fish. They can kidnap humans and hold them for ransom. They are called *nissen*, kelpies, *nikker*, and by other names across Europe.

Die Weissen Frauen are "white women" who are witches. They live in the woods, can aid lost travelers, and are said to be able to read the future. Or they may be evil ghosts or dead goddesses.

ADAM OF BREMEN

In the eleventh century Adam of Bremen wrote that "soothsayers and augurs and sorcerers and enchanters and other satellites of Antichrist live where by their deceptions and wonders they may hold unhappy souls up for mockery by demons."

MORE WITCHES
THAN WIZARDS

The medieval theologian Berthold of Regensburg said that more women went to Hell than men because of the witchcraft practiced by women: "spells for getting a husband, spells for the marriage, spells before the child is born, spells before the christening. . . ." He added that "it is a marvel that men lose not their wits for the monstrous witchcrafts that women practise upon them."

An old German woodcut shows accusers masked lest those they label as witches really be witches and have power to retaliate.

The misogyny of medieval (and later) hatred of witches, the burning time that was a sort of Holocaust, did much to keep women in terror, in what religion and other male establishment forces defined as their place.

THE DEVIL AND THE OLD WOMAN

In the Middle Ages, the art of narration got a boost from the use of *exempla* (illustrative tales) inserted into sermons the way woodcuts were to be later put into printed books. One example of the tales frequently told is the German *Der Teufel und das alte Weib*. Sigrid Brauner in *Fearless Wives and Frightened Shrews* describes the tale as told by Erasmus, Melancthon, and others. Over the fifteenth and sixteenth centuries the tale evolved, The Devil became an *Eheteufel* (Marriage Devil), the tale was turned into drama by Hans Sachs and others, and the women characters became stronger and more controversial, more and more like the witch that emerged in the witchcraft trials. Reality imitated fiction.

In its traditional rendition, the tale opens with an angry Satan venting his frustration over thirty or forty years of vain attempts to disrupt the marriage of a pious couple. In one final attempt, he transforms himself into a wealthy and handsome young man, then waits at a crossroads until an old washerwoman passes by. He makes a deal with her, promising her money or a pair of red shoes if she can sow discord between the pious husband and his wife. The old woman goes to the husband and accuses his wife of infidelity, then goes to the wife with the same mendacious story about her husband. She convinces the wife to use sorcery in order to regain her husband's love, and to cut off a lock of his hair while he sleeps. Meanwhile, she warns the husband that his wife is plotting to kill him in his sleep. A nocturnal confrontation follows in which the wife is severely beaten or killed. In the end, the old woman's lies are usually discovered and she is punished, but in some versions of the tale she collects her reward from the devil, who is so afraid of her power that he flees. In either case, the tale is designed to illustrate the proverb that a treacherous tongue is worse than the devil, and to ridicule superstition while reinforcing marital fidelity.

In the folk tale, note not only the desire to promote what we now call "family values" but the connection in the Protestant mind between sex and The Devil, between misogyny and magic. The red shoes, by the way, which to modern readers may bring to mind *The Wizard of Oz* or the magical shoes in the ballet of that name, to the medieval mind meant an expensive present you might give to a prostitute. A witch was a kind of prostitute, selling her soul rather than her body.

BENEDICT CARPZOV

A learned man of Leipzig, Benedict Carpzov closely concerned himself with the witchcraft prosecutions in Saxony but firmly believed that the Thirty Years War was caused by witches. Where Bavaria boasted a dozen kinds of torture to wring confessions out of wretches, he recommended seventeen. The Caroline Code of Justice (named for Charles V) was replaced by harsher punishments by the Elector of Saxony, Augustus (1579).

ANNA EBELER ACCUSED OF MURDER
AND EXECUTED AS A WITCH

Here from the state archives of Bavaria is a German broadside of 1669 that shows Anna Ebeler, aged 67, being seduced by The Devil at a dance (A), flying with the witches (B) and at their dance (C) and feasting with them

Relation

Oder Beschreibung so Anno 1669. den 23. Martij in der Römischen Reichs-Statt Augspurg geschehen / von einer Weibs-Person / welche ob grausamer vnd erschröcklicher Hexerey vnd Verkürtzungen der Menschen / wie auch wegen anderer verübten Vbelthaten durch ein ertheiltes gnädiges Vrtheil von eim gantzen Ehrsamen Rath / zuvor mit glüenden Zangen gerissen / hernach aber mit dem Schwerdt gericht / der Leib zu Aschen verbrennt ist worden.

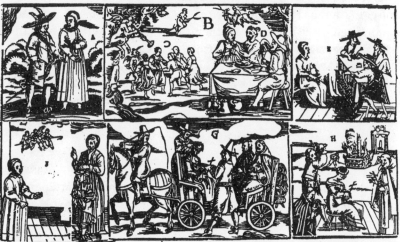

Rstlich hat Anna mit Namen Eberlehrin / gewese Kindtbeth-Kellerin von Augspurg gebürtig / gut vnd betrohlich aufgefaßt vnd bekändt / daß sie vor vngefähr 13. oder vierzehen Jahren / sich mit dem bösen Geist / als er damahlen bey einer Hochzeit in Manns-Gestalt zu jhr auff den Tantz / vnd hernach in jhr Hauß kommen / der gestalt in ein heimlichen Pact vnd Verbündtnuß eingelassen / das sie nit allein demselben sich gantz vnd gar ergeben / sondern auch der Allerheyligisten Dreyfaltigkeit abgesagt / dieselbe verlaugnet / vnd dise zuvor Mündliche gethane all zugrausame vnd höchst Gottslästerliche Absag vnd Verlaugming / auff begehren deß bösen Feinds / nach dem er selbige selbst zu Papier gebracht / mit jhr die Hand gefuhrt / auch so gar mit jhrem Blut vnderschriben vnd bekräfftiget / von welcher Zeit an sie mit dem laidigen Sathan auch manches mahlen Vnzucht getriben: Defgleichen auff antrib desselben durch eine von jhme empfangnes weisses Pülverleins wenigist 5. Personen / vnd darunder 4. vnschuldige vnmündige Kinder elendiglich hingerichtet / vnd vmbs Leben gebracht / nit weniger habe sie jhren leibeignen Bruder durch ein dergleichen jhme inn Trunck beygebrachtes Pülverleins verkrümbt / vnd dardurch sowol demselben als andern Menschen mehr / die eintweders an jhren Leibern Knüpffel oder sonsten grosse Kopffwehe bekommen / zu mahlen dem Vieh durch Hexerey vnd zauberische Mittel geschadet / auch darunder zwey Pferdt gar zu schanden gemacht / Ferners habe sie auch nit allein durch grausam flüchen vnd schworen mit zuthun der bösen Feindts etliche Wetter gemacht / darunder eines zu Günzburg eingeschlagen / vnd grossen Schaden gethan / sondern auch vermittelst Nächtlicher Aufsahrens zu vnderschidenen mahlen bey den Hexen-Tänzen vnd Ver-

samblungen sich eingefunden / vñ darbey dem bösen Geist mit Knie biegen vnd dergleichen solche Ehr bewisen die sonsten GOtt dem Allmächtigen allein gebühre. So hat sie auch über daß noch weiters auffgesagt vñ bekändt / daß sie in Zeit diser jhrer mit dem bösen Feind gehabten gemein vnd Kundschafft einsmahls vngebeichtet das Hochwürdige heylige Sacrament deß Altars empfangen vñ genossen / auch sich vnderstanden / nit allein durch jhr vergifftes Teufflisches Pulver vñ andere / zwey Weibs-Personen vnfruchtbar zunachen / bey deme es aber ausser einer nit angangen seye / sondern auch ein Mägdlein vnd einen jungen Knaben zu den Hexen-Tänzen mit genommen vnd verführet.

Ob welcher vnd anderer verübter vilfältiger schwerer vnd grausamerer Vnthaten / vnd Verbrechen halber ein Ehrsamer Rath mit Vrtheil zu Recht erkandt / daß jhr Eberlehrin obwolen sie denen Rechten nach lebendig verbrennt zu werden verdient hette / dannoch auf Gnaden allein mit glüenden Zangen am Außführen drey Griff gegeben / vnd sie bey der Richtstatt mit dem Schwerdt von blutiger Hand vom Leben zum Todt hingerichtet / auch der Cörper in Aschen verbrandt solle werden.

A   Die Abführung ab dem Tantz / vnd in Anna Eberlehrin Behausung Einführung von dem Teuffel.
B   Die Außfahrung Nächtlicher weil mit dem bösen Feind.
C   Die Bewohnungen der Hexen-Tänzen.
D   Die Heßischen Zamenkunfften vnd Teufflische Malzeiten.
E   Verdörung vnd Außsag wegen jhrer verübten Hexereyen.
F   Verführung zweyer jungen vnschuldiger Kinder / als eines Knaben vnd Mägdlein.
G   Anna Eberlehrin Außführung zu dem Gericht / vnd wie sie mit glüenden Zangen gerissen wird.
H   Die Hinrichtung vnd Verbrennung zu Aschen jhres Leibs.

Zu Augspurg / bey Elias Wellhöffer Brieffmaler / bey vnser l. Frawen Thor.

(D), interrogated for witchcraft (E), leading astray a little boy and little girl (F), carted off to execution (G), executed for witchcraft and her body then burned at Augsburg (H).

PUNISHMENT OF WITCHCRAFT IN STYRIA

Here, from Austria in the seventeenth century, is an example of the incredible barbarities in the persecution of witches in backwaters. At Gutenhag (1673) a 57-year-old woman was made to kneel on spikes for 11 days and nights while her feet were burned with sulphur. She died, says J. B. Holtzinger's *Zur Naturgeschichten der Hexen* (1883), out of her mind with torture. In Meran (1679) a fourteen-year-old beggar boy was tortured until he implicated three others in witchcraft and all four were burned. In Linz (1680) Emerenziane Pichler was burned at the stake and so were two of her children, aged twelve and fourteen. In 1688 a whole family and its servant were burned. In Steiermark (1695) Marianna Schepp was tortured until she confessed to having had sex with The Devil; she was burned.

HEXENHAUSEN

Special jails had to be built to hold witches in Germany. One was built in Salzburg and another, for instance, in Bamburg. In the latter town the Prince-Bishop Gottfried Johann Georg II Fuchs von Dornheim sent some 600 persons accused of witchcraft to their deaths.

OPPONENTS OF THE WITCHCRAFT MANIA

Some sensible men called for reason to triumph in witchcraft cases, as opposed to those who were arguing (for instance) that confessions extracted under torture be admissible. Among rational writers of witchcraft and demonology, the English leader was Reginald Scot (*The Discovery of Witchcraft*, 1584); in Germany the leader was Johannes Weyer (*De Præstigiis dæmonum*, 1563); and in Italy the leader was Samuel de Cassini (*Question de la strie*, 1505).

EARLY GERMAN WRITERS ON WITCHCRAFT
AND DEMONOLOGY

It is only natural that the land that produced the first printing by moveable type should have contributed significantly to *incunabula*, fifteenth-century books on these popular topics. Among other writers we find:

Johannes Nider, Dominican prior at Nurenberg and Basle, *Formicarius* (written 1435)

Johann Hartlieb, physician to the King of Bavaria, *Buch aller verboten Kunst* . . . (*c.* 1456)

Jakob Sprenger & Heinrich Kramer, Dominican Inquisitors, *Malleus malefi-carum* (*c.* 1486)

Ulrich Molitor, law professor, University of Constance, *De Lamiis* . . . (1489)

ULRICH MOLITOR

This learned professor at the University of Constance is one of the big names in this area of study. His *De Lamiis et pythonicis mulieribus* (1489) was one of the first significant books on the subject, had a woodcut that was the first picture ever published of a witch on her broomstick in flight, and was way ahead of its time in urging that the *sabbat* was delusion, not to be punished by death. He writes:

> It is untrue that witches go thousands of furlongs in the silence of the night to gather for the *sabbat*. They are the playthings of dreams or some powerful illusion . . . which the devil has impressed on their minds. Thus deceived by vain appearances, they believe, on waking, that such things really happened to them.

A BERLIN JEW PUT TO DEATH

Under torture, the master of the mint in Berlin (1573), a Jew, confessed that he had killed the elector of the Holy Roman Empire by magical drinks. He was torn apart and the pieces burned with a book on magic, allegedly his.

Jews were slandered as killers of Christian babies. It was alleged that they used the infants' blood to make *matzoh* and for other vile practices. This connected Jews in popular prejudice with Satanists who spilled the blood of infants and engaged in ritual murder.

BAMBERG

The French judge Nicholas Rémy of Nancy boasted of having sent witches to execution on the average of one a week for ten years. What had started him off was that a beggar woman cursed him (when he refused to give her anything) and soon after his son died. However, Rémy's personal record was far outdone by the prince-bishop and his cousin the infamous "axe bishop" of Bamberg in Bavaria. Let us look at him again.

Prince-Bishop Philipp Adolph von Ehrenberg and Bishop Gottfried Johann Georg II Fuchs von Dornheim, in about a decade from 1623 on, sent some 1,500 witches to the stake. The city built a special *Hexenhaus* in which to incarcerate and torture them into confessions, as we noted.

WITCHCRAFT TRIALS

With the exception of books that blame the Jesuits for excesses and similar ax-grinding, there is no one huge volume that covers all the bloody history of *Die Hexenprozesse*. One has to seek out rare volumes specializing in individual cities such as Bamberg, individual states such as Bavaria, or individual areas such as The Tyrol. Debates rage whether this or that hanging (or should we say burning?) judge's score is higher than that one, but 500, 600, or 700 deaths to a judge's "credit" is not unusual and some overachievers are to be found. The dark recesses of the *Schwartzwald* seem to have hatched the craziest people, but even the northern rationality of the likes of Berlin, Bremen, and Hamburg fails more often than one might expect.

Germany seems to hold the dubious record for deaths for dealing with demons. This penchant continued into modern times: the Nazis were very interested in the occult and attempted to enlist evil supernatural forces as well as to bend good ones to their will.

JOHANNES WEYER BLASTS THE JUDGES OF WITCHES

"But when He finally appears Whom nothing escapes—the searcher of the heart and reins Who knows and judges the most hidden truth—your deeds will be made public, you stubborn tyrants and bloodthirsty judges stripped of humanity and far removed from all mercy because of your blindness. I challenge you to appear at the most just tribunal of the Supreme Judge Himself, Who will decide between you and me when the truth that has been buried and trampled underfoot will rise again and oppose you to your face, exacting vengeance for your villainy. Then shall be revealed your understanding of the Gospel truth, which some of you belch forth so excessively. Then you will see how much the true word of God has been with you; then you will be measured by the same standard by which you have been measured." *De Præstigiis dæmonum* VI:4; translated by John Shea.

ONE OF THE TEN MOST SIGNIFICANT BOOKS OF ALL TIME

According to Sigmund Freud, that honor goes to Johann Weir (or Weyer)'s *De Præstigiis dæmonum* (1563, now available in a translation by John Shea, with a useful positioning preface by Dr. John Weber, edited by Dr. George Mora, 1991). In Weir's lifetime (1515–1588) this medical and magical, legal and philosophical masterpiece appeared in six Latin editions (up to 1583) and German and French translations. Weir considers witches to be deluded and far less harmful than sorcerers and he calls for an end to the wildest superstitions of witch-hunters. He gives a tremendous amount of medical and historical, but also superstitious and folklore, material and an insight into the lives of real people in his time, people terrified and confused by magic. This is a contribution to theology, psychiatry, canon and secular law's history, the history of religion, and the history of ideas. Some other relevant books, not so central, yet all significant:

"Agrippa, Cornelius," *Opera*
Ashley, Leonard R. N., *Die Welt der Magie*
Brennan, J. H., *The Occult Reich*
Fascher, E., *Jesus und der Satan*
Hansen, Joseph, *Geschichte des Hexenwahns und der Hexenverfolgung im Mittelalter*
Jung, Carl, *Mysterium coniunctionis*
Obenkid, H., *Der Teufel bei Martin Luther*
"Paracelsus," *De Natura rerum*
Sprenger, Jakob & Heinrich Kramer, *Malleus maleficarum*

FURTHER READING ON WITCHCRAFT IN GERMANY

Hansen, Joseph, *Quellen und Untersuchungen zür Geschichte des Hexenwahns und der Hexenverfolgung* (1901)
_____, *Zauberwahn, Inquisition und Hexenprozess im Mitelalter*
Horst, George, *Zauberbibliotek (1821–1826)* (1900)
Midelfort, H. C. E., *Witch-Hunting in South-Western Germany 1562–1684* (1972)
Ruttenauer, Isabelle, *Friedrich von Spee . . .* (1951)
Rysan, Joseph, *Wilhelm Meinhold's Maria Schweidler die Bernsteinhexe: A Study in Witchcraft and Cultural History* (1948)
Schieler, Caspar, *Magister Johannes Nider* (1885, an author of *Formicarius*, 1475)
Soldan, Wilhelm Gottleib, *Geschichte der Hexenproczesse* (revised by Max

Bauer, 1912)
Stockum, Theodorus Cornelis van, *Friedrich von Spee en de hexen processen* (1949)
Wachter, Oscar von, *Vehmgerichte und hexenprocess in Deutschland* (1882)

GERMAN STUDIES OF EVIL IN THE OLD TESTAMENT

Duhm, H., *Die bösen Geister in Alten Testament* (1904)
Kaupel, H., *Die Dämonen in Alten Testament* (1930)
Scharff, R. R., *Die Gestalt des Satan in Alten Testament* (1948)
Weinel, H., *Die Wirkungen des Geistes unter der Geister* (1899)

ITALIAN WITCHCRAFT

The two most common aspects of Italian dealing in the black arts are connected with *mal occhio* (the Evil Eye that can bewitch at a glance) and *ghirlanda delle streghe* ("witches' garland," better known in English as the witches' ladder).

The Evil Eye is countered by a gesture that extends the first and fourth fingers (to resemble the horns of a bull), by charms of coral or a silver *mano figa* making an obscene gesture, or amulets of other material worn around the neck. In The Kingdom of the Two Sicilies the *jettatore* or persons who could cast the Evil Eye were greatly feared. In Corsica it is called *innoc-*

Devils push a thirteenth-century Italian monk into the Tiber.

chiatura. In Britain the Evil Eye was guarded against or cured by various witches' powders but Italy does not seem to have had recipes for them.

There is not much you can do about the witches' ladder unless you find it and destroy it before the evil it invokes destroys you. The witch ties knots in a length of rope at equal intervals and makes sure there is a feather from a black hen in each knot. Then she buries the "ladder." As it rots, you decline, and eventually you die.

Italian witches were also familiar with poisons, with making wax figurines which, when melted, caused the person portrayed to dwindle in health, and other evil magic common across Europe, but the Evil Eye and the witches' ladder were their specialties.

In the Renaissance, Italian astrologers reached a high degree of respectability, if not accuracy, but today none of the world's leading astrologers is Italian. English astrologers are famous.

The power of the Roman Catholic Church in Italy may have done much to suppress the dealing with evil, but at the same time those who do fight the system gain extra thrills because of their sharp awareness of blasphemies being committed. It is said in some circles that no one becomes a truly potent magician who is not electrified by the irreligious actions she or he is performing.

THE EVIL EYE

Dundes, Alan, *Evil Eye* (1981)
Elworthy, Frederick Thomas, *The Evil Eye* (1958)
Frohmann, Johannes Christian, *Tractatus de fascinatione* (1675)
Gifford, Edward S., Jr., *The Evil Eye* (1958)
MacLagan, R. C., *The Evil Eye in the Western Highlands* (1902)
Maloney, Clarence (ed.), *The Evil Eye* (1976)
Story, William W., *Castle St. Angelo and the Evil Eye* (1877)
Valletta, Niccola, *Cicolata sul fascino volgamente ditto jettatura* (1814)

SACRIFICES TO THE EVIL ONES

Ancient Greeks sacrificed black animals to the gods of the nether world and dogs to Hecate, a witch goddess of the underworld. The Romans inherited many Greek superstitions like these.

MATHESIS

Julius Firmicius Maternus studied magic in the East, principally at Alexandria, and returned to fourth-century Rome to write *Mathesis*. It is chiefly a defense of astrology but is relevant here because of the connection between devils and divination. It deserves more attention.

EVIL GODDESSES OF CLASSICAL TIMES

There are so many books on the gods and goddesses and other supernatural creatures of Greece and Rome that it is quite unnecessary to list their equivalents of devils and demons here. However, although I omit the harpies, destructive Arai, monsters, and some other creatures, you may be interested in this unusual list of evil goddesses from the Greek and Roman mythologies:

Acco, Greek goddess who swallowed the newborn
Acidalia, Greek and Roman goddess of restlessness, disorder
Adiphasia, Greek goddess of gluttony, disorder
Adicia, Greek goddess of injustice, ugliness
Aegiale, Greek goddess of unhappiness, magic
Aetheria, Greek goddess of unhappiness, magic
Androctasia, Greek goddess of slaughter
Brimo, terrifying Greek goddess of death
Campe, Greek goddess guarding the gates of Tartarus
Canidia, Greek sorceress who can bring the moon down from the sky
Cer, Greek destroyer of life
Charybdis, Greek destroyer of life (a whirlpool)
Deino, Greek sea goddess of destructive waves
Dioxippe, Greek goddess of unhappiness, magic
Dysnomia, Greek goddess of lawlessness, disorder
Empusa, Greek vampire goddess of ugliness
Epitymbia, Greek goddess of "death in life"
Eriphyle, Greek goddess of evil
Eris, Greek goddess of disorder, war
Euryale, Greek Gorgon of evil (the others are **Medusa** and **Stheno**)
Gello, Greek female demon of magic and evil
Gorgopa, Greek destroyer of life
Kakia, Greek goddess of vice
Lamia, evil Greek eater of children

Mormo, Greek goddess of evil and immortality
Pandora, Greek "giver of all" evil on earth
Phaea, Greek monstrous sower of evil
Pugna, Greek goddess of disorder
Scylla, Greek "witch of the shoals" (goes with **Charybdis**)

It is odd that the nine Muses are patronesses not only of the arts and creativity, intelligence, etc., but also function as goddesses of evil in some respects. There are other goddesses who include evil among their mixed attributes. Pyrene (for whom The Pyrennees were named) is one of the Greek goddesses who included evil among other attributes. The straightforward evil Roman goddesses are:

Caca, Roman goddess of evil and fire
Discordia, Roman goddess of discord
Fata, Roman goddess of fate and evil
Fata Albina and **Fata Morgana**, sisters in evil
Fraud, Roman goddess of betrayal and deceit
Laverna, Roman goddess of evil, patroness of thieves
Tursa, Roman goddess of terror and evil

IF YOU AREN'T SEXUALLY ATTRACTIVE, YOU DON'T HAVE TO WORRY ABOUT VAMPIRES

Vampires (and predatory female horrors) go back to classical times and sexual fears. James Sheridan LeFanu's lesbian *Carmilla*, Robert Louis Stevenson's sexy *Ollala*, and Bram Stoker's dashing *Dracula* (with all its white throats, heaving bosoms, seductive female vampires), not to mention the studly and slinky creatures that stalk by night with a hunger for sex as well as for blood in modern novels and films—all these make it clear that vampires, heterosexual and homosexual, are undead from the waist down as well.

David Punter in *The Literature of Terror* claims that "one of the principal arguments behind vampire fiction" is "that only for those who are in unfortunate possession of sexual attractions and urges which they are personally or socially incapable of repressing is vampirism a significant psychological danger."

To put it another way, if you are not "hot," those chill reanimated corpses are not interested in you in the least. If you don't turn vampires on, vampires will not turn on you.

That must be some consolation to some people.

HOLY ICONS BANISH SLAVIC VAMPIRES

The undead, despite those classic Greek origins, are forever associated now with Transylvania. Just as in England and other European countries, where an evil spirit can be lured into a bottle by certain ceremonies ("witch bottles" are still to be seen in a few museums), in Bulgaria and other Slavic countries the dreaded vampires can be captured this way.

Summers in *The Vampire: His Kith and Kin* quotes *Walachische Muaeheren*:

> There is yet another method of abolishing a Vampire—that of *bottling* him. There are certain persons who make a profession of this; and their mode of procedure is as follows: The sorcerer, armed with a picture of some saint, lies in ambush until he sees the Vampire pass, when he pursues him with his *Eikon*; the poor Obour takes refuge in a tree or on the roof of a house, but his persecutor follows him up with the talisman, driving him away from all shelter, in the direction of the bottle specially prepared, in which is placed some of the vampire's favorite food [blood]. Having no other resource, he enters this prison, and is immediately fastened down with a cork, on the interior of which is a fragment of the *Eikon*. The bottle is then thrown into the fire, and the Vampire disappears for ever.

Known to everyone is the vampire's aversion to the basic icon of Christianity, the crucifix. In old vampire movies the crucifix burned the flesh of any vampire who was touched with it; vampires fled before it in dismay. More recently, the power of faith or faith itself has waned. The crucifix is simply brushed aside by vampires in modern films. As a Jewish vampire said in a parodic vampire movie: "This will not help."

THE *STRIX* OF THE ROMANS

Petronius writes early of a superstition that was to have a long life, namely that the *strix* could fly in, take away your baby, and leave in its stead a poppet such as the witches made of straw.

THE WITCHES OF HORACE'S ROME

Quintus Horatius Flaccus (65–8 B.C.) in his satires or "conversation pieces" offers us sharp pictures of life in his time and in *Satires* I:8 he describes two witches up to no good in the cemetery on the Esquiline Hill of Rome. They are there by the light of the new moon to collect the necessaries for their evil work, bones and herbs, and because it offers a suitably ghoulish venue for their dirty deeds. Their hair is wild, their gowns all awry, their feet bare.

They dig a hole and over it tear a lamb apart as a sacrifice to the powers of evil. They are raising the dead. They have two poppets or little dolls. One is made of wool and represents a witch. The other is made of wax and represents their victim. The scene is ghastly. The moon turns red as blood. Snakes skitter across the ground. The witches do their evil magic and bury the tooth of a snake and the muzzle of a wolf to seal their awful bargain with the destructive forces. They melt the waxen image. Their victim will pine and die.

BURNING OF WITCHES IN ITALY

Despite being the site of the papacy, Italy did not prosecute as many witches under the Holy Inquisition as did (say) Germany, but in 1485 in Como, 41 women were burned for witchcraft and in 1514 a total of 300 more. Brescia was supposed to have been the site of a sort of Woodstock for witches (the *sabbat* crowd on one occasion estimated at 25,000) and the few witches burned in the fifteenth century were followed by increased prosecutions and persecutions: 140 burned in 1510, for example. The Holy Inquisition got so busy in Brescia that the jails were crammed with thousands of suspects, which local officials resisted burning. In 1521 Leo X's bull *Honestis* excommunicated all officials who resisted the Holy Inquisition and removed all church sacraments and services from communities that did not promptly deal with witches handed over to the civil authorities for execution. The signory of Brescia resisted the pope, setting up its own "blue-ribbon" commission to examine newly arrested and already condemned alleged witches and pointing out to the pope that a great many accusations of witchcraft were unfounded, prompted by malice, revenge, and the desire to get the property of the accused.

Most Italian authorities, however, went along with papal policies, but most witchcraft in Italy was quietly conducted at the village level, where it was more or less appreciated by the peasantry. In the papal court itself, astrologers and even sorcerers were retained by a number of popes at the time, though it is fair to say that these high ecclesiastics were no more superstitious than the average Italian of the period, or, for that matter, the presidents (and their wives) in the United States of the twentieth century.

THEODORE OF GAZA

This famous Humanist, translator of Aristotle into Latin and professor of Greek in the universities of Sienna, Ferrara, and Rome, spent the years 1429 to 1478 (the year of his death) in Italy and enjoyed the patronage of Pope Nicholas V and Cardinal Bessarion.

While Theodore was a priest in the Abruzzi region, a farmer who worked on the parish farm turned up an ancient burial urn and that same night had a dream in which a ghost of gaunt and menacing aspect appeared and threatened the farmer with harm unless the urn was immediately reburied.

When the farmer paid no attention to this threat, his son was found dead, his body drained of blood, and it seemed that the ghost was a vampire, for when he next appeared to the farmer in a dream he was now full of vigor, presumably from having feasted on the blood of the son. Once again the ghost (or vampire) demanded that the burial urn and its ashes be returned to the ground. If not, the ghost said, the farmer's second son would die in a similar grisly fashion.

The farmer took the story to Theodore, who took it seriously. Theodore saw to it that the urn was reburied not only with Christian ceremonies but with all the rites of a pagan funeral of the pre-Christian period. The ghost (or vampire) seemed to be pleased with that and never was heard of again. What is remarkable about this story is that the vampire's body having been cremated in ancient times was not available for him to reanimate it, so he had to come in a dream rather than in the undead flesh to harry the living. In ordinary vampire stories, the vampire is laid by its corpse being staked or dismembered and even burned to ashes, which are scattered. In this case, the ashes enabled the vampire to survive and to preserve their rest the vampire was willing and able to kill the living. Or so the superstitious peasants of the Abruzzi, not to mention the learned Humanist, were convinced.

FRA AGNOLO FIRENZUOLA

This Vallambrosan monk, born in Florence (hence the surname) in 1493— he died in Prato in 1543 after a burst of writing activity following a decade or more of silence—and active in Rome at the height of his career, translated *The Golden Ass* of Apuleius as *Asino d'oro* (1525). Because of the original novel's interest in magic and witchcraft and the fact that in his adaptation Fra Agnolo did not hesitate to change things and include a lot

Devils and demons punish sin in this Italian popular print, eighteenth century. Bassano del Grappa Municipal Museum.

of his own experiences and comments on his own times, perhaps Italian scholars ought to include his work among the neglected writings of the Renaissance which have yet to be assessed in terms of their possible contributions to the history of Italian folklore, witchcraft and the Holy Inquisition, and related topics.

THE DEVIL AT THE CROSSROADS

Rachel Harriette Busk in *The Folk-Lore of Rome* (1874):

> I know a very consistently religious woman, and also singularly intelligent, who appeared to have a salutary contempt for certain practices in which her husband, a worthless fellow, who had long ago abandoned her and his religion together, indulged. 'He actually believes,' she told me one day, 'that if you go out and stand on a cross road—not merely where two roads happen to cross each other, but where they actually make a perfect cross—and if at the stroke of *mezzorgionro in punto* [midnight exactly], you call the Devil he is bound to come to you.'

DON'T ORDER ITALIAN CHEESECAKE FOR DESSERT

St. Augustine was disturbed to hear rumors that in Italy women innkeepers gave cheese to travelers which turned them into beasts of burden. This seems to reflect something of the story of the witch Circe who in the *Odyssey* turned men into swine and was, with the possible exception of Medea, the most famous witch of Greek legend.

ITALIAN EXPERTS ARGUE THE REALITY OF CONTACT WITH EVIL

The Roman Catholic Church *canon episcopi* instructed that alleged contacts of humans with devils and demons were usually imaginary, delusion rather than devil worship, and it attempted to keep stories of the calling up of demons and of exorcisms to a minimum. This has been church policy for centuries, even though some Catholics are unaware of the fact. After the witch hunts of Innocent VIII died down this attitude was echoed by such writers as the lawyer Gianfrancisco Ponzinibio of *De Lamiis et excellentia juris utriusque*, published with Paolo Grillando's *De Sortilegius* (1519).

Nevertheless, various orders within the church took various views. The Jesuits, for instance, tended on the whole to play down demonology, while the Dominicans tended to stress it. For instance, in his *De Strigamagarum daemonumque mirandis* (1521), Silvestro Mazzolini (*Prierius* from his birthplace in northern Italy) took a much more extreme view than Ponzinibio but did not think it was worthwhile to debate theology with a layman like him. Another Dominican, Bartolomeo Spina, took on Ponzinibio in three *Apologiæ*.

By the eighteenth century, Italian thought on the subject of demonology was decidedly in the modern, doubting camp (see C. Grimaldi's *Dissertatione* [1751]). However, as late as the end of the nineteenth century, popes were still being accused of dabbling in the black arts and one was generally believed to have the dreaded Evil Eye so that when he appeared in public in Rome, the average person averted his or her gaze for fear of him. Of course the hotly contested papal elections, which sometimes were bitter and lasted a long time (in modern times the consistory of cardinals is bricked up and pretty much held prisoner in the Sistine Chapel until their selection is made), often produced rumors that this or that candidate was trying to employ infernal powers to get the Throne of Peter. Both popes and political candidates in ancient Rome wore white—

which is where the word *candidate* came from—but it was suspected that some of them lacked the purity this was supposed to signify.

STREGA

This word is known today to non-Italians as the name of a liqueur with an herbal base, somewhat similar to those created by Carthusian, Benedictine, and other monks. The name apparently suggests that this recipe comes from, or was influenced by, the wise women or witches famous for their potions (and also poisons, but the liqueur is supposed to be health-giving).

For centuries these old women practiced herbal medicine, and if they mumbled blessings or curses over their retorts or attached magical conditions to taking the medicines, it only assisted the superstitious to get well. The mystery that surrounds modern medical prescriptions gives them similar additional power, and the very symbol of medicine is a magical wand of Mercury.

It was only when locals turned against these old women out of disappointment with their medicines, or when malice or greed for their few possessions caused people to turn them in to the authorities or lynch them, that the witches were persecuted. Most of the time they were both diagnosticians and apothecaries in their little world, a genuine public service, regarded with respect and permitted to operate more or less publicly alongside church and other institutions, like the *curanderos* in Mexico today.

PALLADISM

Some weird conjunction of Roman Catholic traditional opposition to Freemasonry and superstitious revival produced in the nineteenth century a tremendous fear of Satanism and rumors of Palladism revived in Rome. Dominico Margiotta *La Palladisme: Culte de Satan* (1895) stirred up fears and writers using the pseudonyms of "Papus" and "Diana Vaughan," both French, got on the bandwagon. As was often the case in matters of this sort, the more Italians denied the existence of Satanism in their country, the more this was regarded by those who held crazy ideas as an obvious cover-up.

Secret rituals of any kind, those of Freemasonry or even, say, of Mormonism (which the founder of the Church of Jesus Christ of Latter Day Saints, Joseph Smith, borrowed from his training with the Masons), always give ammunition to those who are looking for Satanic rites.

Palladism was one of those nonstarters that occasionally crop up in imitation of what the ignorant imagine to be the vile and occult practices of

The Knights Templar. That order was uprooted centuries ago and none of the modern imitations have even as much validity as the peculiarly American supposed revivals of Rosicrucianism that have come out of California. The Nazis, with an *Ahnenerbe* (occult bureau) under the notorious Heinrich Himmler, were much interested in The Templars as well as in the spear with which "Longinus" is supposed to have pierced the side of the Crucified Christ. That spear was taken to Germany by Hitler's forces after the *Anschluss* in Austria and returned to Vienna by the victorious American forces in 1946. You can read all you would ever want to know about *The Spear of Destiny* in Trevor Ravenscroft's book of that title (1973), and the bibliography of The Templars (and the Rosicrucians, for that matter) is immense. Like Palladism, it is all part of the unending literature of human superstition and folly.

WITCHCRAFT IN ITALY

Anania, Giovanni Lorenzo, *De Natura demonum* (1581)
Anonymous, *Instructio pro formandis processibus in causis strigum* (c. 1627)
Bergamo, Johannes de, *Quæstio de strigis* (c. 1470)
Carena, Caesar, *Tractatus de offico santctissimæ inquisitionis* (1636)
Ferraironi, Francesco, *Le Strege e l'inquisizione . . .* (1955)
Giacomo, Vittorio di, *Legende del diavolo* (1957)
Grillandus, Paulus, *Tractatus de hereticis et sortilegiis* (1536)
Guazzo, Francesco Maria, *Compendium maleficarum* (trans. M. Summers, 1929)
Menghi, Girolamo, *Flagellum dæmonum* (1582)
Papini, Giovanni, *Il Diavolo* (1954)
Pico della Mirandola, Gianfrancesco, *Dialogo intitolata la strega* (Italian trans. of *Strix* of 1523, 1864)
Ponzinibio, Gianfrancesco, *Tractatus de lamiis* (1563)
Sinistrati, Ludovico, *Demonality* (trans. M. Summers, 1927)
Spina, Bartolommeo, *Quæstio de strigibus* (1523)
Vignati, Ambrogio de, *Tractatus de hæreticis* (1581)
Vitoria, Francisco de, *Relationes XII thelogiæ* (1540)
Walker, D. P., *Spiritual and Demonic Magic from Ficino to Campanella* (1958)

POPE ACCUSED OF DEALING WITH DEMONS

That sounds like a headline in one of the sensational, checkout-counter rags that do much to account for the frightening percentages of Americans who believe that UFOs are real and that the government is keeping something from us. Dealing with The Devil is real in the United States (and elsewhere), or at least the Satanists trying it believe so, and the government doesn't seem to be making a whole hell of a lot out of that fact. The reasons may be political, including a desire not to alarm people who can't do much under the law to rectify the situation anyway.

Political also were many of the accusations of dealing with The Devil leveled at the anti-popes of the Great Schism. Benedict XIII (anti-pope, 1394-1423, not the real one who reigned 1724–1730) was accused of holding "continuous traffic" with evil spirits and of carrying two demons around with him, in a bag. He certainly did collect a nice library of books on magic, but so did other popes building the collections of The Vatican. Benedict IX (1042–1048) was twice deposed and became an anti-pope (to Clement II, no prize package either) and was called a sorcerer. The anti-pope John XXIII was accused of having tried black magic to protect him against the Council of Constance (1414–1417). Some other popes were attacked by black magicians and may have responded in kind. Charges of being black magicians on the papal throne, however, are suspect because of the partisan politics involved. Those could be bitter. There were murder attempts off and on on both sides of many questions and even after you were dead you were not safe: Honorius I died in 638 and forty-two years later they pronounced him anathema. Honorius II and Honorius III were also accused of being black magicians.

Some popes, however, seem to have been accused less politically, more justifiably. Leo III (795–816) sent a book of magic, *Enchiridion*, to the Emperor Charlemagne and is plausibly said to have written it. I explain in *The Complete Book of Magic and Witchcraft* why I think Sylvester II (999–1003) had such a reputation as a magician. It's a good story. I also explain why I think Pius IX (who lived until 1878) was unfairly accused of having the Evil Eye. Of twentieth-century popes, including at least one who disappeared rather too abruptly, I say nothing.

THE WITCHES OF THE ABRUZZI

This notably backward section of Italy has given many immigrants to the United States, so some of the peasant customs of the *Abruzzesi* were well known in New York and other cities, in the last century and survive in some smaller degree today in various cities with Italian-American populations.

Putting salt in a little bag to be hung around a child's neck was supposed to ward off witches. So were, of course, certain Roman Catholic

Mandragoras mas & fæmina.
The male and female Mandrake.

FOEMINÆ

MARIS

Mandrakes were supposed to have magical powers, and many legends were spun about them. One said that a root pulled from the earth would utter a scream so terrible that any person who heard it would go mad. So people tied plants to dogs' tails and ran away. Nicolò Machiavelli wrote a famous play entitled *La Mandragola.*

prayers, the crucifix, holy water (on the hinges of the door, notably), blessed medals, etc. The stink of a sulfur was said to drive off evil spirits, which was odd because they themselves were said to give off a sulfurous smell.

GERONIMO CARDANO

This Italian genius (1501–1576) made great strides in mathematics and natural science (where he anticipated Darwin *re* evolution) and education (signs for the deaf to communicate, a system anticipating Braille for the blind to read, etc.). However, he was prevented from the regular practice of medicine because he was a bastard child. So he turned to medical astrology, and in that occupation was very famous. It also brought him into contact with demonology, but he was, like other Italian thinkers of his time such as Alciati, Porta, and Ponzinibio, skeptical about what the dogmatists and the demonologists claimed about contact between humans and infernal powers. Italian witches, frankly, did not seem to have any important connections with the vast powers the church attributed to mankind's greatest and oldest enemy. Cardano thought that there were medical and psychological uses for potions and ungents and such and that their effectiveness might be enhanced by mumbo-jumbo but that spells and incantations worked on people, not on devils and demons.

The instructions for conducting witchcraft trials issued by the Borghese Pope Paul V (who reigned 1605–1621), a master of the Canon Law, were tempered by the opinions of such men as Cardano. *Instructio pro formandis processibus in causis strigum, sortilegiorum et maleficiorum* by Paul V shows the vast difference between Italian approaches and German approaches such as those in the *Malleus maleficarum*, which by Paul V's time had run to almost thirty editions in a little over a century.

THE OCCULT IN SPAIN

The Golden Age was perhaps the zenith (to use a word we got from the Arabs who held Spain for centuries) of interest in the occult and we see many instances of Spanish beliefs of this sort in the works of Cervantes and the playwrights. (See *Critica hispanica* 19:1, 1993, 117–138 for a survey of the occult in Spanish drama right up to the eighteenth century.) Earlier than the sixteenth century, however, the Spanish were fascinated by occult aspects of both Arab and Jewish thought. Then, of course, there was the emphasis on magic and witchcraft brought about by the Holy Inquisition, the Spanish branch of which remains the most famous, or infamous. In the nineteenth and twentieth centuries, historical novelists and other writers have made much of the sensational aspects of the Inquisition, the magicians of southern Spain, the witches of the Basque and other regions, the mages of the past (among whom they like to include Leonardo da Vinci), and aspects of the magical and even diabolical in the folklore.

A DEMONIC *OLLA PODRIDA*

Before the judges of the Holy Inquisition in Spain (1610) one Juan de Echalár from Navarre gave the recipe for the most disgusting dish of Spanish cooking, Toad & Corpse Stew.

He testified under oath that at the *sabbat* the witches presented toads to Satan (who received them and blessed them with his left hand) and that they were boiled up in a pot with pieces of dead bodies that ghouls had stolen from graveyards. This made destructive magical potions that were distributed to the witches present.

Toads were frequently mentioned in connection with a magical "stone" supposedly found in their heads and with attempts at foretelling the future by examining their entrails, but this is the one and only example (so far as I know) of them as an ingredient in the witches' brew. Traditionally there are toads "broken" at the *sabbat* the way the consecrated host is broken at the Mass, and toads used like that are called *"Philip"* after the French king who put to death the last Grand Master of the Knights Templar, Jacques de Molay, in the fourteenth century. Black magicians will never forget that. They rejoiced at the French Revolution killing a king.

There are other witches' brews that use parts of toads, eye of newt, and so on. There is, in fact, some poisonous element in certain animal parts, of course, and to this witches added plants containing atropine and many other dangerous substances. Modern witches use chemicals rather than animal parts but they do sometimes employ herbs and simples, partly (I imagine) to avoid too modern, too synthetic a pharmacology.

Most people know they do not like garlic or salt but are unaware that witches steer clear of verbena; it is the bane of witches. The witch hazel is just a misnomer: it is a "quick," that is "live," tree not a "magic" tree (although the German name for it now, *Zauberstrauch*, incorporates the word for "magic"). It is never used in witches' brews.

I think I should omit identification of the kind of wood needed for stirring the evil brew. Without that piece of information, even if you get the recipes from some *Cooking Up Evil in Your Microwave* or such, your potions won't work. Anything containing poison will turn out poisonous, naturally, but there will be no magic about it.

There was a cartoon in *The New Yorker* many years ago that showed one witch at the cauldron recommending something in a box she was sprinkling into the water. "It's marvelous," she said, "you just add water." This was about as amusing as the vampire film that began with the revival of a vampire who had turned to dust. Igor poured blood into the coffin and there was Instant Dracula.

WEREWOLF OF THE MONTH

The great Arab physician ibn Sina, whom we call Avicenna (980–1037) and whose medical system (brought to Spain and thence to the rest of Europe) was preeminent in the West for many centuries, was of the opinion that fits of werewolf activity were most likely in February. Was T. S. Eliot wrong when he said April was "the cruellest month"?

DEMONS IN RINGS, BOTTLES, ETC.

In 1523, Don Alfonso Manriquez, Grand Inquisitor, gave orders to arrest "any person [who] made or caused to be made mirrors, rings, phials of glass or other vessels therein to contain some spirit who should reply to his inquiries and aid his projects" It looks as if Christians in formerly Muslim Spain were picking up the idea of an imp in a bottle, the *djin* (as we sometimes spell it) who is "the slave of the lamp," and a lot more hocus-pocus from the fairytales of *The Arabian Nights* and "Aladdin's Wonderful

Lamp." There's an interesting short story you should seek out; it's called "The Bottle Imp."

TO WARD OFF THE EVIL EYE

Certain Spanish witches use an incantation which translates thus:
> The shepherd went to the fountain
> And returned from the fountain.
> Take away the evil eye
> From the person on which you placed it.

SPANISH INQUISITION

Elizabeth J. Moffett, *A Glossary of the Spanish Inquisition* (doctoral dissertation, 1967).

A MAGICIAN OF TOLEDO

Don Juan Manuel (*c.* 1283–*c.* 1350) was a nephew of Alfonso X of Castille and the author of the collection of tales from various sources that comprise a book called *Count Lucanor*. From this very first work of Spanish prose, here is the tale as I summarize it, that his adviser told to the count when the latter was afraid that if he did a favor for someone that person would be ungrateful. The tale involves a similar situation between a magician of Toledo, known as a center for magic in the Middle Ages, and a dean of Santiago.

There was a dean of Santiago determined to learn the secrets of necromancy and he therefore went to visit Don Illan, a magician of Toledo. The magician insisted that the dean first sit down to a good meal with him and, that having been enjoyed, he asked the dean's business. The dean replied that he expected to rise high in the church and wanted the magician's help. He would reward it. The magician sighed and said it was his experience that those who were helped forgot their promises to pay back their benefactors.

"I am not like that," the dean argued, and the magician said he would assist him. First he took the dean to a splendid set of apartments and, on the way, because it was by now nearly time for another meal, the magician told his cook that they would have pheasants, but not to prepare them until given the order.

The magician's private apartments, which seemed to be way down under the River Tagus itself, were full of magical books and instruments.

There the dean and the magician talked at length and suddenly two messengers arrived with news that the dean's uncle, the archbishop, was dying and wanted to see him before he expired. The dean, however, was unwilling to leave the magician until he had learned the secrets he coveted and he sent the messengers away.

Four days later, the messengers returned. They told the dean that his uncle had died and that he might well be selected to be archbishop. They advised him to absent himself in order to increase his chances of election. So he did. Then a week later two squires arrived, kissed his hands, and saluted the dean as the new archbishop of Santiago.

"I am very pleased to have such good news come to my house," said the magician, "and now that the post of dean is vacant perhaps you will look kindly on my son and make him the dean."

The dean declined, saying that he had already promised the post to his brother. He did, however, invite the magician and his son to go with him to Santiago. He said that some post might well be found for the son there.

The magician and his son stayed in Santiago for some time and no post was forthcoming from the new archbishop. Then one day messengers from the pope arrived to say that the archbishop was going to be raised to the See of Tolosa and that he ought to select a replacement for himself in Santiago.

"Please remember your promise," pleaded the magician. "Make my son your successor here in Santiago." But the archbishop said he had already promised the archdiocese of Santiago to one of his uncles.

Two years later, the pope summoned the former dean and subsequent prelate now to be a cardinal. Once again Don Illan asked for a place for his son, but the magician was disappointed once again. The post had already been promised by the fast-rising churchman to still another uncle.

The magician and his son went with the new cardinal to Rome. The pope died and the new cardinal was elected to the Throne of Peter.

"Now, surely, you have so many benefices at your command you can give my son a post," pleaded the magician.

"Let us not rush these things," replied the new pope. "Maybe tomorrow."

"Don't bother," replied the magician, "you will never keep your promise. I have lost all faith in you."

"If you don't watch out," replied the pope, "I shall have you thrown into a dungeon as a heretic."

The magician gave up. All he asked for was money for himself and his son to go back to Toledo. The pope angrily refused to give them anything at all.

"In that case," said the magician, "the partridges!"

And the dean suddenly found himself back in Don Illan's rooms in Toledo, no longer pope, angry, and ashamed.

"You will never keep your promises," said the magician. "I'm glad I did not waste the partridges on you!"

The count's adviser pointed the moral to this little story:

Befriend an ingrate, your reward will be
Not thanks nor riches—do it once and see.

THE DEVIL IN SPANISH EXPRESSIONS

Estár un diablo "there is a problem"; *estudiar uno con el demónio* is said of anyone who is so smart he must have studied with The Devil; and The Devil knows so much not because he is The Devil but because he is so old (and has a lot of experience), *más sabe el diablo por ser viejo que por ser diablo*. Bad luck comes often because The Devil doesn't sleep (*el demonio que no duerme*) and if you give up in despair you might as well give The Devil your flock and your signature on the deed (*dar el diablo el hato y el garabato*). Of reprobates who reform just because they are tired and can't keep up the pace, the Spanish say *el diablo, harto de carne, se metió fraile* — he became a monk.

Very colorful are such expressions as *donde el diablo perdió el poncho*: the place where The Devil lost his cloak is unknown and far away. When there's mucho malice or complication involved, The Devil is there: *aquí hay mucho diablo*. To deplore gratitude you say *así pagar el diablo a quien bien le sarvi*. To those who fritter away time you say *quando el diablo no tiene que hacer, con el rabo macha moscas*. To those who spoil their children you say *tanto quiso el diablo a sus hijos que les saccó los ojos*. He tears out the eyes of his children!

DO DEMONS REIGN IN SPAIN?

One might think that with Toledo as the capital of magic in medieval Europe there would have been a lot of persecution of witches. Except for the Basque Country, where we saw De Lancre was sent by French authorities to clear out sorcerers, there really was not as violent an anti-magic movement as one would expect to find in the country that made the words equivalent to *Holy Inquisition* the terror of millions.

No vast burning of witches in Spain? Holy Toledo!

In 1610 Spanish authorities were alerted to an uproar in an area where nearly 2,000 people, most of them children, were accused of being in league with the demonic powers. They sent Alonso de Salazár y Frias to investigate. He wrote a report of thousands of pages saying it was all nonsense. After that no one was put to death in Spain for witchcraft any more.

Now there are very few Satanist groups at work. They apparently find it hard to recruit Spanish members. Even Portugal seems to be more interested in devils and demons!

My favorite story of Spanish demonology involves Sor Magdalena de la Cruz, a nun of Córdoba. She entered the convent of Santa Isabél there under the age of eighteen in 1504. For nearly 40 years she fell into trances, saw visions, made prophecies, and won her an outstanding reputation even with the proliferation of Hispanic hysterics the sixteenth century contained. They say Saint Ignatius Loyola didn't trust her transcendental flights, and he would have known. When he said Mass they used to have to hold him down by tugging on his chasuble; he had a tendency to levitate at the consecration.

Then came 1543 and Sor Magdalena fell ill. She was told that the doctors could do nothing for her. She was soon going to meet her Maker. At this point she decided to confess to them that all she had been able to do was due to two demons, Balban and Patorrio, incubi with whom she had had glorious sex all these years. The Flying Nun!

The deathbed confession seemed to give her a new lease on life. She didn't die. She recovered. So church authorities, who always resented these nuns who were bypassing ecclesiastical authority and getting visions directly from God (or, heaven forbid!, powers from The Devil), launched a full investigation. The results were not all assembled until 1546. Sor Magdalena was to be put away in a more remote convent (Santa Clara at Andujár) and kept quiet until she died. That didn't come until 1560.

She had had a wild life while it lasted and now, with menopause and contrition, she had had a peaceful old age.

Nothing more was heard of or from Balban and Patorrio.

IBERIA

Arles, Martin de, *Tractatus de superstitionibus* (1517)

Cirac Estopanan, Sebastian, *Los Processos de hecherías en la inquisición de Castilla la Neuva* (1942)

Cirvello, Pedro Sanchez, *Opus de magia superstitione* (trans. into Spanish as *Reprobación de las superstitiones y hechizerías*, 1539)

Henningsen, Gustav, *The Witches' Advocate* (1980, Basques 1609 - 114)
Noacak, B., *Satanás y Sotería* (1948)
Risco, Vicente, *Satanás, historia del diablo* (1956)
Salillas, Rafael, *La Fascinación en España* (1905)
Spina, Alfonsus de, *Fortaliciam fidei* (1467)

ZOHAR

This, translated as (*The Book of*) *Splendor*, appeared among the Sephardic Jews in the thirteenth century where Spanish Jews were studying mysticism as well as medicine and mathematics. Later it was translated into Latin for universal European use by the cabalist Pico della Mirandola. In the sixteenth century Isaac Luria or *Ari* (Lion) was the center of cabalistic learning and had many associates, including (he claimed) the Prophet Elijah. By the seventeenth century the Cabala

A Jew blows the *shofar* (ram's horn) at Rosh Ha Shanah. Thirteenth century. *Bibliothéque Nationale*, Paris.

was known in every Western country and had many exotic adherents, some philosophers, some delving into gematria (numerology) to answer questions ranging from "whom should I marry?" (when was settled: before twenty at the latest if you are male and do not wish to be condemned to a life of misery, even earlier if female and willing to take a chance on that) to "when is The Messiah coming?" Christians, of course, wanted the date of the "Second Coming" of The Messiah.

Because the very nature of Cabala was to be maddeningly obscure, practitioners came up with different answers for almost everything.

THE CABALA

"Fortune, Dion," *The Mystical Qabalah* (reprint 1984)
Regardie, Israel, *The Tree of Life* (1970)
Scholem, G., *The Kabbalah* (1974)
Godwin, David, *Godwin's Cabalistic Encyclopedia* (1979)
Mathers, S. L. Macgregor, *The Kabbalah Unveiled* (1951)
Waite, A. E., *The Book of Ceremonial Magic* (n.d.)

DON'T LOOK IN THE ATTIC!

From Gershom Scholem's *On the Kabbalah and Its Symbolism*:

> It must have been . . . toward the middle of the 18th century that the Polish legend about the rabbi of Chelm moved to Prague and attached itself to a far more famous figure, the 'Great Rabbi' Loew of Prague (c. 1520–1609). Of course the Prague legend may have grown up independently, but this strikes me as very unlikely. In the Prague tradition of the early 19th century, the legend was associated with certain special features of the Sabbath Even liturgy. The story is that Rabbi Loew fashioned a golem who did all manner of work for his master during the week. But because all creatures rest on the Sabbath, Rabbi Loew turned his golem back into clay every Friday evening, by taking away the name of God. Once, however, the rabbi forgot to remove the *shem* (from the *Shem Hameforash*, the ineffable name of God). The congregation was assembled for services in the synagogue and had already recited the 92nd Psalm when the mighty golem ran amuck, shaking houses, and threatening to destroy everything. Rabbi Loew was summoned; it was still dusk, and the Sabbath had not already begun. He rushed at the raging golem and tore away the *shem*, whereupon the golem crumbled into dust. The rabbi then ordered that the Sabbath Psalm should be sung a second time, a custom which has been maintained ever since in that synagogue, the Altner Schul, but buried his remains in the attic of the ancient synagogue, where they lie to this day. Once, after much fasting, Rabbi Ezekiel Lander, one of Rabbi Loew's most prominent successors, is said to have gone up to look at the golem. On his return he gave an order, binding on all future generations, that no mortal must ever go up to that attic . . . .

See also Thomas Witton Davies' *Magic, White and Black* (1910), Bernard Jacob Bamburger's *Fallen Angels* (1952).

THE GOLEM AT THE MOVIES

Gustav Meyrink's novel (1915) about how Rabbi Elijah had made a golem in Chelm in the Middle Ages was quickly made into a film (1917) and another early movie called *Die Golem, Wie Er in die Welt Kam* (The Golem, How He Came into the World) was based on how Rabbi Loew of Prague had made a golem. Then there were French golem movies starring Ferdinand Hart (1937) and Andre Rebaz (1966) as the great clay "shapeless thing"—which is what *golem* means—and American moviegoers will recall such golem masterpieces as the dramatically titled *It!* (1966).

One detail the movies do not seem to agree upon is whether the secret name of God that gives the creature its life is *Shem, Aemaer, Shemamphoras,* or what.

What really gives the creature its get up and go is the dramatic potential in discussing how science can overstep the bounds and create problems it cannot handle. That goes back at least as far as Mary Shelley's animated anatomical anthology in *Frankenstein.* Technology as the demon we cannot cope with is the modern dilemma.

A good read is Chayim Bloch's *The Golem* . . . (1972).

DYBBUK

Pronounced (according to Leo Rosten) to rhyme with "cook," this means "evil spirit" or "incubus." It is thought to be the soul of a dead person possessing a living one. It thus resembles a vampire or revenant in some respects, and it can be put back into the infernal world by a *minyan* (ten Jews met to pray) if one will read the 91st Psalm aloud and have the courage to order the *dybbuk* to be gone. It may be necessary to sound the *shofar* (ram's horn trumpet) to effect the exorcism. S. Ansky (S. Z. Rapoport, 1863–1920)'s play of *The Dybbuk* deals with such an exorcism. It was a standard of the Yiddish theatre in its prime and has been performed in many languages and cultures worldwide.

Rosten in *The Joys of Yiddish* adds a detail I have not seen elsewhere, "that when a *dybbuk* flees a man or woman, a tiny, bloody spot, the size of a pinhead, appears on the pinky of the right foot. Either that, or a window develops a little crack."

Perhaps one ought to have rooms such as the Swiss used to have for bedrooms. In each there was a tiny, extra window through which the soul could exit when a person died. Or one could presumably open a window before the exorcism and prevent cracking the glass that way.

WITCHCRAFT AND BELGIAN FOLK BELIEF

A number of articles for those who can read Flemish and Dutch appear in the journal *Volkskunde* published in Antwerp.

SWITZERLAND

A fact about demonology in Switzerland strikes one much like the uniform of the Swiss Guards: how colorful, how incredibly un-Swiss looking!

Sinners and demons at The Last Judgment. Cathedral of Bourges.

The Dominicans, as was the case elsewhere, actively pursued sorcerers in Switzerland as they did everywhere. (In Italy they got out of hand and Gregory IX had to quiet them down.) In Berne and elsewhere, Dominicans were responsible for sending some malefactors to the stake, but when the Dominicans quarreled with the Franciscans over the dogma of The Immaculate Conception—a question still open to debate until the end of the nineteenth century in the Roman church—they were accused of being in league with The Devil. Sly Franciscans managed to get some Dominicans burned as sorcerers.

The Reformation swept away the rivalry between Roman Catholic orders and the Protestants were less interested in sorcery than in politics and peace.

There has been no execution for witchcraft in Switzerland since the middle of the seventeenth century when a poor woman with a birthmark was accused of bearing The Devil's Mark and was brutally killed.

VAMPIRES OF MONTENEGRO

Montenegro is one of the most spectacular landscapes I have ever visited, so I was glad to hear that its superstitions people it with a host of equally spectacular spirits. In *Voyage historique et politique au Montenegro*, Col. L. C. Vialla de Sommières writes (translated by Montague Summers in *The Vampire in Europe*, 1961):

In no country is the belief in ghosts, in witches, and in evil spirits stronger than in Montenegro. Apparitions, dreams, omens ceaselessly haunt their brains, but nothing equals the terror inspired by *brucolaques*, that is to say the dead bodies of those who died excommunicate, and which are huddled into the earth without any burial rite or prayer. The very ground which has covered them is for ever accursed; the spot is shunned and avoided by all, and if a thought of the place crosses a man's mind he believes that he is being pursued by avenging ghosts. In fine these men who court every danger and endure every peril think of nothing but of witches and of demons; they are for ever discoursing of the terror with which evil spirits inspire them. It would require no mean authority on demonology with a facile pen to write the long narratives of all manner of devils which they never tire of relating and the myriad adventures of this sort that they love to tell.

TAR-CROSSED LEAVERS

If you want bogeymen to depart from your premises, or just leave you alone, the Serbs, the Swedes, and many other peoples say that you should make a cross with tar on the building, especially on barns. Tar crosses were also known in old Scotland and to some extent the superstition was brought to America by Scottish settlers in the eighteenth century.

VRYKOLAKES ON THE ISLAND OF CRETE

A history of the Sphakia district of Crete (1888) is quoted in Lawson's *Modern Greek Folklore*. As he translates the story of vampires:

> It is popularly believed that most of the death, those who have lived bad lives or who have been excommunicated by some priest (or, worse still, by seven priests together) . . . become *vrykolakes*; that is to say, after the separation of the soul from the body there enters into the latter an evil spirit, which takes the place of the soul and assumes the shape of the dead man and so is transformed into a *vrykolakas* or man demon.
> In this guise it keeps the body as its dwelling-place and preserves it from corruption, and it runs swift as lightning wherever it lists, and causes men great alarms at night and strikes all with

panic. And the trouble is that it does not remain solitary, but makes everyone, who dies while it is about, like to itself, so that in a short space of time it gets together a larger and dangerous train of followers. The common practice of the *vrykolakes* is to seat themselves upon those who are asleep and by their enormous weight to cause an agonizing sense of oppression. There is great danger that the sufferer in such cases may expire, and himself too be turned into *vrykolakas*, if there be not someone at hand who perceives his torment and fires off a gun, thereby putting the blood-thirsty monster to flight; for fortunately it is afraid of the report of fire-arms and retreats without effecting its purpose. Not a few such scenes we have witnessed with our own eyes.

This monster, as time goes on, becomes more and more audacious and blood-thirsty, so that it is able completely to devastate whole villages. On this account all possible haste is made to annihilate the first which appears before it enters upon its second period of forty days. Because by that time it becomes a merciless and invincible dealer of death. To this end the villagers call in priests who profess to know how to annihilate the monster—for a consideration. These impostors proceed after service to the tomb, and if the monster be not found there—for it goes to and fro molesting men—they summon it in authoritative tones to enter its dwelling place; and, as soon as it is come, it is imprisoned there by virtue of some prayer and subsequently breaks up. With its disruption all those who have been turned into *vrykolakes* by it, wherever they may be, suffer the same lot as their leader.

This absurd superstition is rife and vigorous throughout Crete and especially in the mountainous and secluded parts of the island.

SOME RECENT STUDIES OF VAMPIRES

In addition to a great many articles in the learned journals on literature, folklore, and other subjects, and collections in anthologies of articles devoted to criticism and short stories about vampires, not to mention the many novels and screenplays about vampires (Anne Rice, Stephen King, and other popular writers), there have been quite a few books on the topic here and abroad and, significantly, the vampire has also of late become a respectable topic for PhD research. Here are some recent, representative titles:

Bennett, Gillian & Paul Smith (eds.), *Monsters with Iron Teeth* (1988)
Bhalla, Alok, *Politics of Atrocity and Lust: The Vampire Tale as a Nightmare History of England in the Nineteenth Century* (1990)
Boone, Troy Monroe, *Unearthing Plots: Vampirism and Victorian Culture* (doctoral dissertation, 1994)
Carter, Margaret L., *Dracula: The Vampire and the Critics* (1988)
_____, *The Vampire in Literature: A Critical Bibliography* (1989)
Colwin, Thomas L., *Magic, Trick-Work, and Illusion in the Vampire Plays* (doctoral dissertation, 1988)
Docherty, Brian (ed.), *American Horror Fiction from* [Charles] *Brockden Brown to Stephen King* (1990)
Giovanni, Fabio, *Il libro dei vampiri . . .* (1985)
Lane, Victor, *Gothic Feminism in Anne Rice's The Vampire Chronicles* (doctoral dissertation, 1994)
Marigny, Jean, *Le Vampire en la littérature anglo-saxonne* (1985)
Olivier, Jean-Michel, *Lautréamont: Le Texte du vampire* (1992)
Perkowski, Jan L., *The Darkling: A Treatise on Slavic Vampirism* (1989)
Rogers, Susan Leigh, *Vampire Vixens: The Female Undead and the Lacanian Symbolic Order in Tales by* [Théophile] *Gautier,* [Henry] *James, and* [James Sheridan] *LeFanu* (doctoral dissertation, 1993)
Senf, Carol A., *The Vampire in Nineteenth-Century English Literature* (1988)
Stuart, Roxana, *The Vampires of Nineteenth-Century Melodrama* (doctoral dissertaiton, 1993)
Toufic, Jalal Omran, *Vampires* (doctoral dissertation, 1993)

While the vampire is not called up in necromancy or sent by The Devil, the folklore emphasizes that serving The Devil in life is the reason the undead are prevented from resting in peace after death. It was once suggested that vampires are the offspring of demons and humans, but it has seldom been thought that vampires are possessed by demonic powers.

GYPSIES IN EUROPE

Erik Victor Gunnemark says there are 6 million gypsies in the world today and some 4 million of them speak Romany as their home language. Some 3 million of them are in Europe, principally in Hungary, the former Yugoslavia, Romania, Bulgaria, and the Czech Republic. There are at least 100,000 in France, and in Britain the gypsies have long been thought to be clever tinkerers, shrewd horse traders, and gifted fortune-tellers. Today you may find gypsies in tea rooms telling fortunes by tea leaves or (as in

America) in store-front "parlors" offering to gaze into a crystal ball, do The Tarot, or otherwise tell your fortune. Gypsies are no longer regarded, as once they were, as likely to be in league with the powers of darkness; now they are more likely to be regarded as confidence men and women. Gypsies no longer are dumb, either, but speak when they tell fortunes. In the old days it was thought in places such as Britain that those who were unable to speak might have special powers of second sight. The English gypsies often pretended they were unable to speak and by hand gestures they indicated one's fortune—after you crossed their palms with silver. Pointing at a finger indicated a wedding ring, foretold a marriage, etc. Most gypsies could, in fact, more or less manage the language of whatever country in which they found themselves. Some developed new tinkers' languages, such as Shelta in Ireland. Most spoke some variety of Romany along with some standard European language.

Gypsy superstitions are colorful and well known. They do not need to be detailed here. It is a long time since any gypsies were connected in popular superstition with devils and demons. Today, whether in Europe or in the Americas (where there are more than 100,000 in the United States and Canada and almost 250,000 in Central and South America), gypsies are not much trusted but are certainly not thought of as diabolical.

Gypsies are not, of course, from Egypt—nor from Flanders (though the Spanish call them *flamencos*), nor from Bohemia (though we have the English word *bohemians*). They come originally from India and their language is related to Punjabi and Hindi. The gypsy language has to some extent entered into colloquial English, especially among barrow boys, actors, and other strollers.

See Ralph Lewis' *Whispers of Witchcraft* (1977). He studies "gypsies, witches, clairvoyants and charlatans."

The gypsies have almost completely given up their original, pagan religion in which there was belief in an evil god who almost totally destroyed the world that the good god first made. The fire (or flood) that the evil god sent, however, was insufficient to eradicate the good.

Gypsies may have been the first to use cards to tell fortunes, cards which later were developed into common modern playing cards (said by some to have been created to amuse a French king). Their original cards may in some ways resemble The Tarot pack: It was a gypsy who told me always to keep my Tarot pack wrapped in silk when it was not being used—to preserve its "strength."

Gypsies have had a bad reputation, and not only from dabbling in fortune-telling. They were once widely believed to steal children and put their own offsprings in the place of better tots when they went around in their caravans from place to place, trading at fairs, repairing pots and pans, and so on. In England, they were accused of filching laundry set out on the hedgerows to dry.

Gypsies and their superstitions appear in many places in older English literature. George Borrow in the nineteenth century is the best but far from the only source. Shakespeare's Othello has a magical handkerchief. This plot-central handkerchief

> Did an Egyptian to my mother give;
> She was a charmer, and could almost read
> The thoughts of people.

There's a magical belt owned by Maudlin (a witch) in *The Sad Shepherd*:

> A Gypsan lady, and a right beldame
> Wrought it by moonshine for me and starlight.

There is much gypsy lore in *Gypsies Metamorphosed* (where one of Ben Jonson's characters reads palms) and in *Endymion* (where John Lyly has a soothsayer named Gyptes) and elsewhere in the Elizabethan drama.

Bowness, Charles, *Romany Magic* (1977)
Clebert, Jean-Paul, *The Gypsies* (1963)
Derlon, Pierre, *Secrets of the Gypsies* (1977)
Leland, Charles, *Gypsy Sorcery and Fortune-Telling* (reprinted 1974)
Loseby, Charles Edgar, *Witches, Mediums, Vagrants and Law* (1946)

GYPSY CURSES

A stock in trade of the Decadents of the last century was the curse that blasted the guilty and sometimes the innocent. The Gypsy's Curse was a favorite. For instance, in the sick fantasies of Jean Lorrain we find a story with a title that may be translated "The Princess under Glass." In this story, the body of a princess, in a glass coffin such as is familiar to those who have seen Disney's *Sleeping Beauty* or some Hollywood morbidity in Forest Lawn Cemetery, falls out of the coffin, lands in a ditch, and has the hands eaten off it by Prince Otto's hunting hounds. Involved in it all, as in Lorrain's other fiction, *Les Noronsoffs* is a gypsy violin that bears a terrible curse.

The Devil is often associated with violins. Paganinni was popularly believed to have sold his soul to The Devil for the skill to play so well. Tartini heard his famous "Devil's Trill" in a dream. In some folklore the gypsy's violin functions like the lyre of Orpheus and puts under a spell animals or persons who hear it played. A recurrent horror story involves the severed hand of a gypsy violinist that "outlives" him and, crawling like a spider, throttles in revenge.

Wandering gypsies, greeted everywhere with the suspicion and dislike of strangers that is common worldwide among the ignorant, appear to have encouraged the fear of their powerful, devilish curses. It helped business. It made others think twice about persecuting them.

CURSES!

There is an almost infinite number of stories about this or that cursed person, place, or thing. All of them involve evil powers, of course, which put the curse into effect and, sometimes, keep it active for a long period of time. Two stories will suffice; one is actual, one a joke.

My selection for a cursed place has to be none of the famous European places but the parish church of Cartago in Costa Rica. Founded in 1570, the church suffered repeated earthquakes until 1841, when it was completely destroyed. Like the inhabitants of Antigua in Guatemala, whose cathedral was destroyed twice, once by fire and once by water because of volcanic eruptions nearby, and now stands cracked by earthquake, the people of Cartago kept on repairing and replacing, determined not to give up. In Cartago from 1862 a Romanesque replacement (designed by Francisco Kurtze, a German-born architect in Costa Rica) was undertaken, but building was intermittently stopped by earthquakes until 1910; then an earthquake pretty much demolished the building. The locals finally got the point. Now its ruins stand in a public park.

The curse? Oh, forget the earthquakes. Local legend has it that the parish priest killed his brother, perhaps over a woman, and that no church can stand on the cursed site. Now it is hoped that the ruined arches won't fall and kill some picnickers in the park.

The joke involves a woman on an airplane who sees her seat mate is sporting a diamond ring that resembles a headlight.

"I couldn't help noticing your ring. What a beauty!"

"Thank you, but this ring you wouldn't want."

"No, why not?"

"This is the famous Goldstein Diamond. With the Goldstein Diamond comes a curse."

"A curse? What curse?"

"Goldstein."

WRITTEN EVIDENCE

The otherwise despicable Paul de Man was right when he wrote that "the basis for historical knowledge are not empirical knowledge but written texts," among which he included "wars or revolutions," not just books. Demonology has a vast record of written texts, mostly from its enemies. It is difficult to get at what ordinary people, rather than biased religious apologists or hanging judges, thought about trafficking with The Devil over the centuries. The peasantry's views of witches, for example—particularly in Italy, where the *strega* with her medicines and love philtres was a pretty well accepted feature of daily life—were not often written down. It was only when a peasant got caught up in the persecution of witches, generally, that she or he became part of any record.

Even the testimony of the allegedly possessed is not balanced by the reports of competent psychiatrists (who in most cases appear to have been more needed than spiritual advisers) and the "evidence" of devils and demons is tainted when obtained under torture or censored by the clerics who quietly edited dictation from hysterical nuns and such individuals. Most importantly, the evidence for active Satanist groups has often been forged or fiddled with so that one does not know what to believe.

Nonetheless, as is the case with God and The Devil themselves, what people decide to write and what people are content to believe are as interesting as facts. What Charles MacKay called "extraordinary popular delusions" and William James called "the madness of crowds," which is to say a great deal of human history, is well worth trying to read and decipher.

SOME KOOKY HISTORIES

For those who would like to see historians of devils and demons at their oddest, there is a long bibliography of incredible publications. As a start, I recommend the one-sided views of true believers such as the "Rev." Montague Summers (*The History of Witchcraft and Witchcraft & Black Magic*). For those who can manage foreign languages, this dozen are representative examples of scholarship in the service of stupidity:

Abner, Théodore, *Les Apparitions du diable*
Caietanus, Thomas, *De Maleficiis*
Delassus, Jules, *Les Incubes et les succubes*
Elich, Philip Ludwig, *Dæmonomagia*
Gerson, Jean, *De Probatione spirituum*
Guazzo, Francesco Maria, *Compendium maleficarum*

Krakowitz, Albert Joachim von, *De Theologia dæmonum*
Mamor, Pietro, *Flagellum maleficorum*
Roskoff, Gustav, *Geschichte des teufels*
Sinistrati, Lodovico Maria, *De Dæmonialitate*
Terrega, Raimundus, *De Invocatione dæmonum*
Villanova, Arnoldus, *De Maleficiis*

SOME RECENT SCHOLARLY WORK ON WITCHCRAFT

Anglo, Sydney, (ed.), *The Damned Art . . . Literature Witchcraft* (1977)
Ankerloo, Bengt & Gustav Hennigsen (eds.), *Early Modern European Witch-craft: Centres and Peripheries* (1990)
Boyer, Paul & Stephen Nisenbaum, *Salem Possessed: The Social Origins of Witchcraft* (1974)
Douglas, Mary (ed.), *Witchcraft Confessions and Accusations* (1972)
Franklyn, Julian, *Death by Enchantment . . . Ancient and Modern Witchcraft* (1972)
Fritscher, John, *Popular Witchcraft: Straight from the Witch's Mouth* (1972)
Haining, Peter (ed.), *A Circle of Witches: An Anthology of Victorian Witch-craft Stories* (1971)
_____, *Anatomy of Witchcraft* (1972)
Hart, Roger, *Witchcraft* (1971)
Hodgron, Pat, *Witchcraft and Magic* (1978)
Hoyt, Charles A. & Beatrice R. Moore (eds.), *Witchcraft* (1981)
Jencson, Linda Jeran, *Neopagan Witchcraft: Cult in Cultural Context* (doctoral dissertation, 1992)
Jorden, Edward *et al.*, *Witchcraft and Hysteria in Elizabethan London* (1991)
Lewis, James R. (ed.), *Medical Religion and Modern Witchcraft* (1996)
Lloyd, Susannah M., *The Occult Revival . . . Contemporary United States* (doctoral dissertation, 1979)
Mair, Lucy, *Witchcraft* (1969)
Melton, J. G., *The Encyclopedia of Modern Religions* (1978)
Ravensdale, Tom & James Morgan, *The Psychology of Witchcraft . . .* (1974)
Russell, Jeffrey B., *Witchcraft in the Middle Ages* (1972)
Sanders, Andrew, *A Deed without a Name* (1995)
Sebald, Hans, *Witchcraft: The Heritage of a Heresy* (1978)

SOME DISSERTATIONS ON WITCHCRAFT AND LITERATURE

Anushiravani, Alireza, *The Images of Satan in Rumi's 'Mathnawi,' Dante's 'Divine Comedy', and Milton's 'Paradise Lost'* (1992)

Craig, Terry Ann, *Witchcraft and Demonology in Renaissance English Literature* (1978)

Dukes, Eugene O., *Magic and Witchcraft in the Writings of the Early Church Fathers* (1972)

Finch, Patricia S., *Magic and Witchcraft in the 'Celestina' and Its Imitations* (1981)

Franz, Philip Edward, *A. A. Perovskij (Pogorel' skil)... (1981)*

Grinnell, Richard William, *English Demonology and Renaissance Drama* (1992)

Hopkin, Charles Edward, *The Share of Thomas Aquinas in the Growth of the Witchcraft Delusions* (1940)

Leuschner, Kristine Jeanne, *Creating the 'Known True Story': Seventeenth-Century Murder and Witchcraft Pamphlets and Plays* (1992)

Pavia, Mario N., *Magic and Witchcraft in the Literature of the* Siglo de Oro, *Especially in the Drama* (1948)

Prior, Moody Erasmus, *Joseph Glanvill, Witchcraft, and Seventeenth-Century Science* (1930)

Ricardo-Gil, Joan-Nancy, *The Practice of Witchcraft and Magic in Fact and Fiction during the French Middle Ages* (1980)

Rumsey, Peter Lockwood, *Acts of God: The Rhetoric of Providence in New England 1620–1760* (1984)

Wolover, Charles Patrick, *Robert Ward's [Opera, Libretto by Bernard Stambler, based on Arthur Miller's Play] 'The Crucible': A Critical Commentary* (1986)

WITCHCRAFT AND YOUNG PEOPLE

John Warren Stewig ("The Witch Woman: A Recurring Motif in Recent Fantasy Writing for Young People" in *Children's Literature and Education* 26:2, 1995) and others have remarked on how witchcraft is a popular topic for young readers, but it should also be noted that the Religious Right and other groups have been outspoken in their objections to anything really occult or perceived as occult in the curriculum or the school library. There have been challenges to the curriculum of American public schools in the nineties in California, Oregon, and elsewhere. Parents' fear of Satanism is especially strong.

The magician's wand, from Francis Barrett's *The Magnus*. On the side shown is engraved *Agla ✛ On ✛ Tetragramaton*. On the reverse should be *Ego Alpha Omega* ("I [am] the Beginning [and] the End").

The pagan temple at Uppsala in Sweden with its great iron chain, tree representing Ygarassill, and the well in which Adam of Bremen reported human sacrifices were drowned.

3

The Far North of Europe

NORTHERN MYTHOLOGY

Hel is the name of the goddess who commands "the army of darkness," punishes the dead, and terrorizes the living. Loki, whom we mention elsewhere, became "the father of evil powers," killer of Balder (the good sun god), and opponent of Thor and fertility. Loki is a destroyer, a trickster, full of evil but rather childish machinations, often somewhat similar to the stupid devil of folklore, seeming to take a juvenile delight in panic, as did the god Pan. With him, we begin our survey of Scandinavia here.

RUDRA

Something of Thor thundering through the heavens with storms and lightning and of the folk tradition of The Devil and his Dandy Dogs, or the Wild Hunt, is in the god of Vedic times called Rudra, an ancient divinity of India. Rudra stormed over the world, destroying with his arrows those who displeased him, and this destructive power is now seen in Shiva, "The Destroyer," and his wife, Kali, goddess of destruction and death. Rudra was perhaps the earliest conception in Indian religion that parallels our Devil. He must have been an inspiration for Thor.

FYLGIA

In Iceland an animal spirit was said to accompany every human being, rather like the guardian angels who protect all Christians in a state of grace. This is something like the *dæmon* of the Greeks but is good, not a demon. It is not unrelated, however, to the animal familiars of witches.

THE MISCHIEVOUS LOKI

Loki, Scandinavian god of fire, talked too much. Once Brock sewed his mouth up, but it didn't help much. He was a kind of uncontrollable demon, mischievous as an imp, something like the Vice in plays of the Middle Ages. Loki was eventually killed by Heimdall, but Heimdall perished as well. In the end a great fire destroyed everything and the whole world sank into the sea, only to rise again "purified at last . . . higher, better, nobler than before."

HÄXAN

Under this title (English release title *Witchcraft through the Ages*) the Danish director Benjamin Christensen (1879–1959) in 1921 in Sweden produced a semi-documentary film that still has not been surpassed by the many attempts at this sensational subject in big-screen and small-screen (television) documentaries. Christensen played Satan in the film, of which Ephraim Katz's *Film Encyclopedia* says:

> The film remains a masterpiece of the horror genre, a horrifyingly vivid record in striking lights and shades of diabolism and Satanic practices from the Middle Ages to the 20th century . . . it was banned in many countries for scenes of cruelty and nudism. . . .

TV has, however, been very influential in increasing the knowledge of and probably the belief in superstition, most recently with a spate of infomercials by "professional psychics." (Are they tested? Licensed? Anything but fools or frauds?) Satanism and witchcraft (even without blood sacrifice and naked coven cavorting) are a bit strong for most of the regular TV programs on "the occult," which tend to prove, if anything at all, that extraterrestrials interested in the human race unfortunately are collecting as specimens from trailer parks and seedy suburbs some of the least educated, least intelligent Americans available. One Harvard professor believes in UFOs, but his colleagues appear to regard him as a disgrace. Partly because of TV, an astounding number of Americans believe in all sorts of superstitions and 2 percent claim to have been abducted by curious aliens. Scandinavians think Americans to be very superstitious.

Satanism and witchcraft are real, if rare. However, they seem to be of less interest to the gee-whiz programs than out-of-body experiences, seeing ghosts, poltergeists, kidnapping by aliens, and such. It may be that Americans prefer to portray themselves as victims rather than as perpetrators these days. Scandinavians feel they are less vulnerable.

LOTS AND SACRIFICE

Shirley Jackson's slick story "The Lottery" is famous. Less well-known is the fact that, as Derolez suggested in *La Divination* (1968), the Old Icelandic words *blotspan* (sacrificial silver) and *blauttein* (blood twig) point to ancient sacrifices. In his *Germania*, the Roman writer Tacitus refers to lots being cast to determine when attacks should be launched, which prisoners should die, and which persons ought to be sacrificial victims. In the *Erbyggia Saga*, there is evidence that a twig or branch was dipped in the blood of the sacrifice and used to asperge the sacrificial altar. Perhaps runes were written on slips of wood, and these were drawn to choose the victim. The runes themselves may have been charged with extra power by writing them in blood.

WITCHES' BROOMS

Norwegians of the Middle Ages described strange structures seen in trees—they were produced by a parasite called *Taphrina betulæ*—as *heksekoster* (witch's broom). The superstitious said these "brooms" could be placed over the bed and would protect against the female spirit called *mara*.

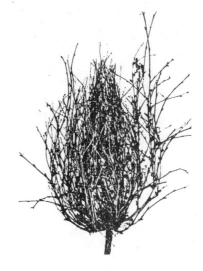

This *mara* (sometimes *marua*) came by night and caused the victim to wake up suddenly, bathed in sweat. The cattle could also be protected by hanging up the "brooms" in the stables. It was further believed that the "brooms" lost their protective power if you carried them across a road down which a corpse had passed.

GALDR

In Norse mythology, the *galdr* was a magical song, probably from the same root as the word for a bird warbling loudly. The *Elder Edda* has Odin saying that he learned *eighteen* of these magical songs from a certain troll and that with the help of these incantations he was able to protect health, attract love, loose chains, extinguish fires, take the edge off sharp weapons, and perform other wonders.

It was believed that when Tore Hund killed King Olaf (later St. Olaf) at the Battle of Strikelstad in Trondelag in the year 1000, it was due to Tore Hund (The Hound) being magically protected by a *galdr*.

The Norse laws, however, forbade the use of these magical songs and anyone who used them was an outlaw, which is to say he had no law to protect him against anyone killing him.

Here are some *galdr* stanzas in Nynorsk (5, 6, and 7 of a long diatribe) written by a woman named Busla who wants to force the king to spare a man named Bosí:

5

Eg skal klemma deg
hardt for brystet,
som om hoggormar
lág der og gnaga.
Orene dine
skal ikkje hooyre,
augene dine
innover vrengast,
om Bose ei blir skána
og Herrod blir frigjeven.

5

I'll squeeze hard on your breast
as if vipers lay there gnawing.
Your ears shall not hear, your
eyes shall be turned inwards,
if Bosí is not spared and Herrod
set free.

6

Nár du rir
skal saumar smuldre,
hestar bli halte
og gampar segne.
Pá gate og gangstig
skal trollhender binde dog,
om ikkje Bose
fár liv og helse
og Herrod blir frisleppt.

6

When you ride the horseshoe nails
shall fail, the horses shall limp,
the stallions fall down exhausted.
In streets and on paths, hands of
trolls shall hinder you, if Bosí
does not regain life and health
and Herrod is not set free.

7

Her skal komma karar seks,
sei meg namna deira,
men loys forst gáta!
Kan du det ikkje
slik som det skal vera,
da skal hundar
gnage deg i hel
og sjela di skal
synka ned i Helheimen!

7

Here shall come six knights: tell
me their names. But first you
must solve the puzzle! If you
cannot do that, as it stands,
then hounds shall gnaw you to
the grave and your soul shall
sink down into hell!

Then come the six obscure words: *Ristil, Sistil, Pistil, Hestil, Mistil, Vistil.*
Nobody today has any inkling what they mean!

From A.D. 350-550, there are ancient runes in Sweden for magical protection. This is a picture of the oldest so far discovered; it came to light in 1903 at Klyver Farm, Stanga Parish, Gotland. The word at the right (*sueus*) is magical because it is the same backwards and forwards. The rune at the right-hand end of the row (resembling a pine tree) is for Thor, six times, for intensifying the power of the inscription.

MISTELL, THISTILL, PISTILL, KISTILL, RISTILL, GISTILL, BESTILL

Ola J. Holten tells me that these secret names, which occur on more than one old runic stone and may be found abbreviated and carved on ancient stave churches, are considered powerful defenses against trolls and other wicked spirits. Further, he finds that the seven words that appear above (found on an old rune stick at Bergen) are interpretable from Norse to Norwegian as follows:

mistell, mistletoe, magical in the story of Balder, among Druids, etc.
tistel, thistle (the Norse word beginning with the *thorn* letter)
epistle, epistle (though in Nordmore dialect it is the word for "person with tiny or weak voice")
kiste, coffer, small chest
plog-spiss, plough edge
Gestill, name of a king of the sea related to the idea of "stranger" or "little guest"

We had best not finish this by explaining *bestill* because solving the riddle is exactly what destroys the trolls who try it. *Aestil* and *vistil* also occur.

SCANDINAVIAN GUARDIANS

In the rich folklore of Scandinavia, spirits are said to live in the forests, streams, mountains, outbuildings of farms—practically everywhere. Some

are benevolent; some are not. The trolls and *tomten*, who are said to look
like small versions of H. Ross Perot in red hats, protect the family—if they
are given respect, bowls of milk, honey and oatmeal mush, and other gifts.
The *nissen* in the water and the gnome-like creatures who live underground
are said to be less friendly and are best avoided.

Living for a very long time, some of these undergrounders (folklore
is sure) have amassed great fortunes in precious metals and gems. There
are all kinds of stories about people getting or failing to get the treasures
of the little people, of dining with them off golden plates inside the mountains, of coming upon buried pots of gold and silver coins, and so on.

Many are the tales that claim that treasures are protected by fierce dragons (as in *Beowulf*) or devils and demons (as in the folktales where those
who try to dig up cauldrons of gold are terrified by horrendous apparitions, loud noises, and threats to themselves or their families back at home).
Many stories repeat that the demons guarding treasure strive to make the
digger *say* something, because if one utters a word while digging up treasure, the whole treasure instantly vanishes. There are other warnings about
speaking of the treasure after one has obtained it.

A Norwegian tale recounts how a man digging for treasure encoun-
ters evil spirits who tell him his farm is on fire or that his wife and children are in danger. When he exclaims and runs off, the treasure vanishes
forever. In another tale a man who is walking through the woods slips on
what he thinks is ice. It is fairy silver. He becomes a very rich man. In a
third tale a troll appears to a farmer and invites him to dinner in an underground palace. He is served dainties on gold and silver plates but soon
learns why the troll has invited him. The troll wants him to move his cow
barn, for the droppings of the cows are falling into the undergrounders'
food. After some discussion, the farmer moves his cow barn and the trolls
make sure he is happy and prosperous from then on. Even in the twentieth century more people than you would credit consult the trolls (they
claim) before situating any building. Not to do so would invite trouble.

Still another tale that has been handed down through the centuries,
producing a number of variants but retaining its core of meaning, deals
with a man who arrives at a deserted hut on Christmas Eve with his pet
bear and asks for food and shelter for the night. The owner of the hut
explains that the buffet he has generously set out is for trolls, who come
to party there each year at this time, and that on this occasion he and his
family flee and leave the hut to the supernatural revelers. The stranger,
with his bear, elects to sleep there anyway. The trolls come and riotously
enjoy themselves, eating and drinking, but the bear is awakened and goes

after them. They flee. Long after, the owner of the hut meets a troll in the woods who inquires after the bear. "O, Pussy has had kittens, and now we have quite a few of her family around the place," the farmer lies. He is never again bothered by trolls taking over his hut for parties.

When visitors to Scandinavia see that amid all the modernity of these advanced countries the country people still put crosses on their barns to protect against trolls and still put dishes of milk in the barns to feed the trolls, the strangers are surprised. The locals point to the fact that the milk is drunk. It is no use to suggest that the farm cat or some other animal may have drunk it.

SOME SCANDINAVIAN FOLKTALES

The history of Iceland goes back to the end of the ninth century and it is told in medieval sagas of which about 30 not only still exist but are read and loved by the Icelanders of today. These tales of duty and destiny, of honor and bravery, bring the story down to the end of the first Christian generation, which is to say almost the middle of the eleventh century. These sagas of great heroes and their families contain some supernatural wonders as well as many facts. When the tales handed down in oral tradition were eventually written down, they were also accompanied by hagiographies, the saints' lives also involving the supernatural world. Sagas deal in the real world, but the folk tales tell of devils and demons.

Here is the folk tale of "The Demon's Son" and how a farm at Bakki moved south.

There was a priest at Bakki who had a beautiful young daughter who was courted by a poor farmer's boy. When the boy was refused, he died of a broken heart. Soon afterwards the girl told her foster mother that the dead boy's ghost was visiting her and that she had become pregnant and did not know what to do. The foster mother went to the grave of the dead boy and spoke with him. He confessed that he was indeed visiting the girl by night and that she would soon have a male child. To complete his revenge on those who would not permit him in life to marry the girl, the boy said that the male child would grow up to be the priest in Bakki, and the very first time the priest gave his blessing from the altar, the priest, church, and all its congregation would sink down into Hell.

The baby was born and grew up and was about to become the priest at Bakki when the old woman who had heard the terrible prophecy about him felt she must act to prevent evil. She made her son promise to kill the new priest before he could pronounce the blessing that would send him and the whole congregation to Hell.

Just as the new priest began the blessing, the woman's son sprang from the pews and stabbed the priest to death. The congregation was in an uproar and seized the man still brandishing the dagger, but they soon realized that the priest's vanishing body (all but a neck bone) and the end of the church beginning to sink (because the priest had managed to utter a syllable or two of the blessing before he died) proved that this deadful violence was against something inhuman.

The area thereafter was so haunted by demons that the farm had to be moved, which is why it is south of where it used to be. And if you go and look at the church you will notice that one end of it is sunken, even to this day.

CARE OF THE BABY

In Scandinavia old superstition said that until a baby was baptized into the Christian faith it was in danger of being stolen for the use of its blood in witchcraft or replaced by devils with a changeling. To prevent this awful fate, the water in which the newborn baby was washed must not be thrown out, the fire must never be allowed to go out in the baby's room, and something of iron or steel (such as a pin) must be attached to the baby's clothes at all times.

Once again the superstitions about iron tend to suggest that the trolls and other wicked creatures have some association with peoples whom the Iron Age, more advanced peoples encountered in the forests of the north when first they ventured into the uncharted area.

When a baby cries like a fiend at baptism, there is cause for worry that it may be a troll child, a changeling. Blaming children who turn out badly on the trolls would be a convenient excuse for many modern parents.

An old Swedish story tells of how you can get your child back from a troll who has left a substitute in its stead. Bake bread three Thursdays in a row and on the fourth Thursday put the baby on the peele and threaten to put it into the oven. The troll mother will return to save it. In one tale she does so with the words, "I have never hurt your baby, so why are you threatening to injure mine?" The troll mother will then vanish with her child. How to get your own baby back is another story.

KATY GRAY

This is the English translation of the name by which, in Swedish folk tales, the female counterpart of The Devil is known.

DANISH AND SWEDISH COMPARED

Some idea of the differences between Danish and Swedish can be obtained by comparing these verses on a popular subject of superstition, the were-wolf:

Midvinterblot (Midwinter Sacrifice). A heathen king offers himself as a sacrifice for the good of his people. A detail of a large painting executed by Carl Larsson for the entrance hall of the National Museum of Sweden, which refused it, 1915.

DANISH

Varulven

En varulv stak en aften af
fra barn og kone og begav
sig til en skolelærers grav.
"Oh, boj mig," ulven hofligt sa'.

Og landsbyskolemestern gnaven
skod låget bort—og steg af graven.
Fromt ulven folded sine bløde
poter for den lærde dode.

"*Varulven*," sa' den gode mand,
í praæsens er-*ulv*, men hvordan . . .
jo, *v.ære-ulv* infinitiven,
futurum: at Du ulv skal blive."

Varulven folte, den fik ondt
og rulled sine øjne rundt
og sa'e: "Det kan jeg ikke bære
er der kun ental af at *v.ære?*"

Den dode måtte blankt erkende,
Hans viden fik for hurtigt ende.
Ulv i dusin, ja, også parvis.
Men "*være*" kun I singularis.

Varulven rejste sig bedrovet,
den opgav sin familje nødig,
men var I bøjning ikke øvet
og takked høfligt og ærbødig.

SWEDISH

Varulven

En varulv lopp från fru m.m.
en vacker afton samt begav
sig till en bymagisters grav
och bad: Var snäll och konjugera

mig!" Byskolläraren stod upp
päblecknamnskyltens mässingsknopp
med svar till den, som satt på pass
med tåligt korslagd tass på tass.

"Jag var-ulv I ta pers. I sing.
du, han, hon, den, det var-ulv. Så
vi voro-ulv, I voren, På
de voro-ulv kom ingenting."

Varulven myste glad åt hur
pers, hadeföljts av sing och plur.
"Fast," bad han, "kan det inte ges ens
en enda pers. i tempus presens?"

Bekänna måste vår magister,
att därvidlag fanns vissa brister.
En varulv sine imperfecto
var contradictio in adjecto.

Varulven satt med tårad lins.
Han visste att han fanns och finns.
Därtill kom också fru m. m.
som även måste existera.

ENGLISH

The Werewolf

One night an errant Werewolf fled
His wife and child and visited
A village teacher's sepulchre
And begged him: 'Conjugate me, Sir!'

The village teacher then awoke
And standing on his scutcheon spoke
Thus to the beast, who made his seat
With crossed paws at the dead man's feet:

'The Werewolf,' said that honest wight,
'The Willwolf—future, am I right?
The Wouldwolf—wolf conditional,
The Beowolf—father of them all!'

These tenses had a pleasing sound,
The Werewolf rolled his eyeballs round,
And begged him, as he'd gone so far,
Add plural to the singular.

The village teacher scratched his head;
He'd never heard of that, he said.
Though there were 'wolves' in packs and swarms,
Of 'were' could be no plural forms!

The Werewolf rose up blind with tears
He'd had a wife and child for years!
But being ignorant of letters
He went home, thankful, to his betters.

MAN INTO BEAR

Dasent in *Popular Tales from the Norse* (1859) writes:

> Even now in Norway, it is a matter of popular belief that Finns
> and Lapps, who from time immemorial have passed for the most
> skillful witches and wizards in the world, can at will assume the
> shape of bears; and it is a common thing to say of one of those
> beasts, when he gets unusually savage and daring, "that can be no
> Christian bear." Of such a bear, in the parish of Oföden, after he
> had worried to death more than sixty horses and six men, it is said
> that a girdle of bear-skin, the infallible mark of a man thus trans-
> formed, was found when he was at last tracked and slain.

QUEEN HEDWIG ELEONORA

She was the daughter (1636–1715) of Frederick II of Holstein-Gotorp and
for dynastic reasons was married off to Carl X Gustav of Sweden in 1654.
She was always a dominant force in Swedish politics for the rest of her busy
life, and after she was queen, she was the chief in the regency of her son
(who became Carl XI) and even in the regency of her grandson (who came
to the throne as Carl XII in 1697). She changed the face of Sweden politically and as well as architecturally (with the building of the palaces somewhat in imitation of Versailles called *Dröttningsholms Slott* and *Strömsholms
Slott*). Nicodemus Tessin, and later his equally talented son, directed the
building of these French-inspired castles for the queen. They are not,

unfortunately, the only reasons that history remembers her. She had constructed in addition to (say) her charming little theater, which still puts on plays, a theater of cruelty which cost the lives of some of her subjects.

The queen had many ideas about changing things. Once the building got under way in 1662 she began to consider changes in society as well, and in 1669–1672 she gave orders to root out witchcraft, particularly in the province of Bohuslän, newly acquired and supposedly filled with magic directed against the good of society and the government of the realm. A treaty executed at Roskilde (Denmark)in 1658 gave to Sweden the territories of Skåne, Halland, Blekinge, Bornholm, and Bohuslän, as well as Trøndelag, now in Norway (that went back to Norwegian land by another treaty made in Copenhagen in 1660). The queen announced her intention of binding these territories firmly to the Swedish crown and of cleaning up witchcraft as efficiently as had been done in Germany and elsewhere on the Continent, by force, since France in the thirteenth century, if not earlier.

In the Nordic countries the mass hysteria and witchcraft persecutions were comparatively minor and not very long lasting, though the outbreak of witch burning or beheading is still remembered in the folklore of Bohuslän and, as we say elsewhere, the children of that province dress up as witches or *påske-käringar* for fun at Eastertide.

Here is the Queen, as Regent of Sweden, ordering the extermination of witchcraft: We translate

> By God's Grace, etc.
>
> Our greatest favor and with inclination to God's grace. We most willingly instruct our servant and governor that against any sort of witchcraft and Satanic superstition anywhere in our realm we act so that, by the grace of God, even greater evils of The Devil come not among the common people, and demand even stricter and harsher means be adopted.
>
> Wherefor we have decided to command your investigations and set up a commission of sacred and secular persons, namely our governor in Gothenburg [Harald Stake], our beloved and faithful Master Per Sparre, together with the president of the same city, trusted Master Gripenklou, and Bishop Zacharias Klingenstierna, who shall assist the responsible clergy who at the same city shall at a time decided by you meet to find the cause of this evil. We must bring wretched and deviant people to the right and true way, to lead them to eternal salvation and from the slough of supersti-

tion. Thus with complete zeal and seriousness we must make them realize that our royal government will bring salvation to our subjects' eternal souls as well as welfare to their persons and possessions in the present.

We command you to do your uttermost to inform such a commission with all necessary authority and to specify the time and place when our own representatives can be sent when you in due time have assembled. There you and the officials of your civic government together with two or three legal counsels to the commission should meet. In this matter this commission should act with less severity than with zeal and dedication to find out evil. What you thereby are able to accomplish will greatly please us.

Queen Hedwig Eleonora orders the suppression of witchcraft in Bohuslän, 1669.

However, if the matter cannot be carried out without the force of law and stiff punishments, we instruct the civic and legal authorities to act decisively under your orders. Sentences after judgment shall be published in the court of Jonkoping in which other criminals are tried. We shall be informed . . . .

In extreme cases when anyone is imprisoned you surely must not leave them unattended so that The Devil might bring them into greater danger. We all these things submit to your skill and commend you to God, Almighty and full of Grace.

Given at Stockholm on the seventh of August in the year 1669.

On behalf of the highborn Majesty the King, our royal and beloved son. . . .HEDVIG ELEONORA . . . .

That is the best English rendition we can make of a document as difficult in language as it is nonsensical in intention. According to such historians as Linderholm, witchcraft executions in Sweden up to 1676 numbered 250 or 300, mostly of women. The last few were in Stockholm and Uppsala, the most (70) in the parish of Angermanland at the height of the persecution and (30) at Kungalv on the island of Tjörn. In every case a confession, usually obtained under torture, was required.

A DOZEN REFERENCES IF YOU CAN READ SCANDINAVIAN LANGUAGES

Alver, Bente, *Heksetro og trolldom* (Oslo, 1971)

Bang, A. C., *Norske Hexeformulater og magiske opskrifter* (Kristiania, 1901–1902)

Espeland, Velle., *Svartbok fra Gudbrandsdalen* (Oslo, 1974)

Forsblom, W. W., *Folktro ock trolldom 5: Magiske folkmedicin* (Helsinki, 1927)

Grambo, Ronald., *De tre legende moyer inorske trollformler* (Oslo, 1974)

Jacobsen, J. C., *Dvævlebesværgelse: Træk af Exorsismens historie* (Copenhagen, 1972)

Lindqvist, Ivar., *Galdrar* (Gothenburg, 1923)

Ohrt, F., *Danmarks Trylleformler* I & II (Copenhagen 1917, 1921)

_____, *Trylleord* (Copenhagen, 1922)

Reichborn-Kjennerud, I., *Var gamle Trollsdomsmedicin* I-V (Oslo, 1927–1947)

Stroraker, J. T., *Sygdom og forgjorelse* (Oslo, 1932)

Tallqvist, Knut, *Månen I myt och dikt, folktro och kult* (Stockholm, 1949)

EIGHTEENTH-CENTURY SWEDISH WITCHES

From documents in G. P. Hallenberg's *De Inquisitione sagarum in Svecia*, published in Uppsala in 1787 and earlier, here is the story of the plague of witches that troubled Sweden from the seventeenth to the late years of the eighteenth century:

> On July 5, 1668, the pastor of Elfvedalen in Dalecarlia reported to his bishop that Gertrude Svensen, a girl of eight, who had come there four years before from Lille Herrdal, a parish of Norrland, and had learned the art of incantation from a servant named Marit Jonsdotter, had stolen for the devil (*abstulerait ad malum genium*) several children of Elfvedalen. She was detected by Eric Ericson, a boy of fifteen, who likewise accused several others, one of whom, a woman of seventy, confessed, and the others denied. The royal officials had likewise investigated the matter and reported that these persons had visited the church on the first day appointed for

public supplication, and had stolen from the sacristy some of the consecrated wine.

The pastor is rewarded for his zeal by the king, March 22, 1669, with promotion to a better benefice. May 22 royal letters are issued to the bishop to appoint some trusty pastors who with delegates from the royal council should bring back the simple multitude to the way of salvation by mild measures, without imprisonment or cruel punishment. June 15 the bishop is ordered to appoint persons to meet at Gahlun on St. John's Day to confer, and further he is to order public prayers throughout the diocese to avert the raging of the devil.

The commission, consisting of members of the royal council and leading local officials, meets. After a brief examination, lasting from the 13th to the 25th of August, they condemn to death twenty-three persons of whom fifteen, convicted on their own confession, are immediately beheaded, August 25, and their bodies burned at the stake. The rest are reserved for further examination by the royal council. Besides this, thirty-six children, who had been seduced by the witches, are beaten with rods; and 200 more are ordered to stand with rods for three Sundays in the porch of the church, and then, for a year from the 13th Sunday after Trinity, to occupy a special position in front of the preachers.

So far was this severity from curing the evil that it seemed rather to scatter its seeds far and wide. September 25 royal letters were addressed to the bishop ordering him to assemble a new commission, as the former one appeared to have accomplished nothing. December 19, other letters ordered a new form of prayer to be used in all the churches of the kingdom, as witchcraft was said to have penetrated as far as Bohusia [Bohuslän].

In 1670 several of these commissions were constituted "in Helsingia (Helsingen), præfectura *Uplandiae Orbyhusensi (Örbyhus?) atque Upsaliæ.*" The president of them was Andreas Stjernbok, member of the council of Dorpat, and a member was Charles Lund, Professor of Law in Uppsala. A letter of Stjernbok to Charles XI describes the horrible apparition of the devil to himself and Lund— which was confirmed by the latter frequently in his lectures, under an invocation to God.

In the parish of Nordingra in Angermannia, two boys, one of sixteen and the other of eighteen, began to preach to other children at play, whence angelic visions began to occupy the minds of all, young and old. A royal commission thereupon made the ordinary inquisition in the parishes of Thorsaker, Ytterlannas and Dahl, in the course of which, during 1674 and 1675, they put to death 71 persons, beheaded first, then burnt. October 16, 1674, Jacob Abraham Euren, Lector of the Gymnasium of Hernosand and afterwards *Præpositus Norensis*, asserted that he was given up to the devil (*ad malum genium ablatum*)—as his own wife testified. In this same year many other persons were put to death on three pyres erected near the town of Hernosand.

In the year 1676 the contagion reached Stockholm, notwithstanding that the inhabitants had endeavored to avert it by a day of public prayer on February 20. By the order of the royal council, the Consistory of the city, March 31, delivered its opinion on the subject, confirming in all respects the public infatuation. Examinations were made by the inferior judges and sentences rendered by the royal council, under which six women were put to death. Then the Regents appointed a royal commission of twelve members, half clergy and half laity, some of the latter being physicians. All the prisons were crowded with the accused; many accused themselves and persisted in it to the death, and the popular excitement was kept up by vigils, fasts and prayers. Several children and three servant girls accused a Finnish woman, Magdalen Matsdotter, of witchcraft, and her own two daughters joined in the accusations, asserting in court that they saw the devil standing beside her. Notwithstanding her denials, she was burned to death, a punishment at that point almost unheard of, and her youngest daughter accompanied her to the stake, vainly endeavoring to the last to persuade her to confess. These same servant girls then accused of witchcraft the daughter of a gardener, betrothed to a tailor, who had given her a silk dress; she confessed and was condemned to death, but before execution it was proved that they had acted from envy and that the Finnish woman had likewise been falsely accused. These and other similar cases at length showed the judges that they should act with more caution when human life was at stake, nor admit the evidence of children. The above-named servant girls were condemned to death and a boy of fourteen, named Johan Johanson, who was supposed to have been the first to bring to Stockholm these magic arts from Gevalia and was proved to have done everything to gain money. Then by order of the king all future prosecutions for witchcraft were stopped.

Christian Thomasius [of Leipzig, 1712] says that one of the assessors appointed by the King of Sweden to sit on the trials for witchcraft, when traveling in Germany, told him that he and the other assessors at the beginning easily [perceived] that there was lack of sufficient ground for an inquisition on the accused, since there was no other evidence than the fantastic talk of children and half-grown boys. But the spiritual assessors, who had the upper hand, disregarded this, while they asserted that the Holy Spirit, which strove to guard the glory of God against the kingdom of Satan, would never permit these boys to tell lies, in support of which they always quoted the Psalm: "Out of the mouths of babes and sucklings has thou ordained strength, because of thine enemies, that thou mightest still the enemy and the avenger." At last, after many innocents had been burnt, one of the boys accused an honorable man of having been at the devil's feast, whereupon one of the assessors, with the knowledge of the others, promised him half a thaler if he would admit that he was in error and had meant to accuse another person, which he readily agreed to do. Then the theologians immediately saw that the Holy Spirit did not speak through the boys, and this one was scourged with rods by the servants of the judges; but the persecution was abandoned too late, for already many innocent persons had been executed.

And one more story from the time before Sweden stopped witchcraft persecutions (1779). One Hauber reported (again we translate):

A letter from Stockholm, December 27, 1732, relates how a young girl performed miraculous cures by prayer and laying on of hands. The authorities of the place arrested her and sent her to Stockholm for judgment, where a judge condemned her to be burnt as a sorceress, but his colleague dissented and she was handed over to the Hofgericht, which on investigation found her to be an industrious person of exemplary life who performed her cures gratuitously, and called in two clergymen to examine her. One pronounced her to be of feeble understanding, the other, who took great interest in the case, regarded her as endowed with miraculous gifts from her close relations with God and Christ — no priest was so familiar with Scripture and her whole conduct was modest and God-fearing. The upshot was still to be determined, but she doubtless escaped the stake.

ANNA i HOLTA

It was June of 1669 in Sweden and one Sören Muremester (Bricklayer) appeared at a court in Marstrand, a seaside town, to lodge a complaint against Anna i Holta of the same town.

He said that one night she appeared at his house, found him in bed, and touched his *hemliga lem* or private part, joking with him, saying she would rob him of his *snopp* or potency. Then she left, but at the door she met Sören's wife and told her, "I just went in and stole your husband's potency."

"Shame on you," the wife scolded Anna.

Sören told the court that immediately his stomach began to feel as if a litter of kittens was running around inside him and he was sure he had lost his manhood. He jumped out of bed and dressed and went to Anna's house and banged on the door. When she opened the door he told her angrily that if she did not at once restore to him what she had taken away that afternoon he would send her on a hell of a journey with "fire to pay her back."

"Dear Sören," she replied sweetly, "I don't know what you are talking about. Why do you come and disturb me like this? Go home and get some rest. I have taken nothing away from you."

But Sören would not rest and soon after Sören's wife went to Anna and demanded she return Sören's manhood to him. She refused. Then one night soon after, at the stroke of midnight, Anna appeared at Sören's door, gained admission to the house, and said she wanted to know what this whole business was about. Why were they accusing her?

Sören blurted out, "If you think I'm lying, come over here and feel this and you'll know what I'm talking about."

Anna touched him on what the court reporter suddenly bursts into German to record: his *Gemecht* instantly regained its full manhood.

In court Anna admitted that she had touched him there and that indeed it did seem to do wonders for him. She checked later and everything was working well. Was she to be punished for that?

Yes, she was. Moreover, a couple of days later the court met again to hear more accusations against Anna. One Signe Larsdotter (Daughter of Lars) testified that a couple of weeks before—it was now 10 June—she had gone to Anna's house and asked for some yeast for her baking. She got none and she was certain Anna had determined to do no good for anyone. In fact, she must have put some kind of curse on Signe's daughter, for the daughter suddenly fell ill and "lay there like a rain worm."

Also Malin i Lunden (From the Bushes) came forward with accusations of witchcraft against Anna. Malin said she had once been in Anna's house when Anna was baking and the cake started to burn and Anna just opened the door of the oven, blew into it three times, and the fire went out. Another time, Malin swore, Anna (in the shape of a cat) had come to her and tried to tear her throat! Malin's husband Lars was similarly attacked by the cat!

Kirstin Anders Mølners (Miller) added that Anna had put some sort of curse on her husband, who sickened and died. That was eight years ago.

Brengda Lars Spelemands (Playmaker) accused Anna of having killed her husband, too. Their two husbands had got into a fatal altercation over a herring net which Brengda had promised she would make but somehow had not had time to get around to. "What sort of a whore of a wife do you have," Anna's husband had demanded, "who won't make a herring net she promised to make?"

"Well," replied Lars, "your whore of a wife has wound up in court!"

When Anna's husband told Anna of that sharp exchange, Anna was furious. Everything in the house, they say, flew through the air. She swore that Lars was going straight to The Devil. The very next day Lars's boat capsized, and he was drowned, with two others, though all the other boats returned safely and with good catches.

Now 21 June rolled around and the court met once more. In came Ingier Persdotter (Peter's Daughter). She admitted that she had no complaint of her own but she wanted to say that twice she had failed to make brandy right but that Anna told her she should try a third time and when she did, Anna coming to her house, the brandy turned out fine.

All this time Anna had been kept in prison and, of course, she was being tortured to see if a confession of witchcraft could be got out of her. She must be dealing with The Devil, but even a minister was unable to get a confession out of her. So they had to call in an expert in witchcraft tests.

On 22 June Anna was given the test of being thrown into water. If she sank, she was all right. If she floated, clearly The Devil was buoying her up. She floated like a swan, the records tell.

Well, the court sessions and the tortures and tests went on and on, but they could not force a confession of dealing with The Devil out of her. And they were cheated of chopping off her head or burning her, for she hanged herself in her cell on Sunday, 4 July, 1669, while supervision was lax because good Christians were at church.

A book on the 300th anniversary of the beginning of the witchcraft scare was published as *Häxorna och trolldomen i Bohuslän . . . 1669-1672*. In that period in that section of Sweden some 300 witches, women and men, were executed. In the area the children's folklore still recall the burnings.

WITCHCRAFT TRIALS IN GÖTLAND 1635-1754

Per Sorlin's doctoral dissertation (Umea, 1993) is *Trolldoms och vidskepelsprocesserna i Göta hovratt, 1635-1754*. As the title says, it examines witchcraft and magic trials in the superior court of Gota in the period mentioned, the only significant period for these matters in the history of Sweden. The trials seem to indicate that foreign folk-belief systems, chiefly German, were at work more than native Swedish ones and a certain amount of vindictiveness in the testimony of witnesses suggests that these trials may have been at least in part motivated by factors other than fear of The Devil and his minions taking over the society.

ICELANDIC WITCH TRIALS

In the history of Iceland, there seems to have been far more men than women dabbling in witchcraft. One source speaks of the execution for witchcraft of twenty-two men and one woman. The last execution for witchcraft in Iceland I know of dates from 1690.

MOSE LAG

The Law of Moses which says "thou shalt not suffer a witch to live" was pretty much in force in Sweden before the *lagbok* or new code that came in 1735. It put to death a number of Swedish witches of whom perhaps the most famous was named Elin. Elin of Pilane on the island of Tjörn was burned at the stake in Myggenäs (27 January 1672) with six other women and a man.

OFF WITH HIS HEAD

The last person whom I can find in the records as having been beheaded for witchcraft in Sweden was Jacob Eriksson Mejer, a smith in Skåne, condemned to death on 16 May 1723.

THE BONES OF THE DEAD

Elsewhere I have encountered people stealing the bones of the dead to work black magic but only in Norway is there evidence of these being sold by the church. Priests used to encourage the practice and tell the *ronkjerringar* (runes workers) to leave a coin in the churchyard wall. When the churchyard wall at Lom was demolished in the nineteenth century, a bag containing coins and human hair, nail clippings, and charred bone was found.

FINNISH WITCHCRAFT

Bishop Rothovius said in a sermon at the new university in Turku in 1640:

> When people fall ill, they seek help from The Devil by laying wax figures, candles, squirrel skins and other things on the altars, and on certain days they sacrifice sheep and coins.

Later in the same century a professor at Turku (Martin Stodius) and two undergraduates (Eolinus Gunnerus and Johannes Arwidi) were hauled before the council on charges of practicing black magic. In 1687 a law was passed making witchcraft and pacts with The Devil capital offenses. In the 1650s there were 50 trials for witchcraft in Pohjanmaa alone.

ACCUSATION IN DALARNA

In 1757 a shoemaker's apprentice (Erik Johansson) accused some people in this Swedish province, notoriously superstitious, of witchcraft and under torture they confessed to a pact with The Devil. The governor (Bernhard Reynold von Hauswolf) doubted the confessions, questioned the suspects more closely, and determined young Erik was lying. He ordered twenty-four "pairs of lashes" for the boy plus a fine of 100 *daler* in silver and set free the convicted. After that Dalarna residents thought twice before accusing their neighbors of witchcraft.

NAILING DOWN EVIL IN DENMARK
AND SOUTHERN SWEDEN

An old *grimmoire* was used in Denmark and Bohusland, etc., well into the nineteenth century. Here's one of its recipes for evil, summarized: Take nails from a coffin exhumed from consecrated ground and as you pull them say: "Nails, I take thee so that thou mayest serve to turn aside and cause evil to all persons whom I will." Then you oddly add: "In the Name of The Father, The Son, and The Holy Ghost. Amen." Then you drive the nails into the footprints left by your victim. You say a *Pater Noster qui es in terra* (on earth, not in heaven), addressed to The Devil as you do so. "Cause harm unto *N.* until I remove thee." The victim will suffer unless and until she or he pulls up the nails with the words: "I remove thee so that the evil thou hast caused to *N.* will cease. In the Name of The Father, The Son, and The Holy Ghost. Amen."

A page of a book of the black arts, from Småland (Sweden), acquired by the *Nordiska Museet* (Northern Museum) in 1910, which took the photograph. The book contains recipes and incantations.

THE FIRE DEMON ÍMI

A runic inscription on a wooden stock from very ancient times in Norway gives us a curse of a sort: It calls upon the fire demon Ími to hinder an enemy's cooking. It would sound like this:

> *Ími stein heitti,*
> *at ari(n)-reykr rjúki!*
> *Aldri seydir sodni!*
> *út yl!*
> *inn kyl!*
> *Ími stein heitti!*

And that means: "Ími heated the stone. Never smoke shall smoke. Never shall the food be cooked. Out with the heat! In with the cold! Ími heated the stone." It is not impossible that in the ancient tongue *ími* meant soot deposited on the walls of the fireplace the way that *imma* is the modern Swedish word for condensation of water on windows, etc. The Middle Ages still seem to have had a lively belief in the ancient demons of the west of Norway and the distant, pagan past.

EYVIND JOHNSON

Born in Borden in 1900, this Swedish novelist wrote a great deal about his own early life in northern Sweden but he also penned important historical novels set in foreign climes and in *Drommer en rosa och eld* (1949) he retold the story of the witches of Loudun. His work is compared to that of Aldous Huxley's *The Devils of Loudun* by Lars G. Warme in the journal *Selecta 2* (1981).

TWO SEVENTEENTH-CENTURY INCANTATIONS

These are from Uppland (Sweden), dated 1646, and typical:

> *Jag står upp en morgon*
> *från alla mina sorger.*
> *Jag binder mig med vredes linda*
> *från man och kvinna,*
> *från svärd, från värld,*
> *från all min ofärd.*
> *Så skall hat och avund smältas*
> *på mig i dag,*
> *som saltet smältes*
> *i friska vattnet.*
> ✠ ✠ ✠ *AMEN.*

> I get up in the morning
> From all of my sorrows.
> I bind myself with a band of wrath
> Against man and woman,
> Against sword, against world,
> Against all my misfortune.
> So shall hate and envy be melted
> On me today,
> As salt dissolves
> In fresh water.

Jag binder daras händer.
Jag binder eras tänder.
Jag binger deras lever.
Jag binder deras lunga.
Jag binder deras tunga.
Jag binder dem med ormegadd och ormenacka.
Mitt fram och deras tillbaka
i alla de sju tusende namn!

I bind their hands.
I bind their teeth.
I bind their livers.
I bind their lungs.
I bind their tongues.
I bind them with snake sting and snake's neck.
I forward and they back
In all the 7000 names!

CHARM TO BANISH NIGHTMARES

Here is an old Swedish verse to banish nightmares:

Mara mara minne
du får ej bli härinne,
förrän du räknat
fäglar i skog,
fiskar i flod,
alla eketräd
och Guds ord.

Nightmare, nightmare mine
You mustn't stay herein
Before you have counted
The birds of the forest,
The fish in the river,
All of the oak trees
And all the works of God.

SIMPLE INCANTATIONS

Every child in America has heard these verses:

Rain, rain, go away,
Come again another day.

Few people think of it this way but the verses are, in fact, an incantation. Here is a simple incantation still used in Småland (Sweden):

Mot Regn

Jungfru Maria hon satt på stätta
hon borsta och han flätta.
hon bad til Gud alena
Att regnet måtte lena
och solen måtte skena,
först på folk ocn sen på fä,
och så på Jungfru Maria
lilla vita knä.

Against Rain

The Virgin Mary sat on a stile,
She combed and braided her hair.
She prayed to God Almighty
That the rain might be kind
And the sun might shine,
First on folk and then on beast
And then on the Virgin Mary's
Little white knee.

THE "WISE WOMAN" CURING SICK ANIMALS

Hard-to-find old Danish verses record a reaction to the "wise woman" Maren Aas trying to cure the priest's cow:

> *Her staar jeg, Maren Aas,*
> *ved din Ko i Baas,*
> *og stryger dig fra din*
> *Nakke til din Hale,*
> *gor det ikke godt,*
> *gor det ikke Skade.*

> Here stand I, Maren Aas,
> At your cow in the stall,
> And stroke from the

neck to the tail,
If that does not do good,
It can't do bad.

Her staar jeg, Pastor Eg,
lænet op til en Vaeg
mit Hasselstok i Hænde
for at varme Maren Aas'es Ende.

Here stand I, Pastor Eg,
Leaning against the wall
With a hazel stick in my hand
With which to warm Maren Aas' end.

NORWEGIAN NAMES OF THE DEVIL

Gammel Erik, Old Eric
Hinmannen, The Other One Himself
Hin Hårde/Hin Håte, The Hard One
Støggmannen, The Ugly One
Puken/Pukjen, Puck

NORWEGIAN PROVERBS ABOUT THE DEVIL

If you take The Ugly One on your back you'll have to carry him.
If you take The Devil into the boat you will have to sail with him.
If you give The Devil your little finger he'll take the whole hand.
The Devil knows his audience.
Morality in the middle, as The Devil said when walking between
   two priests.
Når en snakker om Faen, så kommer han—Speak of The Devil, he
   appears.

CHURCH MURALS OF THE NORTH SHOWING THE EVIL ONE

The northern devil is often depicted as blue or black, covered with fur,
but humanoid. Often he has a tail, bat wings, talons, huge eyes, and a fierce
mouth, and occasionally a single horn on his forehead. He appears in various other forms, such as a firedrake or the dragon that St. Michael the
Archangel defeats or as the evil opponent of St. Goran or St. Margaret or
even St. Olaf (also depicted as tramping down paganism in the form of a

troll named Skalle). The Trønder poet of Norway in 1038 referred to the demons who assailed St. Olaf and "made The Devil laugh" with satisfaction. Halldorr Skvaldri about 1120 mentions "the servants of The Devil," related by others to "trolldom" and "The Devil's delusion" (wisdom given by The Devil to a kind of witch doctor). The twelfth-century sagas mention Satan as the Prince of Darkness. The name Beelzebub also appears in the saga literature of this period as Christianity and older traditions are blended. In the biblical *Stjorn* of the mid-fourteenth century, the familiar black devil with horns and a tail appears. Insane people begin to be described as in the grip of this humanoid creature of evil. Bishop Arne's saga warns that unbaptized children who die may become wandering and dangerous servants of evil powers and bring sickness to the neighborhood if these dead children are not properly buried near, not in, the consecrated ground. The Devil and demons are seen as ever-present and serious threats.

The Devil and sometimes his attendant demons are seen in paintings of Hell and The Last Judgment and in a church in Odense (Denmark) he lies in front of the Savior. He is sometimes shown as tempting Christ, as on a Swedish baptismal font in Skåne. In Gotland he is depicted with Cain and Abel. In Småland he whispers into the ear of the wife of Noah and in Ål church (Norway) into the ear of King Herod (advising him, obviously, to slaughter the innocents). He appears again with Herod in a stave church at Torpo in Norway. The Devil may be shown at a deathbed, waiting to get a soul, or at the suicide of Judas. In an Icelandic drawing, in a Danish church, and elsewhere, The Devil is shown being prevented by angels from seizing the soul of a departed person. The Devil is depicted in frescoes or just chalk drawings, on ceilings, on walls, and in rather obscure places in churches such as a west corner or the room or area where congregants stashed their weapons while they attended services (*vapenhusen*).

As the Middle Ages come along, The Devil is shown more often engaged in everyday life: at a drinking party in Iceland or Sweden, tempting a man to steal or threatening with a sword (in Uppland, Sweden), tipping the scales when souls are weighed, torturing the damned, or listening to Danish women gossiping and noting down their remarks. In Gotland he sits by the door noting down in his tablets the names of those who arrive late for divine service. A similar picture in Roskilde cathedral in Denmark is quite famous. He stands by the wine barrels and the woman milking her cow, he watches women at the churn, and he attacks ships at sea.

One very striking feature is the connection of The Devil in northern folk art with *Sko-Ella* (Shoe-Ella), a woman he is shown in various guises to be rewarding with a new pair of shoes for some evil service. The Devil doesn't dare to come too close to this evil harridan, and he fetches her the shoes on the end of a long rod. The Devil and Shoe-Ella are sometimes seen on opposite sides of the door to the weapons house. The scene is not uncommon in Uppland, Sweden, but also appears in a lot of church painting and at Tovsala, for instance, he seems to be putting evil ideas into the ear of a woman who is brandishing a large knife. In Finland we see The Devil in common life, his followers tempted or threatened, even some of his witches riding off to the *sabbat* on brooms.

In these sometimes crude but often effective depictions of The Devil we can see evidence of the mindset of northern people of ages past. Art speaks to all who see it in these propagandistic illustrations and warnings. My good friend Ola J. Holten writes me from Sweden:

> The idea of the *djevelen* was largely conveyed to the people through church pictures, rather than by rituals in Latin or even sermons. However, *Birgittas åbenbaringer* (Birgitta Revelations), which introduced more southern ideas to the far north, probably played a role, especially among the clergy, who could read, from mid-thirteenth century on, and there demons are mentioned, too. These ideas were reinforced by Peder Palladius in Denmark around A.D. 1500 and with the Reformation especially German concepts of The Devil went north. At that point The Devil became a kind of personality in northern thinking on a wide scale, more so than he had been in religious poems (called *kvaels*) or any pre-Reformation religious playlets or even in the superstitions regarding the incubus. As far back as about 1300, though, the Christian devil got mixed up with native beliefs in ghosts and dragons and mythical sea beasts and trolls and such, the church itself likely encouraging this useful connection of the fairly new religion with the old heathen folk beliefs. In Gothic wall pictures and drawings, demons are conflated with grotesque animal forms, and The Devil enters into the life of ordinary people just as bogeys did in heathen times under such guises as "antagonist," "enemy," "snake" or "dragon," "evil force," even "collector of nails from the dead."

People came to believe that The Devil could go about in human form or take on any one of a vast repertoire of animal forms. There are folk tales about a person wounding a woman or an animal, etc., only to have The Devil himself appear nursing the same kind of wound. In one story, he demands reparations!

As the *Malleus malificarum* and other anti-witchcraft books became known in northern climes, such ideas as pacts with The Devil became ordinary belief and in time the north suffered witchcraft trials, though never as long or as severely as countries more southerly in Europe.

MAGICAL CHANTS OF THE NORTHLANDS

Thirteenth-century Norse literature speaks of *galdr*, a word which has survived to this day in the oldest dialects of the north and west of Norway and chiefly in the area where Norwegian meets Sammish culture. The modern Norwegian word is *galder*, which corresponds to the Germanic *galan* (sing in a loud and shrill voice), so we have evidence of how magical incantations sounded in very distant days.

These incantations are repeatedly mentioned in the ancient literature. Odin says he has learned "strong songs from the son of Bolpórr" and later we hear that with them he can heal, protect against edged weapons, extinguish fires, create love, and deprive troll witches of their powers. Women

The Devil notes down some gossip. Fanefjord church, (Danish) county of Praeste.

were also versed in these incantations. In the saga about the "Weeping of Oddrun," for instance, Oddrun chants over the pregnant Borgny to facilitate delivery of the child. The Lapps appear in the literature as past masters of *galdr* and in the report the Battle of Stikelstad in Trøndelag we hear that Tore Hund was invulnerable, protected by the strong magic of the Lapps (or Finns). Snorri Sturlesson speaks appreciatively of the power of incantations. Though *Gulatinglova* was on the books prohibiting sorcery and outlawing diving, incantations, spells, and *galdr* in general, witches went right on using the magic and apparently were well tolerated until the German executions of witches spread to the north, principally due to Queen Hedwig Eleanora, whom we have introduced to the reader earlier.

CALLING UP A STORM

The witches in Shakespeare's "Scottish play" vengefully call up a storm, and the witches of the Nordic areas were really good at this. Here is a *gandrim* (magic rhyme) for the purpose, which Ola J. Holten found in the folklore of Skåland for me, with my translation:

> *Kom så vantan togna.*
> *Kom så mastra bogna.*
> *Kom så seglet remna.*
> *Kom så båten klemna.*

> Come so shrouds are at the brink.
> Come so that the mast is bent.
> Come so that the sail is rent.
> Come so that the boat will sink.

GAND-FINN

The stories about Finnish *gand* (magic) and *trollskap* (sorcery) go back to the times when the Finns were not at all approved by the Norwegians nearby (*bygdefolket*) who were more prosperous and prejudiced against the Finns. The Norwegians told stories about how some boys shot a reindeer and when a Finn demanded payment for it and was refused, he cast a spell on the boys whose parents would not pay. One boy had to have his foot amputated and the other (an old man from Grunnfarnes at the time the tale was told) almost died. On another occasion a farmer was slaughtering a cow, but the blood would not flow out of the animal. Surely this was due to the magic of a Finn who happened to be passing by. But the farmer remembered the way around this. He remembered a woman named Elin in the Steinfjorden area that kept the blood from flowing from a slaughtered cow until a knife was stuck into the ground. Another Finn had an otter trap at Torsköya and a woman named Hanna complained that one of her sheep had disappeared and must have been caught in the trap. "I have not hurt your animals," the Finn replied, "but after me will come someone who will." The very next summer a bear swam over the sound and started to decimate the flock. The neighbors all pointed out that Hanna's flock was the only one attacked. Obviously the work of the Finn's magic.

There's a story about a Finn coming down to one of the farms at Torsken and asking for bread. The first farmer he asked refused to help him. The second, brother of the first, helped him out. "You are a better man than your brother," the Finn told his benefactor. "He chased me off, but he shall be paid in full for that."

"You shouldn't do harm to the brother of the man who helped you," the benefactor argued.

"Well," said the Finn, "there's something in that. But he must be hurt a little."

And he was. His stable was so ridden with fleas that neither cattle nor people could stay near it.

When autumn came, the farmers rowed to Holmen and whom should they meet but the Finn. "How's your brother?" the Finn asked his friend. "Has he got rid of his little visitors yet?"

Then they tell of a girl at Berg who got pregnant by a Finnish boy. He wanted to marry her but she said no; after all, he was a Finn. He became angry and said, "If you do not become anything for me, you shall not be anything for anyone else"—and the very next day she went insane and stayed that way for the rest of her life.

These stories are from Arthur Brox's *Folkeminne frå Ytre Senja* (Folklore from Outer Senja), a collection from 1990 that Ola J. Holten has translated for me and some of whose tales I tell. Senja is an island far to the north in the Lofoten Archipelago.

In the old days there were a lot of witches there, it is said, putting evil spells on cattle and people, so good folks put a cross on the stable and the boathouse and carried some iron or steel on their persons, for protection. Better safe than sorry. If someone did manage to do you harm and you caught her, it was a quick trip to the fire. Kirsten Andersdotter from Gryllefjord, for instance, was burned in 1620 because she threatened a man from Bergen with an accident. Shortly thereafter he was lost at sea. She went to the stake for it. In Outer Senja they still use the expression *å brenne trollkjerring* (to burn a troll wife) in connection with the bonfire on St. John's Eve and even with regular fires. It was once believed that at *Sanhansbål* the witches flew off to Blocksberg for a *sabbat*. Look for them now in the smoke and flames of bonfires.

These witches, peasants believed, could make themselves invisible. (In another book I give recipes for invisibility, but you won't see one here.) Or they could assume animal shapes, such as that of a troll cat. If you wanted to see a troll cat all you had to do was spin seven Sundays in succession. (Of course you were not supposed to be working on Sundays.) On the seventh Sunday the troll cat would roll across the floor like a ball of wool. Troll cats used to go into the stable and drink the milk from the cows and then sneak quietly out when the milkers came in the morning.

Ola Sørensen in Hopen says there were witches everywhere in the old days, dangerous ones. You had to be careful on sea or land. But they were caught and eliminated, one by one, until a single old hag remained in Medfjorden. Well, when people realized she was a witch they seized and blindfolded her and dragged her off to be burned at the stake. She said that as her last wish before she died, she would like to see, just once more, the light. So they took off her blindfold. Then she chanted:

> *Så langt eg no kan se,*
> *skall det aldri vekse tre.*

> As far as I now can see,
> Never more shall grow a tree.

Of course they immediately put back the blindfold, but it was too late, and ever since that day no tree has grown on that very hill. You can see for yourself.

WITTENBERG AND THE MAGICIANS OF THE NORTH

Hamlet and his friend Horatio were not the only Northerners to study at Wittenberg. This German university (though Shakespeare critics don't know the fact) was notorious for its students of black magic, the way Toledo in Spain had earlier achieved a reputation as a site of cabalistic studies. Recall that Dr. Faustus was a poor boy whose relatives paid for him to study at Wittenberg, where he became a black magician.

In Norwegian today *putre* describes the sound of water boiling, but in Catholic Europe of a much earlier time it was used to describe exhortations to The Devil which renegade priests sneaked into their Latin mumblings. The old meaning still found in some archaic dialects of Norway and Sweden. The Northerners were said to derive their evil learning from Wittenberg.

These priests were said to learn devilish prayers from a *swart(e)boka* (black book) which was full of *trollformler* (magical formulæ), pentagrams, and other kinds of occult knowledge. In Norway they still preserve "black books" such as those from Arenmark, Dovre, Hallingdale, and the *Vinjeboka* from Telemark dated *c.* 1520. One is dated as late as 1722. Many of these "black books" were ascribed to Cyprianus, bishop of Antioch, who, according to legend, tried to seduce the virginal Justina with the aid of demons.

The incantations and spells and recipes found in the "black books" were added to the older Norse magic which is described in the *Edda* of Snorri Sturlusson and are found throughout *Norden* in runic inscriptions of various sorts. All writing must have seemed magical to early peoples, but the runes were thought to have special power. It was only in Christian times that Christian symbols, occult sigils, pentagrams, and even Greek letters found in the "black books" were added to them. Olaus Magnus mentions rune magic in his history of the northern peoples and *lonnruner* were widely used to cast spells on animals and birds, trolls and people. The "black books" fitted in perfectly with a much older tradition.

EARLY NORSE MAGIC

Magic is, of course, about power, and the early Norse magic protected the weak against the strong as well as the natural world against evil from the supernatural world. The Lapps were especially noted for the magic which they used to counter the much greater numbers and strength of their neighbors, and modern folklore of the area is full of stories of how the Lapps used magic against the Swedes and Norwegians.

The old incantations and trances are still used by shamans although certain practices have fallen into disuse. For example, seldom or never now are curses put on the underside of a stone covering a grave. (If the stone were turned over, the curse would strike anyone who wanted to desecrate the buried body, launching evil forces against the disturber of the tomb.) One such grave curse was found on a stone turned up by ploughing at Egga Farm in Sogn (Norway) in 1917. It was written in a language between North Germanic (Proto-Nordic) and Old Norse and probably dates from the seventh century.

This gravestone is worth notice. It is a meter and a half long and covered a man's grave into which (as was customary in Vestlandet in that era) useful items for death's journey were put: an iron knife, a fire steel, and a scraper of flint. The gravestone was elegantly engraved with a horse's head surrounded by lines of runic inscriptions (about 200 runes). Parts of the inscriptions are lost or illegible, but we can see they were ancient magic. The inscriptions warn that the stone must not be uncovered by daylight or moonlight and must not be moved by men. This is what we can translate:

nissolusotuknisAksestAin
skorinnixxxxmaRnAkdanisnip
rinRniwiltiRmanRIAgixx

Not is the stone sought by the sun, nor is the stone cut with the
    [iron] knife.
Nor shall any man uncover it under the waning moon.
Nor shall troubled men move it.

hinwArbnAseumaRmAdepAim
kAibAibormopAhunihuwARob
kamhArasahialatgotnAfiskR
oRfxxnAuimsuwimadefoklxfx
xxxxxxgAlande

This [stone] the runemaster has sprinkled with the sea of the body [blood], scraped with the tole-pins of the boat weary of floating. As from whom came here the god of war [Odin?] to the land of the Goths [mankind?]. Like the fish, swimming out of the river of horrs [?] and like the bird—crying [crying—bird?]

Axxxxsurki

Protection against the evil one.

Note that the inscription, being magical, could not be made with iron but was made with a bone pin or hard stone such as flint. In Setedal (Norway) there is still a tradition that iron nails are not used in making coffins lest they disturb the soul of the deceased. In Nordic superstition, iron drove away trolls. Note also the ancient German superstition about the waning moon, considered to be too weak to bestow power. In the fascinating if unreliable history of *Germania*, Tacitus (at the end of the first century) tells us that the Teutonic peoples held their great meetings and sacrifices at the increasing and full moons. The first full moon after Yule was especially propitious. Julius Caesar wrote in *De Bello Gallico* that the diviners warned that "it was not the will of the gods that the Teutons should win if they attacked before the full moon." All this is relevant to devils and demons driven off by iron and emphasized as creatures of darkness.

In the Far North, dark, moonless nights were of the very essence of death, the time of devils and demons abroad. "Northwards and downwards lies the Home of Fog," says the *Neibelungenleid*.

WITCHCRAFT IN FINLAND

Rath and Achte in *Psychiatria Fennica* (1974) and others have tried to explain why Finland suffered far less of a witchcraft craze than Sweden in the seventeenth century, but it is a fact that in the twenty years between 1665 and 1685 persecution raged in Finland and 152 cases of what Rath and Achte call hexing were brought to the attention of worried authorities. Articles on witchcraft of the Finns in Norway appear in the journal *Tradisjon* (Tradition). In the anthology on *Early Modern European Witchcraft*—which takes up one by one the Scandinavian and nearby countries, including Finland—Antero Heikkinen and Timo Kervinen ascribe Finnish witchcraft persecutions to "the male domination" of the time.

WITCHCRAFT IN LITHUANIA

If asked to guess which neglected area of investigation would produce the most useful additions to the understanding of witchcraft in Europe, I would hazard Lithuania. The pagan past—Christianity came late, with political union with Poland happening in the fourteenth century—and the subsequent battles in print between the Lutherans and the Jesuits may hold fascinating information about magic and witchcraft in the popular imagination, although at least until the eighteenth century the documents of Lithuania are chiefly concerned with linguistic and theological arguments. After Lithuania became part of the Russian empire at the end of

L. M. Svenungsson

Rannsakningarna om

TROLLDOMEN

i Bohuslän

1669–1672

Häxorna · Satan · Rätten

the eighteenth century, Russian folk beliefs had an increasing influence. When we see the dramatic tales from the Russians and the Slavs and what witchcraft meant in Germany in the seventeenth and eighteenth centuries, we must suspect that treasures exist to be found in the area of Lithuania and in the Lithuanian written language whose foundations were established importantly at least as early as the writings of Konstantinas Sirvydas (1580–1631).

SUPERSTITIONS OF THE FAROE ISLANDS

Anyone lucky at fishing in The Faroes is said to *kunna ríkamannareit*, "know the magic spells" to catch fish.

Some Faroese might not touch the flesh of sheep killed this year but might eat meat two or three years old.

The cure for scabies used to be to go out early on Midsummer morning and wash in the dew.

On the thirteenth day after Christmas the islanders seek the omens for the new year and find plenty, *títt sum tortilin*, "nineteen to the dozen."

In The Faroes they say that if you walk barefoot on a newly-sown field it will be bare at harvest time.

In his book on *The Faroes and Iceland* (1905), Nelson Annandale praises these people as having few faults "unless, indeed, we are to include among faults a harmless superstition, which, in the twentieth century, still ventures to believe in trolls and mermaids." He found fishermen very apt to blame tangled lines on mermen and mermaids.

ADVICE TO PREGNANT WOMEN IN THE FAROES

Do not drink from a cup that is cracked or broken or your baby may be born with a harelip.

Do not wear a twisted necklace lest the umbilical cord get similarly twisted.

Do not follow a corpse at a funeral or the child will be born pale—and most people say it is bad to see a corpse at all if you are carrying a new life within you.

HULDREFOLK

A *hulda* has a Norwegian name from the same source as the word for *hidden*, that is occult. These creatures are somewhat like our fairies and they are said to live in the Norwegian *sætra* or chalets up in the areas where the cattle graze in summer. They enjoy this vacation from their underground homes. The supernatural visitors move in when the regular folk go to their winter quarters. The *huldrefolk* are said to dress in the old blue and red peasant colors but especially nasty ones may wear gray or other dark colors.

One still shouts when first arriving near one's chalet in summer and when opening the door. One has to give the *huldrefolk* warning to move out for the season. At Römdalen in the Trollheimen mountains people show you the *haukarsteinen* (shouting stone) where you must stand to broadcast news of your arrival as the *sætra* season begins.

From Trøndelag, this advice from 1749:

> When you lay the cornerstone for a new house you must beat three times with a stick on the stone at the place so that the underground folk will know you are there. If they are living there underneath they will make an odd noise. If they do, you must not build your house there.

These undergrounders, whether using your chalet in your absence or residing under the ground, make good friends but wicked enemies. Don't make demons of them, Norwegians advise.

NORDEN

"Probably less than [fewer than] two-dozen witch trials took place in Norway," writes Rossell Hope Robbins with worse grammar than one might expect of a Fellow of the Royal Society of Literature but all the authority of his fact-packed *Encyclopedia of Witchcraft and Demonology*. The first recorded witch trial was 1592: Oluf Gurdal was sentenced to death in Bergen. Two years later there was another such trial in Bergen and two witches were burned. Robbins lists a few other cases from the seventeenth century and a few eighteenth-century poltergeists. He has no entries for Denmark or Iceland.

Venetia Newell's *Encyclopedia of Witchcraft and Magic*, however, has this:

> The Black School was known in parts of northern Europe, especially Diresland, Denmark and Iceland. The devil taught there and new clergy attended with other students to receive instruction, for, according to this tradition, all clerics are familiar with the black art. Some are very knowledgeable and sell their souls to the devil if they fail to keep various conditions: for instance that they shave only on Saturdays or wear the same woollen vest or one garter for the rest of their lives. Another condition, presumably more applicable to other students than to the clergy, is that they do not enter a church, or, if they do, stay no longer than half an hour. If any of these stipulations is broken, the soul will be lost forever.
>
> Graduates of the Black School can control spirits and exorcise ghosts . . . and are able to travel simply by wishing to be in another place.

In Denmark card-playing, often associated in Protestant countries with The Devil, leads to The Evil One being portrayed as a black cat clutching a playing card (but not a club, which looks too much like a cross).

In Sweden, Charles IX (1608) and Gustav Vasa (1618) passed laws against poisoners and witches, but Queen Christina (1649) said persecuting witches only led to witch hysteria. She instructed that all prisoners not guilty of murder be freed and that witch trials cease. In 1669 a witch scare broke out in Mora. In 1670 a royal commission was appointed to look into witches in Sweden and Finland (then under Swedish control). In 1674–1675, seventy-one persons were beheaded or burned as witches in three parishes, and in 1676 a witch scare struck Stockholm, but when it was discovered that some informers were only after the accused's property, Charles XI banned all further prosecutions. The death penalty for witchcraft was abolished in 1779 in Sweden.

The Finns were famous (like the Lapps, Orkneys, and Shetland isles) for calling up storms by witchcraft. Olaus Magnus says the Finns used to sell magic strings with three knots in them to merchant sailors: loose one, two, or all three of the knots to get greater degrees of wind. Swedes appear to have brought black magic (rather than pagan practices) to Finland and as early as Gustav Vasa (1554) fines of 40 marks were levied on those who did not report to the sheriff witches—or tramps. In 1573 the Synod of Turku excommunicated witches. In 1575 Finland had its first trial for witchcraft and Johan III instructed government officials to look out for witches and idolaters. Around the time of the Mora witches in Sweden there was a witch scare in Finland. Laws of 1683 directed that males be hanged and women be burned for witchcraft. Most witchcraft trials in Finland were in the Swedish-speaking Pohjanmaa and Ahvenanmaa areas. The death penalty for witchcraft was repeated in the laws of 1734 and was abolished at the same time as Sweden's law (1779).

Ms. Newell tells of an Icelander who went to the Black School and decided to defy the tradition that the last student to leave was the property of The Devil. Soemundur the Learned (as he was called) dressed in a black cloak and when The Devil snatched at him The Devil was left holding the cloak. Soemundur got away. When The Devil pursued, he fled into the sunlight; The Devil caught only his shadow. Then he put blood on his head and The Devil, seeing him in the sky with a bloody halo, thought he was dead. Then he filled his shoe with salt water and The Devil thought he was drowned, and with soil, and The Devil thought he was buried. When he learned the truth, The Devil was so proud of the cunning of his pupil that he let him go. Most Icelandic magic involves far less cleverness than this and is regarded by most people as merely quaint, a collection of homemade remedies and old superstitions, although the extensive Swedish research into Lappish customs has revealed a rich and very ancient culture with a religion that may suggest features that come from other parts of Europe in the earliest times.

For a thousand years after Christ, the North was pagan and to some extent pagan practices still are found there along with belief in trolls and other superstitions. In Lapland the shamans still beat their magic drums and practice a religion that is also known among the Inuit and other northern peoples and is of prehistoric origin. As with other religions not our own, we are prone to look upon it as superstition or black magic, especially since the Lapp and similar religions are much concerned with trance states, healing, and divination. Selling one's soul to The Devil was, however, basically a foreign and infrequent idea. Only a few academics were in touch with the witchlore books of the rest of Europe.

SWEDISH DEVILS AND DEMONS

The Swedes turned the forces of nature with which they are confronted into demons centuries ago. However, they have found ways that satisfy them to propitiate these entities. They are ridden with trolls and all sorts of other creatures that visitors are surprised to see, but the concept of The Devil seems very strange to most of them, for that is theology, not folklore, and theology is something in which the Swedes do not seem to have had much interest for many, many years. I have a Swedish academic collaborator who consulted the trolls about the placement of his summer house before he built it and who laughs at people who go to church.

Sweden had a Witch Mountain, fear of sorcerers and poisoners, witchcraft trials (in the late 1670s and eighties, there was a rash of them), and more executions for dabbling in the black arts than you might expect. The seventeenth century seems very far back to them. The last execution for witchcraft was near the end of the eighteenth century, just about the same time that Germany ceased to execute witches. Today some who asserted they were dealing with demons would wind up in a hospital, not a jail.

JULENISSE

We put out cookies and milk for Santa Claus because he may need some refreshment as he makes his rounds on Christmas Eve. The Danes also think of the little spirits outside the house and put out a bowl of rice and milk on Christmas Eve. Maybe the cat eats it, maybe not, but if it's gone the next day you have made friends with the spirits out there.

LAPPISH RELIGION

The Lapps worshipped the god of thunder (*Tiermes*) and his wife (*Akka*, whose name appears in numerous placenames and in *Sarakka, Uksakka, Juksadda*), the sun god (*Païve*), and other deities. Their beliefs included *halde* (underground people) and certain spirits who lived in what the Swedes call *seitar* (strangely-shaped stones). Any such stone found (not made) was regarded as sacred and called *bassi-bá'ki*; I have seen docu-

Tegneta abonodika ärepa Salonia Rotas Belial, Bellsebuleb övers Lusefärdiabolus asonans med alla deras män underhavandes konster varda dövt i Faderns namn, i Guds faders namn, i Guds sons namn och i Gud den Helige andes namn, amen.

A Swedish magical charm from 1870.

mentary film of these stones being worshipped, but never the act in person. One film shows a shaman with his magic drum sprinkling the stone with water, placing ritual objects carefully around it, and then drumming.

Christianity reached the Lapps in the eleventh century, but this film is only about a half a century old and some aspects of the ancient religion still persist, as in *jojking*, what Johan Turi, one of the most important of Lappish writers, has called "the art of remembering people and animals." Creatures are sung about in nostalgia or in hatred.

ESKIMO TALES FROM GREENLAND

The Inuit or Eskimos of Greenland have two kinds of tales they tell, *ogalugtuag* and *oqualvalarut*.

The *oqalugtuaq* stories are very old and mix history and the fabulous but are regarded as the accurate records of the past; as such they are handed down from one generation to another. They prove the relationship of all the Inuit peoples and recount their battles with foreign tribes, their settlements and trapping and hunting activities, their births and deaths, their joys and sorrows, their religion and superstitions, their murders and vengeance and court proceedings and punishments, and so on.

The *oqualvalarut* stories are just "stuff for conversation," exciting tales about personages and great events of the past, but not historical and often not referring to a very distant period.

There may even be a third category, which is Greenlandic fairy tales of a sort, designed to make the hearers go to sleep! At the risk of putting you to sleep, I'll tell you the one about the dwarfs and the giant.

Once upon a time there were some dwarfs who wanted to go out rowing for pleasure in a "woman-boat." As they were about to set out, the oldest woman shouted: "Oh, we have forgotten the skin that we stretched out for drying!"

"What skin?" the men asked.

The woman jumped ashore to take the skin into the house, but just as she did a huge mountain spirit came down the hillside, terrible to behold. The old woman stopped and held her breath. The mountain spirit tried to put a smile on his ugly face and winked at her and threw blueberries at her until she fell to the ground, slid down the slope into the sea, and was drowned.

The others, watching all this from the "woman-boat," dared not go ashore for help. The mountain spirit stood there smiling and flirting with the women in the "woman-boat," for he was a real woman-loving giant!

From the "woman-boat," the others had seen everything and feared worse. The dwarfs did not know how to fight the giant. Surely he was going to kill all the women and the men would be left to lie alone in their beds, with no one to cook their food or mend their clothes or make them new ones, with no one even to tend the oil lamps. Cold and misery would reign in their homes.

Then one old woman, hunched up in the "woman-boat," started to sing a troll song. Here it is in Danish:

> *Den, der sidder i Midten*
> *og giver Barnet Bryst,*
> *aja aja aja aja ja-a-a,*
> *hendes næstyngste Barn*
> *hører man altid græde*
> *aja aja aja aja ja-a-a.*
> *Den lille Kajakmand*
> *har tre smaa Mavesække,*
> *de ligner Fangeblærer,*
> *aja aja aja aja aja.*
> *Oh hun, der roer forrest,*
> *har stor Skildning i sin Navle,*
> *og han, der passer Styret,*
> *har et lille, bitte Haleben,*
> *aja aja aja aja ja-a-a-a.*

Those are the old Danish words, and they translate into something like this:

> The one sitting in the middle
> And giving the child her breast,
> Yah, yah, yah, yah, yah.
> Her next to youngest child
> Is always heard crying,
> Yah, yah, yah, yah, yah.
> The little kayak-man
> Has three small stomachs
> That look like fishing bladders,
> Yah, yah, yah, yah, yah.
> And she who rows in front
> Has a large fissure in her.
> And he who mans the rudder
> Has a tiny little tail bone,
> Yah, yah, yah, yah, yah.

An illustration from a history by Olaus Magnus (1555) shows the equality of women and men in ancient Lapland. A woman joins two men in hunting. They are all on skis!

When the giant heard this song he was so frightened that he split right in half: his legs and feet ran at great speed over the mountain and the rest of him just fell to the ground right there. The old woman's song made a terrific impression, you will agree!

To comment on the story, without getting into the possible sexual references in the little song, we might note that Inuit society assigns very special tasks to men and women: the women build the "woman-boat" and row it, they seem to be so much in charge of daily life that the men would perish without them. This is a theme which is echoed in many Inuit stories—stories which, it may be added, appear to be mostly invented and handed down orally by women, the poets, historians, and entertainers of these people.

GREENLANDIC FOLKTALES

The Danish missionary Peter Kragh was probably the first outsider to hear the folktales of North Greenland and he collected about 50 of them in *Kaladlit Okalluktuallait*. He began collecting in about 1824, and by 1868, he had collected 140 tales from Greenland and Labrador. In the 1850s the Danish scholar H. Rink began to collect the Inuit tales from Greenland, Baffin Land, and Alaska, discovering their common themes and dispersion. In Copenhagen in 1868 he published a pioneering work: *Om grønnnlæn-*

dernes gamle tro og kvad der af samme er bevaret under kristendommen. Missionaries such as Reichel (at remote Station Hebron) and Albrecht (at Station Okak) discovered more about the ancient Inuit (who fought against foreigners and left ruins of stone houses as well as tales of past times). One of Albrecht's tales deals with a person called Akigssak who is featured in a number of Greenlandic tales. Here, from a German version, is the story of Kaujakjuk (*Kaujajaklungmik*), from Labrador:

> Once upon a time there was a pitiful orphan child who in the winter had to sleep outside the warm area of the dwelling and who was forced to eat with the dogs. He was called Kaujajaklungmik. He had only a grandfather and a grandmother and they gave him no shred of love or kindness.
>
> He had a very big nose because they used to pick him up by the nostrils.
>
> One morning he called to his grandparents, frightened: "Grandfather dear, let me in! Grandmother dear, let me in!"
>
> "You are not any better than the dogs," they replied. "You stay outside!"
>
> So he went up the mountain and there he grew up to be a man, big and strong. And one time three polar bears appeared when he was not around and the people shouted and asked, "Where is Kaujakjuk?" Then he appeared and grabbed hold of the bears by the feet and, without any weapon, one by one, he killed the bears. Then he killed the people, one after the other, grabbing them by their feet. But he spared the lives of two women, who had been kind to him. One of them he was in love with and the other he found to be wise.

Well, that's the story of Kaujakjuk or *Kaujajaklungmik* ("about Kaujakjuk"), also known in Labrador as Aklaujak and by other names. In Greenland he is called Kausaksuk (in Julienehaab), Kassaksuk (in Fiskernæsset), Kagssagsusuk (in Godthaab), and Kausasuk (in Umanak). In Kragh's manuscript he is Kauksaksuk. In the basic Greenlandic version of his story, this is the text:

> Once upon a time there was a pitiful orphan. Because his family threw him out of the house, he was forced to live in the corridor, where an old lady took care of him. He was called Kagssagssuk. Whenever he came into the dwelling the others gave him pain and sorrow. They used to pick him up by the nostrils.

Because of that, his nose got bigger but he did not become any bigger himself.

When he grew older he was able to go out alone, and once he climbed up to the top of the mountain, where he met a stranger who spoke to him in a friendly way and promised to give him strength. This came true, but he had to promise to hide his strength until winter came, when the bears would appear.

In time, the bears came. Then Kagssagssuk came running. He took hold of the bears by the feet with his bare hands and he killed them. After that he even killed the people, one after another, bashing them and tearing them into pieces.

He spared the old woman and one other person who had shown him mercy.

SCANDINAVIA, FINLAND

Bergstrand, Carl Martin, *Trolldom och klokscap i Västergötland under 1800-talet* (1932)

Bosi, Roberto, *The Lapps* (1960)

Craigie, Sir William, *Scandinavian Folk-Lore* (1896)

Dalerup, Verner, *Hexe og hexeprocesier i Dänmark* (1888)

Elliott, R. M. V., *Runes* (1959)

Groenwald, F. W., *En Skansk Hexenprocess* (1899)

Hallenberg, George, *Dissertatio de Inquisitione sagarum in Svecia 1668-1677* (1787)

Hertzberg, R., *Hexprocesser pa 1600-talet* (1888)

Linderholm, E., *De Stora haxprocesserna i Svierge* (1918)

Malmquist, H., *Om Hexprocessen di Dalarme 1757-1763* (1877)

Olaus Magnus, *A Compendious History of the Goths, Swedes and Vandals* (1658)

Runeberg, Arne, *Witches, Demons, and Fertility Magic* (1947)

Salomie, Ilmari, *Noitausko ja noitavainot* (1935)

Vorren, Ornulv & Ernst Manker, *Lapp Life and Customs* (1962)

REPRESENTATIVE BOOKS ABOUT
THE FAR NORTH OF EUROPE

Bergsrand, Carl Martin, *Trolldom och klokscap i Vastergötland under 1800-talet* (1932).

Bosi, Roberto, *The Lapps* (1960.

Craigie, Sir William, *Scandinavian Folk-Lore* (1896).

Dalerup, Verner, *Hexe og hexeprocesser i Danmark* (1888).

Elliott, R. M. V., *Runes* (1959).

Grambo, Roland, "A Catalogue of Nordic Charms" in *NIF Newsletters 2* (Helsinki, 1977).

Grohwald, F. W., *En Skånsk Hexeprocess* (1899).

Hallenberg, George, *Dissertatio de Inquisitione sagarum in Svecia 1668-1677* (1787).

Herzberg, R., *Hexeprocessor på 1600-talet* (1888)

Linderholm, E., *De Stora häxprocesserna i Svierge* (1918)

Malmqvist, H., *Om Hexeprocessen di Dalarne 1757-1763* (1877)

Olaus Magnus, *A Compendious History of the Goths, Swedes and Vandals* (1658).

Runeberg, Arne, *Witches, Demons, and Fertility Magic* (1947).

Salomie, Ilmari, *Noitausko ja noitavainot* (1935).

Tillhagen, Carl Herman, "The Conception of Nightmare in Sweden" in *Humaniora . . . Honoring Archer Taylor* (1960).

Vorren, Ornulv & Ernst Manker, *Lapp Life and Customs* (1962).

THE DEVIL AND THE TAX COLLECTOR

Finally, in this section on Scandianavia and devils and witchcraft, a little story I offer in translation from the Norwegian, from *Fanden op Futen*, a folktale that illustrates that to the practical people of the north The Devil is more a figure of fun than fear. Here we see him with another man to be dreaded, the tax collector.

> Once upon a time there was a tax collector, a scourge of the worst kind. One day The Devil came to fetch him. "I never hear anyone saying anything but," The Devil said, "I wish The Devil would take this tax collector! So now you have to come with me. Besides, you already are so evil, there is no use leaving you here; you can't get any worse."
>
> "Oh, if you listen to what people say," replied the tax collector, "you'll get more work than you can do. And if you are so considerate a creature, you'll grant anyone anything they ask for, why then I may be spared even at this time."
>
> The tax collector presented a good case for himself, and the Devil was rather gullible, so at length they came to a compromise: they would walk along with each other for a while, and the first person they met who was cursed with "to The Devil with you," The Devil would take instead of the tax collector. But the curse had to come from the heart.

First they arrived at a cottage where the woman was churning butter. Discovering that she had visitors, she went out to see them. Meanwhile, her little pig was sniffing around on his own, put his snout into the churn, overturned it, and began to eat up its contents.

"There are no animals in the world worse or nastier than pigs!," the woman shouted. "May The Devil take you!"

"So you take the pig, then," said the tax collector.

"Don't you think she'd begrudge me the meat?" asked The Devil. "What would she have to eat in the winter then? No, this is not from the heart."

Then they went along some more and came to another cottage. Here the child had been naughty. "Now I'm fed up with you!," the mother cried. "I never have any time to do anything else but pick up after you! The Devil take you!"

"So take the child, then," said the tax collector.

"Oh, it is never from the heart that a mother curses her child," said The Devil. And so they went on until they came upon two farmers.

"Look at that!," said one. "Our tax collector!"

"May The Devil take him alive, that damned scourge of the peasants!," said the other.

"Now that comes from the heart!" The Devil exclaimed. "So you have to come with me yourself," The Devil said. And this time neither supplication nor argument was of any use at all.

TK.

A dramatic moment at a Salem witchcraft trial as imagined in a lithograph of 1892, two centuries later.

4

The United States and the Rest of the Americas

WITCHCRAFT IN AMERICA

I said in my book on magic and witchcraft, first published in 1986, that there were more covens active in the US then than there had been at the time of the infamous Salem trials. In the last decade, the number of covens has considerably increased. The most active witches in the country are, however, not followers of The Goddess or Satan but "water witches": dowsers are everywhere, though this can probably be thought of as science, not superstition, because it seems to work. The most obvious American signs of witchcraft are the Hex Signs on the barns of the Pennsylvania Dutch, perhaps more decorative than functional in the minds of moderns, however. The great interest in "psychics" on TV and expensive telephone lines is the most publicized of "occult" activities, though this has nothing to do with witches or The Devil. Americans still carry "lucky charms" and believe in age-old superstitions, even (or perhaps especially) as the end of the millennium approaches. Despite the upsurge in Born-Again religion, The Devil is not discussed much lately. Sit in the middle of the room and hold a glass of water in your hand and you will not be struck by lightning. Sure. Who do you know who was doing that when struck by lightning? Read your horoscope in the daily paper and consider that it's marvelous, in a country where every conformist likes to think of herself or himself as a unique individual, where people are giving the most risible names to their babies in the hope of making them unique, people really are ready to accept that there are only a dozen kinds of people in the world and today requires the same advice for all Sagittarians.

Have we come along at all since George Lyman Kittredge's *Witchcraft in Old and New England* of 1929?

MICMAC MAGIC

Vincent O. Erickson reported on "Some Recent Micmac Witchcraft Beliefs" at a Canadian conference in 1977, the proceedings of which were published by The National Museums of Canada, edited by Richard J. Preston (1977).

HAND TREMBLING AMONG THE NAVAJO

All Amerind peoples had some form of shaman or witch doctor and in fact these traditions persist into the present. Among the Navajo certain people were (and are) thought to possess occult powers and were called upon to treat illnesses both mental and physical. They also were asked to divine for water or to foretell the future, to ensure fertility of nature and human beings, or to counteract evil magic by saying where magical objects could be dug up and the spell therefore broken. The witchdoctor (if we may call him that) was said to go into an elevated psychological state accompanied by the trembling of the hands when his powers were in use. In Navajo life, the shamans were not as powerful as psychopomps and political advisers were among certain other peoples of Meso-America and South America, but they were considered to be essential servants of the community. As is still the norm in African and other societies, individual illness was considered among the Navajo to be a threat to the whole community's health and a matter for the attention of the whole community.

DEMONIZING THE INDIANS

To the Puritan founding fathers of the New England theocracy, all other Christian sects were in error and the Indians were worse. The Indians, pagans, were savages, probably in league with The Devil. Cotton Mather and many others thought that the Indians were The Devil's own, that God showed many "providences" to the white man when the Indians were kept by plague or force of arms from wiping out the colonists. The New England colonists were not quite as convinced as the *conquistadores* had been in Mexico that the aborigines were not even human and that anything could and should be done to them, but they demonized the Indians and expected the worst from them. The Indians, in the view of the white invaders, were obviously sent by Satan to try the faith of the Puritans. That was the Puritan conviction.

Winslow in *Good News from New England* (1624) accused Indians of making sacrifices to The Devil and of being in the power of the Evil One. He admits that he had no real proof of this. He writes that the Indians "told me I should see the Devil at those [certain] times come to the vestry; but I assured myself and them of the contrary, which so proved. Yea, they themselves have confessed, they never saw him, when any of us were present."

Of course, just as the Puritans saw the hand of God in everything they also saw the work of The Devil. The Devil was always being accused of knocking this man's hat off in Connecticut or spoiling the crops of that man in Massachusetts, or appearing to this or that Goodwife or Goodman who was ready to swear to the fact. The Devil can, without exaggeration, be said to be one of the principal figures in the first century or so of our history in America. It is not too much to say that The Devil has remained a potent force, or myth, in our particularly American brand of evangelical Christianity. "Get thee behind me, Satan!" is a common phrase in traditional American life. And our hellions "go to The Devil" with startling frequency. When we had more or less dispatched the Indians, we turned to demonizing the Negro. Now the African-American radicals are talking of white persons as "blue-eyed devils."

EVIL (AND NICER) CRONES OF NORTH AMERICA

These include *The Spider Woman, Whistling Grandmother, Wind Old Woman, Witch Woman*, and *Woman Who Fell from the Sky*. Each has a tale attached. Kinder, guardian figures of North American (mostly Amerind) folklore include *Badger Old Woman, Bear Woman, Buffalo Woman, White-Painted Woman*, and the *First Woman* of various peoples. Healers include the *Animal Mother, Ghost-Faced Woman, Heavy Woman*, and *Large Woman*. Weather is in the hands of (among others) *Bright-Cloud Woman, Cold Woman, Corn Maidens, North Wind Woman, Rain Goddess, South Wind Woman*, and *Woman Who Washed Her Face*. There are also a great many female figures with hard-to-pronounce Amerind names more or less mangled by the white man. For details see Martha Ann and Dorothy Myers Imel's *Goddesses in World Mythology*, a stunning compilation.

EVIL SPIRITS OF THE AMERINDIANS

The Native Americans (in Canada, First Nations) had a great number of cultures and evil spirits. Here are the names of some of them. Remember  that Amerinds did not name as we do—any tidal river could be a *Connecticut* in one language, a person could have name changes to mark various areas in his life—and some of these are actually descriptions rather than proper names. Remember also that a familiar placename (such as *Connecticut*) may have had thirty or forty different spellings and these less familiar designations can be spelled in an incredible number of ways. Some tribes or nations have a large number of evil spirits. *The Works of Howard Howe Bancroft* (1886), for instance, lists many he found among the Trinity River Indians of California, which we note here. We have had to be more selective in other cases.

Aipalookvik, malevolent spirit living on the sea bottom (Inuit, Canada)

Angalootarlo, evil spirit who can lure hunters as a seal (Inuit, Canada)

Atlantow, evil spirit of dissension, disagreement, theft, lying (Mohican, New York)

Chahahhee ymasii (Rolling Darkness Wind), brings evil (Navaho, Arizona)

Chinday, evil gods (Navaho, Arizona, and New Mexico)

Eno, "thief and cannibal" (Acagchemem, California)

Eyak, evil spirit (Koniaga, Pacific Northwest)

Ga-go-sa Ho-nun-nas-tase-ta, Mistress of the False-Faces (Iroquois, US Northeast)

Gnaski, seductive and deceitful daughter of incestuous parents (Lakota and Ogala Sioux, South Dakota)

Gnaskinyan (Crazy Buffalo), disrupts love and incites evil (Lakota, South Dakota)

Ha-gweh-daet-geh, the evil brother of the creator (Iroquois, US Northeast)

Ha-ne-go-ate-geh, the evil twin who created poisonous plants, reptiles, monsters (Iroquois, US Northeast)

Herecgunina, chief evil spirit (Winnebago, Wisconsin)

Hobbamock(o), evil spirit of plagues and calamities (Algonquin, Connecticut)

Ibom, taking the form of the "giant cyclone," same as **Iya** (Lakota, South Dakota)

Istseremurexposhe, "if no one is killed in a battle . . .disappointed" (Crow, Wyoming and Montana)

Iya, "chief of all evil beings" (Lakota and Dakota, South Dakota)

Kaliknatek, catches and consumes whales (Trinity River Indians, California)

Keekut, malignant spirit in the form of a hairless dog (Inuit, Canada)

Kees-du-je-al-ity Kah, evil "master of the tides" (Tlingit, Alaska and British Columbia)

Kegangizi, malevolent water monster invoked by evil shamans (Potawatomi, Michigan and Wisconsin)

Kweraak Kutar (Old Blind Man), source of evil and illness (Yuma, Arizona)

Madji ahando, evil spirit causing earthquakes (Penobscot, Maine)

Maho Penekheka, evil power (Mandan, North and South Dakota)

Makalay, one-horned evil spirit—to see him usually means death (Trinity River Indians, California)

Matc(h)i Manitou, great evil spirit (Cree and Potawatomi, US and Canada)

Missabe, maker of cannibalistic Windego spirits who frighten people to death (Ojibwa, Minnesota)

Nanapolo, evil spirit (Choctaw, Louisiana)

Napousney, evil spirit (Trinity River Indians, California)

Nequiteh, evil spirit (Trinity River Indians, California)

Newathie, evil spirit (Mohave, Arizona and California)

Nunasish, usually misshapen evil spirits of the underworld (Chumash, California)

Oke(e), source of all harm and to be propitated (Owhatan and Potomac, Virginia)

O-ke-heh-de, evil spirit in the form of an owl (Mandan, North Dakota)

Omaha, evil spirit who tries to snatch the souls of the dying (Trinity River Indians, California)

Omahank Chike, evil spirit of the earth (Mandan, North Dakota)

Oo-noo-soo-loo-noo, evil spirit (Mohawk, New York)

Othkon (also **Aireskuoni**), devil worshipped and sacrificed to (Iroquois, US Northeast)

Paija, one-legged female evil spirit—to see her is to die (Ihalmiut Inuit, Keewatin District, Canada)

Pishuni, evil spirit of temptation and disease (Acoma, New Mexico)

Skwai il, chief evil spirit of the underworld (Twana, Washington State)

Soksouh, evil spirit (Yokuts, California)

Surgelp, evil spirit (Trinity River Indians, California)

Sye-elth, evil goddess who tempts human beings to evil (Yurok, California)

Tahquitz, evil god of San Jacinto Peak who stole souls an caused misfortune, disease, and death (Cahuilla, California)

t'ciké•cac nádle-hé (Changing Bear Maiden), personification of evil (Navaho, Arizona and New Mexico)

Thau-wisk-a-lau, the principle of evil (Oneida, New York)

tlic do ntithe (Unending Snake), evil destroyer of mind and consciousness, warning against getting into a circle (Navaho, Arizona and New Mexico)

tliistso xastiin (Big Snake Man), evil god (Navaho, Arizona and New Mexico)

Unk, evil goddess fearing only good god Mahpiyato (Lakota, South Dakota)

Vitiko, source of all evil and misfortune (Indians of York Factory, Manitoba)

Wahcondahpishcona, evil spirit (Ottos, Upper Missour, Nebraska, and South Dakota)

Waiabskinit Awase, white bear who is the chief of evil underground gods (Menomini, Wisconsin)

Wakanda-pezi, evil spirit who leads mankind astray (Ponca, Nebraska)

Wakan sika, "evil sacred" subordinate to Wakantanks (Oglala Sioux, South Dakota)

Wanuswegock, evil spirit (Trinity River Indians, California)

Wittakah, source of all evil and misfortune (Churchill area Indians, Manitoba)

xaict'céitsoh, evil god (perhaps of thunder and lightning) (Navaho, Arizona and New Mexico)

KINDS OF FAIRIES

In medieval times ancient spirits of the earth and air, fire and water, were called fairies and were regarded by the Church as demons, what the Scots called an "unseely [unholy] court" of enchanters and sprites. Saints, said Caesarius of Heisterbach (*Dialogue Miraculorum, c.* 1170–*c.* 1240) were plagued by them, while ordinary people might be tempted by their worthless "fairy gold" or have their children stolen by the fairies. The old demons and spirits became *nicors* (the water spirits) or *nymphs*, the eastern *peris* slowly changed from vile temptresses to a kind of guardian angels, and the man-eating *ogre* in time became a mere bogeyman. The earth spirits became, to Paracelsus, *gnomes*, and the ancient underground *kobolds* still were thought to haunt Germany. Many kinds of fairies, including the pleasant *brownies*, were thought to originate underground. The people said they lived in the old tumuli in which prehistoric peoples had been buried. The Irish called them *aes side* (people of the mounds). In time they came out of their hidden fairyland and moved right in with us mortals, becoming household helpers as brownies, leprechauns, etc. In Scandinavia, also, there were similar creatures, called *nisse* and *tomte*. Behind it all were race memories of a prehistoric time when smaller and frightening aboriginals were encountered by the metal-using tribes who moved westward into the dark forests of Europe.

SOME FAIRIES OF AMERICA

Our own American creation seems to have been the "Little People" who were the fairies of the Passamaquoddy Indians here. In *Collier's Encyclopedia* (1984) fairy expert Katharine M. Briggs writes:

They are about three feet (one meter) high, grotesquely ugly, and made of stone. Their function is to defend the [Roman Catholic] Church and punish neglect of Church festivals and feasts. The missionaries of this tribe were French Jesuits, and it is hard to resist the notion that these spirits were wistful attempts by the missionaries to describe the gargoyles that guarded their churches in France.

The gargoyles got their names and shapes from the French, where *gargouille* meant "throat," for out of the throats of these figures, whose heads decorated cathedrals, water ran off from the roofs. In the creation of these grotesque personages all the ingenuity and superstition of the medieval mind found expression. The ancient and terrifying creatures that people's imaginations had created in the early world were co-opted to guard the churches from which Christianity had undertaken to banish them.

And from Europe, Christian missionaries seem to have brought them to keep in line the new Amerindian converts.

FAIRY STONES

In the Blue Ridge mountains of Virginia especially one finds the "fairy crosses" of staurolite, a grayish or brownish silicate that forms in cross-shaped crystals from one-quarter to a full inch wide. These crosses are worn as amulets against witchcraft and other misfortunes.

Two old folk tales give different explanations of how the "fairy crosses" came there. One says that when news was brought to the fairies there of

the Crucifixion they wept so bitterly that their tears were turned into these little stones. Another says that in Powhattan's Kingdom, the crosses once fell from the sky to herald the Christianity that was to come to the Amerindians.

The "fairy crosses" are found also in the Northeast (Maine, Massachusetts, New Hampshire) and farther South (North Carolina, Georgia), but those of Virginia are the most famous. You will see them for sale at tourist and curio shops to this day.

BANNED IN BOSTON

Even before the witchcraft trials in Salem and Littleton, Massachusetts had a trial for witchcraft. In 1688 John Goodwin alleged his four youngest children had been bewitched by Goody Glover, the mother of their Irish laundress. Goody Glover was condemned.

DEVIL DANCERS OF THE AMERICAS

As in many Central and South American societies, Christianity has been imperfectly imposed upon earlier religions; an odd mixture often results. One of my cousins on my mother's side—all Roman Catholics—was a Canadian bishop who told me how astounded he was when, entering a Mexican church in a procession at a Eucharistic Congress years ago, he approached the main altar, took his seat in the choir, and saw coming down the aisle, after the Eucharist under its canopy held by proper little acolytes in red soutanes, a prancing Corn God and other deities from the pre-Christian religion. On the steps of the Christian church at Chichicastenango in Guatemala, I was struck to note the priests, or at least supplicants of another religion, burning incense to pagan gods. Inside the church *curanderos* practiced the old magic before statues of the Blessed Virgin and the saints.

As the good gods of the old religions have survived, so have the evil ones. In Peru, for instance, Christians sacrifice a black llama to the god of the sun, mix the blood with corn meal, and eat it. At the same festival, they dress as the devils of the old religion and dance themselves into a frenzy.

SPOTTING A WITCH

The popular image of a witch is a toothless old hag whose nose and chin nearly meet, dressed in black, with a pointed hat (such as Welsh women used to wear). But did you know that in the past people also looked at those who had red hair (like Jews and Judas) or whose eyebrows met in the middle?

If you think you see a witch, spit over your left shoulder. Avoid her Evil Eye or counter it by extending the second and little fingers of your right hand.

WHEN THE DOG HOWLS

The dog's keen senses gave people the idea that he might be able to smell, hear, or even see the invisible demons that approach, so a dog howling, especially at night, was said to indicate the presence of evil, perhaps oncoming death.

A TWICE-TOLD TALE OF SALEM VILLAGE

Nathaniel Hawthorne's first American ancestor, Will Hawthorne, was a dour Massachusetts magistrate who persecuted the Quakers. William's son John was a hanging judge in the nefarious Salem witchcraft trials. Hawthorne brooded over his Puritan ancestors and declared that "strong traits of their nature have intertwined themselves with mine." Out of that, along with information culled from obscure Puritan "annals" of the colony and books such as those of Cotton Mather, plus a melancholy that dominated his lonely retreat from life which lasted for a dozen or more years after he returned home from Bowdoin College, in 1835 Hawthorne wrote the haunting and ambiguous tale of *Young Goodman Brown*.

> Had Goodman Brown fallen asleep in the forest and only dreamed a wild dream of a witchmeeting? . . . A stern, a sad, a darkly meditative, a distrustful, if not a desperate man did he become. . . . And when he had lived long, and was borne to his grave a hoary corpse . . . they carved no hopeful verse upon his tombstone, for his dying hour was gloom.

SALEM WITCHCRAFT

The notorious witchcraft trials at Salem in 1692 are too well known to be covered in detail here. The best concise summary is in Rossell Hope Rollins's *Encyclopedia of Witchcraft*. For those who want to read a great deal about our own American witchcraft trial of first importance, I append an extensive bibliography. It helps also to underline the unflagging interest of the American public in this comparatively small witch hunt. In all, there were many accused and only a handful convicted of witchcraft, all but two of them were women, for women have always been more blamed in this particular than men. The ringleader of the supposed coven, however, was a man: the Rev. George Burroughs. There was testimony that he had conducted a *sabbat* with "red bread and red drink" and Summers in *Witchcraft and Magic* boldly asserts: "There can be no doubt that he was the Grand Master of the Salem covens."

In fact, there can be plenty of doubt. The whole miserable Salem experience was a blot on American history. Burroughs and the poor women executed were victims of ignorance and fear, and the only hero to emerge from it all may be the wretch who, slowly pressed to death, obstinately refused to confess to what he went to his pitiful death saying were false charges. Some people have tried to diminish his heroism by saying he was simply trying to prevent his property from being seized and not transferred to his heirs, but the laws of Massachusetts at that time did not permit the state or the accusers to benefit materially from a conviction for witchcraft. He acted on principle. So, frighteningly, did most of those who accused and judged him or wrote piously about the evils of devil worship.

Some children, their heads full of superstitions taught to them by a black slave (Tituba) who was a servant in a Salem household, were guilty of starting the whole chain of events. The history of witchcraft in Old England also is full of allegations made by children, many of which were eventually proved to be false and even more of which ought not to have been taken seriously in the first place. Things would have gone further had not charges eventually been laid against powerful people who stepped in and put an end to the nonsense. The accusers overstepped themselves. The results all around were deplorable.

Nathaniel Hawthorne, with that ancestor who was a judge in the Salem matter, brooded over these dark pages in our history. So have many others since then. America is lucky in that in New York, Pennsylvania, and other places more reasonable than Massachusetts in early days, most allegations of witchcraft were dismissed as ridiculous.

Salem is best described in the title of an unrelated engraving (1762) by William Hogarth. It was prompted by one Mary Tofts announcing that she had given birth to rabbits, a fraud which the king's own physician was sent to examine. Hogarth called his picture (and we can call Salem) *Credulity, Superstition, and Fanaticism.*

The points that need to be emphasized about the whole Salem story—and may be discussed by me in full if I ever get around to writing the book on Salem that is necessary for the current generation — include the superstition and the demonizing of Negro slaves in the period, the psychology of the delusion of crowds, the reasons behind the fact that American society seems to be especially prone to witch-hunting and scapegoating, and the way that accusations of witchcraft against the defenseless are so readily taken as excuses for persecuting them, while accusations made against the pillars of society soon bring a witch hunt to an end.

COTTON MATHER

The Rev. Cotton Mather (1663–1728) has been much criticized by the ignorant as a bigoted and stupid Puritan divine; he has been accused of prompting witch hunts in New England. He deserves a brief mention, even a defense here.

As was expectable in his time, from a clergyman especially, Cotton Mather (whose names bespeak his connection to two leading Massachusetts families) saw the hand of God in history and recorded its providences in *Magnalia Christi Americana* (1702). He is blamed for his *Memorable Providences Relating to Witchcraft and Possessions* (1689), which followed his father's (Rev. Increase Mather's) *Remarkable Providences* (1684). It is said he fueled the fires of superstition which resulted in the execution of persons accused of witchcraft. His reaction to the Salem witch hunt of 1692, however, was rather reasonable for the time; he did not approve of all of the trials, and the following year he published his *Wonders of the Invisible World* (1693) and drew down the wrath of Robert Calef in *More Wonders of the Invisible World* (1700).

It is to be remembered that a Protestant of Cotton Mather's stripe, even if not as Puritan as early New Englanders were, is still compelled to accept the beliefs of Cotton Mather that evil exists as well as good, that God and The Devil both are active in the world (the latter with the permission of God), that witchcraft and other consorting with The Devil is not entirely a delusion (though most cases may be) but is entirely possible for human beings, and that those on the side of the Lord have an unavoidable duty to seek out malefactors and to see that they are punished under the laws of God and of man.

Cotton Mather never succeeded in his drive to become president of his *Alma Mater*, Harvard, although he did much to help found the spin-off institution called Yale, but his learning and his piety were equal to most if not all candidates for university presidencies in his era. He was neither a sadist nor a fool, and if others in Massachusetts in his time were one or both, it was not to be laid at his door. Looked at with 20/20 hindsight, he may be seen to have been deficient in various ways, as may, indeed, to a greater extent, greater theological writers in the history of America and other nations. If his views are shocking, so are those of well-meaning if evil-doing writers on witchcraft and demonology from the fathers of the Christian church (and earlier), through the highly respected and greatly delusioned writers and ecclesiastics of the fourteenth through the twentieth centuries.

Superstition and magic, witchcraft and demonology are not subjects on which even the most erudite have consistently been the most reasonable and realistic. Voltaire called for us to banish superstition. His friend, the practical Prussian prince Frederick the Great, assured him that mankind would forever and forcefully resist all attempts to do that. No one could have straightened out Cotton Mather and, if we accept his argument that providence is severe and always overseeing us all, even God did not want to do so.

Some doggerel from Stephen Vincent Benét with a nice rattle to it:

> Grim Cotton Mather
> Was always seeing witches
> Daylight, moonlight.
> They buzzed around his head,
> Pinching him and plaguing him
> With aches and pains and stitches,
> Witches in his pulpit,
> Witches by his bed.

GRACIOUS SOUTHERN HOSPITALITY

For a while Charleston, South Carolina, was the home of a cult of Satanism pretending to be connected with the Knights Templar. In 1801, bringing with him what he asserted was the skull of Jacques de Molay, last Grand Master of the Knights Templar, Isaac Long arrived in Charleston. He operated a secret society there until his successor, Adriano Lemmi, moved it to Rome, where it was a scandal as "the Synagogue of Satan."

What seems to have been involved is some variety of Freemasonry. "Leo Taxil" (Gabriel Jogand) writes one-sidedly about it in *La Francmaconnerie, synagogue de Satan* (1892). The Italian organization was discussed as Palladism.

CUBAN ALTERNATE RELIGIONS

Like most countries of Central America, the Caribbean, and South America where Roman Catholicism was superimposed on native religions and there was a large influx of African elements, there are alternative religions. Lydia Cabrera is among those who have written about them in books such as *La Sociedad secreta abakúa* (1958), *Una Pelea cubana contra los demónios* (1973), and *Yemagá y Ochún* (1974), the last two mentioned being *Nuestra Señora de Regla* and *Caridád del Cobre*. Santa Barbara and the Blessed Virgin are leading figures in some strange local religions, some of which involve sacrifices to demons and devils. See also Fernando Ortiz (*Los negros Brujos*, 1906) and other writers.

These cults of Cuba, along with *Santería* (worth a book of its own), *obeah*, and so on, have been brought to the United States by new arrivals in this century.

WONDERS AND MORE WONDERS

It is instructive to look at the controversy between the superstitious minister Cotton Mather and the realistic clothmerchant Robert Calef (1648–1719) over the witch trials at Salem. Most New Englanders of the time sided with Cotton Mather.

The grandson of the Puritan divines John Cotton and Richard Mather, the son of the famous clergyman Increase Mather (a president of Harvard College who believed wholeheartedly in The Devil and encouraged his co-religionists to collect as many reports as possible on the work of The Devil in the colonies), Cotton Mather started giving sermons to his playmates at the age of eight and grew up to sermonize the public from the pulpit and in print. He gained a dubious place in history outshining all of his ancestors by his involvement in the Salem trials. He created an atmosphere encouraging them in his *Memorable Providences Relating to Witchcraft* (1689). Here he gloats over the condemnation of George Burroughs:

> This G.B. was indicted for witchcrafts and in the persecution of
> the charge against him, he was accused by five or six of the

> bewitched, as the author of their miseries; he was accused by eight
> of the confessing witches, as being a head actor of some of their
> hellish rendezvous and one who had a promise of being a king in
> Satan's kingdom, now being erected: he was accused by nine per-
> sons for extraordinary lifting, and such feats of strength, as could
> not be done without a diabolical assistance . . . .

And on and on. George Burroughs gave the court a paper in which he
claimed that "there neither are, nor ever were witches, that having made
a compact with the Devil, can send a devil to torment other people at a
distance." Nonetheless, George Burroughs was convicted and executed.

Robert Calef was a Puritan businessman who was shocked at the col-
lective madness of his fellows. He circulated a manuscript in 1694 accusing Cotton Mather of sexual advances to one Margaret Rule, whom Mather
claimed to be exorcising, and of working up the public over witchcraft
rumors. Mather sued him for libel but lost. Then Calef in 1700 published
(in London, because no Boston printer would touch it) *More Wonders of
the Invisible World*, his mocking answer to Cotton Mather's *The Wonders of
the Invisible World*. Among others, he wrote about George Burroughs:

> Mr. Burroughs was carried in a cart with the others, through
> the streets of Salem to execution; when he was upon the ladder,
> he made a speech for the clearing of his innocence, with such
> solemn and serious expressions, as were to the admiration of all
> present; his prayer (which he concluded by repeating the Lord's
> prayer) was so well worded, and uttered with such composedness,
> and such (at least seeming) fervency of spirit, as was very affect-
> ing, and drew tears from many (so that it seemed to some that the
> spectators would hinder the execution). The accusers said the Black
> Man stood and dictated to him; as soon as he was turned off, Mr.
> Cotton Mather, being mounted upon a horse, addressed himself
> to the people, partly to declare that he was no ordained minister,
> and partly to possess the people of his guilt; saying, that the Devil
> has often been transformed into an angel of light; and this did
> somewhat appease the people, and the executions went on; when
> he was cut down, he was dragged by the halter to a hole, or grave,
> between the rocks, about two foot deep, his shirt and breeches
> being pulled off, and an old pair of trousers of one executed, put
> on his lower parts, he was so put in, together with Willard and Car-
> rier, one of his hands and his chin, and a foot of one of them being
> left uncovered . . . .

And now nineteen persons having been hanged, and one pressed to death, and eight more condemned, in all twenty and eight, of which above a third part were members of some of the churches in New England, and more than half of them of a good conversation in general, and not one cleared; about fifty having confessed themselves to be witches, of which not one executed; above a hundred and fifty in prison, and about two hundred more accused; the special commission of oyer and terminer comes to a period, which has no other foundation than the governor's commission; and had proceeded in the manner of swearing witnesses, viz., by holding up the hand (and by receiving evidences in writing), according to the ancient usage of this country; as also having their indictments in English. In the trials, when any were indicted for afflicting, pining, and wasting the bodies of particular persons by witchcraft, it was usual to hear evidence of matter foreign, and of perhaps twenty or thirty years standing, about oversetting carts, the death of cattle, unkindness to relations, or unexpected accidents befalling after some quarrel. Whether this was admitted by the law of England, or by what other law, wants to be determined; the executions seemed mixed, in pressing to death for not pleading, which most agrees with the laws of England, and sentencing women to be hanged for witchcraft, according to the former practice of this country, and not by burning, as is said to have been the law of England. And though the confessing witches were many, yet not one of them that confessed their own guilt, and abode by their confession, were put to death.

Then Robert Calef launched into Cotton Mather and the others he accused of perverting religion and destroying society by rampant superstition and legal murder. Here is a bit of his denunciation of the perverted theocracy of New England of his time:

> Mr. Cotton Mather, having been very forward to write books of witchcraft, has not been so forward either to explain or to defend the doctrinal part thereof; and his belief (which he had a year's time to compose) he durst not venture, so as to be copied. Yet in this book of the life of Sir William he sufficiently testifies his retaining that heterodox belief, seeking by frightful stories of the sufferings of some, and the refined sight of others, &c. to obtrude upon the world, and confirm it in such a belief as hitherto he either cannot or will not defend, as if the blood already shed thereby were not sufficient.

Mr. I. Mather, in his *Cases of Conscience*, tells of a bewitched eye, and that such can see more than others. They were certainly bewitched eyes, that could see as well shut as open, and that could see what never was; that could see the prisoners upon the afflicted, harming them, when those whose eyes were not bewitched could have sworn that they did not stir from the bar. The accusers are said to have suffered much by biting, and the prints of just such a set of teeth, as those they accused had, would be seen on their flesh; but such as had not such bewitched eyes have seen the accusers bite themselves, and then complain of the accused. It has also been seen, when the accused, instead of having just such a set of teeth, has not had one in his head. They were such bewitched eyes, that could see the poisonous powder (brought by spectres) and that could see in the ashes the print of the brand, there invisibly heating to torment the pretended suffers with, &c.

These, with the rest of such legends, have this direct tendency, viz. to tell the world that the devil is more ready to serve his votaries, by his doing for them things above or against the course of nature, showing himself to them and making explicit contracts with them, &c. than the Divine Being is to his faithful servants; and that as he is willing, so also able, to perform their desires. The way whereby these people are believed to arrive at a power to afflict their neighbors, is by a compact with the devil, and that they have a power to commission him to those evils. However irrational, or unscriptural, such assertions are, yet they seem a necessary part of the faith of such as maintain the belief of such a sort of witches.

As the scriptures know nothing of a convenanting or commissioning witch, so reason cannot conceive how mortals should by their wickedness arrive at a power to commission angels, fallen angels, against their innocent neighbors. But the scriptures are full in it, and the instances numerous, that the Almighty Divine Being has his prerogative, to make use of what instruments he pleaseth, in afflicting any, and consequently to commission devils: and though this word, commissioning, in the author's former books, might be thought to be by inadvertency, yet now, after he hath been cautioned of it, still to persist in it seems highly criminal; and therefore, in the name of God, I here charge such belief as guilty of sacrilege in the highest nature, and so much worse than stealing church plate, &c. as it is a higher offense to steal any of the glorious attributes of the Almighty, to bestow them upon mortals, than it is to steal the utensils appropriated to his service. And whether to ascribe such power of commissioning devils to the worst of men, be not direct blasphemy, I leave to others better able to determine. Where the Pharisees were so wicked as to ascribe to Beelzebub the mighty works of Christ (whereby he did manifestly show forth his power and godhead) then it was that our Savior declared the sin against the Holy Ghost to be unpardonable. . . .

Pres. Increase Mather (it has been alleged) had Calef's book burned in Harvard Yard. Increase's son, Cotton Mather, characteristically ran to his desk and quickly and loquaciously retaliated for Calef's insult, ineffectually, with *Some Few Remarks upon a Scandalous Book* (1701). For a long time thereafter, Satan was a major figure in the history of the Commonwealth of Massachusetts. Cotton Mather turned out to be in the view of Henry S. Canby, not a brave and devout divine but an ambitious and credulous fool. Canby wrote: "No better illustration of the ego warped by straining to be virtuous can be found . . . he gave the governor advice when he seemed to need it, he bore the sins of the entire community on his own conscience . . . and was one of the most virtuous prigs and well-meaning asses in history."

THE WITCHES OF SALEM

Anon., *A Short History of the Salem Village Witch Trials* (1911)
Breslaw, Elaine, *Tituba, Reluctant Witch of Salem* (1996)
"Castleton, Dr. R.," *Salem* (1874)
Clapp, Patricia, *Witches' Children* (1987)
Drake, Samuel Adams, *The Witchcraft Delusion* (3 vols., 1866)
Forbes, Esther, *Mirror for Witches* (1928)
Fowler, Samuel Page, *Salem Witchcraft* (1865)
Hoffer, Peter Charles, *The Devil's Disciples* (1996)
Hutchinson, Gov. Thomas, *History of the Colony of Massachusetts Bay* (1764)
Jackson, Shirley, *The Witchcraft of Salem Village* (1956)
Kittredge, George Lyman, *Witchcraft in Old and New England* (1972)
Levin, David, *What Happened in Salem?* (1952)
Mathews, Cornelius, *Witchcraft; or, The Martyrs of Salem* (drama, 1846)

Moore, George Henry, *Notes on the History of Witchcraft in Massachusetts* (1883–1885)
Mudge, Zachariah Atwell, *Witch Hill* (1871)
Nevins, Winfield Scott, *Witchcraft in Salem Village* (1892)
Starkey, Marion L., *The Devil in Massachusetts* (1952)
Upham, Charles Wentworth, *Salem Witchcraft* (2 vols., 1867)
Woodward, W. Elliot, *Records of the Salem Witchcraft* (1864)

The witch craze of Salem has become a part of the Massachusetts tourist industry today and contributed to the dark thread of Puritanism that runs through the early literature. James W. Clark, Jr.'s doctoral dissertation on *The Tradition of Salem Witchcraft in American Literature, 1620–1870* (1971) can be supplemented by similar studies of later periods. Salem is not very interesting when one looks at the whole panorama of the lurid history of witchcraft; however, (fortunately) it is the most noted of American instances of what William James called "the delusion of crowds."

For a recent overview of the more-than-twice-told tale of Salem, see Bernard Rosenthal's *The Salem Story* (1993). Better, read the documents in *Witch-Hunting in Seventeenth-Century New England* (ed. David D. Hall, 1991) and draw your own conclusions. Frankly, I find the current American Satanism scare more intriguing and more indicative of the American mind of today, of course.

EVERY DECADE, MORE ON THE SALEM WITCH TRIALS

Boyer, Paul & Steven Nissenbaum, *Salem Possessed: The Social Origins of Witchcraft* (1974)
Hansen, Chadwick, *Witchcraft at Salem* (1969)
Rosental, Bernard, *The Salem Story: Reading the Witch Trials of 1692* (1993)
Levin, David, "Did the Mathers Disagree about the Salem Witch Trials" in *Proceedings of the American Antiquarian Society* 95:1 (December 1985), 19–37

UNITED STATES (OTHER THAN SALEM, MASSACHUSETTS): THIRTY TYPICAL BOOKS

Anson, Jay, *The Amityville Horror* (1977)
"Arthur, Gavin," (Chester Alan Arthur III) *The Wheel of Life* (c. 1970)
Ashton, J., *The Devil in Britain and America* (1896)
Brandon, Ruth, *The Spiritualists* (1983)

Blake, John P., *The Devil or Satan* (1879)
Brown, Slater, *The Heyday of Spiritualism* (1970)
Burr, George Lincoln, *Narratives of the Witchcraft Cases, 1648–1706* (1914, 1979)
Cobbe, Frances Power, *The Devil* (1871)
Conway, Moncure Daniel, *Demonology and Devil-Lore* (2 vols., 1872)
Delbanco, Andrew, *The Death of Satan* (1996)
Drake, Samuel G., *Annals of Witchcraft in New England* (1869)
Graves, Kersey, *The Biography of Satan* (reprinted 1991)
Green, Samuel A., *Groton in the Witchcraft Times* (1883)
Gummere, Amelia Moth, *Witchcraft and Quakerism* (1908)
Holmes, Thomas James, *Cotton Mather and His Writings on Witchcraft* (1926)
Huebner, Louise, *Power through Witchcraft* (*c.* 1968)
Ingersoll, Robert Green, *The Devil* (1899)
Jorgensen, Danny L., *The Esoteric Scene* (1992)
Kluckhohn, Clyde, *Navaho Witchcraft* (1967)
Lyle, Katie Lecher, *The Man who Wanted Seven Wives* (1986)
Lyons, Arthur, *The Second Coming: Satanism in America* (1970)
Mather, Cotton, *Memorable Providences relating to Witchcrafts and Possession* (1684)
Mather, Increase, *Cases of Conscience concerning Evil Spirits* (1693)
Nevius, John Livingston, *Demon Possession* (1895–1968)
Priest, Josiah, *The Anti-Universalist; or, The History of Fallen Angels* (1837)
Puckett, Newbell N., *Folk Beliefs of the Southern Negro* (1926)
Putnam, Allen, *Witchcraft of New England Explained by Modern Spiritualism* (1888)
Randolph, Vance, *Ozark Superstitions* (1947)
Riccio, Dolores & John Bingham, *Haunted Houses USA* (1989)
Scott, Beth & Michael Norman, *Haunted Heartland* (1985)
Scribner, Welford & Armstrong (publishers), *Bibliotheca diabolica . . .* (1874)
Taylor, John Metcalfe, *The Witchcraft Delusion in Colonial Connecticut 1647–1697* (1908)
Thomas, Keith, *Religion and the Decline of Magic* (1972)

NEWS FROM NEW HAMPSHIRE (1685)

Under oath in April 1685, Susannah Trimmings of Piscataqua, New Hampshire, stated:

On Lord's Day 30th of March, at night, going home with Goodwife Barton, she separated from her at the freshet near her house. On her return, between Goodman Even's and Robert Davis's she heard a rustling in the woods, which she at first thought was occasioned by swine, and presently after there did appear to her a woman whom she apprehended to be old Goodwife Walford.

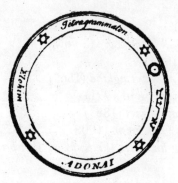

The Magic Circle, from Francis Barrett's *The Magus*.

She asked me where my consort was. I answered, I had none. She said, Thy consort is at home by this time. Lend me a pound of cotton.

I told her I had but two pounds in the house, and I would not spare any to my mother. She said I had better have done it; that my sorrow was great already—and it should be greater, for I was going a great journey, but should never come there. She then left me, and I was struck as with a clap of fire on the back, and she vanished towards the waterside, in my apprehension in the shape of a cat. She had on her head a white linen hood tied under her chin, and her waistcoat and petticoat were red, with an old green apron and a black hat upon her head.

MORE NEWS FROM NEW HAMPSHIRE

Salem and such places are better known in the history of United States witchcraft but Bristol, New Hampshire, also has a distinction you may not know about. It was there during World War I when "The Beast" Aleister Crowley was in the US writing anti-British propaganda, that he promoted himself to the rank of *magus* (magician) and committed the blasphemy of baptizing a toad Jesus Christ and then crucifying it.

The locals were blissfully unaware of this or they probably would have run him out of town on a rail. He would have enjoyed that publicity.

THE DEVIL ALONG THE MISSISSIPPI

John Chesselden and James Arkins claimed that The Devil appeared to them beside The Mississippi on 24 May 1784. The next year John Trumbull printed their *Surprising Account* at Norwich, Connecticut.

RITUAL MURDER IN THE SOUTH

In 1911–1912 there was an outbreak of ritual murder in Georgia, Louisiana, and Texas. It has been studied by William I. Hair ("Inquisition for Blood . . .," *Louisiana Studies* 11, 1972, 274–281). Rumors persist that ritual murder is covered up by authorities in such places as Savannah and Atlanta, the Gulf Coast of Florida and Texas, etc.

"WHEN THE TALK TURNED TO WITCHCRAFT . . ."

So long as the loafers in Bib Tarkey's blacksmith shop discussed crops and politics I paid them scant attention, but when the talk turned to witchcraft I pricked up my ears at once. The old-timers spoke tolerantly of modern disbelief. "Wal," said old Lem Whatley, "I reckon maybe thar *ain't* many witches a-runnin' loose nowadays, but in my day an' time th' woods was full of 'em. My pappy follered gunsmithin' mostly, but he was a witch-master too, an' he shore kilt a many un when we lived up thar on Flat Crick.

"I mind th' time somebody witched our hawgs, so's when I went out t' slop 'em they never come t' th' trough—jest lent back on their tails an' squole. An' th' cow never give no milk, neither, for seven days a-runnin'. Pap he figured it mought be ol' Gram French, whut laid up in a rock-house t'other side o' th' Narrers.

"Funny thing about Gram was, she allus had plenty o' cream an' butter in th' spring-house, but nobody ever seen her do no milkin'. Wal, Pap he snuck over an' bushed up back o' her place, an' peeked in th' winder ever' chanst he got. Finally he seen Gram hang a ol' dirty dishrag on th' potrack an' start in a-squeezin' milk out'n it—she squoze out four big gourdfuls whilst he set thar a-watchin' her, with his eyes a-buggin' out like a tromped-on toadfrog. An' now he knowed how come ol' Muley never give down no milk for seven days a-runnin'.

"When Pap got home he looked mi-ighty solemn. Th' first thing he done was t' git down his ol' silver-mounted witch-rifle, an' th' next thing he done was t' melt up th' dollar an' mold hisse'f a silver bullet. Next mornin', he tuck him a burnt stick an' drawed a pitcher o' ol' Gram French on a peeled sycamore. Hit didn't look much like Gram, but he written her name on it good an' big, so's not t' resk no boggle. Soon's he got th' hull thing drawed an' wrote t' suit him, back he come an' picked up th' ol' witch-killer.

"I was jest a teen-age boy then, an' I got kinder skeerylike, but Pap he'd kilt a lot o' witches in his time, an' he jest stood thar stiddy as a rock. *Bang*, says th' ol' witch-rifle, an' when we run up t' th' pitcher we seen whar th' silver bullet plunked her right squar' in th' middle. We-uns begun t' feel a heap better than, I tell you! An' thet same day, mind you, ol' Gram French fell off'n th' bluff an' kilt herse'f—busted plumb wide open like a rotten apple! Ol' Muley give down lashin's o' milk thet night, too, an' we never had no more trouble with our hawgs, neither."

The blacksmith had stopped his work to listen to old man Whatley's tale, and appeared to be particularly impressed by its happy conclusion. "Witches," he said with feeling, "is for them ol'fellers whut knows how t' handle 'em, like your paw, Lem. Hit's plumb resky for a common ord'nary evr' day feller t' fool with 'em. One o' them Pea Ridge witch-hunters come dang near killin' me one time . . . . Hit was th' year o' th' big freshet, an' th' Bradford boys had lost most ever'thing. They warn't very bright, nohow, an' 'pears like they was loonier'n usual thet fall.

"When their ol' cow died hit jest about wiped out th' Bradford family. It was holler-horn kilt her, I reckon, but Poly Bradford he figgered she was witched. So he went an' got him a silver spoon somers an' loaded up a ol' scatter-gun they had. Then he ambled out in th' flat-woods an' raked up a big circle o'leaves an' bresh—musta been purty nigh sixty foot acrost, I reckon. "Long 'bout midnight he set them 'ar bresh afire, an' then he hid out in back of a big cedar stump t' wait for th' witch.

"Wal sir, it jest happened I was a-comin' home 'crost th' flats thet night—I'd been over a-settin' up t' th' Widder Lane's biggest gal Iny—an' I seen this hyar big fire-ring. I'd orter o' knowed better, but my head was all gaumed up with sparkin', an' I never oncet thought o' witches. Anyhow, I rid rights into thet 'ar ring, an' th' next thing I knowed hyar come Poly a-prancin' out, 'ith th' ol' gun a-p'intin' fa'r an' squar' at my stammick! 'Bib Tarkey!' he hollers out, 'Who'd ever a' thunk *you* was a witch! Wal, anyhow, I got ye now, an' I got a silver bullet in this hyar gun, an' I'm obleeged for t' kill ye!"

"My Gawd, boys, I thought I was sa goner shore, an' th' bar'l o' thet ol' musket looked big as a stovepipe. I lent backwards jest as Poly made his fire, an' th' bullet ploughed a big lane right through my whiskers. Th' horse jumped an' throwed me, too, an' hyar was thet fool Poly right on top o' me, a-swingin' at my head with th' butt o' his gun.

"I dodged him ag'in, though, an' finally I got my thumb in his eye an' wrassled him down. I was purty dang mad by this time, an' I jest churned his head up an' down, an' beat him dang nigh t' death. 'Go on an' kill me, Bib,' says he, 'you've done kilt th' critters, an' me an' Lissie'll starve t' death this Winter anyhow'—an' with thet he begun t' beller like a calf. 'I ain't no witch, you pore ignor'nt, misbegotten eediot,' I says, 'I been over t' Widder Lane's an' I rid into this hyar witch-ring unthoughted-like, 'fore I rightly knowed whar I was at.' Poly he kept on a-grumblin', but he was plumb docile now, so I let him up, an' wiped th' blood off'n his face. 'An' th' next time your danged ol' cow gits witched,' I says, 'you go tell ol' Pap Whatley, an' let him tend to it. You jest leave witches t' th' witch-masters,' says I, 'an' don't you never do no more conjurin' roun' hyar of a night. Hit's too dang resky-like for th' neighbors.'"

With this Tarkey returned to his blacksmithing, but Charley Howard was moved to rehearse the exploits of his cousin Tom, who had wrestled mightily with the powers of darkness in the Eighties. "Hit all happened way back yander afore me an' my wife was married, an' th' first I heerd of it was one day Tom he come over an' told us how their cow was a-comin' home jest plumb stripped, an' Gran' paw Langley was a-follerin' th' critter round all day t' see who was a-milkin' her. Wal sir, he snuck an' he watched, an' finally he seen two big ol' swamp-rabbits a-suckin' her! Sich a thing was never saw nor heerd tell of afore, I reckon, but Gran'paw he up with th' ol' shotgun an' made his fire jest as them two rabbits was a-hoppin' off together. Th' ol' gun was loaded heavy with turkey-shot, an' they warn't more'n thirty foot off, but danged if he didn't clean miss 'em! Right then an' thar th' ol' man seen how things was, an' he come a-runnin' up t' th' house a-hollerin', 'Witches! Witches!' with his eyes a-buggin' out bigger'n duck-aigs.

"Wal sir, Tom he shucked right out an' dug up th' corner post whar th' money was vaulted, an' they melted up a dollar. Gran'paw he run th' bullets hisse'f, a-shakin' like a white-oak leaf in a Christmas wind, an' Mary she loaded up th' ol' rifle-gun afore th' ball was cold scarcely. Tom got a soon start in th' mornin', an' we was all a-settin' on th' stake-an'-rider when he kilt th' ol' she-rabbit—th' buck run off afore he could git th' gun charged. . . . An' then 'bout four o'clock come th' news thet somebody had went an' kilt ol' Miz' Ricketts over in Hell Holler—shot her plumb thorugh th' heart. Doc he never did find th' bullet, but ever'body knowed how it was, all right."

The subject must certainly be exhausted now, I thought, but another hillman, a stranger to me, had something to contribute to the symposium. "Speakin' o' witchees," he said, after helping himself to a big drink of corn from the fruit-jar provided by Whatley, "puts me in mind of a 'sperience Buck Peters had one time when he was berry-pickin' down on Bug Scuffle. Buck was th' loud-talkin'est, drinkin'est, fightin'est feller ever come t' them parts. He'd fight a circle-saw an' turn it hisse'f, an' he warn't skeered o' nothin' in this world or th' next 'un, neither. Thar was a ol' tore-down shanty in back o' Lum Hobart's grocery whar witches had been a-usin' round, an' one day some o' th' boys bannered Buck t' sleep in thar all night. Buck he says if they git him a jug o' right good drinkin' likker he'll sleep anywhar, an' if any witches come round *him* a-lookin' for trouble they'll shore git a lavish of it. Wal, Lum says he'd furnish th' jug hisse'f, pervidin' Buck was still alive come morning', an' they set thar a-drinkin' an' a-jow-erin' an' a-spewin' ambeer over each an' ever', till finally Buck he loaded up with whiskey an' went into th' ol' shanty an' shet th' door. I tuck notice he packed in a -plenty o' candles, too—reckon he warn't a-hankerin' t' fight no witches in th' dark.

"Buck he set thar a long time, a studyin' 'bout witches an' hants an' th' like o' thet, when all of a succint up jumps th' Gawd-awfullest big she-cat ever saw in Arkansas, a-yowlin' an' spittin' like a Injun with his tail-feathers afire! Buck he was feelin' kinder mean an' narvish-like anyhow, so he drawed his ol' horse-pistol an' pulls back th' rooster. Lucky for him he done it, too, for jest a ha'r later th' varmint jumped right squar' at him. Th' ol' gun roared like a Christmas anvil, an' one o' th' cat's hind feet was blowed plumb off. Somers a woman hollers out, 'Oh my Gawd!' an' Buck allus swore he seen a woman's bare foot, all shot up an' bloody, a-wigglin' round on th' table. But jest then th' candle went out. Buck he went out too, right through th' winder, an' never stopped a-runnin' till he got plumb home. I never did blame him none, myse'f. Gawda' mighty! Sich doin's as thet 'ar 'd skeer anybody! . . . Purty soon hyar come a feller name Burdick a-ridin' in for t' git Doc Holton—says his ol' woman has done shot her foot off accidental-like. She up an' bled t' death, though, spite of all Doc could do. They do say she died a-yowlin' an' a-spittin' like a cat. . . ."

At the end of the stranger's story I tore myself away, and repaired to the log residence of Uncle Bill Hatfield and his wife, who provided me with bed and board. After supper I broached the general subject of witchcraft and demonology to Uncle Bill, remarking that I myself gave no credence to such idle superstitions as appeared to obtain in this benighted region.

"I ain't superstitious, neither," said Uncle Bill mildly, "but a lot o' things whut some folks *call* superstitions is jest as true as Gawd's own gospel. An' as for witches, it ain't no manner o' use t' tell me thar ain't none, 'cause I know better. Why, I've been rode by 'em myse'f, many th' time!

"I war jest a-dozen' off one night, in th' ol' cabin way back in up on Leetle Piney, when in come th' purtiest gal I ever seen, with a bran'-new bridle in her hand. She fetched a whoop an' jumped plumb astraddle o' my back, an' th' first thing I knowed she had thet 'ar bridle onto me, with th' big cold bit a-cuttin' into my gooms! An' th' *next* thing I knowed she turned me into a flea-bit gray pony, an' we was a-tearin' down th' road hell-bent for 'lection, with th' spurs a-sockin' into my hams at ever' jump.

"Up hills an' down hollers an' 'crost branches an' through berry-patches we went, till we met up with some furriners a-packin' big sacks full o' money—bankrobbers, I reckon they was, or somethin'. Th' witch-woman she lit down then, an' help them fellers, an' danged if they didn't pile all them big pokes on my back! Hit was all gold money, 'peared like, an' it shore was heavy. Purty soon we come t' a big cave in under a clift, an' she tied me up t' a white oak-saplin', whilst they all tuck th' money inside for t'hide it, I reckon. Atter while th' furriners come out, a-talking' an' a-laughin' 'mongst their se'fs, an' purty soon she come out too, an' rid me back hom ag'in.

"Wal, th' next night she come an' rid me some more, an' we met up with th' same fellers, an' they drug in another turrible big load o' money. . . . An' th' next night th' same an' more of it, an' the next night, too—hit seemed like thar warn't no end t' th' money we-uns toted into thet 'ar cave-hole. Ever' mornin' I'd wake up plumb tuckered out an' brier-scratched; my head was full o' cockleburrs constant, an' my mouth a-tastin' like a cat had done littered in it.

"I never said nothin' t' th' ol' woman 'bout this hyar witch-ridin' an' all, but I shore done a heap o' studyin' over it. I spent a lot o' time a-lookin' for thet 'ar cave, too, but I couldn't make out t' find it noways, so one mornin' I hobbled off down t' ol' Pap Jennin's shanty an' told him th' hull story. Pap he was a witch-master from who laid th' chunk, an' I knowed in reason he'd tell me whut I better do. Th' ol' man he jest pondered awhile, a-shakin' of his head kinder juberous, an' then he sayd: 'Wal, Bill, I reckon you-all better mark thet 'ar cave so we kin find it easy. When you git it marked I'll jest lay for this hyar witch-woman an' kill her with a silver bul-let. Then we-uns 'll git th' gold-money, o' course.'

"The next night, when she hitched me outside th' cave, I jest drapped as many drappin's as I could, an' started in for t' chaw me a good big blaze on th' white-oak saplin', like Pap told me. I chawed an' I chawed. All of a suddint come a hell of a noise an' a big flash o' light, an' then I heerd a lot o' hollerin'—my ol' woman was a-doin' th' hollerin'. . . . Quick as a wink I seen I was home ag'in, an' it seemed like"—and here Uncle Bill stole a furtive glance at his wife, who sat stolidly smoking by the fireplace—"hit seemed like I'd went an' benastied th' bed-blankets bad, an' dang near bit th' ol' woman's laig off!"

The unexpected conclusion of the story "sot me back right smart," and the whole shanty shook with Bill's uproarious laughter. Uncle Bill is one of the very few old-time Ozarkers whom I have heard speak lightly of these matters. They sometimes assert their unbelief, but they don't joke about it. . . . Aunt Lavina told me later that deep down in his heart Bill still believes in witchcraft, but refuses to admit it to any but his most intimate friends nowadays. And so it is with others of his generation.

SPIRITUAL INTERCOURSE

Though the Fox sisters of Hydesville and Joseph Smith, also of upstate New York, succeeded in founding new religions (Spiritualism and Mormonism), more neglected and perhaps more interesting than they was Andrew Jackson Davis, born in Blooming Grove, New York, in 1826. He was the author of extraordinary works on spiritualism and communication from Beyond.

In 1841 he was sent to Poughkeepsie to be apprenticed to a shoemaker, his parents being extremely poor, and the unlettered lad was taken up by a Mr. Livingston who convinced him he had powers of clairvoyance and could communicate with spirits. In 1845, still a teenager, he dictated while in hypnotic trance a huge book of some 500 crammed pages on *The Principles of Nature, Her Divine Revelations, and a Voice of Mankind*. Rev. William Fishbough wrote it all down for him. It was immensely complex and much read and went into a second edition in 1863. Its ideas were expanded in a number of later works that Davis said were given to him by supernatural means. These include the *Great Harmonia* (six volumes 1850–1861), *The Philosophy of Spiritual Intercourse* (1851), *The Present Age and Inner Life* (1854, 1870), *The Approaching Crisis* (a review of Dr. Bushnell on *Spiritualism*, 1852), *The Penetralia* (1856), *The Magic Staff* (his autobiography, 1857), *Morning Lectures* (1867), and more.

Davis did not have the charisma of Joseph Smith and did not gather around him a devoted band, start them to a Promised Land, or think of running for president of the United States. Nor did Davis star on the lecture platform as did Margaret Fox, although she was an utter fake, had a weak voice, and was often drunk. He never wrote anything as internationally popular as Mary Baker Eddy's *Science and Health*, nor did he have her dynamism, which enabled her to found a church that denied the existence of disease and death (but not demons—its seal refers to casting them out). Davis's writings, however, are a strange combination of learning and stunning, if confused, originality. They ought to have earned him a higher place in the peculiar history of spiritualists, visionaries, hypnotists, mediums, religious figures, and charlatans of nineteenth-century America.

PHINEAS T. QUIMBY

Now there's a name that ought to be more famous, as famous as that as the founder of another American-bred religion, Joseph Smith of The Church of Jesus Christ of Latter Day Saints (Mormonism), for it was Phineas T. Quimby of Portland, Maine, who inspired Mary Baker Eddy to found Christian Science. It was Quimby who wrote *The Science of Man*, which had a lot to do with Mrs. Eddy's "the science of divine metaphysical science, which I named Christian Science." It was Quimby whom Mrs. Eddy sought out in Maine. It was Quimby who did much to relieve her of symptoms that had plagued her from childhood, not the least of which were voices that spoke to her and the dead who visited her. It was Quimby who treated her where hard drugs had failed and substituted the discoveries of Franz Mesmer and "a science," she said, that had hitherto not been recognized. It was Quimby who, Mrs. Eddy declared in the local newspaper soon after he treated her, "speaks as no man spoke and heals as no man has healed since Christ." When Quimby died, she eulogized him in a poem entitled "Lines on the Death of Dr. P. P. Quimby, Who Healed with the Truth that Christ Taught in Contradistinction to All Isms." It was only after his death that she healed herself of allegedly serious damage by faith alone and created her own "Ism" and Church of Christ, Scientist with the publication of *Science and Health*. Then she began to pooh-pooh suggestions that Quimby had taught her all she knew.

What *Science and Health* owed to what Quimby called "Science and Health," and the extent to which Quimby was the true founder of Christian Science and not just an itinerant hypnotist and fakir of a sort rather common in the America of his time, whether he was (you might say) the Wizard of Oz or just "that man behind the curtain" faking things, remains or ought to be a subject for heated debate. This is more significant than whether the basis of it all comes from what Charles S. Braden in *These Also Believe* identified as "the Hindu concept of the one Real, and the illusory character of all else." Braden claims of Mrs. Eddy that "her fundamental denial of the reality of evil and suffering is an almost-exact restatement of one phase of Hindu thought." This is about giving credit where credit is due.

Start if you are interested with a few pages on Mrs. Eddy's work in Robert B. Downs' *Famous American Books* (1971) and investigate further in libraries and Christian Science Reading rooms, established in many places and eager to assist the curious. Probably the more important question, granted, is whether faith healing works or not. On that I do not consider myself ready to voice any opinion.

But I do think that Dr. Quimby, whom Mrs. Eddy once adored, has been slighted by history and reviled by her protective followers, and that Dr. Quimby and those who, like him, deny the very existence of evil are interesting in the context of the beliefs about the existence, even the personification, of evil in the world reflected in the long history of magic and witchcraft, of sin and Satanism. Is all evil, is death itself, just illusion?

BIBLE-POUNDING BAPTIST HELL

Flamboyant American rhetoric from William Faulkner on up to Martin Luther King, Jr., owes much to "hellfire-and-damnation" Southern Baptist preaching, which is to Jonathan Edwards's *Sinners in the Hands of an Angry God* what jazz is to études. I thought I would include a sample here, but without the audience response (which tradition has done much to make theater and cinema going less attractive than renting a video to watch in the peace of your own home), and without a lot space to the allow the pulpit pounder to build his effects to a climax, the homespun majesty of it all cannot quite be captured.

This is a street scene in the utopian community of New Harmony, PA, in the early nineteenth century. George Rapp (1770–1847) had a vision of Christ appearing in the US and came here to form a colony in the ConnoquenessingValley wilderness in 1803. Other religious utopians had similar inspirations to found the Oneida, Amana, and other societies of that century.

Still, the preacher's hell needs recognition, for the brimstone lake of *Revelations* has been much elaborated in American folk art. Let me just tell one of my favorite stories of the Deep South. The preacher had taken as his text *Matthew* XIII:49–50 and was doing a riff on "weeping and wailing and gnashing of teeth."

One of the congregation shouted. "Preacher, I ain't *got* no teeth!"

"Brother," came the reply, "teeth will be *provided*!"

OZARK SUPERSTITION

Ozard superstition is worth a whole book. Here we can note one interesting belief: witches are unable to say "For God's sake."

STRANGE GOINGS-ON IN HADLEY, MASSACHUSETTS

In 1684 one Philip Smith, 50, of Hadley fell afoul of one of the poor women of the town who were under his care. Cotton Mather is at pains to assure us that Smith was an innocent victim of a witch's malice. Smith was (Mather testified) the virtuous son of virtuous parents, a man of probity and position (deacon, justice, militia officer, etc.), and that the curse the woman who felt mistreated laid on Smith caused him to be "murder'd by hideous witchcraft." Before he died Smith was tormented by pains caused by "invisibilised" instruments and strange odors and raved in several languages. "There shall be a wonder in Hadley," the dying man predicted. And there was.

THE BIBLE

Many people regard the Bible as the revealed word of God, every word precious and correct. Others read it as poetry open for interpretation (Eve was not actually constructed from a rib nor were all the animals created at one time, the age of the earth is greater and the age of Methusaleh much less than is specified, etc.). Others think of it as a sort of Truman Capote "nonfiction novel" combining historical fact and literary imagination. (There is no proof outside the Bible of the existence of Moses. *Ruth* is a short story, not a biography. The Joshua story is all wrong: the walls of Jericho crumbled a long time before Joshua's day, and of course the sun always stands still, though in ancient times people believed it moved and the earth stood still.) Most people accept some parts of what the Bible says and reject others; they won't eat pork but will wear scarlet, for instance. I personally find most strict fundamentalist, inerrant-Bible believers to be vegetarians in alligator shoes.

Christians believe that the New Testament corrects the Old. Muslims believe the Koran corrects both. A lot of infidels see much good advice in the Bible and revere its wisdom, including that which many believe the Jews borrowed from friends and enemies and Christ got from the Chinese, and so on.

On the subject of witchcraft, see what you can put together from the much-debated words of the Old Testament in:

Deut. XVIII:9–14	**Isa.** VIII:19, XIX:3, XLVII:9–12, LVII:3
Exod. VII:11, XXII: 18	**Jer.** XXVII:9
Lev. XIX:21, XX:6	**Dan.** II:2
I Sam. XV:23, 28	**Mic.** V:12
II Kings IX:22, XXI:6, XXIII:24	**Mal.** III:5
II Chron. XXXIII: 6	

Check also the magical acts manifested in the life of the Savior and the references in the New Testament, principally in *Galatians* V:20, *Acts* XIX: 17–20 (the Ephesians abandoning "curious arts" may mean giving up pagan witchcraft), and most especially several notices in *Revelations*

"Abomination" extends from devil-worship and malevolent sorcery to casting spells, telling fortunes, perhaps necromancy. There are magicians in the Bible but no broom-riding witches. The Witch of Endor may not be a witch with a familiar but a medium with a spirit guide, though still dealing with the dead.

No witchcraft can be practiced by any observant Jew or Christian, and Christians are forbidden all fortune-telling.

Just as some Jews and Christians happily hold views both historically and currently anathematized officially and yet consider themselves devout members of the religions, so many witches ignore the condemnation of churches to which they pay at least lip service, and they go on with both their witchcraft and other religion.

On New Religions see:

Adler, Margot, *Drawing Down the Moon* (1986)
Barton, B., *The Church of Satan* (1990)
Cohen, Daniel, *The New Believers* (1975)
DeParrie, Paul & Mary Prind, *Unholy Sacrifices of the New Age* (1988)
Drury, Nevill, *Don Juan, Mescalito, and Modern Magic* (1985)
"Starhawk" [Miriam Sines], *The Spiral Dance* (1979)
Thorson, Edred, *Rune Might* (1989)

CURANDEROS OF PUERTO RICO

From Puerto Rico, this little song, which suggests that if your problems are not successfully solved by the witch doctor (for that is what we are talking about), then maybe you ought to consult a licensed physician. The "poetry" here is drivel, but I like any Spanish song in which the word *corazón* (heart) does not appear, and there are not a lot like that!

Si fuere dolor de oído
muy bien te puedo aliviar
con el gua de azahar
y un algodón embutido.
Y si antes has padecido
no podrás ser aliviado;
pero antes, resignado
y, vete donde el doctor
te puede aliviar mejor,
todo mal communicado.

"The Great Sorcerer" from *El Primer neuva crónico y buen gobierno*, Felipe Guaman Pomo de Ayala of the early *conquista* period of Peru.

FORTUNE-TELLERS

These are perhaps the most common and least criticized of American practitioners of forbidden or black arts. Today we have Magic Eight-Ball toys for children, "psychics" for adults (or older children), and an anxious, millenarian, fortune-cookie society that would like to have not only "today's news today" but tomorrow's, too, right now.

THE FOX SISTERS

A couple of teenage girls, Margaret and Katherine Fox, started one of America's home-grown religions (which spread around the world,) in 1848 in upstate New York. It was called Spiritualism; but it was really, in cases closely observed, almost always revealed as faked necromancy. In Europe, Elise Müller ("Hélène Smith") talked with Martians!

Despite traditional religious objection to dealings with the dead, séances proved very popular, especially when so many people died of epidemics and in the First World War. Sir Oliver Lodge and Sir Arthur Conan Doyle lost loved ones in the Great War and became fervent adherents of Spiritualism. Their reputations in other fields helped the cause of mediumship. The Fox sisters were said to have confessed to fraudulent table-rapping, but by then mediums were so popular a form of communication and parlor entertainment that nobody listened to their denials.

Houdini in the United States, Guy Lambert and others from The Society for Psychical Research in London, Théodore Flournoy, and others all devoted themselves to exposing fake mediums. The living still went on happily chatting with the dear departed—or demons pretending to be the dead. Being dead seems to be a sad state. Nobody ever seems to say anything original or useful at séances. Music by Mozart and Lizst, dictated to an Englishwoman from beyond the grave, shows the deleterious effect on talent of being dead. It's dreadfully inept. Or perhaps demons are playing jokes on us and our loved ones are silent.

Jehovah's Witnesses, Orthodox Jews, and some others believe that when you're dead, you're dead. Most people do not want to believe in their own eventual extinction. Spiritualism says we have a life after death and that is a very attractive belief. We welcome even ghosts and vampires, anything that says we do not die. True or false, no amount of research or reason could stamp out Spiritualism. It stresses one of the greatest of all appeals of all religions. The frauds of the Fox sisters found people eager to be defrauded. Mediums offering to bring back dead loved ones (especially since none ever reports that she or he is suffering torments in Purgatory, as Hamlet's father was, or worse in Hell) is a comfort to the bereaved.

THE DEVIL FROM THE PINE BARRENS

From Charles M. Skinner's *American Myths and Legends I*:

> Within recent times [1903] the Leeds Devil has ramped about the New Jersey pine region, between Freehold and Cape May, though it should have been "laid" many years ago. Its coming portends evil, for it appears before wars, fires, and great calamities.
>
> Albeit a sober Quaker in appearance, Mother Leeds, of Burlington, New Jersey, was strongly suspected of witchcraft; and suspicion became certainty when, in 1735, a child was born to her. The old women who had assembled on that occasion, as they

always do assemble wherever there is death or birth or marriage, reported that while it was like other human creatures at first, the child changed, under their very eyes. It began to lose its likeness to other babes, and grew long and brown; it presently took the shape of a dragon, with a snake-like body, a horse's head, a pig's feet, and a bat's wings. This dreadful being increased in strength as it gained in size, until it exceeded the bulk and might of a grown man, when it fell on the assemblage, beating all the members of the party, even its own mother, with its long, forked, leathery tail. This despite being wreaked, it rose through the chimney and vanished, its harsh cries mingling with the clamor of a storm that was raging out-of-doors.

That night several children disappeared; the dragon had eaten them. For several years thereafter it was glimpsed in the woods at nightfall, and it would wing its way heavily from farm to farm, though it seldom did much mischief after its first escape into the world. To sour the milk by breathing on it, to dry the cows, and to sear the corn were its usual errands. On a still night the farmers could follow its course, as they did with trembling, by the howling of dogs, the hoots of owls, and the squawks of poultry. It sometimes appeared on the coast, generally when a wreck impended, and was seen in the company of the spectres that haunt the shores: the golden-haired woman in white, the black-muzzled pirate, and the robber, whose head being cut off at Barnegat by Captain Kidd, stumps about the sands without it, guarding a treasure buried near. When it needed a change of diet the Leeds Devil would breath upon the cedar swamps, and straightway the fish would die in the pools and creeks, their bodies, whitened and decayed by the poison, floating about in such numbers as to threaten illness to all the neighborhood. In 1740 the service of a clergyman was secured, who, by reason of his piety and exemplary life, had dominion over many of the fiends that plagued New Jersey, and had even prevailed in his congregation against applejack, which some declared to be a worse fiend than any other, if, indeed, it did not create some of those others. With candle, book, and bell the good man banned the creature for a hundred years, and, truly, the herds and henneries were not molested in all that time. The Leeds Devil had become a dim tradition when, in 1840, it burst its cerements, if such had been put about it; or, at all events, it broke through the clergyman's commandments, and went whiffling among the pines again, eating sheep and other animals, and making clutches at children that dared to sport about their dooryards in the twilight. From time to time it reappeared, its last raid occurring at Vincetown and Burrville in 1899, but it is said that its life has nearly run its course, and with the advent of the new century many worshipful commoners of Jersey dismissed, for good and all, the fear of this monster from their minds.

AMERICANISMS

debbil Negro dialect for *devil*
devil dog tough fighter (Marines in World War I)
devilinski, devilinsky a devilish person
deviled made spicy (as deviled ham, deviled eggs, deviled crab, etc.)
Devil's War World War II
deviltry British *devilry*, action like a devil's
devil's weed hawkweed
devil's piano machine gun

THE DEVIL'S ADDITION

You've heard of Hell's Kitchen (now called Clinton) but have you heard of the Devil's Addition? In *Words Fail Me*, Philip Howard says that "cattlemen used to ride down the last stage of a trail drive into Abilene to the warm consolation of a district known as the Devil's Addition."

GETTING RID OF A GHOST

Among African-Americans in the south, the method was to throw some hairs from a black cat at it and say, "Skit, skat! Turn to a bat!" The Devil was thought, like the vampire, to like the bat form.

AFRICAN-AMERICAN HELL

From H. L. Mencken's "Hell and Its Outskirts" in the *New Yorker*, 23 October 1948:

In Harlem, according to Zora Neale Hurston, the dark geographers have discovered that there is a hotter Hell lying somewhere south of the familiar Christian resort, and have given it the name of *Beluthahatchie*. So far not much has been learned about its amperage, sociology, or public improvements, but its temperature has been fixed tentatively somewhere between that of a blast furnace and that of the sun. These Afro-American explorers also believe that their spectroscopes have found three suburbs of Hell proper, by name *Diddy-wah-diddy*, *Ginny Gall*, and *West Hell*. . . . *Diddy-wah-diddy* is a sort of Long Island, given over mainly to eating houses and night clubs . . ., *West Hell* lies beyond the railroad tracks and is somewhat tacky.

West Hell brings to mind that boondocks Nowheresville that slang colorfully calls *East Jesus*. Personally, a real hell would be one inhabited by a whole population that agrees with some of my more political colleagues who want to rank Zora Neale Hurston and Alice Walker with Shakespeare and Dante.

HAITIAN ZOMBIES

The zombie (walking dead) is not technically a demon, but insofar as to raise the dead in this way, he takes a pact with The Devil, he and deserves a mention here. The *hougan* or evil magician makes that pact in advance, sucks out the victim's soul through the keyhole of his door, and breathes it into a bottle. The victim sickens and dies. The corpse is disinterred secretly with chants of "*Mortu tombo mihi*" ("The dead in the tomb are mine"). The body is carried past its former residence. If it does not revive at that, everything is fine. The soul is put back into the body with spells, incantations, and a shower of acacia leaves. A stiff drink, and the dead man walks again, totally under the control of the black magician. Zombies are perfectly obedient slaves.

Auto-suggestion and mental defectiveness have added much to the zombie legend, especially in a country where black magic is widely believed to be a matter of everyday life at the highest as well as the lowest levels.

With Edgar Cayce having predicted that New York will be under water by the end of the 1990s, with Nostradamus having predicted that this decade will experience nuclear terrorism, and with Mayan predictions that the whole word will end in 2012, you may well find it hard to worry about zombies and Haitian politics.

MEXICAN WITCHCRAFT

There are batches of witches all over Mexico. I have encountered them among American expatriates in Guadalajara and around Lake Chapala, and there are many in other places, such as Catemeco. They meet on the first Friday of March each year for a grand convention and to discuss the profession. Recently the fall of the peso has affected business. NAFTA (they complained in 1992) promised to bring in modern medicine and to "adulterate" the old herbal knowledge and destroy the powers of the *curanderos*. These are still at work. I saw them performing inside the little church of a village near San Cristobal de las Casas with their Coca-Cola bottles of water, candles, chickens . . . .

When last I checked, Tirso Vasquez had a radio show five days a week in Monterey on which he talked about witchcraft. Predicting political upsets has gained him quite a following. In Mexico City, however, António Vasquez Alba says business is slow since the 1995 trouble with finances. Phil Gunson in the *Guardian* for 19 June 1995 says current conditions there are a "Nightmare for Purveyors of Dreams." Interpreting dreams and giving advice on picking lottery numbers seems to be big just now, but I know some witches who are famed for extremely effective curses and spells and are much sought after. One I know offers a money-back guarantee.

PALO MAYOMBE

This African-influenced Mexican equivalent of our devil worship was blamed in 1989 for the murder of Mark Kilroy, a presumably innocent University of Texas student, who was kidnapped and offered as a human sacrifice to these evil gods by Mexican drug dealers. This incident in Matamoros was widely reported in the United States.

WITCHCRAFT OF THE *INDIGENES* OF MEXICO

An unusual story appears in the journal of the indigenous culture of Mexico, *Tlacoan* 7 (1977), in Jon Ek's "A Witchcraft Trial in Guerrero." To the Aztec traditions of witchcraft those of the Spanish *conquistadores* have been added and the result is an amalgam of both cultures, as is also the case in formerly Mexican areas of the United States. See Marc Simmons, *Witchcraft in the Southwest: Spanish and Indian Supernaturalism on the Río Grande*, 1974; Norman G. Thomas' doctoral dissertation on Pueblo witchcraft, *The Nexus of Envy*, and Keith H. Basso's dissertation on the Western Apache and witchcraft, *Heavy with Hate*, both 1968; the journal *El Palacio* published by the Museum of New Mexico; and other sources.

Witchcraft is a theme in a great deal of Meso-American literature and can be seen as central in works such as the novel *Aura* by the leading Mexican writer, Carlos Fuentes.

DEATH BY WITCHCRAFT IN MEXICO

One syndrome that United States doctors have investigated in Mexico is the sudden death of infants attributed by the locals to blood-sucking witches. In 1993 *Social Science and Medicine* reported on forty-seven such cases in Tlaxcala and the *sequelæ* (or impact upon the bereaved families). As in Cameroon or right here in the United States, belief by parents that the sudden death of innocents is always and entirely due to natural rather than supernatural causes is a lot rarer than you might expect.

MAYAN MAGIC AND WITCHCRAFT

Horace Dudley Oeck has edited *Mam Texts on Witchcraft* (1977) and archeological excavations of the Mayan world are continually presenting us with other evidence of the beliefs and practices of the Maya.

WITCHCRAFT IN ECUADOR

Just as the *curanderos* of Mexico carpenter together elements of Christian and non-Christian rites, the superstitious on the northern coast of Ecuador (writes Diego Quiroga in his doctoral dissertation *Saints, Virgins, and the Devil*, 1994) call on all the supernatural forces they know to assist in healing. If one does not work, another may. Little altars may feature statutes or symbols of both the Christian saints and the pagan gods.

THE DEVIL OF THE MEXICANS

Tezcalipoca (also called *Yaotzin*, "The Enemy") was, Bernal Díaz reports in his *Historia verdadera de la conquista de Neuva España*, "the god of hell and had charge of the souls of the Mexicans, and his body was girt with figures like little devils with the tails of snakes." He was said to be responsible for the strange cries heard in the night jungle and appeared to the luckless as a headless and decomposing corpse. But in the chest of this hideous creature were two little doors, and if anyone had the courage to reach into the cavity they protected and seize the black heart of the monster, that person could make the demon give him anything he might desire.

THE MEXICAN QUEEN OF THE WITCHES

Women who died in childbirth became the Ciuapipiltin (Princesses); they came back as demons to harm children. They haunted crossroads, and it was there that propitiatory sacrifices were offered in an attempt to cut down on their depredations. They were offered bread and "thunder stones which fall from the sky." They were white-faced creatures (their faces covered with talc) and wore the costume of Tlazolteotl, the goddess of witchcraft and sorcery, lust and all other evils. She is related to goddesses of the witches in other cultures by her snakes, her connection with the moon, her screech owl, her connection with crossroads, and her broom.

Bernadino de Sahagún in his *Historia universál de Neuva España* says: "when anyone is possessed by the demons, with twisted mouth and feet turned inwards, wringing his hands and foaming at the mouth, they say he has become associated with a demon; the *Ciuateteo*, resident at the crossroads, has taken over his body."

THE MEXICAN LORD AND LADY OF THE DEAD

The Lord of Mictlampa (Region of the Dead) and his consort Mictecaci-uatl (Lady of the Region of the Dead) are represented in the codices that have come down to us—one bishop deliberately destroyed a great many records of pre-Christian Mexico—as cannibalistic and hideous. He is often shown as a skeleton, she decked with the paper pennons put on corpses on the way to cremation. One representation shows her thrusting a mummified body into the earth. One representation of him shows him clutching *malinalli*, grass "associated with witchcraft," Summers says in *The Vampire: His Kith and Kin*. Summers sees vampire characteristics in both these hellish demons.

THE VOODOO CURSE

The voodoo doll is usually placed in a tiny coffin and delivered to the victim with this spell:

> *Zo wan-we sobadi sobo kalisso*
> *Maître Carrefour mwe mem kiriminal*
> *M'a remesye loa-yo Grand Bois, l'uvri*
> *Baye mwe Baron [Samedi] Cimetiéres, l'envoi morts*

Maître Carrefours (Master of the Crossroads), *Grand Bois* (Big Woods), and *Baron Samedi* (Baron Saturday, Master of the Cemeteries) are powerful *loas* (spirits) in voodoo.

MAGIC AND MAGIC REALISM

The recent vibrant literature of South America is full of witchcraft, magic, and other ancient beliefs. One example that can represent what we do not have space to mention is Mario Vargas Llosa's eleventh novel, first published as *Lituma en los Andes* (Lituma in the Andes). In a review in the March 1996 *Atlantic Monthly*, Steven G. Kellman provides a succinct paragraph we can cite. In it he says that:

> *Death in the Andes* [title of Edith Grossman's translation] offers horrors even more harrowing than Shining Path [*Sendero Luminoso* is a violent Peruvian guerrilla movement]. The *serruchos*—mountain people—believe that their rugged terrain is haunted by *apus*, tutelary spirits of the local summits who must periodically be propitiated with ritual slaughter and cannibalism. *Pishtacos*, demons who suck the fat out of living human bodies, are said to wander the mountainside. "In civilized places, nobody believes things like that anymore," Lituma [a Civil Guard corporal, the narrator of this novel] says. But the corporal is not in Piura anymore, and many in Naccos [a remote mining town] believe that the *huayco*, the Andean avalanche that defeats the efforts to build a highway and nearly kills Lituma, has supernatural origins. Lituma interrogates Dionisio, the proprietor of the town's only cantina and the impresario of nightly Dionysian revelries. But neither he nor his wife, Adriana, a devotee of witchcraft, can satisfy a civilized man seeking a lucid explanation for the mysterious disappearances in Naccos.

VOODOO ART AND MUSIC

When an exhibit of "Sacred Arts of Haitian Vodou" was presented at the Fowler Museum of Cultural History (UCLA) in 1996, Prof. Donald J. Consentino said of the fantastically jumbled altars from Port-au-Prince, the brilliant beaded and sequined flags, the sculptures, the primitive and more

Voodoo seals of love, victory in lawsuits, and Baron Saturday (to dispell evil influences).

sophisticated paintings, the tiny decorated coffins, and the rest, "The question is not whether they are handicraft or fine art but whether they are truly magical, powerful as well as beautiful." High and low art, psychology, anthropology, and power are studied in the *vodun* cultures of Benin, Togo, Haiti, etc., in Suzanne Preston Blier's detailed *African Vodun* (1996).

The Smithsonian has La Troupe Makandal's *Rhythms of Raptures* on record. It is the best introduction to the voodoo music of Haiti. Devils and demons will be drawn from everywhere when you play it. Play it very loud and they may come from the apartments upstairs.

ROOT DOCTORS

These American equivalents of African witchdoctors are common in the folklore of the South and are treated in *North Carolina Folklore* and other journals. Medical personnel complain about the problems of treating patients who consider themselves hexed and would rather rely on root doctors than ordinary physicians. Lawyers discuss the problems of root doctoring brought into the courts.

HOODOO AND "WHITE LIVER"

The folk medicine of the poor has often been directed at diseases that superstitious people attribute to hexing, hoodoo, and such. One of these, which closely resembles AIDS but was known long before AIDS has long been known in the African-American population as "white liver," attributed to voodoo.

WITCHCRAFT COLLECTIONS

Important holdings are in the great national libraries in Washington, London, Paris, and other cities, but there is also a large collection of books on witchcraft at Cornell University, thanks largely to a former professor there, Rossell Hope Robbins. He supplied an introduction to Jane Marsh Dieckman's *Catalogue of the Witchcraft Collection* (1977). Researchers should look also in libraries in Philadelphia and in state folklore collections as well as in the state folklore journals of Indiana, Pennsylvania, California, etc.

VOODOO IN THE BIG APPLE

Vodou (as Elizabeth A. McAlister in her Yale dissertation, "Vodou in New York City," 1990, thinks it more polite to call voudoo) flourishes in New

York City among Haitian immigrants. There it had undergone the "creolization" and "economizing of ritual time and space" that this scholar is able to demonstrate. In what we might call "a New York minute," Hatian religion has changed to fit into the new context even as the elements of African religion take years ago from Dahomy and The Congo remain. Voodoo thus becomes a vivid example of the interaction between foreign elements and the New York melting pot or "glorious mosaic."

Whites who admire in art galleries and shops the elaborate, sequined banners and cute little dolls used in voodoo ceremonies know practically nothing of the many herbalist and candle shops and other outlets for voodoo materials in the metropolis, little shops that are almost as numerous as the magical *bodegas* that serve the *Santeristas* of the Hispanic community. Haitian voodoo is one of the most fervent religions of the city but practically invisible to most New Yorkers. It is not a tourist attraction, as in New Orleans. It is an everyday if somewhat underground religion.

The Devil as drawn by the visionary poet William Blake.

5

The Rest of the World

GODS AND GODDESSES OF BLACK MAGIC

China has *Dshi-dshi-garr*, a deity the sorcerer can call on to help him in suppressing demons and *Shang Chieh Fu Kuan Szu Tsai* to protect against demons at funerals. Tibet has so many powers assisting or participating in sorcery that we shall have to leave them to some much longer book. *Enki* was the Sumerian god of purification magic. *Feimata* fights sorcery in Polynesia. *Netekwo* guides the priest in Ghana to counteract witchcraft. *Odani* frees Ethiopians from diabolical possession. Here are other perhaps less healthy powers the magician can call on:

Ablatan, Aliburon, Angob, Anip, Badowado, Daludalum, Doko, Galikom, Halangob, Halibongbong, Halimudat, Halimudong, Humabungol Inadungali, Inaiyuan, Intimitiman, Intudtudu, Kalotkot, Kinipul, Kinlutan, Kuyub, Lobag, Lunge, Manalikan, Manugahung, Manunglub, Monbolboldang, Mondauwat, Numputol, Pinigipigon, (Philippines)

Adantayi, Aglosunto, Aziza, Dadda Langga, Hoho, Loko, Minona, Palada (Dahomey)

ah q'in (Guatemala)

'Alae-a-Hina, Hi'iaka, Kahuila-o-ka-lani, Kane-i-kaulana-'ula, Kane pohaka'a, Kapo, Keoloewa, Ku-ho'one'enu'u, Ku-ka'ili-moku, Ku-waha-illo Maka-ku-koa'e, Pahulu, Uli (Hawaii)

Amana (Surinam)

The Aukis (Peru)

Bagala, Bhairu, Marutha Veran (India)
Begawati (Bali)
Carman, Mongfhinn (Ireland)
Chang Kuo-lao, La-gkyi-la-khu, Mun-ludzi-pu, No Cha, P'u-lla gka-hla, Sheng Mu Ti-mba Shera (China)
Circe, Eileithyia (Greece)
Dja-ma, Lo-ye Ha-ddu, Ssan-ddo, T'u-chi Yu-ma (China and Tibet)
Gollveig, Odin (Scandinavia)
Harohoha (New Guinea)
Heka, Nesert (Egypt)
Heva, Poti'i-ta-rire, Rangatau, Ro'o, Temaru, Teruharuhatai, Ti'i, Tukia (Polynesia)
Ini Andan, Manang Jaban (Borneo)
Kamrusepa (Hittites)
Khyung dung (Bhutan, Sikkim, Tibet)
Laxee, Matlalcueye, Pitao Pijze, Tlacauepan (Mexico)
Mahamayuri, Mahapratisara, Mahasahasrapramardani, Mahasitavati Sitatapatra Aparajita (Buddhism)
Mari, Prakagorri (Basques)
Mikenak, Mistabeo, Mistapiu (Eastern Canada)
Moko-hiku-aru (Maori)
Nyamikeri-mahse (Colombia)
Omaua (Venezuela)
peyák nõta (Bolivia)
Simbi (en Deux Eaux), Simbi Promene, 'Ti [Petite] Kita (Haiti)
Sinthgunt, Vol(la) (Germanic)
Thai-cu-ia (Taiwan)
Toro (New Guinea)
Tuira (Panama)
Tutu (Assyrians and Babylonians)
Unktomi (Spider Woman of the Lakota and Oglala Sioux, South Dakota)
Wazi (Wizard, Oglala, South Dakota)
The we'mawe (Zuñi, New Mexico)
Xu (Kung!, South Africa)

ZAR

In Islamic tradition, this is a demon that possesses a woman and demands jewels, fancier clothes, and expensive presents. Husbands are afraid of it and buy things for their wives. This demon has been reported in the vicinity of expensive shops in the US.

EKIMMU

In Assyrian demonology, this is a person violently "snatched away" who roams the earth as an evil spirit. The *ekimmu* was especially difficult to exorcize.

In the West we have often been told that those who died violently or suddenly return as ghosts. I can understand those rudely snatched wanting to cling to some kind of existence but one would think suicides, who took drastic action to leave, would hardly want to return.

MAGIC IN ASSYRIA AND BABYLON

Some of the most interesting books are not in English:
Contenau, C., *La Magie chez les Assyriens et les Babyloniens* (1942)
Dhorme, E., *Les Religions de Babylonie* (1949)
Fossey, C., *La Magie assyrienne* (1902)
Furlani, G., *La Religione babilonese e asira* (1920 - 1929)

INDIA

The seal of the Egyptian goddess It. See Aleister Crowley's *The Book of Thoth* and *The Book of Lies*.

Crooke, William, *The Popular Religion and Folklore of Northern India* (1896)
Dumezil, Georges, *Les Dieux des Indo-Européens* (1952)
Herman, A. L., *The Problem of Evil and Indian Thought* (1976)
O'Flaherty, Wendy, *The Origins of Evil in Hindu Mythology* (1977)
Weber, Max, *The Religion of India* (1958)

The Egyptian Book of the Dead is interesting to compare with *The Tibetan Book of the Dead*. Like most of the Tibetan magical literature, the latter is unknown here, but some foreigners have written the likes of:

David-Neel, A., *With Mystics and Magicians in Tibet*
Evans-Wentz-W. Y., *Tibetan Yoga and Secret Doctrines*
Grant, J., *The Mysteries of all Nations*

One must be careful not to be misled by Englishmen with aliases pretending to be learned lamas or led astray by other frauds, other gurus.

EVIL GODDESSES OF EGYPT

Anyone with an interest in the occult knows *The Book of the Dead*, the eccentric publications on the "mysteries" of the pyramids (a boon to numerologists when they are not explaining the height of the Washington Monument in terms of Freemasonry), and the fascination of the Egyptians with the preservation of the body, so that we can look Rameses II in the face today. (He looks a lot like old photographs of John D. Rockefeller.) There was a time when mediums who did not favor Indians (American or from the subcontinent) as "helpers," used Egyptian hocus-pocus. The "curse of the pharaohs" and the devils and demons of Egypt are pretty well known with the exception, perhaps of *Heka* ("god of magical words"). Here are some less familiar evil goddesses of Egypt. First in alphabetical order is *Ahemait*, a mixed creature (crocodile, hippopotamus, lion) who devours the souls of evil persons who reach the underworld. *Sag*, another odd-looking creature (head of a hawk, body of a lion, a lotus blossom at the end of her tail), causes drought. At a town called Pselchis, history tells us, the Greeks worshipped a scorpion goddess from Nubia of The Sudan. She was associated with Set (who slew his brother Osiris and married his sister Nephthys, becoming the father of Anubis) and Typhon (in Greek mythology a half-man, half-monster demon of the whirlwind, the hurricane, the volcano and other destruction). She is also associated with—any connection with Lucifer?—the morning star. She was called *Selket* or *Serquet*.

Then there is *Sekhet*, last because there is most to say about her, even in a brief notice. She has the head of a lion, denoting fierceness. She is the daughter of Ra and solar rays are her symbol. Like a pharaoh, she wears the solar disc and the lunar horns, and as *Tefnut*, she is the consort of Shu, destroyer of mankind. She directs the torture of the dead. She is shown with an *ankh* and papyrus staff or with a basket and a warrior's shield. In the northern part of Egypt she is called *Ouati*. Her powers extend over animals and hunting, justice, time, destruction and hell, and in the latter aspect she is called *Beset* or *Bubastis*. She may be an aspect of the reptile goddess *Selk* or even of *Isis*. As *Mehenit* she is the cobra that guards the head of Ra. As *Nesrit* she is a goddess of fire with magical powers. She is related somehow to the queen of the underworld, *Hathor*, who may be her mother-in-law. I include her as an example of the complexity of the study Egyptian gods, goddesses, monsters, etc. E.A.W. Budge, *Gods of the Egyptians* . . . (1969) offers an authoritative introduction to a whole world of divinities and other supernatural creatures, many of whom are as evil and tenacious as any devils or demons of Christian belief.

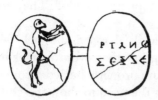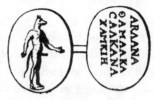

WITCHCRAFT IN ANCIENT EGYPT

The ancient Egyptians used witchcraft to fight the many evil spirits and malevolent aspects of their gods and goddesses and also bend them to their will. They employed talismans and amulets (the eye of Horus, the *ankh*, the "Blood of Isis," etc.). Egyptians went to great pains by these (such as scarabs, symbols of the giver of life) and other means to protect the dead body, so that the soul could visit it when it desired. They were likewise of the belief that the dead could visit the living, and in fear of the evil dead they turned to magical protections. Humans were thought to attain special spiritual power after death. The Egyptians also adopted methods designed to give them spiritual power while yet alive, out-of-body experiences, and in mystery religions, contact with occult powers.

We can trace back to the Egyptian witches the practice of making wax figures of persons you wanted to waste away (you melted the wax), figurines into which you stuck pins (to bring pain to that part of their bodies) or smashed (to destroy their bodies completely), and other kinds of what is called sympathetic magic. It is my belief that one of the Commandments given to Moses the Egyptian, the one that forbade the making of images, was aimed at least as much at black magicians as at idolators, maybe more so.

The elaborate sarcophagi of Egyptian mummies, it should be remembered, were in part designed to protect the contents from devils and demons.

YOU'RE NOT SAFE EVEN WHEN YOU'RE DEAD

The mention elsewhere of a Japanese emperor signing his name in blood reminds me to tell you about the Japanese emperor called Nintoku. He died in 395 A.D., but it took until 427 A.D. for his mausoleum to be completed so he was not officially buried until thirty-two years after his death. The corpses of Spanish monarchs at the palace of the Escurial, outside Madrid, have had to be placed in drying rooms before they eventually go to their eternal rest in the marble sarcophagi provided. They, too, have to wait for final storage.

What's the connection between devils, demons, and such delays? This: After your death you are more susceptible than ever to attack by devils or demons (some people say) until you are properly buried. From this (along with the hope the dead will revive or the need to show the body to prove the death has actually occurred) may come the care with which the body is treated when displayed before the funeral, the crosses or other religious objects, the candles, the sitting by the coffin, and the rest.

FAR-OUT IDEAS FROM THE FAR EAST

In Bali, *leyaks* are werewolves who can turn themselves into animal shapes but also—the Balinese really believe—into bicycles and automobiles.

Wu Tao-tze (Wu, Master of the Way) was born about the year 700 of our era, in China. He became the best painter of the T'ang Dynasty, working best (it was said) when he had had a few drinks. Four hundred years after his death the Chinese emperors still had almost 100 of his masterful landscapes and Buddhist temples were decorated with his murals. Today there is not one of his great works extant anywhere; all he has left us is a legend. Legend says that when Wu decided he had lived long enough, he painted a vast landscape on the wall of a temple, walked into a cave in the landscape, and disappeared forever.

SHEN

The Chinese character *shen* is often put up over a door to keep demons from entering. You can also use garlic flowers (not just garlic, which only keeps away people) or throw on the ground a large quantity of tiny objects, such as fine seeds (which keeps evil spirits counting and deters them from business). Or nail up a crucifix, *mezzuzah*, or some other superstitious sanitizer.

TIBETAN MAGIC

The magicians of Tibet are particularly colorful, not only because they are said to deal effectively with some of the most grotesque and virulent demons, but also because they can produce such incredible public displays at the ceremonies in which they cut open their bellies and expose the

entrails, throw blood all over the spectators, and then close the wounds.
I've seen it done. It leaves no scars.

DEMON FESTIVALS IN JAPAN

Demons are an important aspect of Shinto and other religions in Japan.
On 17 April, for instance, at the Rukuhoji Temple in the prefecture of
Ibaraki, they celebrate the *Madara Kijinsa* (Demon God Event). Madara
and his fellow demons are credited with having rebuilt the temple, after
it burned down, in seven days of intense labor.

On 16 August at Sosa in the prefecture of Chiba, they present the *Oni-Mai* (Demon Dance), a series of seven plays dealing with demons and hell.
This is the same day, by the way, that souls are lit on their way back into
the sea from which they came; at Miyazu there are Bon dances and a festival of lanterns to guide the dead.

The *Onioi-Shiki* (Demon Dispersing Ceremony) is conducted early in
February each year at the Kofukuji Temple at Nara and at the Nagata
Shrine at Kobe. Men dressed as Buddhist priests drive off men dressed as
demons in a lively, beautifully costumed mock battle. This is followed by
a bean-throwing ceremony.

THE CHINESE SOUL-STEALERS

In 1768 there was a tremendous uproar in China about soul-stealing by
sorcery. The vivid story is excitingly as well as authoritatively told by Philip
A. Kuhn in *Soulstealers . . .* (1990).

CHINESE MAGICIAN

In music hall and vaudeville acts, many Caucasians pretended to be Chinese magicians because of the great reputation of real Chinese in real magic.
In C. A. S. Williams's *Outlines of Chinese Symbolism and Art Motives* (third,
revised, edition, 1976), we read of Chung-li Chüan (of the Chou dynasty,
well before Christ) who became the chief of the Eight Immortals of Tao-
ism. He was supposed to have "obtained the secrets of the elixir of life,
the powder of transmution" in alchemy and had a fan that was "believed
to revive the souls of the dead." This goes well beyond the Tibetan magicians I mentioned earlier who, supposedly assisted by devils and demons
but perhaps working with mass hypnotism, give demonstrations of cutting

their bellies open and taking out the guts only to stuff them back in again, wipe off the blood, and show no scar from their razor-sharp swords.

ADDING A CERTAIN SOMETHING

Oriental sages used to recommend that to strengthen the foundations of a Great Wall or a small building a human sacrifice ought to be buried within. This was not unknown in Europe, either, and the remains of poor wretches used for this purpose have been found, though of course no evidence remains of those whose blood was used for similar magical efforts. In China there is a great bell which was said to owe its exceptional quality to a young maiden who jumped into (or was thrown into) the molten metal before the bell was cast. Well, a little extra potassium would have helped the metallurgy, it is true.

SHAMANS OF THE FROZEN WASTES

The Lapps and Samoyeds are, as we say in another place, probably the most renowned shamans (a combination of seer and medical specialist), but the Inuit (who do not like to be called *Eskimos* any more because that possibly suggests cannibalism, although it means only meat-eaters, if that) of the Canadian and American Far North are also much concerned with the drums, doctoring, trances, and dances of shamans. They used to believe that shamans could teleport themselves. They still believe, in some measure, that some men and women have psychic or indeed supernatural powers.

Little known is the fact that some Inuit of the Eastern Arctic have a religion of The Goddess. Their supreme power is Sedna; she gives or withholds the seals on which so much of their lives depend. Sedna is not a devil or a demon; she is a creator and provider.

Recent books such as *Shamans, Priests and Witches* take cross-cultural and serious positions on magical-religious practices, but Anne Rice's *Queen of the Witches* and similar fiction are undoubtedly more popular.

FAUST UPDATED

Richard Schechner, famous for the Performing Garage company of years back, has a new group at New York University (East Coast Artists) that in 1995 produced a pastiche of Faust literature, a television talk show, Adolf Hitler, and the experimental theater equivalent of the kitchen (if not The Kitchen) sink. The old theme of a pact with The Devil still is fresh.

INDONESIA

In an attempt to get officials to refrain from handicapping them with laws against black magic, Indonesian sorcerers put on a demonstration of their powers in December 1993—for police. The *Jakarta Post* reported that policemen were treated to an event in which a person is stabbed but neither bleeds nor feels pain, and nothing was said about blades that retract into the handles or anything like that.

TEETH AND BONES

In the human body, teeth have been destroyed by acid drinks, sand in bread flour, and many other enemies of dental health. Outside the body, teeth are long-lasting. A whole temple enshrines one tooth of the Buddha. Teeth from others who have been dead for centuries survive. So do very ancient magical practices, if now turned into innocuous little customs such as the Tooth Fairy.

It may be because teeth last so well in the grave that people attributed magical powers to them. They, likewise, treasured the teeth (power?) of animals they killed, from mastodons and tigers, to wolves and foxes. They were worn not only as boasts but as amulets.

Magical powers were also acribed to human as well as animal bones, a custom that may have been reinforced by the faithful seeing in splendid reliquaries such saints; relics as the forearm of St. Francis Xavier, the skull of St. Catherine of Siena (with front teeth missing because The Devil had once pushed her down a flight of stone stairs), and so on. Saints' relics could be desecrated in infernal rites. Anyone's bones could be used ground up in magic recipes. The skull on the magician's table was more than a *momento mori* (reminder of mortality) or a theatrical prop; it could hold a candle to light certain black magic ceremonies or have other debased uses. The Scandinavian toast, *skol*, reminds us that Viking victors drank from the skulls of the conquered. Skulls, which once contained the brain and the personality, were the favorite bones of ghouls and nefarious magicians.

It was believed that dragons' teeth were sown to give birth to armies. In China, this led to a great loss to the science of archeology.

In Anyang in the nineteenth century, farmers found old bones in the fields which were peddled as medicinal, ground up for powders to credulous peasants. In scraping the Chinese characters off so that they could be sold as the bones of dragons and grinding them up, the users destroyed what Liu Ngo discovered were ancient inscriptions of the Shang. It was not until about 1928 that such bones, being found with ancient ceremonial bronzes also bearing designs and inscriptions, helped scientists piece together the history of the Shang. Today the great many tombs archeologically examined have yielded up a rich store of funerary treasures, including amazing displays of wealth and art from royal burials. What was lost to history when some old bones were scraped clean of their inscriptions, we shall never know.

Some of those inscriptions would have helped us with the ancient history of magic and divination, not because they were the bones of dragons (always important in magical myth), but because inscribed bones were used for both these occult purposes. There was even an ancient custom of "reading" the cracks made when bones were roasted in the fire, much the way tea leaves are "read" for your fortune today. "Reading" bones, "reading" cracks on tortoise shells, and thrown sticks or arrows were some of the many-*mancies*, methods of fortune-telling, in ancient Chinese culture. The *I Ching* is still widely consulted both within and outside the culture of the East. Today bones reveal information only to forensic pathologists and experts in the fields of evolution, vitamin deficiencies, arsenic poisoning, and so on.

TIBETAN DEVIL DANCERS

The people of Tibet have always lived in a spiritual world replete with many devils and demons. At festivals they don grotesque masks and, on stilts to gain impressiveness, dance to drive away evil spirits. The dances often tell of how Buddhism triumphs over the hosts of devils and demons and no longer offers blood sacrifices to the evil gods as was the custom in pre-Buddhist times in Tibet. Among fierce Tibetan deities are Sridevi (with the head of a dragon) and Yamantaka (with the head of a bull).

CHINA, JAPAN, TIBET

Addis, Stephen (ed.), *Japanese Ghosts and Demons* (1985)
David-Neal, Alexandra, *Magic and Mystery in Tibet* (n.d.)
Dennys, N.B., *The Folk-Lore of China* (1876)
Duncan, Marion H., *Customs and Superstitions of Tibetans* (1964)
Harvey, Edwin Deeks, *The Mind of China* (1933)
Hurwood, Bernhardt J., *Passport to the Supernatural* (1972)
Pott, P. H., *God and Demon in Buddhism* (1962)
Sierksma, Fokke, *Tibet's Terrifying Deities* (1966)
Willoughby-Meade, G., *Chinese Ghouls and Goblins* (1962)

"GEOMANCING THE STONE"

A typically witty headline in *The Economist* (25 November 1995) gives no hint the subject is *qi* (breath of the dragon) and the Chinese "pseudo-science" (as Lillian Too, who has written a book about it, calls it) of *feng shui*, which is about arranging buildings and other objects so as to maximize correct flow of *qi* and thus avoid bad fortune (demons) or achieve good fortune (delight). Wait until American interior decorators start including *feng shui* among the reasons for their imperious decisions! See also Charles F. Emmons in *Journal of Popular Culture* (Summer 1992).

The "white-boned demon" was the subject of a book, *Madam Mao* (1993), reviewed by Stephen R. McKinnon in the *Journal of Asian Studies*, February 1994.

AFRICAN SUICIDES

Just as suicide has occasionally been listed in the reasons vampires are created, in Africa there are various tribes who strongly believe that a suicide may well turn into a demon. Therefore the Baganda and other tribes burn the house in which a person kills himself or the tree from which he hangs himself, as well as the body. And when passing the place where the suicide took place, the natives throw stones or clods of earth to keep any possible demon at bay. In a similar fashion, the graves of witches and others exe-

208 *The Complete Book of the Devil's Disciples*

cuted for black magic are never passed without stones being thrown at the
invisible evil spirits that lurk there.

DEMONS LIKE EXERCISE

Perhaps you know Gilbert and Sullivan's *Ruddigore* with its bad baronet
cursed to perform one evil deed every day to maintain himself, a sort of
Boy Scout in reverse. Mary Henrietta Kingsley (1862–1900) was a British
lady of Gilbert and Sullivan's time who went off to Africa and was as bold
as any man in that age of exploration of "The Dark Continent." She found
some people doomed to be frequently bad. It was she who reported that
some African witches believe they have to keep doing evil deeds just to keep
their hand in, as it were, and that demons, if not put to work, may turn
on their witches.

AFRICAN MEDIUMS

American mediums might be annoyed to be accused of engaging in the
black arts, but African mediums are unashamed to say they are engaging
with devils and demons as well as good spirits in the world on the other
side of life. In Dahomey, there are schools for mediums where people
(mostly women) train to become connectors to the spirit world. When
trained, they undergo a ceremony like a funeral; they are "reborn" in their
new profession, which is to deliver messages in spiritualistic séances from
"the other world."

Mediums may act like the god or devil they are representing, walking
like a pregnant woman, roaring like a lion, or speaking in the voices of others. They impress with special jewelry of occult significance and fancy
robes. They purport to deliver messages from the Beyond and are much
consulted. If a devil or demon should take possession of them when they
are in the vulnerable trance state, they must be cleansed. Like witch doctors, they can prescribe medicines for various ills, and they interpret their
own dreams and the dreams brought to them for analysis.

Africans are more likely, however, to deal in curses and spells (see A.
Castiglione's *Incantation et Magie*, 1951); various compilations of spells,
many of which are non-African; dancing (for example, see A. J. N.
Tremearne's study of demon dancing in North and West Africa, *The Ban
of the Bori*, 1968); and more (see R. F. Fortune's *Sorcerer of Dobu*, 1932, which
sets a pattern that ought to be used for a book on the sorcerers of each
major African society).

LIFE AND DEATH IN MADAGASCAR

In Madagascar they say the Creator asked mankind whether humans should be like the moon or like the banana. The moon remains and goes and comes back. The banana dies, but before it does, it sets shoots that will replace it. As the Psalm of our Western religion has it, "As for man, his days are as grass."

NECROMANCY IN AN AFRICAN TALE

The tale is told of twin brothers at whose birth the mother died. They were brought up by a cruel stepmother who mistreated them. They feared her.

One day they were given gourds by the stepmother and sent to fetch water. One of the boys fell and broke his gourd. The other, not wanting his brother to be punished for the accident when he was not, deliberately broke his gourd as well.

When the boys came home without gourds or water, the stepmother punished them. The boys decided to seek their real mother in the land of the dead.

They found her there and discovered that the other world had two markets, the market of the living and the market of the dead. Their mother took them to the market of the living and bought two new gourds for them there. Then she took them to the market of the dead and bought them some palm nuts.

Returning to the land of the living, the boys gave the gourds and the palm nuts to their stepmother, who eagerly ate the palm nuts, her favorite delicacy. She died.

Speaking through a witch doctor who called up her ghost, the repentant stepmother warned everyone not to mistreat stepchildren and orphans lest they suffer her fate.

A TEACHING OF THE BUDDHA ABOUT LIFE AND DEATH

Once upon a time a man was walking along when a tiger appeared and chased him. He ran to the edge of a cliff and, seizing a vine, he went over the side of the cliff and hung on. The tiger above could not get at him. But then he looked down into the ravine and there was another tiger, waiting.

As he hung on the vine, mice appeared and started to nibble away at the vine. The man would not have long to wait until the vine broke and he fell into the chasm. Seeing a strawberry, the man reached out, took it, and ate it. The strawberry was delicious.

We may add to this wisdom this comment on the folly of magic and witchcraft: attempts to make the tigers or the mice disappear are futile, and malice and revenge taste bitter, while the strawberry is sweet.

BISHOP CALDWELL AND DEVIL DANCERS OF INDIA

Dr. Robert Caldwell (1814–1891) was one of those missionaries who wrote so vividly on the languages and customs of the India of the British *Raj*. He can stand here for many whom we could quote on the devils and demons of the Indian subcontinent and its various religions.

Caldwell was a Scot sent to India by the London Missionary Society. In 1841 he established himself as a missionary at Tinnevelly, of which he eventually became coadjutor bishop under the Anglican bishop of Madras. In later years he translated to and from the Tamil language and did other linguistic studies, but here is a passage from his *The Tinnevelly Shawars* of 1849:

> When the preparations are completed and the devil-dance is about to commence, the music is at first comparatively slow; the dancer seems impassive and sullen, and he either stands still or moves about in gloomy silence. Gradually, as the music becomes quicker and louder, his excitement begins to rise. Sometimes to help him to work himself up into a frenzy, he uses medicated draughts, cuts and lacerates himself till the blood flows, lashes himself with a huge whip, presses a burning torch to his breast, drinks the blood which flows from his own wounds, or drains the blood of the sacrifice, puts the throat of the decapitated goat to his mouth. Then, as if he had acquired a new life, he begins to brandish his staff of bells, and to dance with a quick but unsteady step. Suddenly the afflatus descends; there is no mistaking that glare, or those frantic leaps. He snorts, he swears, he gyrates. The demon has taken possession of him, and though he retains the power of utterance and motion, both are under the demon's control, and his separate consciousness is in abeyance. The bystanders signalize the event by raising a long shout, attended with a peculiar vibratory noise, caused by the motion of the hand and tongue, or the tongue alone. The devil-dancer is now worshipped as a present deity, and every bystander consults him respecting his diseases, his wants, the welfare of absent relatives, the offerings to be made for the accomplishment of his wishes, and, in short, everything for which superhuman knowledge is supposed to be available.

The dancing produces an effect similar to that of the whirling dervishes or the voodoo dancers who go on until they fall in exhaustion or writhe in ecstasy. This is not unrelated to events as different as consulting the oracles of ancient Greece who spoke in trance or the antics of Holy Rollers or other churchgoers of today who are "carried away." This is what the Greeks called enthusiasm, which means "the god in you." They did it with wine in honor of Dionysus, drinking the blood of the grape, the god's blood. Others have done it with the Eucharist, starvation, meditation, or by other means to attain the altered state. "The demon possessed him" says the bishop. Is it diabolical obsession or diabolical possession? Or nothing diabolical at all? "I myself am Heaven and Hell" is the answer found in Fitzgerald's translation of *The Rubaíyat of Omar Khyayyám*. Is it possible that devil dancing or other methods simply allow us to break down barriers to the deeper self, that no one is there but ourselves?

ANTI-WITCHCRAFT FIGURES

Fierce and distorted anti-witchcraft figures guard the homes and lives of members of the Bamileke tribe in Africa. They can be male or female. They are somewhere between a fetish and an idol, somewhere between an amulet and a "keep off" sign.

They can drive away evil, identify witches brought to them, and bring to witches the same horrible symptoms of disease as they are portrayed as suffering.

This is a picture of a twentieth-century version, but such idols or fetishes have been made and believed to have magical powers from time immemorial. Such statuettes are beginning to be made by many African peoples now for sale to Western collectors of primitive art. Africans would not sell genuine statuettes unless they had proved to be ineffective as protection.

AFRICAN WITCHCRAFT

Budge, E. A. Wallis *Egyptian Magic* (1968)

Douttee, Edmond, *Magie et religion dans l'Afrique du nord* (1908)

Evans-Pritchard, E. Evans, *Witchcraft, Oracles and Magic among the Azande* (1976)

Haskins, James, *Witchcraft, Mysticism and Magic in the Black World* (1974)

Legey, Francois, *The Folklore of Morocco* (1935)

Middleton, J. & E. H. Winter (eds.), *Witchcraft and Sorcery in East Africa* (1963)

Parrinder, Geoffrey, *Witchcraft: European and African* (1958)

Scobie, A., *Murder for Magic* (1965)

Williams, Joseph John, *Africa's God* (1937)
and

C. Theodore Binns, *The Warrior People* (1975) (Zulu)

W. Bleck, *Marriage, Inheritance and Witchcraft* (1975) (Ghanian)

Adnee Marie Bradford, *Hell Imagery in Black Literature* (doctoral dissertation, 1980)

Mary Douglas *et al.*, eds., *Man in Africa* (1969)

William J. G. Gardenier, *Witchcraft and Sorcery in a Pastoral Society* . . . . (doctoral dissertation, 1975) (Sakalava of West Madagascar)

Alan Harwood, *Witchcraft, Sorcery and Social Classification* (doctoral dissertation, 1971) (Tanzanian)

James Haskins, *Witchcraft, Mysticism, and Magic in the Black World* (1974) (various)

Harry Middleton Hyatt, *Hoodoo-Conjuration-Witchcraft-Rootwork* (1978)

Simeon Mesaki, *Witchcraft and Witch-Killings in Tanzania* (doctoral dissertation, 1994)

William S. Simmons, *Eyes of the Night* (1971) (Sengalese)

R.G. Willis, ed., *Witchcraft and Healing* . . . *Center of African Studies* . . *Edinburgh* (1969) (various)

WITCH DOCTORS

There has been some misunderstanding about African witch doctors. They have been portrayed as crazed and vicious individuals prancing around with a staff topped with a human skull, screaming curses, threatening evil. In fact, they are generally quite benevolent: they give medical cures to people and cattle, magical amulets to ward off devils and disasters, and talismans to grant fertility and success in various other endeavors. They officiate at rights such as those marking puberty and a boy's official admission to the circle of men. They are often called upon to read omens and foretell the future and to petition the heavenly power. The Sotho people, for instance, use the witch doctor's power to reach Modimo, the creator and ruler of the skies, sender of drought or good weather. Among the Yoruba, the witch doctor can manage the powerful *ofo* (incantations) that work wonders. The witch doctor is part shaman and part physician, part magical and part medical.

But just as they can help, so can they hurt. The witch doctor who can miraculously cure an illness can also cause one by his magic or even point the bone at you and make you fall down dead. He can drive thorns into your flesh from a distance, haunt your dreams, blight your fields or your cattle, and cripple and destroy your body. Those who are assailed by magic usually go to another witch doctor and pay him to fight for them. The stronger magician wins. The evil one, if apprehended, may be put to death.

In societies where the dead ancestors are not only honored (in the poetry of lineages, at altars in the home, at important festivals) but are said to be near in spirit even if God is distant or unreachable, it is only to be expected that there is a great fear of malevolent spirits and a perceived need for plenty of amulets and the services of many witch doctors. A witch doctor, it is believed even by some university graduates in the new Africa, can cure your illness, improve your luck at love or hunting or farming, assist your friends, attack your enemies, and communicate with the dead.

THE BATAK OF SUMATRA

Here is a sample of a small group much feared by their neighbors near Lake Toba not only because they were traditionally cannibals but because they were supposed to be powerful with magic. Their magic consisted of rites to contact and control the spirits of the living and the dead and also to manipulate the souls of anything else in nature, from stones and trees to the weather and wild animals. (Attempting to manipulate the souls of wild animals is a very ancient aspect of primitive magic and explains the prehistoric cave paintings of Europe.) The Batak rituals, mediumship, amulets, and the rest were all considered by their enemies to be black magic. The Bataks are now Christian (Lutherans, etc.), Muslim, and pagan in about equal numbers.

THE BLACK CAT

Summarized from Rev. P. Dehon, a Jesuit missionary among the Uraons, in *Memoirs of The Asiatic Society of Bengal* (1906):

> Cats, vicious creatures (if you have ever seen one with a mouse), have been feared and worshipped since ancient times. The Egyptians mummified them to keep their spirits alive. Cats are on record as being familiars of many witches, even handed down from mother to daughter, and those that are black (the color of evil in our tradition) have often been considered to be The Devil himself or even the witch in animal form.
>
> The Uraons, a hill tribe of Bengal, have a creature called the *chordewa*, which they believe is a witch in the body of a cat. While the soul is in the cat's body, the witch remains in a trance or coma. These witch cats are said to come into houses where people are sick in bed, steal their food, lick their lips, and mortally injure them thereby. Any wound given to these cats appears on the body of the witches they come from. The Bengalis used to execute any person suspected of creating a *chordewa*.

VITALA

The *vitala* reanimates corpses in India or appears as a human but with hands and feet reversed. In Decca, the *vitala* is a guardian and lives in red-painted stones.

AIRI AND *BHUT*

These are two evil spirits of India. The *airi* can scare you to death; it is the evil spirit of a man killed in the hunt. The *bhut* is a particularly malicious creature; it is the evil spirit of a person killed violently, by his own hand or executed, killed in an accident, etc.

SATANISM IN THE PHILIPPINES

There is a long list of native Philippine demons in *The Complete Book of Devils and Demons*, but Christianity has added to the perils facing the natives of these islands. For Satanism there, see numerous articles in the journal *Unitas*, published in Manila.

DEMONS OF MALAYSIA

The *bajang* and *langsuir* are male and female vampires causing illness and death. You detect a *bajang* by scraping an iron pot with a razor; if the suspected person's hair falls out as if the razor were applied to him, he controls the evil spirit. The *langsuir* is often the spirit of a woman who died in childbirth. She sucks the blood of infants. She can also mate with humans and produce monstrous children.

Summers quotes Sir William Maxwell in a Victorian *Journal of the Straits Branch of the Royal Asiatic Society*:

> If a woman dies in childbirth, either before delivery or after the birth of a child, and before the forty days of uncleanness have expired, she is popularly supposed to become a *langsuyar* [sic], a flying demon of the nature of the 'white lady' [usually in the French term, *la dame blanche*] or 'banshee.' To prevent this a quantity of glass beads are put in the mouth of the corpse, a hen's egg is put under each arm-pit, and needles are placed in the palms of the hands. It is believed that if this is done the dead woman cannot become a *langsuyar*, as she cannot open her mouth to shriek (*ngilai*), or wave her arms as wings, or open and shut her hands to assist her flight.

Islamic magic circle.

DISCOVERING WITCHES

In India, they say that you can discover a witch by beating a woman with a castor oil plant.

"A MAGIC WORLD OF SPIRITS, GODS, AND DEMONS"

That is how the general manager of a new hotel in Bali describes the country where a hotel needs a *pedanda* (priest) to "make blood sacrifices to evil spirits" and a *pemangku* (a sort of para-priest) to handle daily spiritual emergencies. Donna Rosenthal reports that "religious beliefs require hotel builders to create a room with a cosmologically correct view" in an article titled "Demons Get a Fast Checkout On Bali" in the *New York Times*, 10 December 1995. It reads:

> When the Four Seasons began building a 47-villa resort in Ubud, Bali, last July, security guards reported seeing leyaks, or nocturnal spirits, floating around the 19-acre jungle site. Most Balinese believe leyaks are living people who practice black magic and transform themselves into spirits—monkeys, birds, even headless bodies. A few skittish guards had been placing offerings of food and flowers under trees to appease them. Others wore amulets to ward them off. Still, the leyaks have continued their nightly visits to the cliff where the partly built villas overlook a meandering river. Because leyaks don't bother non-Hindus, Royal Rowe, assistant manager, hired Moslem security guards.
>
> Then there was the shrine problem. When Mr. Rowe discovered that some stone shrines on the hotel site were blocking access for the army of over 1,500 builders, he turned to a pendanda—a Brahman, or high-caste priest—for advice. The pedanda went into a trance and then transferred the ancestral spirits to temporary bamboo shrines. Then, on an astrologically auspicious day, workers destroyed five shrines. When the hotel is completed next summer, the spirits will be moved again—to permanent new shrines facing sacred Mount Agung, where the gods dwell. "Building a hotel in Bali is a constant eye-opener," said Mr. Rowe when I talked to him on a visit to the island last May. "I've learned we can't use the bulldozer until the pedanda chooses the right day to bless it. When I see a carpenter chanting a mantra in front of a tree, it means he's trying to placate the spirits. To the Balinese, there's no real difference between what we call living and nonliving things."

THE DEVIL IS THEIR GOD

About 20,000 Yezidis live in Kurdistan and elsewhere. They worship the fallen angel we call The Devil. We give them their name from the Persian *ized* ("angel" or "divinity"). They call themselves Dasni or Dasin. They see themselves as descended from Adam alone, thus making them different from the rest of mankind, and their religion (a pastiche of Jewish, Zoroastrian, Manichean, Muslim, and Nestroian elements) is contained in their scriptures, a *Book of Revelation* and a *Black Book*.

Their theology insists that our Satan rules the world. Seven angels, with Malak Ta'us (The Peacock Angel) as chief ruler, preside over all. God is passive. Malak Ta'us rebelled against God and was cast into hell, but his tears of repentance drowned its fires. He is now a force for good, as powerful as other people say God is, and his name is not to be spoken so powerful is he.

This religion goes back at least as far as the Sheik 'Adi, who died in 1161, the prophet of this devil divinity, himself now a divinity. Read about it in detail in Th. Menzel's *Encyclopedia of Islam* (IV:1163–1170), a fascinating story of devil worshippers in the modern world.

RELIGION AND MAGIC

Margaret Murray was taken by many as the leading expert in her day on what she called the Old Religion of witchcraft, what the Italians still call *la vecchia religione*. Still she admitted that she could never precisely delimit the boundaries of magic and religion. Sir James Frazer was sure that the basic distinction was that religion offered prayers and supplications to a personal power and placed taboos on certain things inimical to social order, while magic attempted by force of will to bring impersonal power under its command and to upset the usual rules of order. Thus religion represents the cohesive factors of the community, and magic the individual rebellion against authority. But neither these nor the other common definitions really work. Magic is about the will to power, certainly, but it resembles religion in recognizing another, more powerful authority, and both religion and magic hope to gain something from that authority. The means of doing so (including sacrifice) are quite similar in some respects in both religion and magic. The rituals of religion and magic are often very similar (as in transubstantiation), the more so in Western culture after the clergy played such a large part in defining and denouncing witches and tended to ascribe to them ceremonies and sacraments very like those of the true faith. The Devil himself, defined as The Adversary, becomes a mirror-reversed picture of God Himself. Witchcraft is a kind of religion, and, to return to Margaret Murray, may be the original, more barbaric religion that was the inspiration for and the basis of the Judeo-Christian tradition and the religions of later prophets from Mohammed to the Moonies and beyond.

The discouerie
of witchcraft,

Wherein the lewde dealing of witches
and witchmongers is notablie detected, the
knauerie of coniurors, the impietie of inchan-
tors, the follie of soothsaiers, the impudent fals-
hood of cousenors, the infidelitie of atheists,
the pestilent practises of Pythonists, the
curiositie of figurecasters, the va-
nitie of dreamers, the begger-
lie art of Alcu-
mystrie,

The abhomination of idolatrie, the horrible art of poisoning, the vertue and power of
naturall magike, and all the conueiances
of Legierdemaine and iugling are deciphered:
and many other things opened, which
haue long lien hidden, howbeit
verie necessarie to
be knowne.

Heerevnto is added a treatise vpon the
nature and substance of spirits and diuels,
&c : all latelie written
by Reginald Scot
Esquire.

1. Iohn 4, 1.

Beleeue not euerie spirit, but trie the spirits, whether they are
of God ; for manie false prophets are gone
out into the world, &c.

1584

6

The Devil and Demons, Magic and Witchcraft In Literature and Folklore

HOW PAGAN SUPERSTITIONS CREATED OUR DEVILS

Thomas Wright (1810–1877), when the *Deutsche Mythologie* of Jakob Grimm appeared, "at once recognized the applicability of Grimm's system to the English middle ages when monks and missionaries yet nourished the old heathen notions." So says Richard M. Dorson in his anthology of British folklorists, *Peasant Customs and Savage Myths*. From the second volume of his valuable collection, comes this text from Wright (1846):

> In the earlier ages of Christianity among the Teutonic people, the monks supposed that the elves and fairies of the people were neither more nor less than so many devils, whose business it was to delude people; so that in transmitting to us the outlines of the popular legends they give them a colouring of which it is not always easy to divest them. At later periods, without going so far as to make them absolutely devils, some of the most intelligent writers had very curious ideas about their origin. Giraldus [1146?–1220?] tells us of a fairy who lived some years with a northern bishop as a faithful servant. Before he left the service of his master, he told him who and what he was. He said that the elves and fairies were a portion of the angels who fell with Lucifer from Heaven; but inasmuch as, though they had been seduced and deluded, they were not so criminal as their fellows, their sentence had been less severe:

219

they were allowed to live on the earth, some of them having their peculiar dwelling-place in the air, others in the waters, some again in trees and fountains, and many in the caverns of the earth. He confessed, also, that as Christianity spread, they had much less liberty than formerly. As much of the popular middle-age legends relating to the fall of the angels was probably rooted on the older mythology, this story may itself be the shadow of an earlier article of pagan creed relating to the origin of the elves.

At the same time, as the monks exerted an influence over the superstitions of the people, in modifying them into apparent accordance with Christianity, these superstitions were also influencing the latter, and without doubt gave rise to that multiplicity and multiformity of demoniacal agency which pervades the monkish legends. In their system the whole world was believed to be peopled with innumerable hordes of devils, who possessed only a certain degree of power, which they used in tormenting, seducing, and misleading mankind. Diseases were often the effect of their malignity, and conflagrations and numerous fatal accidents were commonly supposed to be brought about by their agency. They also exerted an influence over the elements, and caused storms, floods, and even greater convulsions of nature. The monks sometimes invented strange stories to account for the influence which the devils thus exerted, because they were not aware of the real source from which they had been adopted. An unedited English poet of the thirteenth century, after explaining in a popular manner the nature of thunder and lightning, proceeds to show how it happens to cause so much mischief. 'When Christ suffered death,' says he, 'he bound the devil, and broken down hell-gates in order to let out those who suffered there. His visit was attended with such terrible thunder, that the devils have been afraid of thunder ever since; and if any of them happens to be caught in a storm, they fly as quick as wind, and kill men, and destroy trees, &c., which they meet in their way. This is the reason that people are killed in a storm.'

Later Dorson quotes from George Webbe Dasent's *Popular Tales from the Norse* (1859) to the effect that "when Christianity came in, and heathendom fell" the giants "more dull than wicked" and the trolls "more systematically malignant than the Giants" were regarded as devils and demons: then godlike races of the Aesir became evil demons instead of good genial powers, then all the objects of the old popular belief, whether Aesir, Giants, or Trolls, were mingled together in one superstition as 'no canny.'" These creatures of the old religion, the sagas, the folk tales, became uncanny and unholy.

> They were all Trolls, all malignant; and thus it is that, in these tales, the traditions about Odin and his underlings, about the Frost Giants, and about sorcerers and wizards, are confused and garbled; and all supernatural agency that plots man's ill is the work of *Trolls*, whether the agent be the arch enemy himself [The Devil], or giant, or witch, or wizard.

He adds an important note about the origin of these creatures not in the story of the War in Heaven but in the struggles on earth of different tribes of early man. Dasent writes:

> There can be little doubt that in their continued existence amongst the woods, and rocks, and hills, we have a memory of the gradual suppression and extinction of some hostile race, who gradually retired into the natural fastnesses of the land, and speedily became mythic. Nor, if we bear in mind their natural position, and remember how constantly the infamy of sorcery has clung to the Finns and Lapps, shall we have far to go to seek this ancient race, even at the present day. Between this outcast nomad race, which wandered from forest to forest, and from fell to fell, without a fixed place of abode, and the old natural powers and Frost Giants, the minds of the race which adored Odin and the Aesir engendered a monstrous man-eating cross-bre[e]d of supernatural beings, who fled from contact with the intruders as soon as the first great struggle was over, abhorred the light of day, and looked upon agriculture and tillage as a dangerous innovation which destroyed their hunting fields, and was destined finally to root them out from off the face of the earth. This fact appears in countless stories all over the globe, for man is true to himself in all climes, and the savage in Africa or across the Rocky Mountains, dreads tillage and detests the plough as much as any Lapp or Samoyed.

SATAN AS THE HERO OF PARADISE LOST

Leave it to Percy Bysshe Shelley, who was thrown out of college because he sent the dean his essay on *The Necessity of Atheism*, to find in Milton's masterpiece a Devil more admirable than God. From Shelley's *Defence of Poetry*:

Milton's Devil as a moral being is far superior to his God, as one who perseveres in some purpose which he has conceived to be excellent, in spite of adversity and torture, is to one who in the cold security of undoubted triumph inflicts the most horrible revenge upon his enemy, not from mistaken notions of inducing him to repent of a perseverance in enmity, but with the alleged design of exasperating him to new torments. Milton has so far violated the popular creed (if this shall be judged a violation), as to have alleged no superiority of moral virtue to his God over his Devil. And this bold neglect of direct moral purpose is the most decisive proof of Milton's genius.

Where Shelley starts off wrong is in saying that The Devil perseveres in "some purpose which he has conceived to be excellent." The Devil is not engaged willingly in any excellent purpose; he is sinful and knows he is sinning. He is, as someone said of the notorious Earl of Rochester, a sort of "martyr to sin." The Devil means to be nasty and destructive. God does not. When God does wrong He just can't help Himself, I suppose, and I am willing to grant He means well, however painful this may be to most other persons.

COUNTRY MATTERS

Considering that it is not long since agriculture was the basic occupation of mankind, it is strange how our language denigrates the dweller outside the city. Such outlanders are considered outlandish, not civilized, not urbane. Look at words like *churl* and *villain* and the use of *farmer* as an insult.

The early Christians in Britain were city-dwellers and the people who lived out in the countryside for a long time after the introduction of Christianity (by St. Augustine) clung to the Old Religion. They lived on the heaths and they were called *heathens*. The Latin *paganus* (countryman) gave us *pagan*.

Naturally, the devils and demons of the Old Religion had some influence on the New Religion and, as always, Christianity turned pagan gods and goddesses into evil spirits. In the long run the Horned God of the earliest Britons was identified with the Devil of the Christians. The countryside in which the Greek god Pan romped became evil (Pan a kind of destructive force, the cause of panic) as Christianity replaced the old beliefs in the supernatural forces dwelling in nature, forests, rivers, streams, and in the mountains. From pantheism to monotheism!

THE HARVEST FESTIVAL

The pagan festivals of the harvest were put down by early Christianity only to erupt in strange forms. In the 1840s, however, an Anglican priest in rural Cornwall, well aware how the pagan traditions had held on there, revived the Harvest Festival now so common in English churches. He was the Rev. R. S. Hawker. Hawker did not go as far as the old Cornish habit of sacrificing to the gods of fertility by sprinkling blood—perhaps human blood—on the fields, but he piled the altar of the parish church with the fruits of the earth and decorated the church inside and out with garlands.

In the west of England and elsewhere old pagan customs connected with harvest time remain. One superstition tells us to make the last sheaf bound up a big one—and to have it bound up by the fertile human, the female. That way the next crop will be large. Also, corn babies (figures made of straw) are put into the house and corn dollies (which are really a kind of talisman) are made and hung up. These may now be sold to tourists to whom they are mere curiosities, but some people still feel that they have power.

Sacrifices to pagan gods are not conducted now. What the Druids did in Britain we do not know. The only reference to them there (as opposed to on the Continent) is a passing mention in the Latin history of Tacitus. Modern Druids (and there are thousands of them in Britain) have to make up their own ceremonies, but sacrifices to demons are not included. Indeed, modern Druidism seems to be more about poetry than pagan gods.

THE DEVIL IN THE PASSION PLAYS

The medieval cycles of didactic, religious plays is perhaps best represented by the York Cycle, forty-eight episodes running from the Creation (with the Fall of Lucifer) to the Last Judgment. The Devil is featured in the very first of them and was there in all his glory, with horns and tail and trident or pitchfork, on the very first pageant wagon to appear when medieval England gathered in York to participate in a celebration of religious and civic fervor. That created a day-long parade of floats (as we might call them now) that presented the city's craft guilds' individual contributions to telling the stories of religion for the edification and enjoyment of the common people.

In "The Creation and Fall of Lucifer," presented by the Barkers (that is to say, Tanners Guild), God Almighty, "Alpha and Omega, the Life," congratulates Himself on creating the universe and gives Lucifer, an archangel, the title of "Bearer of Light," making him God's "mirror." The Seraphim and Cherubim remain loyal to God, but Lucifer is swollen with pride and with no fear of "losing bliss" he rebels against God's control and is promptly aware that "all goes down": he and the other "bad angels" are thrown out of heaven. The second scene of this brief play is set in hell, where Lucifer and devils argue, "mad with woe." The third scene is back in heaven. God creates mankind to finish His creation and the Cherubim praise Him. The Devil is to rest in baleful hell, though in the very next little play The Devil tempts mankind and causes the Fall. The characters of the second play in the series, "Man's Disobedience and the Fall of Man," are God, an Angel, Adam, Eve, and Satan. It begins in hell with Satan "in a whirl" and determined to do evil. He will betray God by destroying His creation, mankind. In the second scene The Devil appears in the Garden of Eden as a "worm," that is to say a serpent. On the pageant wagon he would have sparkled in a grotesque costume. The Devil's evil work here ends with the Angel driving Adam and Eve out of Paradise.

The English plays based on the Bible had their equivalents in France, in Italy's *sacre rappresentazioni*, in Spain's *autos sacramentales*, in German, Austrian, and other versions, too. These plays educated the folk in religion and entertained them as well, creating a secular drama to follow and eventually leading from the participation of amateurs drawn from the guilds to traveling players who were the beginnings of the professional theater as revived in the West after centuries of no theater during the Dark Ages. The verse of the early plays (for decoration and as a mnemonic device) gave way partly to prose, seriousness gave way partly to comic invention, and so on.

If drama is conflict, hardly a better conflict for a play could be imagined than that between God and the Adversary, unless it was that between Everyman and Death, the subject of the most famous of the morality plays which joined the cycle plays in bringing religious drama to the multitude.

DEVILS AND DEMONS IN MEDIEVAL DRAMA

The Greeks had their satyrs (with hairy legs and cloven hoofs) and the medieval Christian drama had its devils and demons (some of whom had cloven feet and horns and tails). The Roman comedy had its clowns and the medieval Christian drama relieved the didacticism with devils and demons in similar carnivalesque roles, roles which eventually produced the disruptive character of the Vice. Just as the good guys had costume traditions—God's face was gilded, angels had wings, saints had halos—so did the bad guys. Their costumes might be funny, or frightening, or grotesque with bat wings or horrible masks. The Devil appeared with horns and a tail and sometimes a trident or pitchfork for tossing sinners into hell.

Devils and demons could be imps or dragons or in a number of other guises, but they were generally costumed in blue, red, or black, colors used for symbolism, being a natural borrowing from the use of colors in the vestments of the church and the stained-glass windows.

Herod, who is said in one old chronicle to have jumped off the pageant wagon and "raged in the crowd" (a modern breaking of the barrier between stage and audience that must have shocked and delighted the crowds gathered in medieval streets to see the procession of plays go by) was the arch villain. The Crusades' enemies were recalled in his crowned turban. Perhaps anti-Semitism accounted for his huge hooked nose. He, like the devils and demons, tended to overact the villain. Hamlet's advice to the players is not to "out-Herod Herod" with what would be called in the nineteenth century (from bad performances of *Hamlet* itself), hammy gestures. Herod was the epitome of exaggerated delivery.

Ironically, out of the rituals of the Roman Catholic Church, which banned the drama and excommunicated all actors because of the rampant obscenity of late Roman comedy, came one of the two strands of medieval drama: the liturgical drama, commencing with the *Quem quæritis?* (Whom Do you Seek?) trope of the Easter Mass. The other source was the native folk drama. Both provided plenty of devil or demon characters for the Miracle Plays, the Mystery Plays, the entertainments at court or in the great halls of the wealthy, the two-boards-and-a-passion entertainments at fairs, the puppeteers and *commedia* mountebanks, the strolling players, the mummers, and all the rest of medieval theater. Devils and demons were naturals for the feasts of fools, the anti-masque, raucous dancing interludes, comedy, horror, rowdy village folk celebrations to blow off steam, and variety (some cycles ran from dawn to dusk, playlet after playlet), among other things. Shakespeare in *Twelfth Night* mentions the old tradition of the Vice "with dagger of lath," cleverness, jokes, a direct descendant of the assistant devils and knockabout demons of the old plays.

But then, in Shakespeare's century, The Devil ceased to be regarded as stupid, and his devils and demons began to be thought of as less clownish and were more feared. Laws were passed against witchcraft, repealed, and passed again. People began to wonder if the devils and demons were so funny after all.

FIFTEEN CLASSIC BOOKS ON EARLY DRAMA

Bridges-Adams, W., *The Irresistible Theatre* (1957)
Cargill, Oscar, *Drama and Liturgy* (1930)

Chambers, Sir Edmund K., *The Medieval Stage* (2 vols., 1903)
Cohen, Gustav, *Le Théâtre en France en Moyen Age* (1948)
Craig, Hardin, *English Religious Drama of the Middle Ages* (1955)
Cushman, L. W., *The Devil and the Vice . . . before Shakespeare* (1900)
Gregor, Josef, *Das Theater des Mittelalteres* (1937)
Mill, A. J., *Medieval Plays in Scotland* (1927)
Nicoll, Allardyce, *The Development of the Theatre* (1937)
Norris, A., *The Early Cornish Drama* (1859)
Purvis, Rev. J. S., *The York Cycle of Mystery Plays* (1957)
Rossiter, A. P., *English Drama from Early Times to the Elizabethans* (1950)
Stratman, Rev. Carl J., *Bibliography of Medieval Drama* (1954)
Wickham, Glynne, *Early English Stages, 1300–1660* (1959)
Young, Karl, *The Drama of the Medieval Church* (2 vols., 1933)

THE DEVIL IN LITERATURE

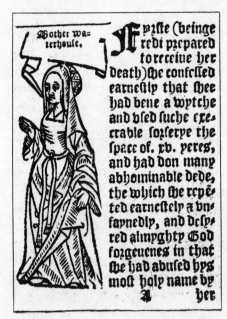

Mother Waterhouse, says an old English pamphlet, was executed because she "had bene a wytche."

Half a Hundred Short Stories, English and American:
Allingham, Margery, "The Wink"
Asimov, Isaac, "The Brazen Locked Room"
Beerbohm, Sir Max, "Enoch Soames"
Belloc, Hilaire, "The Story of St. Dunstan"
Benson, A. C., "The Slype House"
Blackwood, Algernon, "Secret Worship"
Bloch, R., "How Like a God"
Bradbury, Ray, "The Burning Man"
Buchan, John (Lord Tweedsmuir), "Watcher by the Threshold"
Cabell, James Branch, "Some Ladies and Jurgen"
de Camp, L. Sprague & F. Pratt, *"Caveat Emptor"*
Carter, L., "Out of the Ages"
Collier, John, "The Devil, George, and Rosie"
Coppard, A. E., "The Martyrdom of Solomon"
De Quincey, Thomas, "The Dice"

Derleth, August W., "Mr. Ames' Devil"
Edward, Lord Dunsany, "Three Infernal Jokes"
Edward, Lord Lytton, "The Lawyer Who Cost His Client Nothing"
Ellison, Hal, "Deal from the Bottom"
Fast, Howard, "Tomorrow's *Wall Street Journal*"
Garnett, Richard, "Madame Lucifer"
Harte, Bret, "The Devil and the Broker"
Hawthorne, Nathaniel, "Young Goodman Brown"
Heinlein, R. A., "Magic, Inc."
Housman, Laurence, "Little St. Michael"
Irving, Washington, "The Devil and Tom Walker"
James, Montague Rhodes, "Count Magnus"
King, Stephen, "Jerusalem's Lot"
LeFanu, James Sheridan, "Sir Dominick's Bargain"
Leinster, M., "The Devil's Henchman"
Lovecraft, H. P., "Horror at Red Hook"
Lumley, B., "What Dark God?"
MacCreagh, G., "Dr. Muncing, Exorcist"
Machen, Arthur, "The Great God Pan"
Marriott-Watson, H. B., "The Devil of the Marsh"
Melville, Herman, "The Lightning-Rod Man"
Mitchell, E. P., "The Devil's Funeral"
O'Sullivan, V., "The Bargain of Rupert Orange"
Pei, Mario, "The Devil's Christmas"
Poe, Edgar Allan, "Never Bet the Devil Your Head"
Powys, T. F., "The Devil"
Roach, M. K., "The Witch of Wellfleet"
Scott, Sir Walter, "The Fortunes of Martin Waldeck"
Smith, Lady, "Tamar"
Summers, Montague, "The Grimmoire"
Thackeray, William Makepeace, "The Devil's Wager"
Twain, Mark, "The Mysterious Stranger"
Wells, H. G., "The Devotée of Art"
Wren, P. C., "The Devil and Digby Geste"
Wyndham, J., "Technical Slip"

Also consider:
Bowen, Elizabeth, "The Demon Lover"
Defoe, Daniel, "The Friendly Demon"
Garnett, Richard, "The Demon Pope"

Jagendorf, M. A., "The Demon and the Rabbi"
Priestley, J. B., "The Demon King"
Singer, Isaac Bashevis, "The Last Demon"
Turgenev, Ivan, "Bubnoff and the Demon"

In addition, there are English translations of foreign stories. Sample French authors:
de Balzac, Honoré, "The Devil's Disciple"
Baudelaire, Charles, "The Generous Gambler"
Gautier, Théophile, "Two Actors for One Role"
de Maupassant, Guy, "The Legend of Mont St.-Michel"
Rabelais, François, "How a Junior Devil Was Fooled . . ."
There are also plays from the York Cycle (*The Fall of the Angels*, *The Harrowing of Hell*, *The Temptation of Christ*) to David Mamet (*Bobby Gould in Hell*), poems, etc.

DEVILS AND DEMONS IN LITERATURE

A full account under this rubric would be a huge tome, but we can say briefly that The Devil has been a major figure in literature (especially in the works of Marlowe, Milton, and Goethe), that demons are welcomed in horror fiction and have greatly impacted the monsters of science fiction, and that probably the most familiar theme is, in Samuel Taylor Coleridge's famous phrase, "woman wailing for her demon lover." A tony read is Toni Reed's *Demon-Lovers and their Victims in British Fiction* (1988).

THE SCRIPTURES

"There was a war in heaven: Michael and his angels fought against the dragon; and the dragon fought, and his angels,

"And prevailed not.

"The great dragon was cast out, that old serpent, called the Devil, and Satan, which deceiveth the whole world." *Revelation of St. John the Divine* XII:7–9.

"Be sober, be vigilant; because your adversary, as a roaring lion, walketh about, seeking whom he may devour." *I Peter* V:8.

"Satan came also.

"And the Lord said unto Satan, Whence comest thou? Then Satan answered the Lord and said, From going to and fro in the earth, and from walking up and down in it." *Job* I:6–7.

"And the Lord God said unto the serpent, Because thou hast done this, thou art cursed above all cattle, and above every beast of the field; upon thy belly shalt thou go, and dust shalt thou eat all the days of thy life." *Genesis* III:14.

"Put on the whole armor of God.

"For we wrestle not against flesh and blood, but against principalities, against powers, against the rulers of the darkness of this world, against spiritual wickedness in high places.

"Wherefore take unto you the whole armor of God, that ye may be able to withstand in the evil day, and having done all, to stand." *Ephesians* VI:11–13.

THE BOOK OF COMMON PRAYER

"From all blindness of heart, from pride, vainglory, and hypocrisy; from envy; hatred and malice, and all uncharitableness,
    Good Lord, deliver us. . . .
    From all the deceits of the world, the flesh, and the devil."

THE KORAN

"Whoso has done an atom's worth of good shall see it; and whoso has done an atom's worth of evil shall see it." *Sura* 99:7–8.

THE DEVIL IN DANTE'S HELL

Three is the dominant number in Dante's *Commedia*, which we praise as *The Divine Comedy* (1310–1321). It is written in three-line stanzas (*terza rima*) and has three sections (*cantiche*) of thirty-three cantos each (plus one more for the perfection of the number 100). At the bottom of the *Inferno*, farthest away from God in heaven, is Satan, the Adversary, whom Dante thinks of as Lucifer. Dante gives him a triple set of wings and three heads: in one mouth he munches Judas Iscariot and in the other two a couple of Italians, Brutus and Cassius. These surely were not worthy of being the equals in betrayal of Judas but Dante had personal axes to grind; he thought of himself as much betrayed by fellow Italians as was Julius Caesar.

    Because the traditional fires of hell did not sound unpleasant to early Europeans freezing in the north, the northern hell was icy. Dante manages to get both fire and ice into his *Inferno*, though that name stresses fire. His Devil, however uncomfortable home may be, is more of a homebody than an active, rampaging, restless Devil as usually portrayed in demonology and witchcraft.

Dante's Devil nonetheless, is a striking figure and most cleverly conceived. But one would expect that from Dante, a writer so brilliant he managed to put a pope he didn't like into hell when he wasn't even dead at the time of Dante's writing. Read *Inferno* to see how he does it.

THE DEVIL AND THE CRONE

All through the Middle Ages folk tales were repeated about The Devil and old women, greatly affecting popular belief in witches and giving the witch a character with which she is still saddled today. In the time of Erasmus, Melancthon, Hans Sachs, and others in early modern Germany, the tales of the old woman and The Devil took interesting new turns (as is demonstrated in Sigrid Braunder's doctoral dissertation edited by Robert H. Brown as *Fearless Wives & Frightened Shrews*, 1995). The late Prof. Brauner taught courses on witches at the University of Massachusetts at Amherst, putting the witch into the lively modern feminist discussions. It is not too much to say that the witch represented a way in which women could challenge the Establishment and that the persecution of witches had a lot to do with the Establishment defending itself and, likewise, giving vent to its prejudices against females.

Tom, Tennessee Williams's autobiographical character in *The Glass Menagerie*, vents his spleen on his annoying mother by calling her a witch. *Bitch* and *witch* both have long histories in connection with misogyny. I say elsewhere but it is worth repeating here: the history of witch persecutions is part of the history of the persecution of women. The witchcraft trials and executions oppressed all women and for ages thereafter, and they go a long way toward explaining the need for and the nature of modern women's movements for identity and independence.

SHAKESPEARE AND THE SUPERNATURAL

Shakespeare may indeed be, as his friend Jonson said, "not of an age but for all time," but he was also greatly in tune with his audiences because he shared their beliefs, including the Elizabethan and Jacobean convictions about magic and witchcraft, a world of good and bad angels, a world full of devils and demons. His world is studied by scholars along those lines in such books as T. A. Spalding's *Elizabethan Demonology*, Dame Frances Yates's *Giordano Bruno and the Hermetic Tradition*, and A. D. J. Macfarlane's

Witchcraft in Tudor and Stuart England, to name but a few. It is also clearly visible on the stage in his plays, with the ghosts in *Julius Caesar* and *Hamlet,* Lady Macbeth calling on demons in what superstition prefers to call "The Scottish Play" and her husband coping with witches, Caliban having a witch for a mother in *The Tempest* and a sorcerer for an employer, and so on. Witchcraft is also in *Henry VI, Antony and Cleopatra,* etc.

The people of Shakespeare's time loved Christopher Marlowe's *The Tragical History of the Life and Death of Doctor Faustus; The Witch of Edmonton,* with the popular Thomas Dekker as one of the collaborators; Robert Greene's *Friar Bacon and Friar Bungay,* which has a marvelous talking, severed head; Thomas Heywood and Richard Broome's *The Late Lancashire Witches;* Thomas Middleton's *The Witch;* and more. The list could go on and on.

Shakespeare's is a dramatic world in which the supernatural is deeply ingrained. That people have changed only superficially about the supernatural is well illustrated by the fact that none of the Bard's old-fashioned beliefs stand in the way of modern audiences understanding and appreciating his works. We even grasp *The Winter's Tale.*

See also Thomas Arnold Spalding's *Elizabethan Demonology* (1880).

THE ESSENCE OF WITCHES

The great English playwright John Webster, author of *The Duchess of Malfi* (in which, you will remember, one of her atrocious brothers succumbs to lycanthropy), brilliantly sums up witches' motivations in a sentence in his posthumously published *Displaying of Supposed Witchcraft.* He asserts that The Devil prompts them to let loose their "hatred, malice, revenge and envy" and turn poisoners and worse.

And *why* do they sin?

"Who knows what sin is," asks Charlie Chaplin as his *Monsieur Verdoux* (1947), "born as it was from Heaven, from God's fallen angel; who knows what mysterious destiny it serves?"

SUPERSTITIONS

How superstitiously we mind our evils!
The throwing down of salt, or crossing of a hare,
Bleeding at nose, the stumbling of a horse,
Or singing of a cricket, are of power
To daunt whole man in us.
—John Webster, *The Duchess of Malfi*

Holinshed's *Chronicles* showed Shakespeare's, Macbeth, and Banquo meeting The Weird Sisters. The "blasted heath," however, has a flourishing tree, such as that under which these *norns* lived, according to Norse mythology. (They are "weird" because one of them is named Urd in Norse.)

WITCH WEATHER

The three witches in *Macbeth* say they cannot go as far as drowning at sea the husband of a woman who repulsed them with "aroint thee, witch"; but though his ship "may not be lost/Yet it be tempest-tossed." For a long time witches were thought to be able to bring not only bad luck but bad weather. In defiance of Mark Twain's dictum that "everybody talks about the weather, but nobody does anything about it," the witches, with incantations and dance, were *doing* something, though never anything good.

Just as they could bring disease or death on man or beast, they could also affect the elements, ruining crops, and (despite Shakespeare) sink ships and cause other grievous damage. Audbjorga, in *Gisla-saga*, ran around a house widdershins (symbolizing the reversal of good in nature), sniffed to the cardinal points of the compass (drawing in the winds), and caused such snow, sleet, winds, floods that twelve people perished before she was done.

SHAKESPEARE'S WORLD

In her book entitled *The Scythe of Saturn*, Linda Woodbridge of the University of Alberta, shows that "early modern science was often piggybacked on magical beliefs" and that the world and work of Shakespeare (and his contemporaries) was riddled with magical beliefs. She puts it this way: "Magical beliefs of his culture still washed daily against his mental shores." However far from the old religion's superstition the vaunted rationalism of The Reformation was, however anti-ritualistic and reasonable, the people continued superstition, scapegoating sacrifices, and age-old fears of The Devil and his infernal ministers. The power of magic to overturn the laws of nature was greatly feared, and over all it ruled Satan and Saturn, the latter being the god of the saturnalian orgies, death and resurrection, fertility and the eating of his own children, and charivari and chaos.

In the opportunities imagined for the lowest to overthrow the highest by powers derived from The Devil lay a powerful threat.

Some people even today are attracted by the possibility that the last shall be first, the downtrodden shall be revenged upon their masters, the young will reverse the domination of the old, the poor that of the rich. Shakespeare's time may superficially look very different from our "more advanced" age, but we still connect the supernatural with political assassination (as Shakespeare did in his "the king must die" tragedies) and fertility rituals with love stories (as Shakespeare did in his comedies). We still see what he saw in "the language of seasonal magic." We still see ghosts, as Macbeth and Julius Caesar and Hamlet did. We still have our tinpot imitations of Prospero. We still are confronted with witches on the desolate heaths of our melancholy, and they still want to spread seeds of evil that can grow if the soil there is fertile. We are still exposed to "the equivocation of the fiend that lies like truth." We consult "channelers."

AN ELIZABETHAN STORY OF THE DEVIL

From Philip Stubbes's *Two Wonderful and Rare Examples* (1581) in the old spelling for a change:

> And nowe I will proceede to shewe onen other as straunge a judgement happening in Leicestershire, in a towne called Donnington, where dwelt a poore man named Iohn Twell, who deceased, owing vnto one Oswalde Bowcer the summe of fiue shilling, which the sayde Oswalde did forgive the sayde man before named, as he laye vpon his death bedde; but the sayde Oswaldes wife, called Ioane, would in no way forgiue the sayde Twell, as long (she sayde) as she had to live. Whereupon, not long after, the Deuill appeared vnto her in the form of the sayd Twell deceased, expressing all the lynea-

mentes of the body of the dead man: which might well be, for we reade in the Bible, in the like order did Satan counterfeit the body of Samuell. But to proceede to the matter: this euill spirit uttered vnto her these speeches, and said he had brought her money from Iohn Twell deceased, and willed her incontinent to disburse the sayd money vnto her husband for his paines. Which she, with as covetous a desire, receyved, saying, God thanke you. She had no sooner named God, but the money consumed away from betweene her handes, as it were a vapour of smoake, tyll it was all consumed: wherewith the Deuill, giving her a most fearfull and sore stroke, vanished out of her sight. Wherewith her whole body became as blacke as pitche, replenished all over with a moste filthy scurfe and other things.

FROM THE TRAGICAL HISTORY OF
THE LIFE AND DEATH OF DOCTOR FAUSTUS
by Christopher Marlowe

[*Enter Valdes and Cornelius*]
Faust. Valdes, sweet Valdes and Cornelius,
Know that your words have won me at the last
To practice magic and concealèd arts;
Yet not your words only, but mine own fantasy,
That will receive no object, for my head
But ruminates on necromantic skill.
Philosophy is odious and obscure,
Both law and physic are for petty wits,
Divinity is basest of the three,
Unpleasant, harsh, contemptible, and vile,
'Tis magic, magic, that hath ravish'd me.
Then, gentle friends, aid me in this attempt,
And I, that have with concise syllogisms
Graveled the pastors of the German church,
And made the flowering pride of Wittenberg
Swarm to my problems, as the infernal spirits
On sweet Musæus when he came to hell,
Will be as cunning as Agrippa was,
Whose shadows made all Europe honour him.
Vald. Faustus, these books, thy wit, and our experience

Shall make all nations to canonize us.
As Indian Moors obey their Spanish lords
So shall the spirits of every element
Be always serviceable to us three:
Like lions shall they guard us when we please.
Like Almain rutters with their horsemen's staves,
Or Lapland giants, trotting by our sides;
Sometimes like women, or unwedded maids,
Shadowing more beauty in their airy brows
Than in the white breasts of the queen of love;
From Venice shall they drag huge argosies
And from America the golden fleece
That yearly stuffs old Philip's treasury,
If learned Faustus will be resolute.
Faust. Valdes, as resolute am I in this
As thou to live; therefore object it not.
Corn. The miracles that magic will perform
Will make thee vow to study nothing else.
He that is grounded in astrology,
Enrich'd with tongues, well seen in minerals,
Hath all the principles magic doth require.
Then doubt not, Faustus, but to be renowned
And more frequented for this mystery
Than heretofore the Delphian oracle.
The spirits tell me they can dry the sea
And fetch the treasure of all foreign wrecks—
Ay, all the wealth that our forefathers hid
Within the massy entrails of the earth.
Then tell me, Faustus, what shall we three want?
Faust. Nothing, Cornelius. O this cheers my soul!
Come, show me some demonstrations magical
That I may conjure in some lusty grove
And have these joys in full possession.
Vald. Then haste thee to some solitary grove
And bear wise Bacon's and Abanus' works,
The Hebrew Psalter and New Testament;
And whatsoever else is requisite
We will inform thee ere our conference cease.
Corn. Valdes, first let him know the words of art,
And then, all other ceremonies learned,

Faustus may try his cunning by himself.
Vald. First I'll instruct thee in the rudiments,
And then wilt thou be perfecter than I.
Faust. Then come and dine with me, and after meat
We'll canvass every quiddity thereof;
For ere I sleep I'll try what I can do:
This night I'll conjure though I die therefore.
[*Exeunt.*]

THE DEVIL AND DANIEL WEBSTER

The Devil has appeared in much modern literature. Although he has been written about by much better authors (Shaw among them), Stephen Vincent Benét's slight short story called *The Devil and Daniel Webster* may hold pride of place as being the most familiar.

Not much superior to Washington Irving's *The Devil and Tom Walker*, Benét's *The Devil and Daniel Webster* was a little story for *Saturday Evening Post* that made it into an anthology by Benét (*Thirteen O'Clock*, 1937), captured the public imagination, and was made into a one-act opera (score

Folk art of Emilia (Italy), Church of Santa Maria del Monte, sixteenth century. The Madonna exorcizes demons for the peasantry.

by David Moore) and a popular film (*All that Money Can Buy*, 1941).

The plot of *The Devil and Daniel Webster* involves Jabez Stone, a New Hampshire farmer, who sells his soul to The Devil for ten years of prosperity. (Leave it to a Yankee; such deals usually are for seven years.) When the time comes to pay up, Stone wants to get out of the deal and calls upon the great New Hampshire orator, Daniel Webster (1782–1852), to defend him before a jury of notorious villains that The Devil assembles. Webster wins the case. The Devil (here called Mr. Scratch) is bested; it is a long folklore tradition.

For devils in more substantial works, try any of the Faust tales, *The Devil is an Ass* by Ben Jonson, or *The Screwtape Letters* (delightfully witty and wise) by C. S. Lewis. The Devil appears as Mr. Applegate in the musical *Damn Yankees*. I've played him.

SALEM IN NINETEENTH-CENTURY LITERATURE

Anon., *The Salem Belle: A Tale of 1692* (1844)
Anon., *Caroline Hargrave, The Merchant's Daughter* (1845)
Barker, Benjamin, *Zoraida* (1845)
Barker, James Nelson, *Superstition* (1824)
Child, Lydia Maria, *Hobomok* (published anonymously, 1824)
DuBois, Constance Goddard, *Martha Corey: A Tale of the Salem Witchcraft* (1890)
Felt. Joseph Barlow, *Annals of Salem* (1827)
Hawthorne, Nathaniel, *The House of the Seven Gables* (1851)
Longfellow, Henry Wadsworth, *Giles Corey of the Salem Farms* (1868)
Mackie, Pauline B., *Ye Little Salem Maide* (1898)

THE MARRIAGE OF HEAVEN AND HELL

I have to confess that Blake, not Milton, wrote what I consider to be the best poem on Satan. For the background of William Blake's poem on Satan, whom he considered the prince of this world, there are literary articles such as Peter A. Schock's in *English Literary History* (Summer 1993) and the many books on this Romantic poet. Blake made Satan into a sort of pre-Byronic, Romantic hero and totally revised our concepts of hell and The Devil's fall. Moral and political values both were redefined in Blake's masterwork, not as obscurely as in *The Four Zoas* and *The Book of Thel*. Read Blake, the thinking man's Milton. This English writer's mind is worthy of comparison with Goethe's.

THE MONK

So famous was his ripping yarn called *The Monk* (published when he was twenty), that Matthew Lewis (1775–1818) is almost always remembered as "Monk" Lewis. *The Monk*, a milestone in the history of the Gothic novel, came from a hint Lewis found in the annals of the Inquisition. The book is demon-haunted, ornately written but swift for all its length. It is a real rouser.

A Dominican prior of Madrid has been involved with a randy nun. They are arrested by the Holy Inquisition and tortured for confessions. She breaks under duress and is condemned to the stake. Will he ever see her again? Wait. Don Ambrosio holds out longer.

She was in fact a witch and she appears to him in his cell saying he can sell his soul to The Devil and escape the church's punishment. She leaves him a magic book with instructions to read the first four lines of page seven. She vanishes. He is then dragged from his cell and threatened with torture and gives in. He is condemned to be summarily executed.

Back in his cell, he takes the book and reads the passage indicated. The Devil appears and bargains for his soul. Don Ambrosio signs a pact yielding his soul to The Devil. Big moment. Tableau.

The walls dissolve (a nice touch onstage) and The Devil flies away with the evil monk to the mountains, but then The Devil drops him into a ravine. There, in terrible agony, he dies, and the waters rush his body away to—what?

ALL HALLOWS' EVE

Charles Williams's novel (1945) about "the essence of evil" centers on a priest in London called Clerk Simon, another Simon Magus, another Jewish magician with a grateful following because of his cures and apparently peaceful message. But he has alter egos in China and Russia and with them he intends to dominate the world. Betty, like her mother Lady Wallingford, is under Clerk Simon's power, and he proposes to murder to provide him with a link to the world of spirits. He is checked on this by someone in the world of the dead, which parallels the world of the living in this complex book, and Clerk Simon goes to hell. The other Jewish magician, Jesus, prevails. "Thou hast conquered, O Pale Gallilean!" Christ remains to meet the next and final antichrist.

Bernard MGinn writes: "As portrayals of the conflict between essential good and evil, Williams' novels occupy a special place in modern English literature." A novel with The Devil himself as a character might be as unconvincing as one that features the Vampire Lestat or some other such creature, but Clerk Simon is eerily believable despite all the mystery and mysticism in *All Hallows' Eve*. Damien of *Omen* fame couldn't even rack up platinum records as a rock star, let alone dominate the world credibly in *The Final Solution*. Clerk Simon comes surprisingly close to dominating the world, and we worry and wonder at how close he came to success.

WILLIAM HARRISON AINSWORTH, WRITER OF ROMANCE

Ainsworth (1805–1882) was trained in the law in both Manchester and London but early turned to literary pursuits as a writer and a publisher. His thirty-nine novels were chiefly historical, but from the beginning of his writing career (with a melodrama reminiscent of Charles Maturin and graveyard reveries and stories echoing "Monk" Lewis), there was always as much of the Gothic in his work as there was of Sir Walter Scott. Scott supported Ainsworth's first novel in 1826 and contributed poetry to one of Ainsworth's annual periodicals. The master helped the neophyte.

Ainsworth reached the height of his popularity with his tales of the highwayman *Jack Sheppard* (1839), of Lady Jane Grey in *The Tower of London* (1840), in *Old St. Paul's* (1841), *The Miser's Daughter* (1842), and *Windsor Castle* (1843). In both *Rookwood* (1834) and *Jack Sheppard*, Ainsworth encouraged some sympathy for breakers of the law. Clearly he was fascinated by the violent outsider, and so were his many readers. This penchant rules in the work most relevant here, Ainsworth's tale of *The Lancashire Witches*, a three-volume novel of 1849.

In this historical novel based on real witch trials in the reign of King James I (1613), already used as sensational material by such dramatists as Thomas Shadwell (1642?–1692) and commented on by Sir Walter Scott in his *Letters on Demonology and Witchcraft*, Ainsworth tries to keep an objective point of view but

A protective pentacle, "The god hath covered." Put a copy of this pentacle in a white pocket made of a white handkerchief boiled in 3 cups of water (with one pinch of salt) for 9 minutes, dried, and sewn together. Wear it under your outer clothes, the design outward. Pray as you pin it on, "I am surrounded by the pure white light of God. Nothing but good shall come to me. Nothing but good shall go out from me. I give thanks."

seems, if anything, to come down on the side of the witches. He does not doubt their crimes: he believes they really were witches, not deluded women, and that they were vicious, not victimized. As David Punter puts it in *The Literature of Terror* (1980), in the novel, "the good liberals are all on the side of the witches, and try to defend them against harassment," but because Ainsworth believes in dangerous witches, this "makes the good liberals appear rather foolish."

This sympathy for the downtrodden in Gothic novels aimed at a proletarian public is still to be seen in popular novels about witchcraft. There is no doubting that those who deal in the diabolical are evil, but at the same time, there is an alleged attractiveness in them and the good people who are dedicating themselves to rooting out evil are often portrayed as nasty and narrow minded, of doubtful motivation, and tainted with pleasure in persecution.

GERMAN ROMANTIC TALES

Many of these deal with The Devil, demons, and other aspects of the supernatural and are treated with casual objectivity as in the work of Ludwig Tieck (1773–1853) or in a bizarre way as in the works of E. T. A. Hoffmann (1776–1822). A good example is Hoffman's *Die Elixiere des teufels* (*The Devil's Elixirs*, c. 1815, translated by R. Taylor, 1963). Offenbach's opera *The Tales of Hoffmann* is well known. Less well remembered is the fact that Hoffmann wrote an opera of his own with a libretto by the Freiherr de la Motte Fouqué. It is *Undine* (1813), based on Fouqué's story of the same title (1811), and it is about a water sprite who marries a mortal, a subject taken up in the modern French play *Ondine* (Jean Giraudoux, 1937) and elsewhere.

The influence of German tales of the supernatural was especially strong on American writers of the beginning of the nineteenth century.

For folklore, see Werner Harald Wagner's *Teufel und Gott in der deutschen Volkssage* (1930).

A FEW RARE BOOKS ON THE DEVIL
IN UNITED STATES LITERATURE

Cranch, Christopher Pearse, *Satan: A Libretto* (1874)
Draper, John W., *History of the Conflict between Religion and Science* (1874)
Dunn, Nathaniel, *Satan Chained: A Poem* (1875)
Green, J. W., *Satan Conquered; or, The Son of God Victorious* (1844)

North, Sterling, *Speak of the Devil* (1945)
Stein, William B., *Hawthorne's Faust . . .* (1953)

POSTMODERN TAROT

Brian Williams in the *PoMo Tarot* plays with the ancient deck: the Hanged Man is "All Tied Up," Justice is "Just Desserts," and for all I know, the Broken Tower may be one of the two traditional American political parties, struck by lightning. The most famous deck remains the rather off-putting one designed by Aleister Crowley. The Tarot works. However, the miraculous part is not the magical power from outside, but the fact that human beings are conscious of their own existence and have a whole world of inner space that we are just beginning to explore. The best book on this fascinating subject of inner exploration is by Bill Butler.

WHAT ARE THE CHILDREN READING?

It is significant that modern children are brought up not so much to fear the night's dark agents of the grim Grimm Brothers' horrendous stories as to enjoy the non-threatening witches in the juvenile literature of today. Today's kids learn that witches are little, "not-so-witchy," funny, like the cartoon *Broom Hilda*. Retellings such as Ann Petry's *Tituba of Salem Village* do not try to be frightening. Here are many more or less randomly selected titles now almost all in print in America:

Adams, Adrienne, *A Woggle of Witches*
Barry, Margaret, *Simon and the Witch*
Breslaw, Elaine, *Tituba, Reluctant Witch . . .*
Bridwell, Norman, *The Witch's Christmas*
Briggs, K. M., *Kate Crackernuts*
Calif, Ruth, *The Over-the-Hill Witch*
Chew, Ruth, *Witch in the House*
Civardi, Anne, *The Wacky Book of Witches*
Coombs, Patrick, *Dori and the Pin Witch*
Craig, Janet, *The Boo-Hoo Witch*
Dahl, Roald, *The Witches*
DeLage, Ida, *The Old Witch and the Dragon*
Dicks, Terrance, *Meet the MacMagics*
Fitzgerald, B., *Winkie, The Cross-Eyed Witch*
Freedman, Don, *Space Witch*

THE VAMPIRE AND SEX

The vampire legend has enabled many writers in repressed societies (such as Victorian Britain) to write about sexual violence, sadism, and masochism in printable ways. Bram Stoker's *Dracula* reeks with incubus overtones and lesser writers in the genre make the sexual component even more obvious, sometimes combining it with deliberate pornography. Modern vampire films have often commercially combined sex and sensationalism with stalking vampires.

The Argentinian playwright José Gonzalez Castillo in *Los Invertidos* (The Inverts) makes the connection between vampirism and homosexuality, clearly debatable but examined by David William Foster in *Latin-American Review* 22:2 (Spring 1989) more frankly than is usually the case.

A gay vampire appears in Roman Polanski's film *The Fearless Vampire Killers*, and there is a considerable amount of "camp" in other vampire films. Regarding sexual targets as food is a principal component of pedophiliacs ("chicken queens"), and gays refer to sailors as "sea food." It smacks of sympathetic magic.

"THE BEAST" ALEISTER CROWLEY IN LITERATURE

It is not surprising that, having striven so hard to make himself a colorful figure, Aleister Crowley should have been taken up by W. Somerset Maugham and put into such fiction as *Of Human Bondage* (1915), where Crowley appears as Cronshaw, and *The Magician* (1908), where he appears as the "mystic mountebank" Oliver Haddo. In the same book, Rose Kelly, who married Crowley two weeks after she met him and was fascinated by him for six years thereafter (when she divorced him and married someone else), appears as Margaret Dauncey. Julian Symonds thinks Crowley also inspired Dr. Trelawney in Anthony Powell's series of novels *A Dance to the Music of Time* (1951–1976).

MR. ISAACS

Marion Crawford met in Simla around 1880 an "interesting man" whom he made the protagonist of the novel *Mr. Isaacs* (1882). The man was Alexander Jacob, an astrologer and magician, conjurer and con man, spy and dealer in precious stones, and "a man who knows more of the mystic secrets of India than any other man," according to Col. Newnham Davis, who put him (as Mr. Emmanuel) in *Jadoo* (1898). Rudyard Kipling called Jacob "Lurgan Sahib" in his novel of India, *Kim* (1901). Jacob died in 1921.

THE HAUNTED CASTLE

This is not only the title of a book of literary criticism of the Gothic novel published by Eino Railo (1927), but it is also one of the favorite locales of Gothic fiction. The castle, like the convent, in these frightening novels is often the site of diabolical rites conducted in the dead of night. If the castle or convent or ancient house is partly in romantic ruins, all the better. Ruins held (and still hold, in fact) strong appeal for lovers of the Gothic and the occult.

In these decaying environs, one of the most common plot devices used is the decay of virtue (or sense) and the pact with The Devil, always sure to bring in important figures (The Evil One himself or some demonic delegate) and crucial action (the selling of an immortal soul) in a satisfying atmosphere of superstition and dread. *The Haunted Castle* is particularly good on Matthew Lewis and the terrible pact in *The Monk*, but it, likewise, places that sensational success in the context of the pact tradition, which often serves to hold together the rather loose, if often thrilling, episodes of the typical Gothic novel. Most of all, the pact must have a predictable and moral end to it, so the final destruction of the villain who deals in deviltry and death is expectable and can be counted on to lend closure to a series of thrills that toy with the taboo but must be punished and otherwise would go on interminably. Just as the doomed House of Usher, cracked, must fall down in the long run, so the doomed signer of a terrible pact will one day meet his end, too, and in no less dramatic a fashion. In the end, it teaches the lesson that the temporary success of the transgressor is and must of necessity be followed by dire retribution.

U. Graf, *The Hermit and The Devil*, Swiss copper engraving of 1515.

DR. JEKYLL AND MR. HYDE

This short novel by Robert Louis Stevenson (1850–1894), wrote John Mason Brown in an introduction to the Limited Editions Club version

(1952), is "melodrama, sulfurous and appalling, which by the sheer black magic of its telling is lifted into literature." It is, in fact, a less subtle but far more famous story than Stevenson's other great tale of evil and guilt, *Markheim*, and it is one of the most famous discussions of the good and evil in our human composition ever penned. Moreover, it is a thrilling read: I wrote notes for the Enriched Classics edition (1972) and know how popular the book was in the schools.

The result of one of Stevenson's nightmares ("I was dreaming a fine bogey tale" he said when his wife woke him) rapidly recorded the next morning, destroyed, then rewritten, this "strange case" was first issued as a shilling paperback in 1885. It was almost instantly a bestselling novel and a play (T. R. Sullivan dramatized it in America in 1887, Richard Mansfield played it in London) and has been the subject of more than thirty significant movies, television shows, odd adaptations (with a bisexual protagonist, for instance), comic books, and cartoons. John Barrymore and Spencer Tracy essayed the role, Fredric Marsh won an Oscar for his portrayal of it in 1932, and many others have been attracted to the meaty part of the respectable doctor turned hellion by night. In the 1941 film version, Ingrid Bergman introduced a sexual element: she played a barmaid that Mr. Hyde met on his "adventures." In a later version, the good doctor goes into drag as Ms. Hyde, showing a side not as ferociously fiendish as James Gumm in clothes made of women's skins in *The Silence of the Lambs* but, for its time, very startling.

Stevenson said, rather ungratefully, that of all his writings *Dr. Jekyll and Mr. Hyde* was the worse, a mere "shocker." He condemned the public for taking it so to their bosom. However, it is this study of the duality of personality and the dark recesses of the human psyche that Stevenson will continue to be known for, even more than for his children's classics such as *Treasure Island, Kidnapped,* and *The Master of Ballantrae.*

Dr. Jekyll and Mr. Hyde stresses the old Roman Catholic doctrine of original sin, the Calvinist awareness of human depravity, and the familiar violence of Hyde's "ape-like spite." Stevenson, a life-long invalid and a Scottish Presbyterian, much given to brooding not only over the state of his frail health but also the state of his soul, found within the rich and respectable doctor in his elegant townhouse the evil Edward Hyde, who lurked in a wretched room in Soho and committed atrocities with diabolical zest. Stevenson wants to do much more than the horrid little child in Dickens who delights in making "your flesh creep." At one point Stevenson says of Mr. Hyde, "That child of Hell had nothing human; nothing lived in him but fear and hatred." Mr. Hyde is all too horrendously human.

Most recently, the old Jekyll and Hyde story has been retold through a minor female character, *Mary Reilly.*

THE DEVIL AND THE POETS

With devotion's visage
And pious action, we do sugar o'er
The devil himself.
—William Shakespeare, *Hamlet*

Wherever God erects a house of prayer,
The Devil always builds a chapel there;
And 'twill be found, upon examination,
The Devil has the largest congregation.
—Daniel Defoe, *The True-Born Englishman*

Here lie Willie Machin's banes;
O Satan, when ye tak him,
Gie Him the schoolin' of your weans,
For clever deils he'll mak them!
—Robert Burns, *Epitaph on a Schoolmaster*

How then was the Devil dressed?
O, he was in his Sunday best;
His coat was red, and his breetches were blue,
And there was a hole where his tail came through.
—Robert Southey and Samuel Taylor Coleridge, *The Devil's Walk*

We be all good Englishmen.
Let us bang these dogs of Seville, the children of the devil,
For I never turned my back upon Don or devil yet.
—Alfred, Lord Tennyson, *The Revenge*

The Devil, having nothing else to do,
Went off to tempt my Lady Poltagrue.
My Lady, tempted by a private whim,
To his extreme annoyance, tempted him.
—Hilaire Belloc, *Epigrams*

Till the Devil whispered behind the leaves,
"It's clever, but is it Art?"
—Rudyard Kipling, *The Conundrum of the Workshops*

The Devil and me, we don't agree.
I hate him and he hates me.
—Anonymous Salvaation Army hymn (Nineteenth Century)

Sneeze on a Monday, you sneeze for danger.
Sneeze on a Tuesday, you'll kiss a stranger.
Sneeze on a Wednesday, you sneeze for a letter.
Sneeze on a Thursday, for something better.
Sneeze on a Friday, you sneeze for sorrow.
Sneeze on a Saturday, see your sweetheart tomorrow.
Sneeze on a Sunday, your safety seek.
For The Devil will have you the whole of the week.
—Traditional (date unknown)

PROVERBIAL WISDOM ABOUT THE DEVIL

The Devil finds work for idle hands.
The Devil is God's ape.
Give The Devil his due.
What's got over The Devil's back must be spent under his belly.
The Devil bides his day.
You would do little for God if The Devil were dead.
The Devil always leaves a stink behind him.
The Devil hates holy water.
It is easier to raise The Devil than to lay him.
He who sups with The Devil must have a long spoon.
The Devil paints himself black but we see him rose-colored.
    The Devil was sick, The Devil a monk would be.
    The Devil was well, the devil a monk was he.
When the priest's away, The Devil will play.
Only The Devil can cheat a Jew.
When The Devil himself tried to study Basque, he learned only
    three words in seven years.
The Devil divides the world between atheism and superstition.
The Devil has three children: Pride, Falsehood, and Envy.
The Devil's children have The Devil's luck.
The Devil lurks behind the Cross.
If you are afraid of The Devil you will never be rich.
The Devil is not so black as he is painted.
The Devil is kind to his own.

The Devil gets up to the belfry by the vicar's skirts.

The Devil comes where money is; where there is no money, he comes twice.

The Devil wipes his tail with the poor man's pride.

Where The Devil cannot come, he will send.

When it rains while the sun shines, The Devil is beating his wife.

Better The Devil you know than The Devil you don't.

Speak of The Devil and he'll appear.

CZECH VERNACULAR LITERATURE AND THE DEVIL

"The Devil's Stench and Living Water . . .," by R. B. Pysent, is a study of Czech demons and adultery in the Middle Ages and Renaissance. Few articles are noted in this book, but in this case, we must mention this piece in the October 1993 *Slavonic and East European Review* because it is in English and shows the rich and relevant folklore of this part of Eastern Europe. Seek it out.

FOREIGN-LANGUAGE SCHOLARS OF THE DEVIL AND DEMONS IN ART

Cocchiara, G., *Il Diavolo nella tradizione populare italiana* (1945)

Grillot de Givry, Émile, *Picture Museum of Sorcery, Magic and Alchemy* (trans. J. C. Locke, reprint 1963)

Levron, J., *Le Diable dans l'art* (1935)

Michel, W., *Das Teuflisch und Groteske in der Kunst* (1919)

Reisner, E., *Le Démon et son image* (1964)

Turnel, J., *Histoire du diable* (1931)

Villeneuve, Robert, *Le Diable dans l'art* (1957)

PICTURING THE DEVIL AND HIS DEMONS

The ancient Greek misconception that the ugly soul has an ugly body (and *vice versa*) has led to the portrayal of The Devil and demons in grotesque forms borrowed from the basilisk and other monsters of classical times, including bats, birds, bulls, centaurs, dogs, dragons, goats, lions, satyrs, and serpents. The Devil is also associated with the skeleton and other symbols of death. Evil creatures are imagined to be hairy, scaly, pig-nosed, and fanged, sporting fierce talons (green or yellow like a frog or reptile, or black or blue) and often possessing what one witchcraft newsletter in the US was once called a *Cloven Hoof*. The Christian devil tends to remain anthropomorphic if grotesque. Minor devils and demons get more grotesque still. *El sueño de la razón produce monstros*: "The sleep of reason produces monsters." The demons of Asian religions are the most grotesque.

The Devil and demons, however, need not be repulsive in appearance and sometimes beauty facilitates their evil work.

Barbara Allen Woods's dissertation has appeared in book form as *The Devil in Dog Form* (1955); in folklore, canine disguises are said to be a favorite of The Devil. The devils with horns and tails are most common in Christian art, and The Devil himself is a common figure in depictions of the Temptation of Adam and Eve, of Jesus in the desert, and various saints (especially St. Anthony). The Devil has had his portrait painted by German artists such as Bosch and Dürer, Dutch artists such as Memling and Breugel, as well as Goya, James Ensor, John Martin, and others.

Traditional depictions of The Devil with certain saints were established over time. The Devil was shown enchained by St. Bernard of Clairvaux, St. Colum Cill, St. Séverin, St. Dympne, and others. The Devil was held by pincers in the hands of St. Dunstan and St. Eloy. He tries to hide from St. Wolfgang and flees from St. Cyprian of Antioch. St. Martin of Tours was shown talking with The Devil on his deathbed, defying evil. With St. Oswald, The Devil is shown sitting nearby on a rock. Mary Magdalene and many others are depicted with him, too.

Because Satan is connected to Cerunnos, the Horned God of pre-Christian Celts, and because goats have a reputation for being lecherous, Satan is often portrayed as a goat and some witches swore, after torture, that they saw him in that form.

SUNDALS-RYRS
GAMLA KYRKA

That's Swedish for "the old church in Sundals-Ryrs." It is a thirteenth-century church that fell into disrepair and would have been demolished in the last century were

German illumination (*c.* 1020) of a passage in a manuscript of *The Apocalypse of St. John the Divine*. The fifth trumpet sounds.

it not for the labor involved in moving the large stones. So it was abandoned and was replaced in Dalsland by a newer structure. Since the seventies, however, it has been restored, though it is used only in the summer. In the winter, it is too cold.

I mention it here because it has a large painting on the roof that is one of the most dramatic you could ever see regarding The Devil and the damned. Central is the monstrous figure of *Horn-Per* (Horned Peter), The Devil. He has a pitchfork and is pushing a nude woman into a fiery hell already full of suffering humanity. Some good people have escaped him and are headed for heaven.

The changing iconography of The Devil and the damned over the centuries of Christianity is a subject for a colorful book of its own. It was with striking pictures such as this that the congregations of the past literally had the hell frightened out of them. It was also from the ignorance of symbolism that the peasants took the crude representations as factual and came to believe in a devil with horns, a tail, a pitchfork, and talons, and hell not as a state of mind but as a geographical location, fiery hot, full of sulfur and brimstone.

A Texan who did not much enjoy the scorching summers of the Lone Star State once said that if he owned hell and Texas, he'd rent out Texas and live in hell. For the medieval Northmen, the freezing Finns, the numbed Norwegians, and the shivering Swedes, however, a hot hell might have looked preferable to an icy one. Remember Robert Service's Sam McGee, comfortable in Hades after life in the Arctic:

> Since I left Plum Tree, down in Tennessee,
> It's the first time I've been warm.

DE MORTUIS NIHIL NISI BONUM

We are told to say nothing but good of the dead (lest they revenge themselves on us), yet we seldom realize that among native tribes in Australia and many other places a dead person is never, never mentioned by name (lest that raise the ghost). In many cultures those who share a name with the dead change it lest the dead person be summoned by its use among the living. Should the name of the dead be the same as or even too closely approximate the sound of the name of a common object, the word must be dropped from the vocabulary.

"The same reluctance to utter the names of the dead appears to prevail," writes Sir James Frazer in *The New Golden Bough*, "among all the

Indian tribes of America, from Hudson Bay Territory to Patagonia. . . ."
The relevance here is that knowing and using the names of the dead, devils, and demons enables one to put them to work (as on amulets) or call
them up; that a child may become a reincarnation of a dead person if named
for that person; and that naming a child after a supernatural personality,
whether a saint or a demon, summons that supernatural person to take a
special interest in the namesake. Names of rulers and other high officials
used to be kept secret lest sorcery be attempted on them. The Jews believe
that changing the name of a sick child will prevent the angel of death from
finding her or him. Some changes of names are to protect the bearer.

It seems obvious that if indeed infernal powers exist and have names
of power that sorcery could use, sorcery is much handicapped by the fact
that the names that are bruited about are simply arbitrary ones (or mere
descriptions looking like proper names to those to whom the languages
are obscure). Why should, for instance, the Jews and some French or Italian Roman Catholic nuns, who claim to have met demons, get to give them
names that are clearly fictitious, derived as they are from languages far more
modern than the day of creation on which God made the angels who
became devils and demons? Alright, let us say those are the names that the
infernal powers gave them (speaking in their languages). But are those the
real names? Demons lie. God is just evasive: "I AM."

If you had God or Satan's real name, then you might be able to do some
real magic. If somehow or other you do manage to conjure up a demon
(maybe you conjured it, but more likely it just came *per accidens* because
your foolishness was putting you as Mephistopheles tells Marlowe's Faustus "in danger of being damned"), your first question ought to be what its
real name is. I doubt if it will tell you, for there is mighty power in names.

NAMES OF THE DEVIL

Robert Southey in chapter 139 of *The Doctor* ("written between 1834 and
1837") argues that names are "serious things" and, *inter alia*, he lists many
names for The Devil. H. L. Mencken, in the second supplement to his standard *American Language*, remarks:

> With the decay of theology most of [those] . . . have passed out,
> but there are some that certainly deserve revival, if only for use as
> objugations, *e.g., Cocabelto, Kellicocam, Motubizanto, Ju, Arraba, Lac-
> ahabarraiu, Oguerracatam, Buzache, Baa, Kelvoryvyhegg, Leileranny,
> Cnocknatratin, Drung* and *Knockadawe.*

A talisman for love.

For ways to avoid using the name or term *devil* see E. C. Hills, "Exclamations in American English," *Dialect Notes* V:7, 1924. Throughout this work, I have cited chiefly books, not dissertations or articles, but there is nothing like this in any book I know. There are also American evasions for *hell* (blazes, Sam Hill, Jesse, Jo, tarnation, etc.).

THE NAME OF THE DEVIL

In the same spirit as the evasive exclamations such as *Gosh!* and *Gee Whiz!*, common speech refused to name The Devil directly; it refers to him as *Old Nick*. But no one knows why he might be called *Nicholas*. Perhaps it's because he "nicks" souls; in British slang, one of the meanings of *nick* is "to steal" (probably from the Anglo-Saxon). Samuel Butler in *Hudibras* (1663) attributed the nickname to the evil reputation that had attached itself to the Italian Renaissance writer Niccolò Machiavelli:

> Nick Machiavel had ne'er a trick
> Though he gave his name to our Old Nick.

The Devil has other nicknames. Some people, not knowing the correct origin (in Anglo-Saxon *eke name*, "extra name"), even say that a nickname is one you have so that Old Nick will not be able to get you by your real name. The Devil is called by many nicknames from The Black Man to The Old Enemy of Man. *Old Harry* used to be in frequent use, both as a nickname for The Devil and as an equivalent of "Hell" ("I'll knock the Old Harry out of him!"). There's an old oath, "By the Lord Harry!" and Mr. Tulliver in George Eliot's novel, *The Mill on the Floss*, exclaims: "This is a puzzling world, and Old Harry's got a finger in it."

DEVILS IN OUR LANGUAGE

"To play the devil" is to send to rack and ruin. "To go to the devil" or "to pull the devil by the tail" is to be dissolute and ruined. "Devil-may-care" is heedlessness. "Devil's delight" is chaos and confusion, and "the devil's own luck" is extraordinary and probably undeserved good fortune. Gambling was disapproved of before lotteries, casinos, and riverboats became a major feature of US life. Cards were "the devil's playthings," dice were "the devil's bones," and gambling was "the work of the devil." We don't bedevil people or give them a devil of a lot of trouble about such things today.

"To bedevil" is to bother. "To be devilish" is to be both clever and evil or deucedly naughty. "What the deuce!" avoids the direct mention of The Devil. The fires of hell suggested to slangsters that a firecracker is a "devil." The hard work of the assistant to The Devil caused apprentice lawyers and especially the errand boys of printers to be called "devils." To be evil and get away with it was to "get away with the devil" or "whip the devil around the stump," but usually one is punished for evil and there is "the devil to pay." Some expressions, such as "devil's tattoo" (drumming your fingers idly or impatiently on the table) and "devil's *pater noster*" (grumbling) are obsolete. Nobody alive now says "The devil a bit says Punch," instead of "no" or "negative". "The Devil's Own" were the Eighty-eighth Regiment of Foot in the Peninsular War; "The Devil's Sharpshooters" were said to be clergymen who fought in our Mexican War. We still say "speak of the devil" when someone being mentioned turns up but "speak of the devil and you'll see his horns and his tail" is out of fashion.

These and "the devil knows what" more are or have been in our speech, reflecting our attitudes toward The Evil One. As for the ones not mentioned, "to the devil with them."

Related are the expressions including *demon*. They indicate that we have regarded a demon as swift ("speed demon at the typewriter"), very skilled ("demon bowler" in UK cricket games), or persistent. Australians used to call prison guards the "demons" who kept them in a hellish place.

Our language and slanguage are a hell of a lot richer due to the concepts of devils and demons. "The world is all the richer for having a devil in it" in all respects, said the American philosopher William James, "so long as we keep our foot upon his neck. As far as language is concerned, the old superstition that to name a person or thing is to make it draw near suggests we ought not to mention (while always being careful about) devils and demons.

YELLOW AND BLACK

Servants used to wear liveries, uniforms in the colors featured on the coat of arms of their masters. The liveries of The Devil were said to be yellow and black.

Yellow was connected with heresy: Prisoners on their way to be burned at the stake for heresy were forced to wear "San Benito" garments rather

254 The Complete Book of the Devil's Disciples

like the white robes of the Ku Klux Klan; they were yellow. Yellow was the color of the Star of David that Jews were forced to wear. Orientals used yellow as the royal color and believed it had powers to drive off evil, but the West often took contrary positions, perhaps with some long-forgotten objection to rival Sun-God religions. Connected also with wisdom (especially as it verged on orange) and intellectuality, yellow may have been thought by some to have been in opposition to faith.

Black has always been associated with ignorance and night, with nihilism and evil.

WHO BELIEVES IN SATANISM?

Archbishop Samuel Harsnett, mentioned elsewhere in connection with giving Shakespeare some names of devils to mention in *King Lear*, said those who believed in Satanism can be put into "one of these five ranks: Children, Fools, Women, Cowards, sick or black melancholic discomposed Wits." I discuss Satanic cults in *The Complete Book of Devils and Demons* for such—and others.

BLOOD

Even the red markings on the black widow spider give some men the idea of evil associated with menstrual blood. For the use of blood in magical recipes and the folk beliefs in the connection between witches and blood, see the strikingly-titled "*La Cuisine des sorcières,*" by Claudine Fabre-Vassas in *Ethnologie Française* 21:4 1991), 423–427. It's an eye-opener.

HOW TO DEAL WITH A SWEDISH WEREWOLF

In Uppland they tell of a marriage at which the bride and groom, the minister, and all the guests were suddenly turned into werewolves. (I have seen voracious appetites at the receptions, but not at marriage ceremonies.) The werewolves rushed out in a pack and attacked villagers and their cattle. One villager noted that a black werewolf had a white spot at its throat where a minister's stock would be. He asked, "Could you be Parson Salvander?"

"Yes, I am," replied the creature and instantly he turned back into the minister, who then rushed off home to write a sermon.

If you meet a Swedish werewolf, just call him by the name of the person who assumed the horrible shape. The creature will then be restored to human form.

THE CELEBRANT

In 1562 the English clergy (by a vote of 59 to 58) decided that the priest at "common prayer should turn his face to the people." About 400 years later the Roman Catholic Church decreed that the celebrant at Mass should face the congregation. Previously, he faced the altar, which is why copes and chasubles were so decorated on the back, not the front.

In the Black Mass, everything is reversed, so traditionally the celebrant has faced the congregation and put his back to the tabernacle. Now that the Roman Catholics have turned around, do the celebrants of Black Masses have to face the altar to be different?

And if you are not Roman Catholic, could you have a Black Prayer Meeting or a Black Synagogue Ceremony (at which participants stand up and promise proudly not to contribute specific amounts to charity)?

DEVILS AND DEMONS ON THE MAP

There's *Satan's Kingdom* in both Massachusetts and Vermont, *Satan Pass* in New Mexico, *Satan's Toe* in New York, and more. There's *Lucifer Peak* in Oregon, *Lucifer Point* in Arizona, and more. There are hundreds of *Devil* places, including the *Devil's Tater Patch* in North Carolina and Tennessee but only a handful of populated places with "Devil" in the name. I like *Devil's Town*, Ohio, and *Devil's Hate*, New Mexico. *Demon Creek* in Arkansas is the sole US placename with *demon* in it. *Belian Village*, Pennsylvania, is not close enough to *Belial*, but there's a *Mammon Mine* and two places called *Leviathan Mine* in Arizona. *The Witches* is a sand bar in New Hampshire and there are *Witch* pools and lakes scattered around, no *Sorcerer* at all, and just one *Magician Lake*, Michigan.

Canada and Australia have their "Devil" places like the US, and Britain has *Devil's Bridge* in Cardiganshire, where there are (in point of fact, as the Brits say) three bridges over one of the most beautiful chasms in the British Isles. The West Country and Yorkshire are famous for their magic wells and witches and wizards—Merlin was supposed to have been at Tintagel, in Cornwall—but the word "Devil" is not important in the British toponymic vocabulary.

"Devil" seems to occur chiefly in description of a place wild or dangerous or of something fantastic which only The Devil could achieve, like the *Devil's Postpile* and *Devil's Tower* , which are both national monuments, in the US or, say, *El Diablillo* on Tenerife in the Canaries. In the US there's even a *Devils Den Nature Reserve* in Connecticut.

Folklore attaches stories to some places that tell of devils and demons in Britain; but quiet county towns (such as Chelmsford in Essex) have almost forgotten their history of witch burnings. Dark doings of old were reported in the New Forest and the forests of Epping and Dean.

THE DEVIL'S ACRE

From Gillian Avery's *Victorian People in Life and Literature*:

> [Henry] Mayhew, collecting material for the *Criminal Prisons of London* (1862) visited Tothill Fields. . . . restricted to female prisoners and boys under the age of seventeen. It was a house of correction—that is, it held short-term prisoners—and it stood in the "Devil's Acre," the moral plague spot of the whole kingdom, a contemporary called it—behind the House of Parliament.

In America we are less expansive: we had half-acres. From Irving Lewis Allen's *The City in Slang*:

> Slum enclaves and whole slum neighborhoods in New York and other cities were called infernal names such as *The Devil's Half-Acre*, *Hell's Half Acre*, or most famously *Hell's Kitchen*.

THE DEVIL IN MISSOURI

To be specific about "Devil" placenames in one state, let's take Missouri, where they have been thoroughly studied by Robert L. Ramsay and more recently, and as importantly, by Gerald L. Cohen. Missouri has, with counties in which they occur, these names and more:

Devil's Backbone (Jackson, Montgomery, Oregon, Phelps, Ripley)
Devil's Boot Cave and **Devil's Washbasins** (both Warren)
Devil's Elbow (Butler, Pulaski)
Devil's Tea Table (Cape Girardeau, Miller)
Devil's Toll Gate (Iron)

> Robert L. Ramsay wrote in *Our Storehouse of Missouri Place Names*:
>
> A large proportion of the territory of Missouri . . . is still recognized as the property of the Devil, if place names are sufficient evidence of ownership. More than 30 localities attest the healthy respect we have for His Satanic Majesty . . . and the *Devil's Race Ground*, a difficult rapid in the Missouri [River], was mentioned

with awe as long ago as May 24, 1804, in the journals of the Lewis and Clark Expedition.

Gerald L. Cohen in the second volume of his *Interesting Missouri Place Names* explains that both places named *Devil's Elbow* are difficult, dangerous turns in rivers (the Butler one in the Black River, the Pulaski one in the Big Piney River). Long rafts of the lumbering industry had trouble with these abrupt bends.

KEY TO THE DEVIL IN FOLKLORE

One of the most useful guides to the study of folklore is the half-dozen volumes of Stith Thompson's magisterial *Motif-Index of Folk Literature*. You might be interested in G 303 (The Devil), M 210 (Bargain with The Devil), G 242 (Witches in Flight), G 224 (Witch's Ointment), as well as others.

FOLKTALES ABOUT WITCHES

Stith Thompson also has classification systems and many details in *The Folktale*. Here's a folktale that W. T. Wintemberg collected from Germans settled in Canada. Leonard W. Roberts has a version of it in the US in *South from Hell-fer-sartin*. Here's how it appears under the title "An Alsatian Witch Story" in Tristram P. Coffin and Hennig Cohen's anthology *Folklore in America*:

> The witches held monthly orgies or festivals. In Alsace the chimneys of houses are very wide, and it was through these they left the house without being seen. At a certain farmhouse there were two women— mother and daughter—who were witches. With them lived an inquisitive young farmhand. He had noticed that something unusual was taking place in the house every month, so one night he hid in the kitchen and watched. About midnight the women came and stood naked before the fireplace, beneath the chimney, and after annointing themselves with an oil which the Germans call *Hexenfett* (i.e., witches' fat), uttered some magic words, and up they went through the chimney. The young man then emerged from his hiding place, and seeing the vessel containing the oil, he annointed himself to see what effect it would have on him. He had scarcely pronounced the mystic words when he went up the chimney with a suddenness that was surprising, and when he reached the ground he found himself astride a large black sow which carried him with

great speed across the country. They soon arrived at a broad and swift-flowing river, but this did not hinder the onward advance of the sow, for it cleared the broad expanse of water at a single bound. The young man looked back, and, admiring its leaping powers, he said to the sow, "That was a long leap you made," but as he spoke the spell was broken, the sow disappeared, and he found himself in a strange country many miles from home.

HOODOO

Hilda Roberts collected hoodoo superstitions from Iberia Parish, Louisiana. Here's how to sell your soul to The Devil to gain the power of hoodoo people.

To become a hoodoo you must sell your soul to the Devil. To do this on the darkest night of the month go out alone into a field and wait for him to appear. He will do this exactly at midnight in the form of a black bird or shadow. After you have made your agreement with him he is your master, but he will help you to accomplish anything within his power.

WITCHES AND THE CHURN

If there are witches around, you may not be able to make butter. To counter them, throw a pinch of salt into the fire or drop a silver coin into the churn.

SIGNS OF EVIL

If the fire or the candle burns blue, there is evil near. Also, if your thumbs tingle. Remember Shakespeare's witches in what actors refuse to name (calling it "The Scottish Play" lest it bring them bad luck):

By the pricking of my thumbs,
Something wicked this way comes.

By the way, quoting *Macbeth* also brings bad luck.

DEMONIC POSSESSION

A major theme of folklore is not only The Devil tricked but The Devil possessing a person.

Possession and exorcism are dealt with in the companion volume, *The Complete Book of Devils and Demons*, but in summary here we may say that the sociodemographic factors everywhere and at all times appear to be sex (most possessed persons are young and female, especially those suffering from childhood traumas and repression), suggestibility (often combined with greater than usual intelligence—or imagination), and a strong superstitious element in the society (most possessions being involuntary visitations by feared evil entities). Possession has often being the diagnosis when the truth lies in organic, psychiatric, or psychosomatic illness and there is a high percentage of attention-grabbing and faked symptoms. It is striking that while symptoms vary considerably from one culture to another, alleged victims seldom or never report or exhibit symptoms other than those which are disapproved by and hostile to the norms of good behavior in their culture. It is also striking that possession occurs most often in societies—for example, the Ibibio of Nigeria—that attribute almost all ills to supernatural causes and like to blame evil others rather than themselves for all problems. Scapegoating of those thought to be possessed is common. Finally, the depth of belief in possession and other aspects of the supernatural varies from one place and time to another, but it exists in all societies, however educated and sophisticated, even though it may be denied. Problems must be solved by working with the patient rather than on the patient and in the context of modern medical understanding. While it is considered unethical by medical doctors to involve witch doctors and such, modern psychiatrists are often advised to bring in more or less traditional religious figures appropriate to the patient's ethnic and religious background or at least not to dismiss the patient's beliefs out of hand. If you believe in baptism, you believe in demonic possession.

STEMMING THE BLOOD IN NORWAY

The stemming of blood was life-saving and magical. If you were swearing at the time of being wounded, you had to use "troll words" to stop the bleeding; if you were not swearing, you could use Christian magic formulæ. These formulæ were always whispered very low in the ear of the person to be helped. If others heard the magic, it would not work.

Here is an old formula from Drevja (Norway) handed down for generations in the same family and clearly equating the flow of blood with the flow of water in the River Jordan:

> *Kristus og Sankt Peter*
> *gikk over en bro,*
> *talte så meget*
> *om kristenmanns blod*
> *Rind flod,*
> *stans blod*
> *likesom den mann*
> *i helvete stod*

> Christ and St. Peter
> went over a bridge.
> They spoke many a word
> About a Christian's blood.
> Flow, River,
> Stop, Blood,
> Just like the man
> Standing still in Hell.

Another such formula, also from Drevja:

> *Jesus gikk til Jordans flod,*
> *at døve verk og stilla blod.*
> *Statt ditt blod*
> *som den mann i graven stod*
> *og som den mann i helvete stod.*
> *I navn Gud Fader, Amen.*

> Jesus went to Jordan's flood
> To ease the pain and stop the blood.
> Be still, you blood
> Just like the man who stood in the grave
> And also like the man who stood in Hell.
> In the name of God the Father. Amen.

Or, more briefly, from Vefsn in the north of Norway, and right to the point:

> *Stemmer blod,*
> *stemmer blod,*
> *so det stod i Jesu side.*

> Stem blood,
> Stem blood,
> As it did in Jesu's side.

None of these formulæ worked on menstrual bleeding, or if one tried to use them on oneself, or if one was heard using them by any but the bleeding person, as I noted above.

The Christian formulae simply adopted and adapted pagan magical recitations and sometimes seems to have involved The Devil in his incantations. Witness this from Krødsherad in Ostlandet, which was still around in 1853 and was centuries old then:

> *Stat Blod*
> *stil Blod*
> *som den Mand, der smurte sine Sko*
> *paa Langfredag*
> *og gik til Things*
> *og svor sin Ed*
> *Faus, Paus, Belsebub*
> *Grav du din Grav,*
> *Helvetes Grav*
> *der skal du staa fast til Dommedag.*

> Stay, blood!
> Be still, blood!
> Just like the man who greased his shoes
> On Long Friday
> And went to the Thing [parliament]
> And swore his oath:
> Faus, Paus, Beelzebub,
> Dig your grave,
> Your hellish grave,
> Where you will be stuck fast until Doomsday.

SEXUAL POTENCY AND WITCHES

Witches are on record as having confessed to rendering males impotent by tying knots in pieces of cord. They also have charmed males into believing that their penises have been stolen, as is mentioned in the *Malleus maleficarum*. Taking this a step further, rumors circulated that witches cut off and hoarded penises, hiding them in the nests of birds or keeping them in boxes and feeding them with oats and corn.

In his *Discouerie of Witchcraft* (1594), Reginald Scot tells of a young man who was emasculated and went to a witch for help. She told him to climb a certain tree and to choose any replacement he wished. He chose the biggest and heaviest and brought it to her for attachment. She said he could have any one but that one. That one was reserved for the parish priest.

At the *sabbat* The Devil was said to have intercourse with the witches using his huge, scaly, and bifurcated phallus (so that they could be penetrated fore and aft at the same time). Witchcraft trials contained testimony of sex with The Devil and reports that it was painful, cold, and unreproductive.

We use the Latin slang *phallus* (sword) and *vagina* (sheath) instead of the four-letter English words, and this may be the source of the Welsh way of getting a woman by William Wirt Sikes in *British Goblins* (1880):

> Enter the churchyard at midnight, carrying a *twca*, which is a sort of knife made out of an old razor, with a handle of sheep or goat-horn, and encircle the edifice seven times, holding the *twca* at arm's length, and saying, '*Dtma'r twca, p'le mae'r wain?*' Here's the *twca*—where's the sheath?

The Devil will arrange for you to marry the first woman you meet after that. Or you can try the spell quoted in Robin Sketon's *The Practice of Witch-craft Today* (1988): "This I lay upon you: when we meet put your mouth to my mouth, and, furthermore, this I lay upon you: when we meet put your breasts to my breast, and, furthermore, this I lay upon you: when we meet open your thighs and call me into you."

Ritual Magic by "David Conway" gives instructions for preparing a magic mandrake to advance a love intention but it is a demanding proce-dure and he suggests also a simpler charm, the Magic Rose. In June, get up some morning between 3 and 4 A.M. and pick a full-blown red rose. Bring this home and hold the rose for a full five minutes over a chafing dish in which you are burning sulfur and brimstone. The flower is then to be folded in a piece of paper bearing your name and the name of the person you love, sealed with three seals, and buried under the rosebush where you got the rose. Mark an *A* (for *Amor vincit omnia*, "Love conquers all") over the rose's little grave. On 6 July you dig up the rose and put it under your pillow "and you will enjoy dreams of great portent." If that does not work, try boiling fennel in water and then soaking vervain in it for a considerable time in an airtight bottle. The herbs, "Conway" says, must be "gathered on a Friday, preferably during the passage of the Moon through the first ten degrees of Taurus or Virgo. The Moon should also be well aspected with Saturn and Venus." If all goes well you will have a potent *potio priapi* or herbal aphrodisiac.

My next book will include many more recipes.

Some say vervain and fennel can be added to a bottle of vodka and shaken regularly, kept airtight for a month or two, and a potion will be created that works. If you are in a great hurry, propose marriage or an expensive vacation or offer flowers and flattery.

SEDUCTIVE DRINK

From *The Gospel of Bartholomew*, apocrypha of the fifth century or so, translated by Montague Rhodes James, The Devil speaks:

> I took a phial in mine hands and scraped the sweat from off my breast and the hair of mine armpits, and I washed myself in the springs of the waters whence the four rivers flow out [of paradise], and Eve drank of it and desire came upon her: for if she had not drunk of that water I should not have been able to deceive her.

SIR FRANCIS DRAKE, THE WIZARD

Sir Frances Drake (*c.* 1540–1596), of all the famous Britons whispered about as having been sorcerers (Roger Bacon, Owen Glendower, Sir Walter Raleigh, Oliver Cromwell, and more), is the best example to discuss here not because that allegation is so well known today, but, because of all of those suspected, he is the only one about whom there is still a lively legend: if England is in trouble, sounding Drake's drum will call him back to her aid (they say) as he came to her aid when the dreaded Spanish Armada threatened in 1588. Sir Henry Newbold has a poem, "Drake's Drum," that I learned years ago in elementary school. It was just at that time that the drum was said to have been sounded in the dark days of World War II.

Other tales about Drake include the one about him playing bowls on Plymouth Hoe when the news of the Armada reached England. He is said to have taken a piece of wood and cut shavings from it. He threw them into the sea, at which point each one became a wooden ship that could defend the country.

Another legend tells that after he had been away from home, circumnavigating the globe for years, his wife (or, in another version, his fiancée) decided he was dead and undertook to remarry (or marry). The day of the wedding Drake was on the other side of the earth, but his special powers let him know what was happening at Combe Sydenham back home. He fired a cannon into the sea. The cannonball went right through the earth and came up in front of the bride-to-be at the altar in the church. "That is Drake's shot," she exclaimed, and the marriage was off.

After many adventures on the Spanish Main, reaching the Golden Gate in California, fighting off Florida, and bringing disconsolate settlers back from Virginia along with tobacco and potatoes (to mention his American connections), Drake and Sir John Norreys harried the enemy in Spain and Portugal. Then Drake retired to Plymouth and served as a member of parliament from there. He brought the town a water supply. Legend says he did that by riding his horse a far distance to a spring, saying a magic formula, and riding back—with the water following him all the way to Plymouth.

There is a also a legend of "Sir Francis Drake and The Devil," but for that see, Katharine Briggs's four-volume *Dictionary of British Folk-Tales* (1970–1971).

THE DEVIL IN DEVON

At Shebbear in Devon, every year on 5 November they have a ceremony of turning over "The Devil's Boulder" under an ancient oak. This is claimed to be one of the oldest folk customs in Britain. The large stone is supposed to have been dropped there by The Devil, and if it is not turned over on that date, bad luck will follow the inhabitants of the town for the rest of the year.

In many countries, there are things like this to do to avert bad luck. Behind the traditions is the very pleasing idea that although bad luck threatens we know exactly whom to blame and, moreover, there is something we can do to avoid it. It gives one a sense of power, just as children like the "fact" that they could—if they wanted to—revenge themselves on overbearing grownups by stepping on the cracks in the sidewalk.

DEVIL'S BIT SCABIOUS

British folklore is chock full of references to The Devil and his friends, and plants offer some protection against him. The Devil, however, is said to have reduced the efficacy of Devil's Bit Scabious (*Succisa prætensis*). Legend has it that the root of this plant, which was used to treat skin diseases (as "scabious" suggests itching), used to be even more useful until The Devil nastily bit off most of it. Actually the Latin *Succisa* refers to "bitten off" and the rest tells you it grows in the meadow.

CUTTING YOUR NAILS

In certain parts of Britain, a baby's nails did not used to be cut for the first year. Some say this was to keep the baby from growing up to be a thief. Others say it was so witches could not get hold of parts of the body to work evil on the infant. Grown-ups, too, were wary about hair and nail clippings, and Anne, Countess of Westmoreland recorded in her diary that she carefully collected nail clippings and burned them, lest they fall into the wrong hands.

DRIVING AWAY EVIL SPIRITS

Small windows in some very old British churches are said to have been put there for the benefit of lepers who, not permitted to enter the church, could look in at divine services, receive alms, or make confessions at these windows. When a funeral was conducted, lamps were placed in these little windows to drive away evil spirits attracted by the dead. A great deal of incense, holy water, and other means were used to keep devils and demons at bay at the wake, the arrival of the corpse at the lich gate of the church, the funeral services in the church and at the grave, and during and after the burial. Even the spirit of the dead was feared, which is why the corpse was carried to the grave with lighted candles and feet first. That way the corpse would not know the way back to the living.

DEVILS AND DEMONS IN RUSSIAN FOLKLORE

Russian folklore offers a whole world of *cherti* (devils or demons), from the hideous witch hag Bab Yaga to swan maidens, from spirits of the woods and the water and domestic spirits (*demovye*), who can be mischievous like pixies or brownies but never truly malicious, to demons who ride the whirlwind and bring terrible destruction in their wake (*vozdushnye*). There are equivalents of trolls and giants and particularly evil dwarfs (*karliki*). Now there is only one God in Russian theology, but once upon a time, there was an almost Persian dualism with both white (good) and black (evil) gods. W. R. S. Ralston's *Songs of the Russian People* (1872) and *Russian Folk Tales* (1873) present many of these devils and demons in action in the folklore of the last century, some of which still survives in the peasantry's imagination. Ralston, who worked for the British Museum as an expert on Russian books, brought to English readers the collection of oral literature made by P. N. Ruibnikof and others who wrote down the ancient poetry from the traditional blind ministrels called *kalíki*. The dwindling few of them still left by mid-nineteenth century performed poetry for the common people. These poems had been handed down from one generation to another and might have died out had it not been for folklore collectors inspired by the success of the Brothers Grimm in Germany in preserving the evidences of the national past.

RUSSIAN LITERATURE

Mikhail Yur'evich Lermontov (1814–1841) is unusual among Russian writers of demons and devils (a group which included Gogol, "Maxim Gorki," and many others) in that he gives his demon an oriental cast and a Romantic tinge. He began a long poem on a demon in 1829 and finished it a decade later in exile, but because of its content it was not published until 1856, long after his death in a duel. The theme is the longing of a demon impossibly in love with a mortal. The tone is bitter and pessimistic, but the oriental coloring gives it charm. The subject was considered irreligious or blasphemous in its day.

Nyet, ye na Byron (No, I am not Byron) wrote Lermontov as the title of one of his works, but his *Demon* shows he shared Byron's sympathy with the outcast evil one. He is, he says, himself a Byronic "outcast, with a Russian soul." So is his demon.

CHARMS FOR CHILDREN

> Rain, rain, go away,
> Come again another day.
> Little Johnny wants to play.
>
> Come, butter, come,
> Come, butter, come;
> Peter stands at the gate
> Waiting for a butter cake.
> Come, butter, come.

TOADSTONE

In *As You Like It* (II, I, 13–14), Shakespeare repeats the old superstition that,

> The Toad, ugly and venomous,
> Wears yet a precious jewel in his head.

This stone was supposed to be sovereign for ills that medicine could not address. It had other uses as well. Sir Walter Scott, who claimed descent from "The Wizard" Michael Scott and was fascinated by the folklore of the Highlands, wrote (4 April 1812) to Joanna Baillie. Her play called *The Family Legend* had not long before been a tremendous hit at Drury Lane and Scott wanted to mention a family legend of his own, "a toadstone—a celebrated amulet." It belonged to his mother and she had repeatedly lent it to new mothers to protect their infants from the predations of jealous, bad fairies.

People think of fairies as rather sweet characters, but think of the Wicked Fairy in fairy tales or the Wicked Witch of the West in *The Wizard of Oz*. Fairies can be, tradition says, mean-spirited and vengeful. Look what happened when one was not properly invited to the christening of a princess: the poor female grew up to be cursed to prick her finger and cast into a coma from which only Prince Charming's kiss could awake her!

And, speaking of a fairy-tale prince, more than one was by some wicked spell changed into—a horrid toad!

Fairies can be devils and demons writ small, very nasty pieces of work.

IT'S HARD TO GET GOOD HOUSEHOLD HELP

Just as kobolds and knockers help with work in the mines, so pixies and brownies and other spirits are said to assist with household tasks (although they may get out of hand and start throwing pots and pans and dishes around, like poltergeists). In Russia there are different sorts of household helpers: one for the kitchen, one for the privy, and so on. Hilton Hall in England was said to have a pixie who complained he was not getting sufficient reward and announced that if he did not get new clothes he would no longer be helpful:

> Here's a cloak and here's a hood.
> The cauld lad of Hilton will do no more good.

CALLING UP THE DEVIL IN ENGLISH FOLKLORE

This was easy. You drew a chalk circle and threw your hat in it. You said the Lord's Prayer backwards. There are a number of folktales that suggest that merely saying "The Devil take it" in a fit of pique might bring him to do so.

BEN JONSON AND THE WITCH FINDERS AND DEVIL EXPERTS

Unlike his friend and rival Shakespeare, Jonson preferred contemporary follies as the subject of his satire. He ridiculed the con men and their dupes in *The Alchemist*. He pilloried evangelical zealots in *Batholomew Fair*. And in *The Devil Is an Ass*, he deals again with greed, confidence tricks, and "projectors" such as witch finders and those who say they can cure demonic possession. One of the characters in the play tries to evade the law by pretending to be bewitched and there is an actual demon on the loose, one Pug, a minor imp let out of hell for a one-day vacation to see what hell he can raise on earth. The demon discovers he is no match for the evil humans and he winds up in jail. Of all the comic treatments of The Devil in English, including the stories of Friar Rush (German *Rausch* suggested drunkeness) and Robert Greene's play of *Friar Bacon and Friar Bungay*, this is probably the best. Shaw's Devil in the "Don Juan in Hell" segment of *Man and Superman* is amusing but is probably to be put down as the most philosophical rather than funniest Evil One in our literature.

THE DEVIL IN TEN ENGLISH CATCHPHRASES

as The Devil said to his knee-buckles UK used when "there's a pair of us"

(come on) be a devil the British equivalent of US "go ahead and live it up"

The Devil is beating his wife it's raining, but the sun is shining

dimple in chin, the devil within more a proverb than a catchphrase, perhaps

God's good, and The Devil's not a bad 'un UK for "all things are in the lap of Allah"

if The Devil cast his net . . . UK "what a bunch he would get with this lot"

shore saints and sea devils UK of captains meek to employers, hard on their crews

Sunday saints and Monday devils UK of hypocritical churchgoers

where The Devil got the friar UK wherever it happened to be

THE DEVIL IN ANTIQUE ENGLISH SLANG

Devil among the tailors noisy row
Devil catcher clergyman

Devil dodger clergyman

Devil's bedposts four of spades

Devil's books playing cards

Devil's claws broad arrow marking UK government property and convicts

Devil's delight disturbance

Devil's dozen thirteen

Devil's guts length of chain (especially a surveyor's)

Devil's neckerchief hangman's noose

Devil's own anything particularly difficult or unpleasant

Devil's own luck very good luck (or, infrequently, bad luck)

Devil's picture gallery face cards or playing cards in general

Devil's smiles uncertain April weather, clouds and sunshine

Devil take the hindmost "last one there is a rotten egg"

Devil's teeth dice

A Terrible and seasonable Warning to young Men.

Being a very particular and True Relation of one *Abraham Joiner* a young Man about 17 or 18 Years of Age, living in *Shakesby's* Walks in *Shadwell*, being a Ballast Man by Profession, who on *Saturday* Night last pick'd up a lewd Woman, and spent what Money he had about him in Treating her, saying afterwards, if she wou'd have any more he must go to the Devil for it, and slipping out of her Company, he went to the *Cock* and *Lyon* in *King Street*, the Devil appear'd to him, and gave him a Pistole, telling him *he show'd never want for Money*, appointing to meet him the next Night at the *World's End* at Stepney ; Also how his Brother perswaded him to throw the Money away, which he did ; but was suddenly taken in a very strange manner ; so that they were fain to send for the Reverend Mr. Constable and other Ministers to pray with him ; he appearing now to be very Penitent ; with an Account of the Prayers and Expressions he makes use of under his Affliction, and the prayers that were made for him to free him from this violent Temptation.

The Truth of which is sufficiently attested in the Neighbourhood, he lying now at his mother's house, etc.

On the left, The Devil appears to a lecherous young man. On the right, Rev. Mr. Constable and other ministers pray for the lad. From an eighteenth-century chapbook.

CURSED BAKING

American housewives used to believe that if the cake fell or the bread burned a witch's spell was responsible. The "cure" was to burn a loaf deliberately. That was supposed to make the witch come to your house. She would ask to borrow something, but one had to be careful to give her absolutely nothing, not even a courteous word, otherwise one would lose all power to counteract her spells.

This superstition and "trying for a witch," attempting to find out who in the neighborhood was responsible for bad luck and bad baking, must have led to a lot of unfriendliness, discourtesy, and inhospitality.

MILK UNDER A SPELL

It was a custom in early America, if one thought one's cattle were under a spell, to get back at a witch by throwing the milking into the fire. Or one could have one's revenge without losing the milk if one dropped heavy stones into it or chopped it with knives.

A DOZEN ITEMS IN FOLK TRADITION

Devil's apple (*Datura stramonium*), thorn apple
Devil bird several kinds of birds, including the swift and an owl from Sri Lanka
Devil's bit (*Chamælirium luteum*), a member of the lily family, blazing star, fairyweed
Devil in a bush (*Nigela damascena*), a garden flower
Devil carriage, one for moving heavy artillery
Devil's club (*Fatula horrida*), a prickly, araliaceous plant
Devil's coach-horse (*Staphylinus olens*), the large trove beetle of repulsive appearance
Devil's fig (*Opuntiæ*), prickly pears
Devil fish, several kinds of alarming-looking fish, especially rays
Devil's needle, (*Libelluninæ*), dragon flies
Devil's nut (*Castanea equina*), horse chestnut
Devil wood (*Osmanthus americanus*), particularly hard wood

GOOD FENCES MAKE GOOD NEIGHBORS

Folklore tells us that just as a ring of strawberry plants around your property will keep all snakes out so a row of red flowers—in British lore called "soldiers," recalling the redcoats—will keep witches away. To keep a person in a room, try and reduce to a powder the hearts of a wolf and a horse. Put some of the powder on the doorstep.

THINGS THAT GO HUMP IN THE NIGHT

No less an authority than St. Augustine (*De Trinitate* III) states firmly that "devils do indeed collect human semen, by means of which they are able to produce bodily effects; but this cannot be done without some local movement, therefore demons can transfer the semen which they have collected into the bodies of others." Roman Catholics spread the rumor that Martin Luther's father was a demon. It was a part of folk belief for a long time, and may still be in some benighted places (say, rural Greece), that demons and vampires can and do have sex with and reproduce with mortal women.

A mother who is a demon is considered less likely but also possible, asserts the folk tradition.

BLACK ANNIS OF LEICESTER

Until recent years, Leicester children living near the Newarke were afraid to pass at night through Rupert's Gateway, leading to the castle, because a witch called Cat Anna was reputed to lurk there. This seems to be corruption of Black Anna or Annis who lay in wait in her "bower," a cave in the Dane Hills, for young children. Those she caught were scratched to death with her long claws, then their blood was sucked and their skins hung up to dry. As a poem by John Heyrick put it:

> Where down the plain the winding pathway falls,
> From Glen-field vill, to Lester's ancient walls;
> Nature, or art, with imitative power,
> Far in the Glenn has plac'd *Black Annis's Bower*.

> 'Tis said the soul of mortal man recoil'd
> To view Black Annis's eye, so fierce and wild;
> Vast talons, foul with human flesh, there grew
> In place of hands, and features livid blue,
> Glar'd in her visage; whilst her obscene waist
> Warm skins of human victims embrac'd.

To be more precise, the Dane Hills were an expanse of rough, hillocky ground off Glenfield Road, Leicester, which remained partly open until after the Second World War, when houses were built there. Part of the area, near to the present Convent of St. Catherine, was known as Black Annis' Bower-Close. On Easter Monday a fair was held there, attended by the mayor in his scarlet gown and other officials, accompanied by the waits. In the morning there were various entertainments and sporting events, followed by a hare-hunt at noon. Originally a real hare was hunted, but later the hounds and huntsmen followed the trail of a dead cat soaked in aniseed. Traditionally, the trail ended at the mayor's door, so the hunt went in full cry through the streets of the town. The custom was already ancient when it was first mentioned in the town records, in 1668. It seems to have fallen into disuse about a century later, though the fair continued. Even this was opposed, as the *Leicester Journal* reported in 1826: 'Within the last few years attempts have been made by the Proprietors and occupiers of the 'Dane Hill Closes' to put an entire stop to any diversion upon the Grounds during Easter Week.' Nevertheless the festivities continued at least until 1842, when the *Chronicle* noted: 'The Dane-hill fair was crowded with visitors, principally young people of the working classes, and the fields beyond the spot where the fair is held were also thronged with merry-makers.'

The same ground was used for family strolls, as one man wrote: 'As a child I remember walks to Black Anna's Bower, said to be a witch who lived in a tree somewhere near the present Dominican convent at Danes Hill.' In the twentieth century the area could still be reached on foot, though only by a narrow footpath, called 'The Black Pad.' In one of the mounds there was a cave, half-hidden by thorn bushes, with a stunted oak close by. Black Anna was reputed to have dug the cave with her own fingernails. She was also said to have been the same witch that warned Richard III of his fate (see page 13), and to have lived in cellars under Leicester Castle, linked to her bower by an underground passage. The delay in building on the Dane Hills was attributed to a suggestion that a witch was buried there, and another belief was that the area had been a Danish battleground, with the dead having been buried where they fell. Until recently, any particularly unpopular woman was referred to as Black Anna, and a spiteful one as Cat Anna.
—Ray Palmer, *The Folklore of Leicestershire and Rutland.*

CARTFULLS OF MAGIC POWER

In Iceland and other countries of *Norden*, the far north of Europe, it was an ancient custom to build carts and offer them to the *vanir* (fertility gods), especially to Lytir. A story goes that one King Erik had two such carts driven to a place where the god Lytir might find them. They were left overnight, but the god apparently had rejected them. They were left a second night, but still they were not noticed by the god. After a third night, however, sacrifices continually being made, the god accepted the gifts and the carts became so heavy (presumably with gods in them) that the oxen could not draw them.

The carts somehow got to Uppsala, however, and the king feasted in his great hall with the gods and asked them important questions, which it is said they answered for him secretly.

Thus in olden times people got a freight of information from divinities. There were indeed such carts. Examples have been found preserved in the peat bogs of Denmark and elsewhere. They date from the Iron Age. An elaborate cart that archeologists think was used for magic like this was found in the Oseburg ship burial.

SAMPO

Another magical object is the *sampo*, probably some kind of gem to which magical properties were attributed, maybe an opal. Finnish legends tell of expeditions to the frozen wastes to get a *sampo* from an old witch.

HOLDING UP THE SKY

Today people are beginning to recognize that women "hold up half the sky." Among the Samoyad Yuraks, reported the Finnish explorer T. Lehtisalo, the pole that held up their tents represented the "column that held up the sky" and out in the fields men placed certain stones to "hold up the sky" and worshipped them as idols.

In Old Norse belief every man was supported, held up as it were, by a female spirit (*kvinne-fylgior*) that accompanied him, and at least she was mostly benign. In the *Droplaugarsona-saga*, we read that Helgi was warned in a dream by such a female spirit (sometimes called *kona*) of enemies that appeared as ravenous wolves. In the *Víga-Glúms-saga*'s ninth chapter a female spirit in a dream appeared to him in a figure so large she filled the valley in which she woke. On waking, Glúm figured that this was probably the female spirit that had accompanied his maternal uncle and that he must have died for the spirit to be loosed. Her large size obviously was to be interpreted as meaning she was very powerful. And now Glúm was going to get, as it were, the luck of the family (*hamingja*). She would henceforth hold him up and strengthen him. No need for Glúm to be glum!

MAGIC TO DO HARM

The *Grimorium Verum* (*True Handbook of Magic*) is a version (probably eighteenth century but typically pretending to be early sixteenth century and written by a certain Alibeck the Egyptian, at Memphis) of the famous *Key of Solomon* that was medieval (though supposedly, as the title suggests, written by Solomon) and was on the Roman Catholic *Index Prohibitorum* in the Renaissance.

For reasons I cannot explain, this *Grimorium Verum* was what magicians in Denmark and southern Sweden seemed to prefer into the nineteenth century. Here is one of the "recipes" it offered, repeated for you:

Take nails from a coffin exhumed from consecrated ground and pull them with the formula, "Nails, I take thee so that thou mayest serve to turn aside and cause evil to all persons whom I will." Oddly, then you must add: "In the Name of The Father, The Son, and The Holy Ghost. Amen." You then drive nails into footprints left by the person you would injure, this time praying to Satan: "*Pater noster upto in terra*," a parody of the "Our Father," for this time he is "on earth," not "in Heaven." The nail is driven right into the footprint and the order is given: "Cause harm unto *N*. until I remove thee."

The victim will suffer until he or she finds the footprints and removes the nails, reciting these words: "I remove thee so that the evil which thou hast caused to *N*. will cease. In the Name of The Father, The Son, and the Holy Ghost. Amen."

CHARM AGAINST TOOTHACHE

There are all sorts of folk remedies for a toothache, but this one is folk magic, not folk medicine. It's from Norway.

On a long, narrow piece of paper write these words:

> *Agerin—Nagerin + 2*
> *Wagaerin—Jagerin + 2*
> *Spagerin—Sepia + 2*

Cut the paper into three parts and put one part to the aching tooth overnight, throwing the paper into the fire the next morning. Use the other two pieces in a similar way the two following nights. Not only will your toothache disappear—it will never return.

ODD CHARM FROM NORWAY

Norwegians "bind the neck" with a charm that translates thus:

Neck, neck! Nail in water!
The Virgin Mary casts steel into
    water.
Do you sin, I flit.

POWERS OF STONES

In *The Complete Book of Superstition, Prophecy and Luck*, I say something of the magical powers attributed to certain gems, ideas that are at least as old as Marbod, Bishop of Rennes, who nearly a thousand years ago wrote a *Liber lapidum*. In that it was claimed that holding a sapphire while praying made prayers more pleasing to God or wearing a diamond made a man invincible. Strange as it may seem, even today people believe that wearing an amethyst can ward off drunkeness, that opals are unlucky (except to those whose birthstone it is), and that an opal wrapped in a bay leaf can make one invisible.

Well, have you ever seen anyone with an opal wrapped in a bay leaf?

In Scandinavia there are many folk beliefs in the "powers" of certain stones. Americans use crystaels.

Hortus sanitatis (Mainz, 491) was one of many magical books printed early and fairly widely circulated in Europe. This illustration is from its chapter on the powers of stones.

THE DEVIL AND SANTA CLAUS

In Austria, on the Feast of St. Nicholas (our Santa Claus because of the Dutch in earlier America) folklore links two figures into a rather odd couple, Santa Claus and The Devil. Santa gives presents to good children; The Devil (*Krampus*) punishes the bad ones. The Finns claims they invented Santa Claus.

DEFENDING YOURSELF AGAINST DEVILS AND DEMONS

A good start is to be born on the Sabbath. Children born on that day are said to be immune to the depredations of devils and demons. Sunday's children may not be as pretty as children born on Monday—you know the old rhyme that begins "Monday's child is fair of face"—but they will be safer, "blithe and bonny, good and gay." That's in the old sense of *gay*, one supposes. For best results, be born at night and under a full moon. Old superstition says that if you are born "in the dark of the moon" you may not live to reach puberty. Be born at midnight and you may have the power to see the spirits of the dead. Born at sunrise, you will live long. Born at sunset, you will be lazy. Born on Christmas Day you may not get birthday presents along with your Christmas presents, but you will be psychic. Call the seventh son of a seventh son, "Doctor."

A FEW BOOKS ON RELIGION AND MYTHOLOGY

Altheim, Franz, *A History of Roman Religion* (1937)
Ames, Delano, *Egyptian Mythology* (1965)
Betz, Hans Dieter (trans. 6 ed.), *The Greek Magical Papyri . . . Spells* (1996)
Fairbanks, A., *The Mythology of Greece and Rome* (1907)
Ferm, Vergilius, *Ancient Religions* (1950)
Hurston, Zora Neale, *Tell My Horse* (1938)
Oldenberg, H., *Ancient India* (1896)
Osborne, Harold, *South American Mythology* (1968)
Parrinder, Geoffrey, *African Mythology* (1967)
Peeters, Hermes, *The Religions of China* (1941)
Thomas, Keith, *Religion and the Decline of Magic* (1971)
Thompson, R. Campbell, *The Devils and Evil Spirits of Babylon* (1903)

BRITISH SIN-EATERS

So that the dead would rest easy—and not walk—there was an old custom in England and Wales of sin-eating. At the funeral some poor person was given a loaf of bread and a pot of drink and paid sixpence or so to eat and drink the sins of the departed, taking them upon himself. This protected the corpse from devils and demons entering into it. Sir James Frazer in *The Golden Bough* speaks of people in other countries who take on the sins of the dead to free their souls. Christ took our sins.

IRON

Gold and silver will give you what you want from people. Iron will accomplish what you want from devils and demons, which is protection.

The priests of the Sabines and the Romans could not shave with iron; they used bronze. The Druids cut mistletoe but never with iron. When an Arab sees a *jini* he says, "Iron!" to protect himself. Some people put an iron nail on corpses or on food carried from one place to another, or use such a nail in other ways to ward off demons. An iron horseshoe is nailed up to protect premises (always with the points *up*, unless you want "the power to run out of it"). The very mention of iron can drive away evil spirits at sea, and fairies and pixies on land. The use of iron to drive away demons was forbidden as heresy by the Jews and Coptic priests. In some other religions, iron (preferably a knife) can protect against demons; in some societies an iron knife is placed under a sick person's pillow and it used to be a custom in Teutonic countries, and elsewhere, to put such a knife into a childbed "to cut the pain" and to ward off evil.

The Temple of Solomon was built without the use of iron, as were the altars of the ancient Jews. Iron should come nowhere near the making of magical altars today, particularly those intended for black magic (these must face north). Steel is recommended by some ritual magicians for the ritual sword, but I would suggest that except for ceremonies involving Aries (whose metals are iron and steel) iron is contraindicated.

Of course, ritual magic can be performed in various circumstances, with various equipment, and at various times, but the proper preparations and materials make any job easier and *taiijas ttva* (21 March to 21 June) is the best season with *vayu tattva* (21 June to 23 September) next best, the Hindus say. If I were you, I would stay away from iron in ritual magic. From ritual magic, too, perhaps. As the Bible says in another connection, the iron might enter into your soul.

PARSLEY

In Devonshire they say if you transplant parsley there will be a death in the family and The Devil will take over the garden.

For magic in plants all across Europe, see Isidoor Teirlinck's *Flora diabolica* . . . (1925) and the many books on the folklore of herbs, etc., medicinal, plants, etc.

COMMON NAMES FOR PLANTS

The impact of witchcraft on people's sensibilities is reflected by such things as these common names for plants: witches'-broom, witches' thimbles, witchgrass, witch hazel, etc.

The name of witch hazel comes from the twigs used by witches in divining. Magic wands were sometimes made of this wood as well, but yew, ash, or elder is preferable.

MAGIC FROM FOLKLORE

Are these old customs dealing in black arts or just harmless superstitions?

To see whom you will marry: Go to the north side of the church and take three tufts of grass (as rank as possible), put them under your pillow, and in your dream the person you will marry will appear. Or you and other girls can toss a cowslip ball back and forth while you run down the names in your Rolodex; when the ball falls to the ground, that's the one. If you want to marry within the year, pick St. John's Wort with the dew on it (but not naked, or you will conceive). If you just want to know who your best friend is, put yarrow in a flannel bag under your pillow and recite:

> Thou pretty herb of Venus tree, thy true name is yarrow.
> Now whom my bosom friend must be pray tell thou me tomorrow.

Don't pick devil's bit: it will make The Devil come to you at night.

To cure the baby of measles: Tear a piece of linen into nine strips. Spread each piece with garlic from nine bulbs. Wrap them around the baby for nine days. Bury the strips in the garden and the baby will be cured.

Aphrodisiac: Endive will work only if dug up with a stag's horn or a piece of gold, and only if dug up on the Feast of St. Peter (27 June) or of St. James (25 July). In the west of England, you can just pin on a sprig of valerian. Any root shaped like genitals must be good.

Angelica: Blooming on the Feat of St. Michael, it is a protection against demons and devils. It is also associated with the Holy Spirit.

Rowan: Folklore says this tree has many magical powers. Find one that no one else has cut this way and with a household knife cut some twigs from it. Be sure to bring them home by a route different than the one you took to the tree. They will bring protection to the home against devils, demons, and disease. Hawthorne and mountain laurel, however, are very bad to bring into the house. Even daffodils and other flowers that "hang their heads" are unlucky in the house, along with white chrysanthemums.

Primroses: Never ever pick fewer than thirteen primroses for the house bouquet. Indeed, make all bouquets with an odd number.

Dill: This banishes witches, but early America chewed the seeds as Meeting House Seeds because chewing them relieved the boredom of interminable sermons.

Elder: This tree has many magical properties, it makes a good magic wand, planted near the house it keeps witches away, it can be used to point out local witches, it provides twigs that (when notched with the number of warts and buried) cures warts, and has many other uses. Don't cut an elder tree down without reciting the magical rhyme to gain its pardon or you will deeply regret it. It's as powerful as an apple tree, an oak, or even an ash. They should never be cut down.

THE ELDER TREE

Whole books have been devoted to the superstitions attached to trees, but here the elder can serve as an example. It was sometimes wrongly called the Judas Tree, assuming that Judas Iscariot hanged himself from one, and the mushrooms that grew on it were Jews' Ears or Judas' Ears. In the *Anatomy of the Elder* (1653) and other curious old books, there are superstitions about carrying elder twigs in your pockets to prevent your rump from getting sore when you ride too far or too fast, using elder twigs in the creation of amulets to protect children (but don't beat your boys with an elder rod—it hinders their growth), or putting a twig through a hole made in a lame pig's ear to cure it. Of chief interest here is the use of elder branches to ward off witches and demons.

WHAT THE DEUCE!

Dusius was the name of a kind of incubus or succubus known among the Gauls. When we say "What the deuce!" we may be remembering that or, just as likely if not more so, using "Deuce" as equivalent to "Devil," just as we exclaim "Jeepers Creepers" instead of "Jesus Christ."

SAINT MAHOUN

In some of the early mystery plays in England, Satan is called "Saint Mahoun." *Mahoun* seems to be a disrespectful way of referring to the prophet Muhammad. In popular speech St. Mahoun is obsolete but we still say Old Nick, and Americans used to say Mr. Scratch and other names. One such name, now forgotten, was Old Boots, preserved in the antique expression, "It is raining old boots," meaning, "It is raining like The Devil."

WARLOCK

This is a Scottish word, a sixteenth-century version of the Middle English *warlow(e)*. It simply means a male witch (once called a *wicca*, a *magus*, or *mage*), though *witch* is now used pretty much for both sexes. Buried in the origins of these words is the concept of truth deceived, the wizard being a wise man using his wits for evil and sorcery (originally a diviner casting lots). The Devil is called the equivalent of warlock in ancient English writings.

YEW

The yew is a good example of the ambiguity of evidence when it comes to examining the supposedly magical powers that folks attributed to trees and plants.

Yew was traditionally planted in churchyards. It may have been planted in churchyards (says Sir Thomas Browne's musing on urn burial, *Hydrotaphia*) because, evergreen, it was taken as a symbol of eternal life and the Resurrection. It may have been taken over from certain pre-Christian rites connected with the dead. Or because archery was at one time the principal sport encouraged by the state—so that there would be a large supply of bowmen in time of war—and yew made excellent bows. Yew trees may have been grown within the walled churchyards simply because the cattle could not get at the leaves then, and so the trees were protected.

MOTHER SHIPTON

Mother Shipton (whom we met in an earlier chapter) appeared in many "true chronicle" sensational chapbooks of the seventeenth century and in a play by Thomas Thompson, *The Life of Mother Shipton*, largely based on the legends. A demon hears her complaints about being poor and marries her in the guise of a rich and handsome nobleman. She gains magical powers from the demon (whose name is Radamon) and becomes famous as a wise woman throughout Yorkshire. When demons come to claim her, she outwits them and is saved, so the play is a comedy and the old lady, charming in two senses of the word, triumphs. Such a positive picture of a witch or wise woman is seldom seen. One seldom deals with demons and gets off scot free. A lesson witchcraft emphasizes: everything costs.

MELODRAME ON THE PARISIAN STAGE

In the nineteenth century, demons and sorcery were big draws in Paris. Hits included *Les Templiers* (Raynouard's play about the Knights Templar),

Charles Nodier's epoch-making *Le Vampire*, Alexandre Dumas's *Urbain Grandier* (about The Devils of Loudun), and Jules Bois's *Les Noces de Sathan* (by a follower of the Abbé Boullan). At the turn of the century "The Divine Sarah" Bernhardt starred as *La Sorciére* in a play by one of the giants of the French popular theater of the time, Sardou.

See Alfred Mortier's *Le Démon dans ses incarnations dramatiques* (1924).

FRENCH DRAMA AND MELODRAMA ON THE ENGLISH STAGE

The simplicity with which works from the Parisian stage could be stolen and translated for London audiences— particularly the early melodramas and the great hits by Eugène Scribe and Victorien Sardou which followed— almost stifled British dramatists in the nineteenth century. Indeed, I wrote *Nineteenth-Century British Drama* (1968) to show that it was untrue, as so many still said in the sixties, that "there is no British drama between Sheridan and Shaw." When the anthology was reprinted in the eighties many still clung to the old opinion.

Dickens shows us an Englishman asked to translate a French play for immediate use by a tacky theater company. Many such plays dealt with demons, vampires, ghosts, and other sensational topics. Charles Selby, our example here, adapted one for the respectable Adelphi Theatre. "Right up the alley" of this present book, it was called *The Mysterious Stranger* in English and was printed immediately after its stage success in the National Acting Drama Series (vol. 3, no. 6). The original was a two-act *vaudeville* by Louis-François-Nicolaie Clarville and E. Damarin called *Satan; ou, Le Diable à Paris* (1944). Today it is practically unknown, as are most of these popular entertainments of both the Paris and London stages. None of those were grappling with the profound moral questions of the sort raised by Mephistopheles in *Faust* (in which Gounod and others found material for operas as well), such as his "I am a part of that force that always wishes to do evil and yet produces good." No, it was just good, sensational, thrilling "meller." In the US it was "ten'-twent'-thirt'" (from the popular prices in cents).

THE DEVIL IN THE MINOR FOREIGN CINEMA

From Italy we have had *Un Angelo per Satana* (a 1966 film, set in the 1870s), *La Maschera del demonio* (1950, based on a story by Gogol), *La Leggenda di Faust* (1948), *Santana* (a silent epic of 1912 released with the English title *Satan; or, The Drama of Humanity*), *Baba Yaga* (1973), and more. From France come a number of films of French and Italian collaboration as well as characteristically French cinema products with The Devil or Satan in the titles, which are really stories of crime and twisted love, "the devil in the flesh," and so on. But there are also the likes of *Thank You, Satan* (1989), in which a 14-year old girl sells her soul to The Devil to help her family. From Argentina, Spain, and Mexico there are a number of films in Spanish, but titles such as *Gritos en la noche* (1962) are misleading when rendered as *The Demon Doctor*, *The Awful Dr. Orlof*, and *The Diabolical Doctor Satan*, because the doctor is a mad scientist, not a mad Satanist. Brazil offers, unexpectably, little on native devil-worship, but Germany has *Brenn Hexe Brenn* (1970, with a sequel on the mark of The Devil), *Magdalena von teufel besessen* (1974, about demonic possession), and *Tod und teufel* (1973). There are devil pictures from Hungary, Czechoslovakia, and Poland, little seen elsewhere. Examples are *Ordogi kisertetek*, *Hratky s certem*, and *Diabel*. British filmgoers have enjoyed *The Devil Rides Out* (1967, also known as *The Devil's Bride*) and many more, though the vampire and monster horror films have been more popular. I have not seen the Egyptian film called variously *Al-Bidaya*, *Satan's Empire*, and *The Empire of Satan* (1989), but the characters who crash in the desert do not, I think, include The Evil One in person.

THE DEVIL AND DEMONS AT THE DRIVE-IN

Minor American efforts featuring The Devil on screen include D. W. Griffith's *The Sorrows of Satan* (1926, where The Devil appears as a manipulating nobleman), Bernard McEveetey's *The Brotherhood of Satan* (1970, also as *Come In, Children*—Wild West witches), John C. Higgins' *Daughters of Satan* (1972—three witches in an old painting cast a spell on the buyer's household and kill him), Fritz Weaver in *King Cobra* (1979, also as *Jaws of Satan*—Satan appears at an inopportune moment, as a big cobra), and *The Devil* (1908), *While the Devil Laughs* (1921), *The Masks of the Devil* (1928), *Devil Doll (The Witch of Timbuktu*, 1931), *Traffic with the Devil* (1946), and many more.

The word *demon* in a title is often a reference to a speed demon, a sex demon, or such, but you may find the diabolical in the likes of *Le Démon au feminin* (1994, Algerian story of exorcism that goes wrong), *The Demon Lover* (1976, a Michigan Satanist vows vengeance as his flock cools off), *Demon Wind* (1991, a Satanist cult again), *The Evil* (1978, The Devil moves into a psychologist's new home), *Night of the Demon* (1957, based on M. R. Jame's *Casting the Runes*), *Satan's Mistress* (1980, though the bored housewife teams up not with Satan but a demon), and *Yashaga ike* (1979, in which demons are released from a pond in Japan).

To this list you can add: *Maid of Salem* (1937), *The Satanist* (1968), *The Witchmaker* and *Succubus* (both 1969), and *Daughter of Satan* and *Sata-*

nis: The Devil's Mass (both 1970. Maybe someone will stage a Devil Film Festival!

THE CONCEPT OF EVIL AND THE THEATER OF DREAMS

Motion pictures have been for a century now one of the most important evidences of and sources of American fantasy life, so Stanley Rothman's article on religion and the movies, "Is God Really Dead in Beverly Hills?" (*American Scholar* 65:2, Spring 1996), is important. He concludes that religion has "played rather poorly in Hollywood movies for the past 40 years" though the movie moguls cannot really find any truly useful substitute for the traditional good guys/bad guys way of looking at the world. A shrewd student of social change, Rothman sums up:

> Insofar as we never fully succeed in mastering our violent anti-social drives, and insofar as the child continues to function within the adult, it can be argued that most human beings require some mythic structure if they are to function effectively as responsible adults. The myth of the inevitable triumph of good over evil may seem simpleminded to the sophisticated Hollywood producers and directors, who believe that they themselves do not need such myths. They are, in fact, little different from the audiences they serve. They cannot find a satisfactory substitute for religion, though they continue to try. Their failure is reflected in a plethora of films that document the triumph of evil, an evil which, as in *Alien*, often emerges from the bowels of the victim. One suspects that these themes are, at least partially, symbolic of a feared loss of control of the evil impulses within the self.

Typical of modern cinema in some respects was the porno flick *The Devil in Miss Jones*. Likewise typical are the regular films, filled with sex and the sicker pornography of violence, that seem to say that The Devil exists and is inside Joe Sixpack and every other modern person.

As Pogo said in cartoons (which Hollywood films increasingly have come to resemble) a generation or so ago, "We have met the enemy and he is us."

MELMOTH THE WANDERER

Charles Robert Maturin (1782–1823) was the author of sensational plays and novels drenched in *delectatio morbosa*, the most famous of which was *Melmoth the Wanderer* (1820), a masterpiece of the Gothic novel. Let Mario

Praz in *The Romantic Agony* (second edition reissued, 1970) give highlights of the plot, which involves a pact with The Devil:

> Melmoth has made a bargain with Satan, by which, in exchange for his soul, his life is to be prolonged; but he can still escape damnation if he succeeds in finding someone to share his fate. He wanders thus for more than a hundred years from country to country, spreading terror with his eyes, which no one would wish ever to have seen, for, once seen, it was impossible to forget them. Wherever there is a man reduced to desperation, there appears Melmoth to haunt him, in the hope of persuading him to entrust him with his fate: he explores the asylum, the prison, the frightful dungeons of the Inquisition, the houses of the wretched. Like a tiger in ambush, he peers in search of evil and sin; he has something of Goethe's Mephistopeles, something of the Byronic hero, something of the Wandering Jew [cursed because he did not assist Christ with His cross], something of the vampire. . . .

Melmoth finds an innocent lover in Immalee, who wants to share his fate and is married to him "at dead of night, by the spectre of a monk, among the ruins of an ancient monastery." She and her child die. To return to Praz's description of the plot:

> Melmoth, after wandering the earth for a hundred and fifty years, returns to his ancestral castle, and there is seized by devils who hurl him into the sea. . . .

A footnote to all this: Oscar Wilde, in exile in Paris after his life was wrecked by scandal and jail, took the name "Sebastian Melmoth." Melmoth in the novel says: "I have traversed the world in the search, and no one, to gain that world, would lose his own soul!"

MINOR WORKS ABOUT THE OCCULT

PLAYS

Baxter, J. H., *The Devil and Mr. Mulcahy*

Buchan, A., *The Devil's Bargain*

Sand, George, *The Seven Strings of the Lyre*

Schenk, L. L., *A House for David*

Walcott, David, *Ti-Jean and his Brothers*

Witkiewicz, S. I., *The Beelzebub Sonata*

NOVELS

Barr, Amelia E., *The Black Shilling*

Peterson, Henry, *Dulcibel: A Tale of Old Salem*

Taylor, M. Imlay, *Anne Scarlett: A Romance of Colonial Times*

PAGAN SONGS

Tod, Alan et al. *Carry Me Home*

THE KING OF THE BLACK ART
[Condensed version by K. Briggs 1977]

There was once an old fisherman, and one day as he was fishing
he drew out a long box, and inside was a baby boy. He took it home
to his wife, and they brought it up as their own. When the boy
was fourteen years old, a ship came to land, and on the bridge there
was a man dressed as fine as a king, juggling with three poison-
balls with spikes on them. The stranger came to shore, and seemed
to take a great fancy to the boy; he offered to take him away for a
year and a day, and to teach the boy his art. He wheedled so that
the fisherman and his wife agreed, and the boy went away with the
stranger. In a year and a day the ship was back, and the boy was
back, tossing seven poison-balls. The old couple were so pleased
that they allowed the stranger to take the boy for another year and
a day, but he did not come back. So the old wife sent the fisherman to look for him. The fisherman traveled on and on, until in
a wee hut in a wood he saw an old, old man, who asked him in for
the night. The fisherman told the old man his story, and the old
man said, "There's little doubt that the King of the Black Art has
your son, and there is no more I can tell you; but maybe my eldest
brother can help you. He lives a week's journey from here. Tell him
I sent you." So the next morning the fisherman set out, and he jour-
neyed for a week to the older brother's house. And if the first old
man was old, this was three times older. But he asked the fisherman in, and gave him food and lodging, and told him what to do.
He was to go on to the King of the Black Art's castle, and ring the
bell and ask for his son. They would laugh at him, and the King
would tell him to choose his son from among fourteen pigeons that
he would throw up into the air, and he was to choose a little, weak,
raggety-winged one, that flew lower than the rest. The fisherman
did as he was told, and chose the raggety-winged pigeon. "Take
him, and be damned to you!" said the King, and his son stood
beside him. They went away together.

"I'd never have got free if you'd not come for me," said the
boy. "The King of the Black Art and his two sons are at the head
of all the wizards in the country. But I've learned something, and
we'll get something back from them. Now, we're coming to a town
where there is a market, and I'll change myself into a greyhound.
All the lords and the gentry will offer to buy me, but don't you

sell me till the King of the Black Art comes. You can take five hundred pounds from him, but mind you, father, for your life, do not sell the collar and strap, but take it off me." So, in a moment, he'd turned himself into the finest greyhound dog that ever was seen, and the fisherman led him into the market. Knights and nobles were crowding round him to buy, but he would take no offers till the King of the Black Art and his two sons came into the place, and he would not let him have the dog under five hundred pounds. Then he took the strap from round the dog's neck, and tied a piece of string round it instead, and walked away. As soon as he was out of the town, there was his son beside him, for he had been the strap. They went on to another town, and the son turned himself into a grand stallion horse, but he warned his father not to sell the bridle with him, whatever he did. The knights and nobles came round him as before, for no such horse had ever been seen in those parts; but he would not sell him to anyone till the King of the Black Art and his two sons came, and he asked a thousand pounds from him. "He looks worth it," said the King of the Black Art, "and I'll give it if he is as good as his looks. But no man can buy a horse without trying it." The fisherman stood out for a while, but the King said, "Come to this wee house, and I'll show you the gold you'll get. But I must just ride him round the fairground." The glint of the gold was too much for the fisherman. He said, "Just ride him round the ground then," and the King leapt on the horse's back. The fisherman turned to look at the gold, and it turned to dung before his eyes, and when he looked back, the horse was gone.

The King of the Black Art rode the horse back to a stable where he was fastened at with other horses, and they were fed on salt beef, and not given a drop to drink till their tongues were swollen and coated. One day the King and his sons had gone hunting, and the boy spoke to the groom who brought their food, and begged to be given a drink. The groom was frightened, but the horse begged until he had compassion on it, and led it out to the stream. The horse begged him to loosen the bit so that he could drink, and when he did so it slipped its head out of the bridle, and slipped into the stream as a salmon. As he did so, all the bells of the castle rang, and the magicians dashed back from the hills, turned themselves into otters, and swam after the salmon. They came closer and closer, until they were almost on him, then he leapt into the air, and turned in to a swallow. The otters turned into hawks, and pursued him. The swallow saw a lady sitting in a garden, flew to her, and turned into a ring on her finger. The hawks swept round her and flew away. Then the ring spoke. It said, "Lady, in a few minutes three labourers will come here, and offer to build up your dyke. When they have done it, they will ask for the ring from your finger for payment. But say to them that you would rather throw it into that bonfire, and throw it as you speak." The lady said she would do as he told her, and in a few minutes the three labourers arrived. They built up the walls as if by magic, and when she offered them money, they asked for the ring, but she threw it into the fire. The labourers turned themselves into three blacksmiths, and began to blow up the fire, but the ring hopped out on the other side into a pile of corn, and turned itself into a grain in the pile. The magicians turned into three cocks, and began to eat the corn, but the boy turned into a fox, and snapped off the three cocks' heads as quick as thought. So the King of the Black Art was defeated, and the boy rejoined his father, and they lived prosperously all their days by his magic art.

A PLAY ABOUT THE EVIL EYE

Despite the fact that Italians, especially the peasantry, are famously superstitious, there has not been a very great deal of the occult in popular literature. There seems, in fact, to be more about Italian superstition in the English and French melodramas of the nineteenth century, a period in which the *banditti* and other colorful characters of Italian life furnished a lot of material for popular drama. The absence of references to superstition in Italy itself may be due in part to various kinds of censorship, such as the concordat between Mussolini and the Vatican to keep off the stages of Rome in Fascist times any matter that would outrage or embarrass Roman Catholic authorities.

Ettore Schmitz, a Jewish writer who was famous under the pseudonym of Italo Svevo, was an outsider in many ways—Prof. Connell of Glasgow described him as "a businessman who loved literature, an Austro-Hungarian subject who loved Italy, a pacifist in the middle of a world war, a Jew"—and felt free to write about one long-standing Italian superstition. His work *Il Malocchio* (The Evil Eye) was discussed by Beno Weiss in a paper delivered at the Third Annual Conference of the American Association of Teachers of Italian (New York, 1986).

TUESDAY, MAY 18, 1897, AT A QUARTER-PAST TEN O'CLOCK A.M.,

WILL BE PRESENTED, FOR THE FIRST TIME,

DRACULA
OR
THE UN-DEAD

IN A PROLOGUE AND FIVE ACTS
BY
BRAM STOKER

Count Dracula	Mr. JONES.
Jonathan Harker	Mr. PASSMORE.
John Seward, M.D.	Mr. RIVINGTON.
Professor Van Helsing	Mr. T. REYNOLDS.
Quincey P. Morris	Mr. WIDDICOMBE.
Hon. Arthur Holmwood (*afterwards Lord Godalming*)	Mr. INNES.
M. F. Renfield	Mr. HOWARD.
Captain Swales	Mr. GURNEY.
Coastguard	Mr. SIMPSON.
Attendant at Asylum	Mr. PORTER.
Mrs. Westenra	Miss GURNEY.
Lucy Westenra	Miss FOSTER.
Mina Murray (*afterwards Mrs. Harker*)	Miss CRAIG.
Servant	Miss CORNFORD.
Vampire Woman	Mrs. DALY.

SYNOPSIS OF SCENERY

Prologue: Transylvania.

SCENE 1.—Outside the Castle.	SCENE 6.—The Count's Room.
2.—The Count's Room.	7.—The same.
3.—The same.	8.—The Chapel Vault.
4.—The Castle.	9.—The Count's Room.
5.—The Ladies' Hall.	

Act I.

SCENE 1.—The Boudoir at Hillingham.	SCENE 4.—The same—Night.
2.—Dr. Seward's Study.	5.—The same.
3.—The Churchyard, Whitby.	

Act II.

SCENE 1.—The Boudoir - Hillingham.	SCENE 8.—The same.
2.—The same.	9.—The same.
3.—The same.	10.—Mrs. Harker's Morning Room.
4.—The same.	11.—Room in the Berkeley Hotel.
5.—Outside Hillingham.	12.—Mrs. Harker's Drawing-Room.
6.—Lucy's Room.	13.—The same.
7.—The same.	14.—Outside the North Hospital.

Act III.

SCENE 1.—Lucy's Tomb.	SCENE 3.—Lucy's Tomb.
2.—Room in the Berkeley Hotel.	4.—Outside the Tomb.

Act IV.

SCENE 1.—Room in the Berkeley Hotel.	SCENE 6.—Renfield's Room.
2.—Dr. Seward's Study.	7.—Mrs. Harker's Room.
3.—The same.	8.—Dr. Seward's Study.
4.—Carfax.	9.—Room in the Piccadilly House.
5.—Dr. Seward's Study.	10.—Dr. Seward's Study.

Act V.

SCENE 1.—Dr. Seward's Study.	SCENE 4.—Outside the Castle—Night.
2.—Room in Hotel - Varna.	5.—The same—Before Sunset.
3.—Room in Hotel—Galatz.	

Stage Manager	Mr. H. J. LOVEDAY.
Musical Director	Mr. MEREDITH BALL.
Acting Manager	Mr. BRAM STOKER.

Dr. Jeanne Youngson's Count Dracula Fan Club library has thousands of items relating to vampires and other evil creatures. Here is pictured one of the rarest of collectors' items: the program from a single performance (actually a sort of reading of his novel, for copyright purposes) at Sir Henry Irving's *The Lyceum* in London, 18 May 1897.

INNOCENT BLOOD

"Whosoever eats my flesh and drinks my blood shall have life eternal." It was the Body and Blood of Christ, created in the transubstantiation of the Mass, that gave life. The Eucharist continued the older Jewish concept that "the blood is the life," and the Christian doctrines led to superstitious use of human blood. Gabriel Ronay in *The Dracula Myth* (1972) is just one of the scholars who attest to the connection made between the Eucharist and even more ancient pagan beliefs and the fact that in Europe the blood of humans continued into Christian times to be regarded as life-giving. The mad Hungarian Countess Bathory had young girls murdered so that she could bathe in their blood in her efforts to preserve her youth and beauty. Anti-Semites spread rumors that medieval Jews were killing innocent children to use their blood to make magical *matzohs*!

The blood of virgins was prescribed by learned physicians as a cure for many diseases. It was an ingredient in magical elixirs. Pacts with The Devil were signed in blood. It was drunk at the Black Mass and occasionally the congregation was sprinkled with blood rather than with holy water. A drop of a person's blood was eagerly sought by those who wanted to work evil against a person (though a lock of hair or a finger-nail clipping would do in a pinch).

"Contaminated" blood, especially from menstruating women, was said to be dangerous and powerfully evil, and was used in certain magical recipes for that very reason. It was, in fact, a lot easier to obtain than the "innocent" blood of virgins or (as Macbeth's witches put it) "new-born babes." Why blood connected with sexuality should be regarded as "impure" and that connected with virginity "pure" reminds us of the deep-seated sex-negative aspects of Christian thought, but that is another subject for another day.

BLOOD SPEAKS

It was long a folk belief that if the murderer touched the corpse of his victim it would bleed to accuse him. Shakespeare says that murder speaks with "miraculous organ" and "murder will out," of course, still is a part of common speech.

Blood can reanimate vampires, it is alleged. Modern allegations of Satanic rituals, however, seem to play down the use of blood in these nefarious operations and seldom is it said children are murdered for their blood. This may be too horrible to contemplate.

Readers of *The Odyssey* will recall that when Odysseus wants to reanimate the spirits of the dead, he pours the blood of sacrificed black rams into a ditch. This gives the ghosts the strength and power of speech they need. This is one of the less disgusting examples of the use of blood in necromancy. I spare you others of recent madness.

DEMONS OF THE NIGHT

Under this title, Joan C. Kessler has edited and translated tales from nineteenth-century France by such famous writers as Balzac, Dumas, Gauthier, Maupassant, Prosper Merimée, Gérard de Nerval, and Jules Verne, as well as historically important but lesser known fictions such as Charles Nodier's *Smarra* (1821), said to be the first French exploration of dreams and unconscious.

However, the tales deal primarily with vampires, psychic, and "real," not with demons. The vampire and associated monsters such as the lamia, horla, and so on, are not devils or demons. Vampire literature is already huge. We need not add to it in this present book. Both demons and vampires are said sometimes to take the shape of bats to suck human blood.

We must add that werewolves are not devils or demons any more than vampires are, but things get confusing when both demons and humans (sorcerers, werewolves, etc.) both take animal shapes.

The principal connection of devils, demons, vampires, and werewolves is the sexual one. Even ecclesiastical writers and pseudo-ecclesiastical experts (such as Montague Summers, who has remarkable books on witchcraft, vampires, and werewolves) get into the sexual symbolism and lust that lie not very deep under these related topics.

FAMILARS

If you look into it, you may wonder why Violet Tweedale's *Ghosts I Have Seen* ever reached a second edition (1920), or even a first. But some people believed her stories of the familiar who accompanied everywhere the Polish nobleman Laski (who visited England in the reign of the first Elizabeth and was known to Dr. Dee and others involved in the occult)—it was called Buisson—and the one another nobleman (this one a Prince Valori) picked up at a *sabbat* in France and could not shake.

NECROMANCY

Nathaniel Hawthorne wrote importantly about dealing with The Devil (*Young Goodman Brown*) and other aspects of the occult, but his work on necromancy, *Feathertop*, is less known and well worth seeking out.

It may be that the *locus classicus* in Spanish literature is in the *Cantigas de Santa María*, a masterpiece of medieval Galician literature, by Alfonso the Wise, number 125.

OUTSIDERS

Of all the images of evil attractive to the outsiders, the young radicals, the self-proclaimed enemies of the system, the vampire is the most popular. The biggest cliché of independent, small-budget films is—the vampire. The best of these "indie" productions so far is *Near Dark*. You may have a lot of trouble finding it. Big-budget *outsider* films abound.

THE CLASSIC AMERICAN STORY OF THE DEVIL

This is *Young Goodman Brown*, written in 1835 by Nathaniel Hawthorne, who was haunted by Salem's story. We have noted ancestor Will

Hathorne (as the name was then spelled), a dour Massachusetts magistrate who hounded Quakers and his son John, a hanging judge in the Salem trials. "Strong traits of their nature have intertwined with mine," wrote Hawthorne, and his reclusive, brooding personality, shot through with the dark thread of Puritan pessimism that characterized all American literature of his century, influences this ambiguous fable (was it all a dream?) in which the young fellow loses his wife (Faith) and meets The Devil and his followers.

THE BEST STORY OF A CURSE

This surely must be *Casting the Runes* by Montague Rhodes James. You will find it in my anthology *Tales of Mystery and Melodrama* or somewhere else. Don't miss it. It is a masterpiece, better even than W. W. Jacob's terrorizing tale of *The Monkey's Paw*.

Various devices the French call the equivalent of "devils": two devices for moving loads, a kitchen gadget, and a jack-in-the-box and bolo.

THE DEVIL IN SPANISH EXPRESSIONS

Estar un diablo means "there is a problem"; *estudiar uno con el demonio* is said of anyone who is so smart he must have studied with The Devil; and The Devil knows so much not because he is The Devil but because he is so old (and has a lot of experience), *más sabe el diablo por ser viejo que por ser diablo*. Bad luck comes often because The Devil doesn't sleep (*el demonio que no duerme*) and if you give up in despair you might as well give The Devil your flock and your signature on the deed (*dar el diablo el hato y el garabato*). Of reprobates who reform just because they are tired and can't keep up the pace, the Spanish say *el diablo, harto de carne, se metió fraile*— he became a monk.

Very colorful are such expressions as *donde el diablo perdió el poncho*: the place where The Devil lost his cloak is unknown and far away. When there's much malice or complication involved, The Devil is there: *aquí hay mucho diablo*. To deplore ingratitude you say *así pagar el diablo a quien bien le sarvi*. To those who fritter away time you say *quando el diablo no tiene que hacer, con el rabo macha moscas*. To those who spoil their children you say *tanto quiso el diablo a sus hijos que les saccó los ojos*.

HALF A DOZEN FRENCH EXPRESSIONS ABOUT THE DEVIL

In every language there are expressions, proverbs, and other references to The Devil. To take half a dozen examples from French to parallel those we note from English:

Le diable pourait mourir que j n'heriterais pas de ses cornes (The Devil could die and I wouldn't even inherit his horns). I never have any luck at all.

Il mangerait le diable et ses cornes (he could eat The Devil horns and all). He's a great trencherman/glutton.

C'est le diable à confesser (it's The Devil to the confessional). It's a damned hard thing to do.

Bruler une chandelle au diable (to burn a candle to The Devil). To act dishonestly to get something.

Le diable bat sa femme et marie sa fille (The Devil is beating his wife and marrying his daughter). It's raining but the sun is shining.

Le diable chant grand'messe (The Devil is saying High Mass). The hypocrite is pretending to be virtuous.

VOODOO IN LITERATURE

Voodoo for a long time has been both a religious and political force in such countries of African legacy as Haiti, Cuba, and Brazil and has entered not only their folklore but their literature (which is hardly known in English-speaking countries). Michel S. Laguerre has written on *Voodoo and Politics in Haiti* (1989) and Joseph Ferdinand on "The New Political Statement in Haitian Fiction" (in *Voices from Under: Black Narrative in Latin America and the Caribbean*, ed. William Luis, 1984). In the on-line MLA bibliography, one can easily locate work by Charles Asselin ("Voodoo Myths in Haitian Literature"), Sal Scaloura ("A Salute to the Spirits"), Andrew-Marcel d'Ans ("*Legende historique et identité haïtienne . . .*"), Janis A. Mayes on the fiction of Marie Chauvet, and the writing of other scholars. Voodoo, a mixture of pagan African and Christian European religion—see Leslie G. Desmangles's *The Faces of the Gods: Voodoo and Roman Catholicism in Haiti* (1992)—has become a part of many syncretic American cultures, including that of the United States. Here it has influenced writers in New Orleans (such as George Washington Cable and more recent horror novelists) and elsewhere (in the work of Richard Wright, for instance, as well as film scripts for horror fans). It also colors Spanish-American literature (such as Alejo Carpentier's *The Kingdom of this World*) and the magic realism of South American novelists and short-story writers.

"Devil" flowers from a German encyclopedia.

MAGICAL HERBS

Wise women, often suspected of being witches, served their doctorless communities with a pharmacopæia of potions, poultices, and incenses. People still make Hot Foot Powder and Get Away Powder to make people leave, and other magical powders for Luck, Love, and Psychic Abilities; Attraction, Black Cat, Lucky and, other oils; conjure bags, dolls, and *mojos* containing plant material; infusions, teas, and medicines that are magical when taken at the full moon or some other propitious time; colored and scented candles, and so on. They also use graveyard dirt and Gold Magnetic Dust, nutgalls and witch's grass or witch's salt to increase the power of any mixture, Altar Oil and Success Oil for rituals, patchouli to break any jinx, and ginger or the dangerous Spanish fly to perk up any aphrodisiac. It is all about power, of course. The most common desires are love, winning at gambling or in court, getting money, and revenge. Among herbs and other plants believed to attract evil spirits (especially when burned) are absinthe, aloes, asafœtida, balmoney, mullein, sandalwood, and tormentilla. These must sometimes be used with the correctly colored candles or involve certain ceremonies, invocations, or times.

To protect against evil spirits, people use African ginger, agar-agar, agrimony, ague root, alkanet, anise (most especially star anise), basil, bay leaves, benzoin, betony, black cohosh, blood root, broom, burdock, cinnamon, cinquefoil (five-fingers), cowslip, elder, hawthorn, High John the Conqueror, hyssop, kava kava, mint, nettle, nutmeg, purselane, poke root, quince, rosemary, Solomon's seal, St. John's wort, southernwood, stone root, valerian, verbena, wahoo bark, and wormwood, among others. The long list of protective plants testifies to the deep fears people had and still have about curses, spells, jinxes, and devils and demons attacking them.

There are rules regarding each preparation: for instance, only the seeds of quince are used and (like some other charms) worn in a bag around the waist. Others have to be prepared at the waxing or the waning of the moon (people still plant crops after consulting their almanacs), left in dark places to work for a number of days (often seven), put under the bed or pillow or in the four corners of a room, sprinkled on the doorstep, and so on. There is a whole art to the magical use of plants and it is imperfectly known by almost all would be practitioners. "Donna Rose"'s *The Magic of Herbs* has sold for about twenty years and yet is as inaccurate as it is illiterate. A knowledgeable and readable book is needed. Some day I may write one. I would include the scientific names of plants whose folk names are sometimes confused. I might stress the superstitious nature of it all by including the incantations that many charms and spells require, omitted by writers who think of all this as folk medicine rather than magic.

To summon good spirits you can burn various sweet-scented incenses such as frankincense, use rose hips or place sea spirit in water (with a moonstone and at the full moon), burn yarrow, or anoint or bathe yourself with certain oils and extracts. Some other summoning agents (such as wolfbane, brimstone, and sulfur) may get you evil instead of good spirits. Datura, hellebore, henbane, and such are burned only to summon evil presences. Many substances burned in ritual magic are hallucinogenic. Small wonder people see shapes in the smoke! Some substances seem to have suggested themselves simply because of their names, such as angelica, archangel root, blessed thistle, Devil's bit, holy herb, sacred herb, and *yerba sante*, but things may work if you believe enough in their efficacy, especially in matters which involve confidence and boldness. In magic, you first convince yourself.

The use of plants also involves astrology, which is closely involved with all superstition and early science. You often are asked to prepare oils, powders, and potions at appropriate times and even with the colors associated with various planets (as in ritual magic). Each sign of the Zodiac has certain herbs and other plans (as well as the much more familiar gems) associated with it. My own sign (Sagittarius), for instance, would suggest I add betony to any charm prepared to unhex or "uncross" me, burdock to cleanse the magical altar at the new moon each month, red clover to all other cleansing potions, dandelion to all charms designed to increase my spiritual and psychic powers, and pine to add strength to all concoctions. Those who have a personal addition to the standard recipes naturally increase their belief that they will work. It is then custom made for you.

Now, there was more to this folderol than simple superstition. In this homemade herbal practice there was often some medicinal value and the old "wise women" were sometimes really wise. Moreover, from the theory of "signatures" (heart-shaped leaves of digitalis are good for heart troubles, and so on), some useful medications were discovered. Jesuit's Bark, now called quinine, was used in magic by aborigines in the Americas long before it was brought home to Europe by missionaries as a medicine. The Mexicans and Chinese, among many other peoples, use plant materials that are foreign to most of us but are quite effective medicinally and ought to be more fully investigated by science. It is when one goes beyond chemistry to say that Devil's bit sprinkled around will assist you to make more money on the sale of your home or that heartsease will bind a lover to you if you burn it with the loved one's sock at the full moon, that one moves from science to superstition.

HERBS FOR MAGIC AND MEDICINE

Dawson, Adele G., *Health Happiness and the Pursuit of Herbs* (1980)
Joice, Jean, *Some Bygone Garden Herbs and Plants* (1977)
Latorre, Dolores L., *Cooking and Curing with Mexican Herbs* . . . (1977)
Schendel, Gordon, *et al.*, *Medicine in Mexico* . . .(1968)
Scully, Virginia, *A Treasury of American Indian Herbs* . . . (1970)

The Horned God at *Sabbat*, by Francisco Goya.

7

Superstition in the Modern World

MODERN BELIEF IN THE DEVIL

In a seventies poll on the subject, one-third of Americans questioned said that The Devil was impersonal evil, and one-third actually said they believed that crimes where "The Devil made me do it" were credible. In the eighties, there was a rash of accusations of Satanic content in heavy-metal rock and other shocking actions of teenagers. In the nineties, Robert Simandl (a Chicago crime expert) gave seminars to law enforcement officers in which he identified Satanism as "the crime of the nineties" and the sheriff's association guessed that 1.4 million Americans were involved in Satanic worship. In the last ten years (this is written in 1996), accusations of the most publicized aspect of Satanic crime, Satanic child abuse, have dwindled.

Nonetheless, as Martin E. Marty reported in the *Encyclopedia Britannica Yearbook 1990*, "modernity did not purge the world of devils or belief in Satan" and "underground religion" has its attraction "in an era of rebellion and lawlessness" like ours. The millennium is likely to see an increase in superstition.

THE DEVIL OF A PROBLEM

You encounter it all the time, the problem of how God could have let this or that terrible thing happen. All hell breaks loose, we say.

Says the badly injured victim of a car crash, "I wasn't killed, thank God!" Should he or she thank God for the car crash, too? Who's responsible for accidents and anything else that happens?

In Dunblane, Scotland, in 1995, an apparent madman brought four guns into a local gymnasium and killed a teacher and fifteen schoolchildren, wounding others. Then he killed himself—enraging some who would have enjoyed exacting revenge for this horror.

Faced with what one paper at least called "the worst massacre in British history," the Rev. Colin McIntosh preached a sermon in which he said that "our only comfort lies in knowing that it was not the will of God that the children should die."

Which brings us to the question: Whose will was it? What is being done against or without the will of God, and why? If there is evil, is God powerless to stop it? Why does He permit it if He can stop it? What is He up to? Why this evil?

St. Thomas Aquinas neatly defined evil as "the absence of a due and necessary good," and many will contend that that explanation lets God off the hook and answers charges that God is either not omnipotent (thus able to stop evil from happening) or not good (permitting evil to happen). The position of the *Summa theologica* is that evil exists only in those areas in which God chooses not to operate. So, evil does not come from God, and God is good. To which some respond: What's good about not operating to put down evil in certain areas—areas where you could put down evil if you were good enough to take an interest in doing so? Shouldn't mankind fight evil? Shouldn't God? And the traditional religious response is that God works in mysterious ways. That is certainly true.

All of this underlines the problem we all have with why "bad things happen to good people" and indeed, permit me to stress, even why (in the context of a loving God and a religion of forgiveness, such as Christianity) bad things happen to bad people. Why is there evil? What is The Devil doing?

Enter those who believe that Satan is no longer (if he ever was) the employee of God but a powerful personage in his own right. Looking at the world, these persons assume that Satan is winning and therefore they cast their lot with the Evil One.

At least they are not in the dilemma of the Rev. Mr. McIntosh, who told the surviving children that "even the grown-ups do not understand why this has happened." Satanists say they know.

When the Dunblane horror—the press likes to call this kind of thing "tragedy," but it is not—struck, says the Rev. Mr. McIntosh, "God's heart was the first of all our hearts to break." For Heaven's sake, why? Surely God cannot be surprised. He knew it would happen, all along. He must know everything The Adversary does—and He has known since before He created Satan in the first place. What could He have been thinking? God knows! Neither the local clergyman nor the Queen (head of the church as well as of the government, who arrived with sympathy on the scene four days after the events) seems to know the will or the whim of God.

Those who do not like what He does can go to The Devil!

DEVILTRY IN OUR TIME

Nietzsche said that "God is dead." Albert Camus added that "Lucifer has also died with God." But George Bernard Shaw saw both God and The Devil as necessary even now to explain the inexplicable mix of good and evil in the universe, and he wrote: "The invention of Satan is a heroic advance on Jahvism. It is an attempt to solve the Problem of Evil, and at least faces the fact that evil *is* evil." He went on in *Far Fetched Fables* to suggest the continuing need for what he considered to be a myth. I think we may call fair use quoting a couple of sentences.

> Thus the world, as we imagine it, is crowded with anthropomorphic supernatural beings of whose existence there is no scientific proof. None the less, without such belief the human race cannot be civilized and governed, though the ten per cent of persons mentally capable of civilizing and governing are too clever to be imposed on by fairy tales, and in any case have to deal with hard facts as well as fancies and fictions.

This is of a piece with Shaw's firm conviction that "every grade of human intelligence can be civilized by providing it with a frame of reference peculiar to its mental capacity, and called a religion." The struggles with this "tying us back" to our origins may not be easy.

The struggles of the Curé d'Ars (whom we mentioned in an earlier chapter) in the last century were comparable to the terrible fight attributed to St. Anthony against temptations by day and night. St. Paul told the Corinthians (on what basis is unclear) that God does not allow The Devil to taunt and tempt mankind beyond human limits, but why God permits it at all has been a constant subject of theological debate. This debate continues in the twentieth century without a universally accepted basis let alone an agreement. Neither the Roman Catholic Church (which has been formally and increasingly battling Satanists since the bull *Vox in rama* 1233 and essentially since its inception), nor the Satanists have settled each other's hash as yet. It may be that the greatest interest shown in the matter today lies with evangelicals in between these extremes.

For many, this is not a matter worthy of tolerance, touted as the panacea for our divided societies. *The Royal Bank [of Canada] Letter* for September/October 1995 addresses "The Struggle for Tolerance" generally and concludes that:

> It is difficult to live tolerantly in a time like the present. The old familiar ways of life that once gave people a feeling of certainty and security are steadily receding into history. It is natural to look around for someone to blame for disturbing our lives. . . .

The Age of Faith is gone and the Age of Anxiety has given way to an Age of Antagonism. We are blaming other people, not The Devil, for the evil in the world. The newest use of the word *devils* is in the bitter interracial battles that split us asunder as a nation. The problem is not white and black magic but white and black racism. Or maybe just seeing things here, or in China or Bosnia or Israel or wherever, in black and white terms.

THE NEWEST RELIGIONS

In history, religious almost always seemed to come out of the East; in America today, many come out of the West—out of California. Traditional denominations are regarded by many as too old-fashioned or too demanding, despite the fact that some of the new substitutes (Jesus Freaks, Hare Krishna, Scientology, etc.) demand a great deal of their adherents. They do, however, give the bored a full-time activity and keep them off the streets (if not out of the airports). Easier, no-fault religions are more attractive still, especially if you can write your own commandments on corrasible paper or go with half of the old quotation, "Do what thou wilt. . . ."

The most documented of the new religions is involved not with the rise of spiritualism and of self-declared "psychic friends" but the manufactured, eclectic "takes" on pantheism and other pagan rites. Neopaganism now tends to be a smorgasbord of polytheistic and polyecological notions with the evil gods played down, and even the good gods played down in favor of goddesses. Neopaganism is somewhat connected with the feel-good and earth-friendly modern witchcraft movements, many of which are centered tightly around dominant individuals. (Thus far the United States has produced no Aleister Crowley or Gerald Gardner, and modern equivalents of Mme. Blavatsky or Aimée Semple MacPherson are rare.)

Modern witchcraft (usually called Wicca) is free for the most part of solitary hags. It tends to attract more or less well-preserved divorcées. It is one of the main outlets for feminine spirituality, though in the Protestant communion women are achieving positions of significance, while still barred from the priesthood of the Roman Catholic Church.

There are many all-female, some all-lesbian covens, partly driven, perhaps, by the same sentiments that produce on T-shirts in New York such statements as "A Woman Needs a Man like a Fish Needs a Bicycle" and "Men Are Only Good for One Thing—And Who Cares about Parallel Parking?"

Rebellion against established values is also seen in American Judaism. It keeps up with the times not only by inventing a *bat mitzvah* ("so little girls won't murder their little brothers out of jealousy over the *bar mitzvah*," one friend has explained to me), but by becoming a more "user-friendly" faith. There seems to be a movement away from the strict demands of Orthodox Jewry. Many Jews describe themselves as "non-religious Jews." I cannot understand what this may mean, for if Judaism is not a religion, what is it? Certainly not a race, whatever Hitler said. Religious Jews are increasingly disturbed at the large number of Jewish men in the United States who marry non-Jews and so their children are technically not Jewish. Hasidim, Lubavitchers, and other ultra-religious sects are something of an embarrassment to those Jews who have not drifted off into Ethical Culture or Unitarianism or such, but are Jewish principally in connection with ethnic foods and Zionist politics. There are Jewish congregations that are so "reformed" that they have female rabbis, or are gay.

Practitioners of the true black arts and the impressive rituals of ceremonial magic (a very demanding pursuit), condemned first by the Jews and then by the Christians, are few. Like Satanists, they are invisible. True Satanists, with their ritual murders and human sacrifices, are fortunately even fewer. Most of those who are hurtled into the headlines are mere psychopaths who use The Evil One as an excuse for the evil within.

Magic and witchcraft used to offer elaborate costumes and scenery as well as secret plots which did much to bring drama to little lives. There is a need for ritual; moderns are starved for it. So there are all kinds of secret and not-so-secret societies offering everything from community service to the wisdom of the ages by mail. Modern imitations of Rosicrucianism and similar secret societies can hardly be called religions, however, any more than Freemasonry or the Kiwanis or Rotarianism can be. With the Ku Klux Klan and such, the definitions are more blurred.

302 *The Complete Book of the Devil's Disciples*

The Nation of Islam is a black religious and political movement that bears little resemblance to the religion of traditional Muslims but is a notable force in our society. So are certain packagings for American consumption of religions of the Orient and of India, many of which are taken up as fads by the trivial, as in the past swamis and gurus that did well, especially on both coasts. Real conversion to Oriental religion is, however, rare. As one eccentric Greenwich Village poet used to jump up on cafe tables and recite,

> In winter I'm a Buddhist
> But in summer I'm a nudist.

The magical practices of Asian religions are not taken very seriously in America, any more than the principles of Baha'i and similar movements, though their messages appear to be having a little more influence all the time in the most successful of American churches. The growth is in churches stressing charisma and evangelical fervor. This is especially true of store-front churches where the congregations take a very enthusiastic part in the services. Holy Rollers may be making a comeback. The laying on of hands is a feature in many churches. Miracles are sought. Native practices such as snake handling are confined to a few isolated and rather backward areas. Voodoo, Santería, Obeah, and similar imports with an African heritage have, however, reached the underclasses of urban areas and in some places are vital forces in their everyday lives.

A surprising number of Americans attend church, synagogue, or mosque regularly, almost as many as religiously read their horoscopes. However, within the churches there is disagreement over old values (the Roman Catholics defying the papal pronouncements on birth control and other sex-related issues, for example) and change in old customs (in most Jewish congregations now, women sit with the men, though as far as I know they are unwelcome in a *minyan*, the traditional ten Jews required for certain prayers, and the orthodox men still thank God every morning in prayer that they were not born female). In witchcraft much has been adopted or adapted to suit modern tastes, despite the fact that in such countries as Britain there is a more learned and traditional approach to the heritage. In France some nineteenth-century magical groups still quietly survive. In Germany there are some active underground organizations left over from fascination with the occult in Nazi and even earlier times. In some European countries people are just now getting around to dabbling in spiritualism with the excitement that once reigned in the United States and Britain, in the last century. In the US, we have yuppie religions..

Americans like to make things new, to change the rules. Some religions have been altered to suit American laws: Mormons now (mostly) have but one wife, and so do our Muslims. Amerinds may be restricted from using drugs in their ceremonies. And of course some age-old practices of witches and warlocks would get people arrested—if they were made known publicly. Nobody is threatening to kidnap and de-program witches. They are no longer feared or scapegoated. They are hardly even laughed at any more. They are regarded as simply "doing their own thing" in the style of hippies, which at this distance from the Summer of Love looks to Americans like age-old tradition.

The Age of Permissiveness, after some difficulties, has given way to a New Age. That New Age has brought in all kinds of "alternative" ideas in "alternate lifestyle," "alternative medicine," etc. In a few ways this has encouraged ancient transgressive practices of witchcraft. On the whole, however, witchcraft has ceased to be regarded as an affront to religion or a threat to society—that place has been taken by Satanism and in the minds of a few by televangelism—so most of the practitioners are out in the open about their harmless superstitions. Arguments over whether magical potions work are quite similar now to disagreements over the efficacy of vitamin supplements. If it makes you feel good—why not?

Meanwhile, unorthodox religions such as witchcraft offer a kind of cheap celebrity with photo opportunities in quaint robes, a little publicity. Publicity works magic for Americans. Only occasionally does publicity reveal horrors, as in the case of deaths attributed to Satanism or to crazed cults (Rev. Jim Jones and the Peoples Temple, for example). Then there will be a wave of protest against what is considered the work of The Devil. Very soon after that, something else will seize the headlines and be the hot topic for talk shows, Net chat, and *Time* lead articles.

You have to offer something kookier than "I Am a Witch" to get on Geraldo, Sally Jesse Raphael, Oprah, and other TV shows these days. Maybe "I Am a Witch Who Killed a 15-Year-Old Boy's Mother by Voodoo so That I Could Marry Him After He Got Me Pregnant and Gave Me AIDS" might just do it.

ALTERNATIVE RELIGIONS IN AMERICA

The proliferation of alternative religions (often dismissed as cults) is only partially explained by the radicals who challenge the Establishment in all its manifestations and who like to recognize no authorities other than their own "gut" feelings. Something also must be attributed to the burning desire for individualism in extremely conformist society and for the increasing tendency of those who feel the odds are against their success in the regular games to think up games of their own where they can declare themselves winners. Most of all, people want companionship.

Witchcraft has hardly been revived. Rather, calling itself witchcraft, or more often Wicca, a series of more invented rather than revived practices has stressed the currently popular themes of Women's Liberation, Environmentalism, Back to Nature, and New Age notions. Most so-called witchcraft now is more paganism (polytheism with an emphasis on goddesses as well as gods) and naturopathy. Almost all American witches claim to be "good witches" and to practice "white magic." Nobody levitates and nobody flies, although a number of pseudo-occult groups and individuals use drugs. Few modern witches bother to find out what traditional witches did; almost none declare themselves to be in league with The Devil. That is Satanism, and (as is suggested elsewhere in this book) even modern Satanism, is chiefly fraudulent. Modern witches know nothing and care less about the traditions of ceremonial magic. They make up their own feel-good rituals much in the traditional of the homespun marriage ceremonies of the hippies of the radical sixties, as I said.

Neo-pagans attempt to revive the pre-Christian religions or, more usually, piece together odds and ends of Egyptian, Tibetan, Celtic, or other religions to make something personal and comfortable. They are seldom or never at odds with Christianity. They like to feel in harmony with everything and everyone. They usually ask only to be allowed another sixties throwback—their "space." They, too, are weak on research and strong on newly created and undemanding practices and beliefs. They do not offer human or even animal sacrifices. Where witches occasionally meet in naked covens, neo-pagans are drawn to flowing robes.

There are modern substitutes for the Illuminati, Rosicrucians, and various famous orders especially the Knights Templar and the Order of the Golden Dawn, all unconnected with the past, freshly confected, and strongly American in tone, but with pretenses (like the Freemasons and some other organizations) to extremely ancient origins. Many are given to the elaborate robe of "secret" organizations and the high, astounding titles of fraternal organizations of American manufacture. Like the Masons, they do no one much harm and perform a good deal of charitable or other work of benefit to the community, but they do not engage in magic or witchcraft.

There are some groups professing black magic. Gini G. Scott in *The Magicians* (1984) wrote a journalistic report of the search for power in black magic groups and interviewed a number of participants. Danny L. Jorgensen in *The Esoteric Scene* (1992) offered a more in-depth, sociological study of a group of magicians, but T. M. Luhrman's *Persuasions of the Witch's Craft* (1989) still is the best analysis or report of their way of thinking and goals. Practitioners speak for themselves in *Witchcraft Today* (Charles S. Clifton, ed., 1992), though not very profoundly. Many sound silly.

Probably the most noticeable aspect of modern American approximations of witchcraft is the stress on escaping from what feminism defines as the phallocentric. This feminism permeates Margot Adler's *Drawing Down the Moon: Witches, Druids, Goddess-Worshippers and Other Pagans in America Today* (1987, now outdated) and the less sensible but certainly influential writings of a dedicated feminist who named herself "Starhawk," notably *The Spiral Dance* (1979) and *Dreaming the Dark* (1989). There have been books designed to compete with these more recently, but none has equaled the impact of these early statements of witchcraft as feminist politics. The psychological explanations of this are soberly set forth in M. D. Faber's *Modern Witchcraft and Psychoanalysis* (1993).

Aidan Kelly wrote a history of modern (most feminist) Wicca 1939–1964 in *Crafting the Art of Magic* (1964), and many more recent publications have been attempting to supply rationales and rituals. Husband and wife teams often write together as in Janet and Stuart Farrar's *The Witches' Way* (1984) and the published lessons in Wicca offered by mail or otherwise. But feminism is always dominant. Men are supposed to be sensitive, not superior. The female has been promoted from being the altar at a Black Mass to being the celebrant of Goddess ceremonies.

Bibliography is extensive. See J. Gordon Melton and Isotta Poggi's Garland bibliography, *Magic, Witchcraft and Paganism in America* (1992).

Necromancy in the form of Spiritualism, *ouija* boards, and channeling; witchcraft in the manifestations of faith-healing; Voodoo; various imported *obeah*-based religions; and *Santería* among Hispanics especially, round off the religions in America today that are relevant here. People are more likely to say they have sold their souls to Microsoft or IBM than to The Devil. Americans speak of saving the planet's limited natural resources with the fervor they used to speak of saving their immortal souls.

SATANIC HUMAN SACRIFICE

This (along with a funeral for a gay teenager dead of AIDS) was part of the Haunted House setup for Halloween 1995 by the Abundant Life Christian Center in Arvada, Colorado, to show evils of the modern world. There were no reported cases of Satanic human sacrifice in Colorado in 1995.

HONK IF YOU HATE DEMONS

At modern weddings there may be a lot of automobiles honking horns and this may be more than unbridled enthusiasm. It may, in fact, be a distant echo of old customs such as the shivaree (our American version of *charivari*), where a lot of noise was made to drive off demons who might object to a couple getting married to produce new souls for God.

Noise to banish evil spirits is common in many cultures. The Chinese explode firecrackers to rid themselves of demons. From that old custom the West derived gunpowder, and a great deal of harm has been done with it that demons must applaud.

GAY WITCHES

Along with a number of lesbian covens dedicated to The Goddess, there are gay pagan groups. For instance, *The Crucible* is a magazine for "gay pagans," and there are east and west coast newsletters such as *Queer Pagan* and *Lavender Pagan*, both in California. Active groups include "Black Leather Wings" out of Northern California and the TAZ circle of the Zcluster in New Orleans. There is some sadomasochism in these "leather" groups in the tradition of Gardnerian witchcraft (itself reflecting the British public-school flogging kinkiness), but no Satanism, and the "pagan" rituals are more Radical Faerie than orthodox witchcraft, generally made up and not researched. These are not devil-worshippers, just "urban aboriginals" and "alternate-lifestyle" thrill seekers. Sex is a part of some ritual magic, but none of these gay or lesbian groups are "into" so esoteric and demanding a matter as ceremonial magic. These "pagans" are simply attracted by Aleister Crowley's bad-boy reputation and the anti-social-restriction promise of "do what you will." They have no intention of selling their souls to The Devil, just enjoying their bodies in unorthodox ways and rejecting Christianity, which largely rejects their sexual habits. Leo Martello was one of the earliest self-proclaimed modern "gay witches."

HELLFIRE CLUBS

Particularly in eighteenth-century England, Scotland, and Ireland, and at both Oxford and Cambridge, debauchees calling themselves members of various "Hellfire Clubs" met in public houses (taverns) and private houses, outdoors and in ruined abbeys for drunken parties, sex orgies, and very seldom for Satanic rites. In snobbish Britain, some of these decadent louts were given special attention because they had noble titles. The most flamboyant if not evil of these Hellfire beaux was Sir Francis Dashwood, Bart., later fifteenth Baron Le Despencer. He lived 1708–1781 and was famous for debauchery both on the Continent and in England. In the latter place he founded the riotous Monks of Medmenham Abbey, the most notorious of the Hellfire Clubs (1749). He died as an official of the post office, having long since been worn out by his wild life.

The "monks" were generally just playing with the trappings of the occult, as are most occult organizations, both sober and sexually wild, today. They were simply the products of the century of the Count (in popular usage promoted to Marquis) de Sade and a foretaste of the "marvels" of late eighteenth-century French dandyism and the bucks of the English Regency period. They were no more Satanists than the attendees at various Hell-Fire Club meetings in Chicago, New York, and so on are today (who practise homosexual sadism and masochism). They may have been outrageous, but they had not dedicated their souls to The Devil any more than the average sinner has.

A good rule may be just this: If you have heard about it, it is not a real Satanist society. Satanists seek no publicity. Like any other persons engaged in practices that are not only shocking but distinctly illegal, say necrophilia, they are out there but usually solitary. They contact each other only with the greatest caution. Identification can mean incarceration, in jails or in insane asylums.

AUTO-DA-FÉ

One reason people liked public executions of witches was that it was public entertainment. As I write, a videotape called *Executions* is the best-seller in the United Kingdom. A great many people argue that public executions would reduce crime. I disagree. I think they would only feed the basest desires of humans as diabolical as demons used to be said to be. It used to be that we could blame devils and demons who were out to wreck havoc. Now it's horrendously common Americans who are so scary.

Demons are not pushing mothers to murder their innocent children so that the mothers can be more attractive to sleazy boyfriends who want sex but no brats. Demons are not forcing children to murder father and reload to murder mother. Demons are not raping and keeping score as if it were a game. Demons are not possessing Jeffrey Dahmers or the murderers of Jeffrey Dahmers. Demons have nothing to do with women who attack sleeping husbands with a knife "in self-defense" or set fire to their sleeping husbands' beds "in self-defense." Demons are not racked with hideous diseases and deliberately spreading them because they can't answer truthfully the "why me?" question of suffering. Demons are not involved in the cases of people who arm themselves heavily and go out to kill masses of strangers on trains or in malls or offices. Demons cannot be blamed for bombs in the mail, deliberately derailed railroad cars, or downed airplanes.

People now are more obviously frightening than devils or demons used to be. Rappers talk more filth and hate now than possessed nuns used to spout. Too bad we cannot still believe the evil is attributable to Someone Else. The Enemy is our terrible fellow men and women. Devils and demons may be afraid to walk among us now.

SOCRATES

In the *Protagoros*, Socrates flatly declared that no one who knew good could intentionally commit evil. It is, in this view, impossible to do evil for evil's sake. Here is journalist Ron Rosenbaum "Staring into the Heart of the Heart of Darkness" for readers of the *New York Times Magazine* (4 June 1995):

> One of the most useful recent analyses of this question is by an Aus-tralian philosopher S. I. Benn. Benn rigorously examines the box within the Chinese box of categories of wickedness and finds him-self hard-pressed to prove the innermost box is not empty. Strug-gling against Socrates' decree that knowing the good and doing evil is impossible, and against Kant, who, as Benn puts it, "denies that human beings can adopt as a fundamental maxim, informing all rational choices, as a kind of perverse moral law, the maxim 'Do evil for evil's sake!' Benn parades the usual suspects from literature— Milton's Satan ("Evil be thou my good,"Iago [in *Othello*] and Clag-gart in "Billy Budd." But he cites no examples from history or daily life. (Hitler, he says, fell into a lesser category he calls "conscien-tious wickedness," doing evil but convinced he was doing the right thing). And Benn has trouble finding some psychological basis for conceiving of such a person. "The unalloyed wickedness of malig-nity presents a logical or a psychological problem."
>
> In the end Benn has to fall back on the Prince of Darkness. Mounting a counterattack on Kant's denial that human beings can consciously adopt "evil maxims" and do evil for evil's sake, Benn seizes on (what I would consider) Kant's throw away line on the

question that only "a *devilish* being" could behave that way. And tries to pin Kant to the ground with it. If he believes in "devilish beings," that is, wicked satanic spirits, Benn argues, "I cannot see why human beings cannot also be satanic."

Here, then, at the furthermost reaches of the innermost four-chambered heart of darkness, even the most rigorous of philosophers is thrown back on theology. And we witness, in the dryest of dry dispassionate analyses, the rebirth of Satan.

We are, as we have always been, superstitious people. We fear devils and demons. We even fear saints.

In our new, popular and nondenominational feel-good churches, whose parking lots and service committees are full of successful people who find that there is still something painfully lacking in their lives, what appears to be sought is an enhanced connection to other people, not to God, not mystical Theology but comforting camaraderie. They pray some, but above all, they seek *involvement* not with God but with fellow humans who have much but not contentment. They seek happiness, not salvation.

THE DEVIL IN BRITAIN TODAY

Mary Reed in *Weatherwise* (June/July 1995) suggests that prosecutions in Britain are more likely to be for fraudulent mediums and other rip-offs "whereby people are deluded and defrauded" than for Satanism. There is no "war of witches" such as one writer found among "the contemporary Aztecs" of Mexico; in fact, the public interest is in witchcraft in new plays and films and old TV reruns such as *Bewitched*. There is some resurgence of spiritualism but nothing like the US heyday 1880–1920 surveyed by Deborah J. Coon in the *American Psychologist* for February 1992. Britain tends to look on haunted houses and spirit mediums mostly as things of the past, part of the eccentric history. The most famous British medium is still a fictional one, Madam Arcati of *Blithe Spirit*, a hearty old soul as portrayed by Margaret Rutherford in the film version, forever indelible on the mind of any who saw her peddling uphill on her bike in a velvet evening gown and beads. As Sir Noël Coward put it in another great creation of his, a song:

> And if anyone spots the Queen of Scots
> In a hand-embroidered shroud, we're proud
> Of the stately homes of England.

Britain is, nonetheless, an avid market for the history of devils and demons and will, I hope, like this present book, like others of mine.

HALLOWEEN

Not only ghosts and fairies but also evil witches and demons are supposed to be especially active on All Hallows' Eve. Ordinarily, the witches have frequent meetings on the *sabbat* and major celebrations on the four big holidays of the Old Religion. This is the biggest US holiday after Christmas.

HALLOWEEN BANNED

No, not the atrociously violent and apparently unending series of schlock films. The holiday. In the American tradition of the separation of church and state, quite logically (if disappointingly for the children) the Los Altos, California, school board added Halloween in 1995 to the list of holidays that have underlying religious meaning and therefore are forbidden. Brooklyn College ignores Christmas and Easter but insists no significant work take place in classrooms on days when Jewish students have to absent themselves. Citizens on Long Island make the town remove Christmas decorations. And now the Celtic feast of the god of the dead (Samhain), which the Christians took over as Halloween (All Hallows' Eve), is banned.

At Halloween the souls departed were supposed to be revered and the dead were supposed to be placated lest they trouble the living. But the Grateful Dead are just rock history, and in 1995 its venerable Jerry Garcia died. In the Bay Area the kiddies will no longer dress up at school as ghosts and goblins or devils and demons. There will be no costume parades, no drawings of witches on broomsticks on their way to the Sabbat, and no skeletons on the school windows.

Outside of school the holiday can continue, but already the children ringing the doorbells for candy, like their parents, have forgotten they are supposed to represent the dead coming back. Children are more likely in their tricking or treating or parades to be dressed not as devils or ghosts but as Ninja Turtles or Power Rangers. In New York's Greenwich Village, the Halloween celebrations are more for drag than demonology.

The old games for fortune-telling with apples and by other methods at Halloween are things of the past. No one today listens for the wind, blowing over corpses, to rattle their windows and warn them they will die within the year. No one sits on a three-legged stool at the crossroads now to hear, at midnight at the dreary end of October, ghostly voices read the list of those who are going to die in the coming year.

If you are a gambler, you can try the old method of improving your luck at Halloween. Hide under a blackberry bush until midnight and then invoke the aid of Satan.

A GEM OF A STATUTE

The superstitious have created birthstones and connected them to planetary influences and have attributed to various gems and minerals various magical powers. In demonology, jade has a number of uses, for example. Sapphires are said to keep away demons. The largest sapphire ever found weighed over 2,000 karats. It was carved into a bust of President Eisenhower that weighs 1,444 carats. That ought to keep away a lot of demons. It also bids fair to repel art critics.

HEALING BY FAITH ALONE

The United States has not only its own faith-healing established religion (codified by Mary Baker Eddy as Christian Science) but also a long tradition of snake-handling (where poisonous snakes represent the powers of The Devil) and faith stopping blood, curing "thrash" (which is what they call both "red" and "yellow" throat inflammations in Appalachia), and taking the "fire" (burning sensation) out of bad burns. The techniques, it is said, come naturally to the seventh son of a seventh son (political correctness has recently added daughters) and some others; but they also can be learned and, tradition says, taught to two or three other people, provided they are not related to you.

Or you could try stopping blood by reciting *Ezekiel* XVI:6, substituting the sufferer's full name for each "thou" or "thee." This can be done even over the telephone, maybe on the world wide web. As with all magical spells and incantations, no word must be wrong.

To draw "fire" you pass your hand over the victim's body, brushing away the pain, slowly, three times, and blowing gently on the burn, as you recite the magic words exactly. Here they are as given to the editors of *Foxfire*, a journal dedicated to plain living in the mountains of the South by a woman who said that "it might be of some use to you when I'm gone. I believe in th' healing power because th' Lord has healed me. I know He has. That's the greatest thing they is, is th' healin' power of th' Lord Savior." The words as she wrote them down are these:

Thair came an angel
from the East bringing
frost and fire. In frost out
fire. In the name of
the father the Son and
of the Holy Ghost.

Some people would call this white magic, some black, and some would say it is not magic at all but suggestion or a power given to people mentioned in the Bible and exercised ever since by some Christians who would have "no truck with The Devil."

These homespun cures raise large questions worth thinking about. What is magic and what is the faith that can move mountains? What is superstition and what is religion? What is dealing with The Devil and what is of God? Some Christians are forbidden to use any magical spells or incantations whatsoever: a medieval pope bound all Roman Catholics by a bull *ex cathedra* forever. Others use them in the name of God and point to successes. Still others speak of auto-suggestion and deny the miraculous, even at Lourdes and such places to which many flock for cures. But auto-suggestion has always been a major element of magic, black and white.

POPULAR ENTERTAINMENT

It is from horror movies and creepy, crappy television shows and gruesome, violent comic books and the like, not from the study of theology, that modern young people gain their considerable knowledge of evil creatures of the supernatural world. That's where they meet Count Dracula and Barnabas Collins, the reluctant vampire of *Dark Shadows*, and the likes of Aven Hunter, who combined the appeal of the Western movie with that of the horror movie in *Devil Wolf of Shadow Mountain*. In case you missed that 1964 masterwork, Aven Hunter was out hunting, killed a deer, shot a wolf to protect his deer and—his big error—drank water from the wolf's footprint. So he became a werewolf and harried his fellow ranchers until they figured out he was never around when the werewolf was seen and must be the rampaging terror. His brother shot him. With a silver bullet, of course.

In a world of The Blob, The Fly, Diabolo the black cloud of evil, Count Alucard (spell it backwards) and Blacula, The Mummy, The Werewolf, Things from outer space, and more, the devils and demons of the superstitious past live again. Evil continues to be embodied and seen in terms of aliens who pop out of our own bodies, or take over the minds of our children, or roam the earth thirsting for blood, souls, and more. Our very automobiles turn malevolent. Vampires and serial killers want us to hear their personal stories. Then just when you thought your loft was safe from intruders, along comes diabolical possession or an ancient curse attached to some trinket you bought cheap at a flea market.

The relevance here? Only that books on demonology are not nearly so out of touch with the interest of the non-readers of today as most hard-copy, hard-to-read tomes are. The supermarket checkout counter newspapers (with the highest circulations of any newspapers anywhere) have helped to make the average American a firm believer in demons as well as diets, and devils and angels as well as low morals in high places.

MODERN AMERICAN WITCHES

For that reason, modern American couples on (say) Long Island who get into the newspapers (see Nat Friedland's *The Occult Explosion* or your latest periodicals) or give correspondence courses in witchcraft from the depths of the South, or modern purveyors of *gris-gris* and other charms, or modern operators of occult bookstores and magical bodegas and such, in fact, all modern witches, wizards, and "experts" you are likely to hear about boast no contacts with devils and demons, which makes them not a little boring and certainly outside the interests of this present book. Your Psychic Friends may be deleterious to your pocketbook or even your grip on reality, but they are not doing the work of The Devil. Or God.

AMERICAN WITCHES TODAY

Serious ones don't try so hard to get their names in the paper as these "high priestesses" do:

Lady Sintana, who battled to use her house as a church in Atlanta, Georgia; her real name is Candy Lehrman

Beth Gurevitch, youngest of the seven Mother Witches of Britain

Devi in Los Angeles, **Lisa** in Michigan's Upper Peninsula, and others who do not like to give their full names (who can blame that?)

Shawn Poirier, an "ordained witch" whom many in Salem, Massachusetts, took to their bosom

Cheryl St. John, of Manassas, Virginia, who claimed to be in charge of three covens in 1990

Sybil Leek

will teach you how to transmit and receive thought messages!

As we head toward a breakdown of normal communications, Sybil Leek sees telepathy re-instating itself as a practical tool.

The world's most famous psychic, therefore, offers to increase your abilities with a brand new, complete, and easily understood guide.

In the process of teaching you how to broaden your telepathic effectiveness, Sybil Leek will bring you up-to-date on recent academic and scientific research in the field. She'll revi~ ~telep-a~~ ~ire history, an~ ~ate ~any intri ~htr

The British "gypsy" Sybil Leek presented herself in the United States in the sixties and seventies as "the world's most famous psychic."

Zsuzsanna Budapest, who got into San Francisco papers by writing a pamphlet on how to use witchcraft on your boss at the office and is always ready for a feminist fight

Circe (J. B. Cather), who had to move to Toledo, Ohio, because spells didn't keep off the car thieves of Detroit, Michigan

Joyce Siegrest, of Our Lady of the Roses Wiccan Church in Rhode Island

Jerrie Hildebrand, a witch who lives near Boston

Janelle Wade, who converted to Christianity in 1977 and told *USA Today* for Halloween in 1990 that witchcraft was dangerous

Why do the majority of US witches have weirdo forenames? Can it be that they are just publicity-seeking types?

Of all the serious witches I happen to know, none has ever given an interview, been the subject of a journalistic profile, or sought public attention. None has gone to court after being fired from her or his job because the wiccan or wicked truth came out, unlike Mary Silcox (who promptly sued Shell Oil), Jamie Kellam Dodge (who settled with the Salvation Army out of court), and others who get into the papers.

None of the fairly large group of New Orleans adepts has ever met Anne Rice (who moved from pornography to vampires and certainly is famous), though she lives in the same neighborhood as most of the NOLA witches. Maybe witches are afraid of the evangelicals who fulminate against witches, gays, and other unusual people in New Orleans and San Francisco (Larry Lee from Texas launched a crusade there one Halloween not so long ago, without effect).

I SEE A LOT OF FORTUNE-TELLING IN THE FUTURE

Connecticut in 1993 wiped off the books the law passed in 1808 banning all forms of fortune-telling in the state. It's open season for gypsy tea rooms, storefront "readings," and Tarot and cheiromancy experts. Of course all Catholics, some Protestants, and most Jews are forbidden by a higher law from getting involved in any such stuff. New Agers are not.

TEXTBOOKS ON WICKEDNESS?

Across the country in the early nineties there was a rash of PTA meetings protesting the introduction of witchcraft into the elementary school curriculum (or so it was said) by the adoption of textbooks from Harcourt Brace Jovanovitch. HBJ books got parents up in arms in Florida, Ohio, Illinois, and all over. HBJ went to court and got a judgment that their books were not pernicious, but some parents remained unconvinced.

THE OCCULT EXPLOSION

It's now more than twenty years since Nat Friedland, a journalist in California, published a book with the above title that featured Anton LaVey and noted that Isaac Bonewits had recently been graduated from the University of California at Berkeley with the allegedly first major anywhere in Magic. Today my friend Dr. Jeanne Youngson continues with her Count Dracula Fan Club, New York has some lesbian covens (thought the gay Baphomet organization was wiped out, partly by AIDS), and all over the place there are believers in UFOs, but hardly any ritual magicians who can produce anything but a headache in a room filled with the smoke of thorn-apple branches on fire. Yes, there is an interest in the irrational, ESP, Tantric Yoga, and what-all, and there are many more people interested than ever before in taking correspondence courses in The Craft, joining secret organizations, and generally participating in New Age (or age-old) sensational activities.

But neither *demon* nor *devil* is featured in Friedland's index, and there are few indeed in the US who are seriously studying demonology or performing devil worship. Britain is another story. So far, I have encountered no US coven that is doing much more than mooning about The Goddess or practicing more ecology than blasphemy. In Britain, however, there are a few truly dangerous collections of individuals that I know about and perhaps many more of whom I am, as the Brits say, clueless.

Are your occult friends dealing with the half-dozen Authors of Wickedness? They are: *Acteus*, *Lycas*, *Magelsius*, *Mimon*, *Nicon*, and *Ormenus*.

Do they claim to be able to summon any of the devils and demons we have mentioned elsewhere? Have they any experience with more minor ones we can note in passing here, such as *Abac*, *Chameron*, *Densor*, *Estiot*, *Ist*, and *Valefar*.

What would they do were you to sic on them Asmodeus, Astaroth, Belial? Have they spilled the life blood of innocent children to bind them to The Devil and signed a pact in their own blood? They are likely just interested in kinky sex, astral projection, Ouija boards, and things like that. They have not joined The Enemy of Man. They might even want simply to argue that the name ought to be The Enemy of Persons.

If they are not serious, don't worry about them. They are not ready to risk their lives or their souls. They probably do not have the patience to call up demons. It takes fasting for more than a week, assembling a lot of Stuff, and calling the demon's name eleven times. In the age of sound bytes and quick-fix, what average American has *time* for such things? They are just having fun in their fancy costumes—or more traditionally in the nude—and are doing no more harm than Shriners in their temples, or the Elks. They may even be helping the tourist trade.

THE OLD LADY WHO BELIEVED IN THE TROLLS

The Swedish dairy firm of Arla puts various interesting tidbits on their milk cartons and this way you learn about Swedish folklore and other things as you eat your breakfast. Here is a story from that source. Ola J. Holten, my collaborator on a book of Scandinavian folklore, and I translate it for you:

The Old Lady Who Believed in the Trolls

"She has trolls up in her loft," people used to say of the old lady of Timbolholm, far outside the town of Skovde. So they did not put much trust in her stories about trolls running around a hill, lighting it up with golden staves on Thursday nights. But the old lady stuck to her beliefs. And then late in the month of November in 1904 the secret of the grave mound was revealed: 7 kilos of rings and spirals of pure gold came to light. That is to this day the greatest single golden treasure ever found in Sweden. It was discovered by the serving maid Sjöe-Lotta and the servant boy Blue Peter, whose names quickly became "Rich Lotta" and "Gold Peter." This famous Timbolholm Treasure you can see for yourself in the Historical Museum in Stockholm.

JORDENS SKATTER

GUMMAN SOM TRODDE PÅ TOMTEN.

—Hon har tomtar på loftet, sa folk om den gamla gumman på Timboholms gård utanför Skövde. De gav inte mycket för hennes historia om tomtegubbar, som sprang runt en kulle och lyste med guldstavar månljusa torsdagsnätter. Men gumman stod på sig. Och sent i november 1904 avslöjades kullens hemlighet - sju kilo ringar och spiraler i rent guld. Det är Sveriges hittills största guldskatt, upphittad av pigan "Sjöe-Lotta" och drängen "Blue-Per", som snabbt döptes om till "Rike-Lotta" och "Gull-Per". *Timboholmsskatten kan du se på Historiska museet i Stockholm.*

FRANKINCENSE AND MYRRH AND SOMETHING STINKS

The Jews played pleasant music and danced for their God and burned precious substances to please Him and to create an atmosphere of holiness, driving off evil spirits. The modern world has come up with "a room spray compounded of frankincense and myrrh, whose effect is to 'bless' premises sprayed with it." In *BAD, or The Dumbing of America*, Paul Fussell puts this down (along with Creation Science, Nostradamus, "pentagrams and similar talismans," "readings" of various occult sorts, *chakra* balancing, astral projection, horoscopes, and so on) as "worse than bad." He explains: "They are BAD because they represent an overweening urge to impose one's little wishes upon a solid, unyielding actuality" and they play to "New Age patsies." The ignorant people who fall for this stuff are Paphlagonians, ninnies. David Hume in *Of Miracles* (1748) noted that the second-century false prophet Alexander was careful to "lay the first scene of his impostures in [the backward Roman province] of Paphlagonia, where. . . . the people were extremely ignorant and stupid, and ready to swallow even the grossest delusion." Paul Fussell excoriates the dupes of Florida, Illinois, Missouri, Utah, North Carolina, and other places today. He quotes *Matthew* XXV:41: New Age frauds will all fry in Hell. He says they are doing the work of The Devil with their astrology, channeling, and rip-off religions.

METEORIC FALL

There is a wonderful magic book that is so obscure in its language and organization that it has baffled most students, but it begins with something
extremely clear, a fundamental principle of magic: *as above, so below*. This
is a theory of correspondences, illustrated most easily by recalling that when
a crucial new life began on earth in Bethlehem, a bright new star shone
down upon it.

So people influenced by the astrologers and magicians of ancient Babylon and Assyria, from the Jews to the Romans and beyond, have always
scanned the skies for comets, meteors, showers of fire, signs, and portents.

The appearance of a comet, probably because of burning itself out, was
usually considered inauspicious. A meteor, perishing more quickly, was even
worse. After seeing one, Julian the Apostate joined battle with the Parthi-
ans, despite the fact that he had seen a vision of the mournful Roman
Empire as well as the falling red star. He was killed and, "Paul Christian"
(Paul Pitois, an interesting French historian of magic) says, "with his body
the ancient gods laid themselves to rest . . . he died in the arms of Max-
imus and Priscius, the last two masters of ancient Magic."

With his passing, the old ways of reading the stars were not to be abandoned but the whole known world, visible and invisible, would come to
be seen in a new light. There would be a new God triumphant and all sorts
of new devils and demons to counteract. It was a thousand years before a
pope, issuing orders that traffic with these devils and demons was to be
absolutely forbidden, officially recognized their existence. With the death
of Roman religion, a new religion and new hierarchies above and below
were issued from Rome.

ASTROLOGY

Indubitably the moon, for instance, has important effects upon us on earth.
Any woman will tell you that the lunar cycle is truly significant. But the
exactly calculated movements of planetary bodies (a kind of science) gets
fuzzy when magic enters in. Then we go well beyond the sort of argument
that says that the earliest days of a child, if dark and wintry, produce a different person than one whose earliest impressions are of warmth and sun.

Here are some comments on the influence of the moon from an
eleventh-century manuscript in the Vatican that E. Svenburg quotes in *De
Lastinska lunaria* (1936) and V. I. J. Flint brings to my attention:

The fourth day of the moon. Let blood in the morning. This is a good day on which to begin undertakings and to send boys to school. Whoever tries to run away will be speedily recaptured and whoever falls ill will quickly die, with almost no hope of recovery.

I would have thought that dying (quickly or slowly) there was absolutely no "hope of recovery." But to finish the passage:

Boys born on this day will be fornicators and so will girls. If you have a dream on it, good or bad, it will come true.

Now, after the first sentence, which is no more superstitious than old books on medicine or the instructions in farmers' almanacs from Pliny to today that tell you when to plant or reap and so on, this goes beyond observation of nature into the realm of magic. As with all horoscopes, ask "who says so?" and "on what basis?" and "how does this work?" Astrologers I have encountered offer no explanations of *precisely* how the stars affect us (with the exception of one Renaissance writer whom I'll mention to you later). Nor does a horoscope ever tell me *why* next Thursday will be a bad day for me to close a business deal and a good one to be nice to my mother-in-law. Always ask *why*.

Magic and astrology have become inextricably intertwined. This has been bad for magic (which receives an unnecessary load of garbage thereby) and for astrology (which has sometimes been linked with the black arts, to its detriment). Ritual magic depends crucially on the right conjunctions for ceremonies, and there is much fuss with the metals, colors, and incenses of "ruling planets." But magic has an explanation of how effects are achieved, what works. Astrology lacks anything but assertions. Both of course can have an effect on the gullible whether there is anything to them or not. Both are forbidden by most traditional Western religions (though the average person doesn't know this or care about it).

Astrology is not uninteresting, if only as a chapter in the exciting history of human folly. It deserves a whole book, or library, of its own. Here I can take space to say only that some dealing with devils and demons depends upon astrological calculations somewhat similar to those that permit horoscope makers (provided they have the precise longitude and latitude of the place and the time of birth to the second) to "read" character and predict "destiny."

However, the calculations magicians need are comparatively easily done. I find that practically no horoscope-makers have the skills to work with the necessary astronomical and mathematical information to bring what one might call serious astrology to the aid of either ceremonial magic or personal prognostication. They give pseudo-science a bad name.

I want to add that it is my belief that even pseudo-science has something to teach us; it ought not to be dismissed out of hand. But the horoscopes in the daily newspapers and the "You and The Stars" mindless magazines make fools of millions. This adversely affects science and would-be science such as parapsychology and magic because the acceptance of astrological foolishness lowers respect for the intelligence of the general public and encourages charlatans to batten on their stupidity.

AN INNOCENT BEGINNING

The bull *Summis desiderantes affectibus* (1484) of Innocent VIII effectively launched the "clean-up" of witchcraft in Germany and caused the deaths of tens of thousands. I think encouraging astrologers and self-proclaimed psychics can move from innocent entertainment to dangerous irrationality.

CHARMING

Two Dominicans' handbook for prosecuting witches sat on practically every judge's desk at the height of what one historian calls "the witchcraft craze." Some hint as to its thinking may be found in its attitude toward charms. These are permitted to Christians, say the learned priests, provided there is no pact with The Devil involved, no superstition (only belief in the power of God), no pagan "passes" (only the Sign of the Cross), and only phrases from Scripture, that is names from the Judeo-Christian tradition.

Modern astrologers pretend to science and yet also hold superstitious, unscientific views. They try to appeal to religious people and they play down the fact that though astrology and religion have often been linked, they are contradictory. If you are a Christian—no astrology!

YOUR HOROSCOPE

I have noticed that the popular horoscopes in the media deal in bland, congratulatory, upbeat platitudes. When did you last look at your horoscope to see "There is no hope for anything good for you today. Despair"? It's about time for you to have the unvarnished truth, so here is my authoritative reading of Your Horoscope. I predict you won't like it. Astrology, of course, has been implicitly believed by millions of people worldwide for uncounted centuries, so you just know it has to be true.

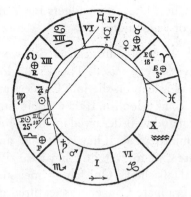

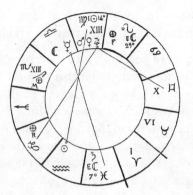

Horoscope of Louis XVI: nativity (day-time) 1754

Horoscope of the death of Louis XVI, 1793

Aries (The Ram), March 21 through April 19. People born under this sign of the ram are hardheaded and too often horny. They are creative, imaginative, and lie a lot. Aries people are hot tempered and, once they have stumbled into an intellectual position, stubborn. However, it is important to know what they think because they are unerring guides to the exact opposite of what you ought to do or believe. The old ones are the worst. They whine a lot about their health, which deteriorates from age seventeen onwards. They tend to be too late for the early bird special.

Taurus (The Bull), April 20 through May 19. Taureans are usually sex-obsessed, but they can hardly ever get it up. They are often able to say the right thing at the right time, but something usually prevents them from doing so. They are never lucky. Being born under Taurus is the earliest, but not the worst, of their misfortunes. I know you are going to expect me to say they are full of bull. I don't. But they are usually repulsive morally and have loser names that begin with "J," like *Jennifer, Jessica, Jason, Joel,* never *John.* You can easily pick them out in a crowd because all their clothes match but their shoes are cheap.

Gemini (The Twins), May 20 through June 20. Geminis are often two-faced, schizophrenic, bisexual, double-crossing, or beside themselves with rage. Their governing planet, Mercury, makes them unreliable and down in winter. They are of two minds—neither of them very powerful. Nobody of any real significance was ever born under the sign of Gemini. Famous Geminis never deserve their fame and serious investigating would reveal why, but nobody cares. Geminis make fair secretaries but bad word processors. Geminis commit adultery with persons more obnoxious than their spouses. In divorces, it is always their fault. They like gadgets but can't light barbecues. They may be Trekkies or vegetarians.

Cancer (The Crab), June 21 through July 22. Who wants cancer? No wonder people born under this sign are universally despised. They crab a lot. Even with a Virgo, a Cancer tends to fall asleep on the job. Cancers are frequently hurt by some imagined slight. This is foolish. If they would simply pay attention they would learn of real and well-deserved insults. Most Cancers can't cook, and worse, they think they can. They run to fat, and the ones who strive to keep thin substitute spite for weight. They wear silly sunglasses. Cancers appear on sensational talk shows. One family once succeeded on *Family Feud*. A high-school graduate Cancer was featured on *That's Incredible!* Look for them on real-crime shows, like *Cops*.

Leo (The Lion), July 23 through August 21. Leos think of themselves as born leaders but no one wants to follow them (except another nightclub act). Leos seek the spotlight. That always shows them up. They like political office and cookouts. They are prone to jealous rages and klutzy love-making, but this is seldom important because few nice people ever want to get involved with a Leo. Almost all Leos have herpes, hair they can't do anything with, and relatives who want to borrow money from you. You can always tell a Leo, but (all together now!) you cannot tell him much. They wear K-Mart or Ralph Lauren clothes. They think displaying the logo on their underwear elastic is fashion.

Virgo (The Virgin), August 22 through September 22. There are a few exceptions, but Virgos tend to be people conceived out of wedlock after office Christmas parties. Figure it out. The fathers are inevitably employees from the mailroom, not the front office. Virgos grow up virgins because child molesters shun them. Virgos smell bad. Nonetheless, people like Virgos around (at a distance) because it is always fun to have people to look down on or to point out to your children as bad role models. Attila the Hun, Freddie Prinze, and possibly Vera Hruba Ralston and other show-biz types were Virgos. Mother Teresa has been photographed slapping a few Virgos and the Pope giving them the finger.

Libra (The Scales), September 23 through October 22. Because Libra is the sign of justice, people born under this sign never get anywhere in life. They are prejudiced, narrow-minded, obdurate, and disagreed with your position on the O.J. verdict. They never win lotteries, always have halitosis, and are prone to cost taxpayers big money for their bypass surgical operations. They predominate among welfare cheaters and those whose houseplants die of neglect or over-watering. Those born on the second decan of Libra are slightly superior to the rest, but nobody but Librans would take an interest in such a trivial distinction. Librans are bad at stock market timing and all sports.

Scorpio (The Scorpion), October 23 through November 21. Sure, you want a Scorpion in your bed. No one ever heard much about Scorpios until the invention of the internal combustion engine, at which point Scorpios emerged as the world's worst drivers. A few manage financial independence by a combination of wealthy Sagitarian parents and a total lack of ethical behavior, but most squander whatever money comes their way. They think delicatessen is gourmet food and that Las Vegas is American theater's heart. Scorpios tend to lose money in boom-and-bust real estate. More Scorpios than you would believe have sex with vibrators or ugly animals.

Sagittarius (The Archer), November 22 through December 21. Sagittarians can't spell and are vain and egotistical. They turned to this paragraph immediately—but it won't do them any good. All they will learn here is that the rest of humanity is laughing at them behind their backs. At least humanity does not condemn them for taking drugs. If you were a Sagittarian, you would turn to Prozac or something illegal, too. Most Sagittarians are attracted to morons born under the sign of Virgo or with big hair. It's social climbing, but it seldom gets them anywhere. In public, Sagittarians pick their noses; in private, their toes. Sagittarians like Wayne Newton, Newt Gingrich, and Gin and Tonic.

Capricorn (The Goat), December 22 through January 20. Born at times that simply ruined the holidays for their parents, Capricorns obviously are inconsiderate people. This is the birth sign of Jesus and a number of other people who died violent deaths because they trod on other people's sensibilities. Most modern Capricorns are too lazy to get into big trouble. They were the original couch potatoes. They enter all the direct-mail contests but never win anything and never suspect the whole thing is a Post Office ploy to get people to buy overpriced stamps. Old Goats are the most pitiful and annoying. Their suspicions they are suffering from a mysterious, fatal disease are usually well founded.

Aquarius (The Water Carrier), January 21 through February 19. Born when winter is at its worst and the most repulsive people go to Florida and such benighted places, the Water Carriers are constantly seeking a better life but deep down know they do not deserve it. In Britain, the slang phrase "the bloke that carries the can" means "the loser." In America, the Age of

Aquarius was proclaimed by the hippies of the sixties, but they were several generations off target. Aquarians get all the menial jobs and are, regrettably, not very good at them. They love to wear badges that say "Security" and to have petty powers to inconvenience the general public. They are model husbands only in the sense that a *model* is defined as "a small imitation of the real thing."

Pisces (The Fish), February 20 through March 20. This sign includes those born on the last day of February in leap years, people who get birthday presents less often than the rest of us. Pisces is last in this list as in most things. It's only fair. People tend to rely on the sympathetic ears of Pisces to unload all their troubles and complaints on them. The naiveté of Pisces also makes them useful targets for unrepayable loans. Many Pisces work in fast-food establishments, but never as managers. They are plagued by misfortune. It was a Pisces in a McDonald's in Alaska who served a Coke with too much ice. The customer spilled it on herself, sued McDonald's for pain and suffering, and collected millions. The Pisces had to go and work in a Friendly's, a longer commute.

If you were born on an odd-numbered day, your lucky numbers are 5840, 4339, and 7771. If you were born on an even-numbered day, you have none. Persons born in the Year of the Dragon in the Chinese zodiac are luckier than others, but no one is ever sure of their year in that system. This is perhaps fortunate, for the Year of the Rat is terrible. The advice "do not marry a dog," however, is always sound. Bad years begin in a one or two. Good years end in no estate taxes. Avoid making mistakes on weekends. Watch out midweek (Monday through Friday). Do not send money without reading the prospectus first and deciding not to invest. Do not remove the tag from your mattress on a day ending in "y." Hope for the best always: nobody loves a character who says "I told you so."

MY OWN HOROSCOPE

I calculate that the planetary positions at my birth (which was distinctly premature—I wonder if I should have waited for a more propitious time and place!) were:

Sun	12 degrees of Sagittarius
Moon	27 degrees of Virgo
Mercury	5 degrees of Sagittarius
Venus	21 degrees of Capricorn

Mars	5 degrees of Cancer
Jupiter	1 degree of Taurus
Saturn	20 degrees of Sagittarius
Uranus	3 degrees of Aries
Neptune	1 degree of Virgo
Pluto	17 degrees of Cancer

So my sun sign is Sagittarius and my moon was in Virgo. Fire 4, Earth 4, Water 2, Air O. Retrograde planets 5. Venus, Uranus, Neptune rule the Ascendant. The Part of Fortune falls in the 10th House.

This Horoscope ought to give me confidence in my psychic abilities but I have to say I cannot predict what the experts on astrology out there might make of it. With Mercury ruling the 9th House and the 12th House, I ought to be a seer—but I don't think I am. Nor, even though Lilith in the 10th House supposedly gives me mediumistic powers, do I intend to employ them to get any answer. If you like, write to me in care of the publishers and give me your comments, predictions, arguments, etc. I know from previous books that I cannot undertake to answer all letters but I read them all, correct errors in future editions when possible, and am glad to be in touch with my readership. I usually say this in prefaces. I repeat it here for those who never read prefaces.

If anyone's predictions turn out to be as the British say "spot on," I will gratefully acknowledge that in the next edition. I cannot even predict if there will be a next edition. At the moment, I'm confused. Some English lady claims there's a 13th sign of the Zodiac. I may not be a Sagittarius after all!

HOW ASTROLOGY WORKS (YOU READ IT HERE)

Or you may have read it in my book on *Elizabethan Popular Culture* (1988). I expect you did not find it (as I did) in the obscure work of John Maplet, who died in 1592. In *The Dial of Destiny* (1581), Maplet published the only attempt to explain that I have ever seen *how* the stars impel or compel our lives.

You are frequently told that conjunctions of planets, etc., affect human lives. How? Here is Maplet's extraordinary explanation:

> In the head of man there are seven Pores or holes, allotted to diverse and sundry offices, as of the which every one of them is subject to a sundry Planet. As that Pore or hole which is the right ear appurtaineth to Saturn, that in the left, to Jupiter. Mars also

hath the government of that [nostril] which is in the right side of the nose; Venus of the contrary [nostril]; Sol is master over that which holdeth the strings of the right Eye; Luna over the other in the left Eye; and all the whole workmanship [of the mouth?] is proper alone to Mercury.

I added there, "For those of you who believe implicitly in astrology, you have holes in your heads." I did not bother to ask how Maplet (or anyone else) discovered which planet affected which part or to remind people that since Maplet we have discovered more planets. Doesn't that complicate matters and invalidate all horoscopes that do not take Uranus and Pluto into account?

The next time you are told that this or that planet is in this or that house, Scorpio is rising, the Moon is in Aries, or some other arrangement exists to impact your personal life, ask how the mechanism works, precisely, both in getting the influences down here to you and then within you and the world around you. Astrology never seems to answer these basic questions. Astrologers simply say, "Watch out for a dark woman." If you should happen to reply, "She's blonde," the clever ones counterattack with, "Oh, well, I meant dark *in character.*"

GOD, DEMONS, AND DISEASE

In the Judeo-Christian way of looking at things, disease and death began with the transgression of Adam and Eve and was directly related to the action of The Devil. It might be sent by God Himself as a punishment (the plagues of Egypt) or a test (Job), but it was also frequently attributed to devils and demons, as was often the case (and still is the case) in a number of pagan religions. God was considered to be in charge of life and health ("I kill, and I give life; I wound, and I heal," He is quoted as saying in *Deuteronomy*), and the god of the Jews is said to have given mankind both threats of death and public health advice, dietary laws, directions on sanitation, rejection of surgery (except for circumcision), and so on.

With Christianity came more suspicion of doctors (as in the gospel of Mark, monks were forbidden to practice medicine after the Council of Clérmont in 1130), more prayers to saints for intercession, and more interest in relics, penances, and miraculous cures. From miracles could come even resurrection from the dead, and from magic, the exilir of life, immortality. For a very long time medical men were as mixed up with magicians as chemists were with alchemists, or astronomers were with astrologers.

It was always believed in the Judeo-Christian tradition that prayer and the Hand of God could cure any disease and, to some extent, that disease was a sign of the presence of evil. The bodies of saints, it was believed, remained uncorrupted even after death. The bodies of sinners, some saints were quoted as saying, filled the nostrils of the holy with actual and repulsive odors of evil. Spiritual health and the health of the body (regarded as the temple of the Holy Ghost, not to be defiled or diseased) went hand in hand.

The connection in the minds of many between spiritual and physical led the thinkers on whose ideas Mrs. Mary Baker Eddy founded Christian Science to rely on the soul to cure the body. Disease was not even to be given a reality by certain Transcendentalists; Ralph Waldo Emerson said we must "never name disease," and (of course) he died, but his way of thinking still lives. As for Mrs. Eddy, criticism has been as direct (though perhaps never as damaging) as that of Mark Twain in his attack of 1907 on her and her church, but Christian Science has grown into a major American religion and has spread worldwide.

In the concept that disease can be banished by faith, prayer, and what tone popular preacher used to call "the power of positive thinking," disease is related to The Devil, his demons, and other evil creatures such as vampires—all the evil that cannot assail a true believer unless *invited in*. Rather than saying that suffering makes some victims extremely nasty— and this may be the hardest part of trying to help the sick and the dying, as many care-givers have discovered in the plagues of the past and AIDS in the present—this rather reverses the situation and blames the victim: Where have you sinned in order to have the deserved disease? Why have you invited the devils and demons into the house of the soul? What are you going to do to expel the negative, the evil in you? If you do not succeed in doing that, in what way is your faith deficient?

SPIRITUALISM IN CZARIST RUSSIA

The strong grip of the Orthodox Church did nothing to prevent the superstitious peasantry and, more often, the decadent aristocracy from playing at spiritualism, following self-proclaimed gurus (of whom the "Mad Monk" Rasputin was among the last and the most dangerous), and toying with fortune-telling, ouija planchettes, and the like. Spiritualism is reflected in the work of writers such as Nikolai Semenovich Leskov, Count Leo Tolstoi, and Feodor Mikhailovich Dostoevsky. Thomas E. Berry (in a *Festschrift* for Victor Terras, *The Supernatural in Slavic and Baltic Literature*, 1988) and others have traced the fascination with mediumship in Russian literature of the nineteenth century. Russian writers were as concerned with Spiritualism as were American ones in that period (Poe, William Dean Howells, Henry Thoreau, Sarah Orne Jewett, and others) and Britons (John Ruskin, Lord Tennyson, Sir Arthur Conan Doyle, and others). There were those—though they were few in Russia—who mocked the idea of table rapping and communications from the Other Side. Spiritualism may have been as significant a home-grown religion in its day as were such other American ideas as Mormonism, Christian Science, and Theosophy, but Mark Twain dismissed Spiritualism as a mere amusement "when other amusements fail."

SPIRITUALISM

Braude, Anne, "News from the Spirit World:
A Checklist of American Periodicals, 1847–1900," *Proceedings of The American Antiquarian Society* 99:2 (October 1988), 399–462)
Crow, Charles L. ed., *The Haunted Dusk* (1983)
Doyle, Jean Conan, (forward), *The Quest for Sir Arthur Conan Doyle* . . . (1987)

EVANGELINE ADAMS AND FRIENDS

This astrologer guided many in the American stock market and politics in the early part of this century. The headlines in 1914 declared that in court she had proved the efficacy of astrology. In 1929 she was advising everyone that the stock market could go nowhere but up and up. The crash proved her wrong. Like Miss Dixon, whose date for the beginning of World War III proved to be wrong, she nonetheless held on to many adherents. In 1996 several other astrologers, including a woman who used to be a professor of mathematics before turning to the stars, are peddling advice in the market and guaranteeing to predict the exact dates of highs and lows.

HOLY WATER

The *Journal of Irreproducible Results*, a scientific publication with several Nobel laureates on its editorial board, reported that in recent experiments seeds watered with holy water did no better than seeds watered with ordinary water.

"PAUL CHRISTIAN"

The author of *L'Histoire de la Magie, du monde surnaturel et de la fatalité à travers les temps et les peuples* was baptized Jean-Baptiste Pitois on 15 May 1811 in the Vosges area of France. As a young man he had a fling at becoming a Trappist monk, led an uprising against slavery in the Dominican Republic (then a French colony), and became interested in magic through his friend, Charles Nodier, librarian at The Arsenal in Paris. He himself eventually became a librarian and pored over books on the occult. He wrote three volumes of "walks" in *Historic Paris* (1837–1840) and other journalism. He wrote a two-volume *History of the French Clergy* (1840) and memoirs of his service in Morocco skirmishes under Marshal Bugeaud, 1843–1844. He edited journals, wrote a *History of The Terror* of the French Revolutionary period, eight volumes of *Heroes of Christianity*, and much more, from Celtic translations to Catholic devotional works and French history, leading up to his history of magic (1870). Along the way he used pseudonyms such as "Dom Marie-Barnard" (for the *Heroes of Christianity*) and "Charles Moreau." As the historian of magic, he was known as "Paul Christian" and declared he brought his "offering without expecting any gratitude." In addition to this work, there remains an unpublished document said to be "10,000 lines" long on magic. It may, like the history published, have a strong element of astrology in it which would recommend it to a pretty large audience today.

Introducing James Kirkup and Julian Shaw's English translation of *The History and Practice of Magic* (1963), edited and emended by various hands, Ross Nicholls writes:

> *The History of Magic* was at once received as a standard work in this period which . . . was filled with occult interests. Christian's preoccupation with intuitive divination by means of the letters which spell out a name or question, which he called the Prenestine Fates, both reflected and intensified the taste of the time. The work became widely known abroad and Madame Blavatsky referred to it in 1888 in the *Secret Doctrine* [I:93 in the first edition].

"Paul Christian" concludes by suggesting a position between the credulous and the skeptical:

> Is divination a universal but sterile error, or a powerful and fruitful truth? Will it disappear before human logic, or will it one day take its honored place amongst serious studies?

That is a decision on which it is hardly likely that a decision will be arrived at.

In some respects the opposing sides seem to be equally matched . . . .

Divination is a star shining and dimming like the beam from a lighthouse; it leads us and it refuses us, in its own time, its capricious intuitions.

Is it diabolical or celestial? Where does it come from? Who shall say what it is or what it is not?

Seen close at hand, it is a card-reader, the last incarnation of a contagious stupidity; seen at a distance, it is a manifestation of the Divine Mind in a Hermes or Zoroaster, in an Elijah or a Daniel; it is the majesty of the Magi and the prophets; it is the mystery of the Sybils and the Vestals; it is the poetry of the Druidic virgins and the nymphs of Hercynos; it is the eternal Tomorrow which passes in the vibration of an electric current.

Ah, I repeat, let us beware of premature negations.

Let us walk softly on the path between abysses, the path which separates error and truth.

PREDICTIONS

Predicting the future has traditionally been considered dealing with The Devil. Still, everyone seems to be trying to do it. Every year the tabloids at the check-out counter offer plenty of predictions for the coming months. But who cares if Marlo Thomas and Phil Donohue divorce (predicted as early as 1981), if Michael Jackson marries and divorces, or what happens to Tori Spelling? The tabloids have been wrong in their timing on all of those topics and many more.

In Washington, Miss J.was right about President Kennedy being assassinated but wrong about the beginning of World War III. In Calumet, Michigan, Louise Helene was right about the assassination of President Sadat, but got the wrong year. She also has been wrong for more than fifteen years now that "Castro will die of cancer." He may yet.

A retired math professor offers to sell me astrological predictions of the next market crash. Sorry, but I called the 1987 one myself a few days even before Elaine Gazarelli. However, I'm not infallible; I got out of the present market far too early; at this point there's no use going back in, or knowing when the crash will come, until it does. I'm ready for the Depression, Recession, or Downturn in the Upswing. I hit the top with silver. I haven't believed for 20 years the dire predictions that gold will hit $2,000. I'm still waiting for Franz Pick's prophecy that the government "will change twenty old dollars for one new hard dollar" to come true; I am not holding my breath. He made that prediction about 1980. I predict the Dow will go down, then up, then down. See if I'm not right. World War III will come before World War IV.

If you knew the logical and psychological factors both, you could use financial market predictions to your advantage. If your psychic frauds and crisis investors and Greenspan gurus knew, would they tell you, though? If you knew, you could plan. If you knew when you are going to die, you could plan. But you don't want to know that, do you? Why not just plan to die and leave the date open? Death is foreseeable.

And—get this—if the future is foreseeable, it is fixed; and if it is fixed, whether you know what will happen or not, there is not a thing you can do to change it. Nothing. So what is the use of occult powers by which you can read the headlines and obits in next week's or next year's newspapers? Or the news bytes they manage to squeeze in between the time-wasting schmoozing of inane TV personalities or those stupid teams of net nerds on the screen.

What I really want to know is why they need more than one anchorperson to read the teleprompter. Or why so many news events, from the outcome of a presidential election to the

Death and The Fool, from John Daye, *The Booke of Christian Prayers* (1578).

latest terror bombing in the Middle East, Oklahoma or Atlanta, come as such a surprise. I say: watch The Coast.

THE DEAD

The dead may be more than a little peeved at their forced departure from this plane of existence or lack of respect or remembrance, but people believe they can be placated and remain useful members of the community in some societies. The spirits of strangers, however, may plague the society as devils and demons do. Worse, those who were powerful in life become more powerful in death, freed of human limitations. They can be fearsome if they seek to bring the living into the world of the dead with them. Proper funerals followed by respectful propitiation may keep the dead placated.

In some societies, Polynesia for example, the dead are thought to be generally implacable and malevolent. They function as devils and demons do in some other traditions. Other societies boast their ancestry, call on their ancestors to intercede with the gods for the living, even invite the dead to feasts and celebrations. One hopes for what the Romans thought of as *manes*, beneficent spirits of the departed. The Chinese hope for beneficial work by dead ancestors honored in the burial place, the home shrine, and family temples; traditionally the Chinese established lists of names for generations at a time so that an ancestor would be able to work for the good of his descendants by name in the spirit world.

In many societies, however, the dead are to be treated with the care and caution given to devils and demons, for they are considered equally disturbed and dangerous. They demand sacrifices or can be malicious, especially those whose journey to a state of peace has not been properly accomplished. In the Malagasy Republic, for example, where the religion is centered on ancestor worship and Zanahary (The Creator) associates closely with the dead, it is believed that the dead enforce the justice of the supreme being by rewarding or hurting the living according to their deserts. The dead are, therefore, treated with the highest respect. It is not quite clear (as in many cases of animism) what the relationship of the spirits of the dead is to the spirits said to inhabit trees and rocks and certain animals.

The dead are of immense importance, and it is only very recently that they ceased to be the majority of mankind. Moreover, we shall all join them in the long or short run. We hope to become saints rather than devils, peaceful souls rather than tormented demons. If the fathers of the Christian church are to be believed—and I, for one, would much prefer to doubt them—our prospects are poor: the elect will be only a tiny fraction of mankind and the damned will be almost everyone.

At least in Christianity we stay in hell once damned, although we suffer. We are not put to work, as in some other religions, to work evil against the living. God has fallen angels, devils, and demons for that work, millions and millions of them (so the story goes), all highly specialized and experienced. He may even be able to downsize effectively.

DESECRATING CEMETERIES

This outrageous act is a simple way to commit sacrilege and shock the public, like drawing swastikas on synagogues, but those who disturb graves, and the living as well, these days may have other motives. They may be Satanists.

January 1990: A teenager from Springfield, Virginia, stopped by police for speeding, is found in possession of an unearthed skull and a coffin handle. In the same month, a family cemetery in Vinings, Georgia, is struck by Satanic vandals.

October 1991: Satanists desecrate Washington Cemetery, reports the *Houston Post*.

June 1994: In Arlington County, Virginia, pentagrams, dead cats, bloody handprints, and other evidence of Satanic cult meetings are found in a vandalized mausoleum.

December 1994: "Satanic Ritual Suspected at Cemetery" in Edwardsville, Illinois, reports the *St. Louis Post-Dispatch*. The sheriff says vandals wanted a "skull."

July 1995: Bill Yates of Brazonia County, Texas, asks authorities to limit access to the local cemeteries to cut down on Satanic cult activities.

New York City cemeteries are frequently vandalized, but the newspapers prefer to play this down, and anti-Semitism rather than Satanism is the way to get desecration noted, if at all. Cemeteries are openly used for magic in such places as New Orleans. Dirt from graves for magical use is collected there and wherever voodoo flourishes. Parts of bodies are also stolen from big city morgues and once in a while at accident sites when police are not looking. Ghouls hit the beaches after TWA 800 crashed.

If you are not going to be cremated, spread the news that you are having a powerful curse put on your tomb. Put it on your gravestone. It worked for Shakespeare!

THE PROCTER & GAMBLE TRADEMARK

A rumor that P&G was a Satanist company, with blatant symbols of the Beast of *Revelations* (666) in its very old trademark of a man in the moon brought issues to court which filled the newspapers for some time. P&G finally dispelled these unfounded rumors—but it altered its trademark, too.

THE DEVILS

Christians are commencing to object to sports teams with this name. For example, in Rockcastle, Kentucky, in November 1990 the Mt. Vernon Elementary School hotly debated whether the devil mascot could be permitted to continue. In these days when Amerinds object to "Indians" and "Chiefs" and similar sports names, it is not very remarkable that "The Devils" should come under attack. What are we to do about the likes of the Tampa Bay Devil Rays? *Ray* spelled backwards, some Floridians have pointed out, is the name of a "satanic canine," *Sports Illustrated* reported in April 1995. After Ronald Wilson Reagan—count the letters! 666!—what next?

SPIRITUALISM AND NECROMANCY

Brandon, Ruth, *The Spiritualists* (1983)
Cerminara, Gina, *Many Mansions* (1967)
Doyle, Sir Arthur Conan, *The History of Spiritualism* (2 vols. reprinted 1975)
Flournoy, Théodore (ed. Sonu Shamdasani), *From India to the Planet Mars* (1996)
Gurney, E. and F., W. H. Myers, & Frank Podmore, *Phantasms of the Living* (2 vols., ed. L. R. N. Ashley, 1968)
Knight, W. F. J., *Elysion: Ancient Greek and Roman Beliefs . . . Life after Death* (1970)
Marwick, Max (ed.), *Witchcraft and Sorcery* (1982)
Myers, F. W. H., *Human Personality and Its Survival of Bodily Death* (completed by R. Hodgson & A. Johnson, 1903)
Oppenheim, Janet, *The Other World: Spiritualism and Psychical Research in England 1850–1914* (1985)
Podmore, Frank, *Modern Spiritualism* (1902)
Tyrrell, G. N. M., *Science and Psychical Phenomena* (1961)

CORPSES AND BLACK MAGIC

Stealing the hands of executed criminals (to make Hand of Glory candles, supposed to render the user invisible) was once a fairly common practice.

The blood of sacrificed babies we noted is called for in black magic recipes and rites. Even today parts of corpses are obtained in various nefarious ways and for various nefarious purposes. Those who can stand the gory details about dying, autopsies, cannibalism, "secret rites," and "religious ceremonies" can read *Death to Dust: What Happens to Dead Bodies* (1995) by Kenneth V. Iserson, MD.

"MARGERY" THE MEDIUM

"Margery" was perhaps the most debated medium America has ever produced, an extremely clever, downright fraud, although Sir Arthur Conan Doyle announced that she was the misunderstood martyr of the "new revelation" of psychic science, and others who desperately wanted to believe (such as Hereward Carrington) hailed her for producing ectoplasm at séances.

She was born Mina Stinson in Canada in 1888. She moved to the United States at an early age and her second husband was a Boston Brahmin, Dr. LeRoi Goddard Crandon. The two of them were not able to fool Houdini, himself no slouch at tricks. Though Margery's dead brother William (who was killed in an accident in 1911) appeared at a séance to say, "Houdini, you God-Damned bastard, get the hell out of here . . .," Houdini stayed, and to all intelligent people revealed "Margery's" phony psychic powers after she won a prize from *Scientific American* in the twenties. Here is the cover of his famous "pink pamphlet" debunking her and another fraud of the time.

"Margery" has been the subject of numerous reports, including the book *Voices in the Dark*. She has been eclipsed by newer frauds.

HUNGARY

This item is not so much about devils and demons as about the atmosphere of superstition in which they flourish. Randi, the stage magician, offers a prize for the best investigation of the paranormal, and in 1993 it was won by two Hungarian students. Robert Dallos and Gabor Takacs. They managed to create one of those wondrous crop circles that have people so concerned about extraterrestrials to fool all the "experts," who declared the phenomenon genuine and inexplicable. When the lads appeared on television and disclosed their prank, however, the convinced tended to remain convinced. Britain and a number of other European countries continue to experience these so-called evidences of UFO activity, though UFOs do seem to prefer to hover over trailer parks and other colorful US locations. As I note elsewhere, a certain percentage of Americans claim to have actually been abducted by extraterrestrials and the story that the United States Air Force found a crashed flying saucer and a variable number of its tiny crew members will not go away.

NOSTRADAMUS IS BACK

The cover story in *Omni* for December 1993 on Michel de Nóstre-Dame (1503–1566) has been followed by more and more interest in his prophecies. Rather than deal with the dead in necromancy or at a séance, you can get *The Complete Prophecies of Nostradamus* (H. C. Roberts, 1947) or a more recent rehash and try to figure them out for yourself. It's very New Age, and fuzzier than the *I Ching* or The Tarot or tea leaves.

"HOW MANY NEW YORK RESIDENTS WILL GO TO HELL?"

Find an opinion on this in Bruce Handy's "Hell of a Town" in the *New York Magazine* for 19 December 1993. It is striking how more and more and more Americans today are being drawn to Christian Fundamentalism and yet fewer and fewer of them accept the fundamental Christian view that almost everyone is irretrievably non-elect. To put that a little more directly: damned to hell. Whether it's the hell of Hieronymus Bosch, Baptist fire and brimstone, or just (thanks to Jean-Paul Sartre) simply "other people," the odds are against you. Learn about devils and demons. They will be the constant companions of practically all of mankind—excepting me and you, of course!—for eternity, and starting comparatively soon.

SHOPPING FOR DEVIL WORSHIP MATERIALS

This is done in tiny *bodegas* in Hispanic neighborhoods (*Santería* being the chief religion of devil worshippers in America) rather than in tourist traps such as the witchcraft museum in Salem or the tiny Historic Voodoo Museum in New Orleans. The latter, according to *Consumer Reports* (September 1991), "stages rituals and has magic potions, voodoo dolls and other artifacts; it's worth a visit for the postcards." New York City has Morrigan's Magick, other shops, and several occult bookshops, many *bodegas* with candles for all good and evil intentions, and so on. The Magickal Childe bookshop is a popular place and there are stuffier dealers in "The Occult" as well as well-stocked "occult" shelves in the mass-market chain bookshops. Those areas are good places to pick up superstitious people. Tell them you knew you'd meet them.

BRAZIL

Allegations fly that witchcraft is involved whenever there is one of those rather dubious elections in Central or South America. Sometimes the charges are true. I cannot decide one way or the other on the case in the state of Paruna in the United States of Brazil where, in 1992, the mayor's wife and his daughter were among those arrested for alleged Satanic rituals calculated to effect the mayor's re-election. Certainly one little boy was murdered. As a sacrifice? I don't know. What is significant is that the Brazilians were expected to take the allegations seriously, and they did.

AMERICAN WITCHCRAFT ORGANIZATIONS TODAY

It is not in the nature of Satanists or covens of "good" witches to advertise, but churches are above ground. In Seattle, for example, there is the Aquarian Tabernacle Church (founded 1979 by the Rev. Pete Davis), a neo-pagan congregation. In New Bern, North Carolina, Gavin and Yvonne Frost set up a Church and School of Wicca in the pseudo-druidic style, and in the 1970s published *The Witch's Bible*, *The Witch's Guide to Life*, and *The Magic Power of Witchcraft*. They influenced many with correspondence courses on *wicca*. Various groups formed under the influence of Margot Adler's *Drawing Down the Moon* (1986), a boost to the ever-growing worship of The Goddess. None of these claim devil worship (as did Anton LaVey's Church of Satan in San Francisco) and would be swift to deny any such thing. A great many organizations have a short life. One example (though it lasted longer than most) is the group dedicated to Gardnerian witchcraft that started as a course taught by James Broughton at San Francisco State University (1967), became Full Moon Coven (1969), blossomed into the New Reformed Orthodox Order of the Golden Dawn (with no connection to the Golden Dawn of which A. E. Waite, W. B. Yeats, et al. were once members), and dissolved in May 1976, though covens inspired by it may still exist. *Gnostica's* mailing list is 40,000 +.

ZAMBIAN WITCHCRAFT

Witchcraft is expectedly rife among native religions but it was a surprise when Silvio Cardinal Oddi in Rome in 1992 leveled a charge against Archbishop Emmanuel Millingo of Zambia. The archbishop was described by the cardinal as not only a "clown" but a devil worshipper.

DEVIL WORSHIP IN THE UNION OF SOUTH AFRICA

It took a 1995 murder of a woman (her breasts and genitals mutilated horribly) on vacation in Durban to draw foreign attention to white Satanism in South Africa. Actually, it is centered on Table Mountain in Cape Town, according to a report in the *Washington Times* of May 1990.

THE SAVAGERY OF SOUTHERN AFRICA

While some leaders of African nations (such as Jonas Savimbi in Angola in the late eighties) have been accused of employing black magic against their enemies, it is not safe to take all reports at face value. General Noriega was accused in our part of the world (Panama) of employing black magicians and working with them; then it turned out he was working with the CIA before his downfall. So was the rebel leader, also feared as a wizard, who fought against the return of the ex-priest Aristide in Haiti; he also was in the pay of the CIA. Maybe the CIA employs not only psychics but black magicians. I hope so, if they advance our interests. We need whatever assistance we can muster. Just to be believed to be using black magic is help, especially in such benighted places as some of the backward nations of Africa.

Actually, witchcraft news from Africa is that hundreds of witches or people accused of witchcraft have been murdered there, some with the notorious "necklaces" of burning rubber tires so dear to the heart of Nelson Mandela's horrific wife. Meanwhile, *sagomas* (witch doctors) are a fact of life in a great many African societies. Witchcraft is also a useful accusation to get rid of political enemies, who may or may not be employing black arts. In 1989, for instance, eleven high officials of Liberia, including the minister of defense, were charged with ritual murder as part of a plot to overthrow the government.

In July and August 1994, forty-four men and women in Kenya's Kisii district were burned as witches. Some fifty arrests were made but burnings were reported in British newspapers as continuing to take place "almost one a week." By the same time that year seventy-one witches had been reported burned in the northern part of the Transvaal, some by the same hideous method. The *New York Times* noted that no one had been tried for these murders. In 1995 ritual murders were rife in the Union of South Africa, and in recent years hundreds of people may have been murdered as suspected witches.

As African societies begin to collapse under AIDS and other plagues, and foreigners are more and more hated for interference in tribal warfare that is killing hundreds of thousands and tearing nations apart, it is not unusual for foreigners to be accused of being evil magicians and worse. Dan Fountain, a medical missionary in the chaos of Zaïre, was accused, the *Washington Post* reported on 22 May 1995, of creating the outbreak of the dreaded Ebola there, by witchcraft.

In Motonawabaloi (Place of the Witches) in northern South Africa, 122 people accused of witchcraft, were huddled in exile. "In the surrounding Northern Province," wrote *The Economist* for 9 December 1995, "in the ten months to February this year, 146 'witches' were stoned, burned or bludgeoned to death. . . . Over the past few years, there has been a resurgence of the ancient practice of witch-burning in South Africa." See *To Live in Fear: Witchburning and Medicine Murder in Venda* by Anthony Minnaar et al. (1992).

"Medicine murder" refers to *muti* (from Zulu *umu thi*, "tree"). *The Economist* explains:

> In Venda tradition, a new chief could sanction murder to obtain parts of the human body for a *muti* brew. By drinking the *muti*, the energy and strength of the dead person would be transferred to him. To be effective, the parts had to be removed while the person was still alive . . . . One young man [reported a witchcraft commission recently] . . . went to a *sangoma* for medicine to make him strong. He was advised to kill another man, and cut off his genitals. He was then told to eat the roasted penis and to rub the ashes of the charcoaled testicles into his skin.

South Africa has age-old traditions that must be eradicated if the country is ever to become civilized. The head of the witchcraft commission says: "The custom of witchcraft is too deeply rooted" to be extirpated soon, and the government policy calls for modernizing, while respecting, African traditions. One other Venda tradition: *zwivhuya*, the idea that there is only a certain amount of material and spiritual goods to go round. So if one person is seen to have more than another, this can be only at other people's expense. In this view, success cannot be earned; it is the result of witchcraft.

AFTER THE IRON CURTAIN

In the dislocation following the collapse of the USSR, black magic sprang up (or came forward) in former Soviet lands. On 25 November 1994 the *Guardian* in Britain reported: "Witches and Wizards put Magic back in Moscow." Russian papers began to carry stories along those lines, extremely rare under communism. Earlier the same year the *Guardian* had been among the first to notice the likes of Angelo del Bertini in Budapest and other witches coming to prominence in former countries of the Eastern Bloc. Despite the strong hold of Catholicism, there is a good deal of black magic in Poland. The East German witches are once again united with their West German colleagues. Spiritualism has long been of interest to Slavs. Satanist serial killers are rarer than in the US, and accusations of Satanic child abuse are almost unheard of in former Soviet republics and other political units formerly dominated by the USSR.

LIFE FROM THE DEAD

In a documentary *Faces of Death*, a gruesome survey by Alan Black, Dr. Francis B. Gröss, thanatologist or expert on death, speaks of a weird cult he found "on the outskirts of San Francisco" that believes "the power of everlasting life" is to be obtained by eating "the internal organs of the dead."

The film shows cultists feasting on the organs of a corpse, "a gift that will enable us to outlive and outlove any contemporary human being on this planet," according to their leader. They bathe in blood, eat the corpse. . . .

Having witnessed the gruesome ceremony with its magical ideas and trappings of sorcery, Dr. Gröss presents it to us on film but adds, "I realized that I was dealing with a maniac" and a group of "dangerous individuals whose minds are controlled."

One hopes he has given their names to the police. In ancient times sorcerers and others may have eaten the dead or sacrificed the living, but to find this in the twentieth century must terrify many, magicians and witches included.

A CANADIAN POLTERGEIST STORY

In 1878 in Amherst, Nova Scotia, there was a terrible fuss over one Esther Cox who, raped and abandoned by a boyfriend, went into depression and then suddenly was said to be the victim of poltergeists who flung things around and created havoc, even starting fires. Then a barn caught fire, and Miss Cox was arrested for arson, tried, and jailed. The poltergeist activity stopped.

Canadian folklore journals have a few useful articles on Canadian witchcraft and superstitions, but not as many as you would expect. Satanism seldom makes Canadian headlines.

DEFENSES AGAINST THE DEAD

If you place a coin in the coffin, the dead person will be able to pay the fare across the River Styx and will not return to haunt the living. This is the belief that led to people being buried with a penny on each eyelid. My grandmother (of Victorian vintage) used to say of light-fingered people, "They'd steal the pennies off a dead man's eyes." It took me years to discover what that really meant.

If you carry the corpse out of the house feet first, it cannot look back and beckon some member of the family to follow it soon into the next world.

If you pin a vampire to the ground with a stake through the heart, him cannot rise to bother the living.

Make sure your loved one is not the first to be buried in a new cemetery. The Devil is said to claim the first person so buried and may send him back to harm the family.

The dead are best placed on an east/west axis facing east (where the sun will rise on the day of Resurrection) and on the south side of the church. This helps to protect them from demons and you from them. To keep the dead from getting up, place a cairn of stones or one heavy stone (a headstone) on the grave. Put a cross on it to keep away devils and demons.

Sometimes the dead return asking you to do work they left unfinished or to undertake other tasks. You can oblige them and then you have the grateful dead on your side. Annoy them by refusing to carry out their wishes (or by such improprieties as dancing or urinating on their graves) and they may seek revenge on you.

I discussed these and other superstitions in *The Complete Book of Superstition, Prophecy, and Luck*. If you don't think superstitions surround the dead,

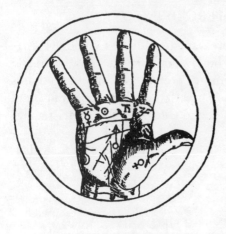

think for a moment that alleged communication with them, first by table rapping and later in séances, is the basis for one of America's home-grown religions, Spiritualism, a product of the last century, which also saw belief in phrenology and other quackeries and other new religions. Spiritualism isn't dead yet either.

I conclude this section on witchcraft in the modern world with Spiritualism because it is probably the most widespread kind of witchcraft practiced today in civilized nations. Witchcraft? Yes. Spiritualism is necromancy. Palmistry is only pseudo-science, like phrenology (once extremely popular, now abandoned).

SPIRITISM AND ALL COMMUNICATION WITH THE DEAD IS EVIL

Put away your Ouija board, cease to go to séances, and maybe it would be wise to stop certain kinds of prayers to favorite saints, because all communication with the dead is evil. It is of The Devil, say many conventional religions (but of course not the Spiritualists). In 1856 the Sacred Congregation of the Holy Office had the last word on the matter for Roman Catholics:

> That to evoke the spirits of the dead, to receive answers from them, to seek knowledge of unknown facts or of events happening at a distance, and all superstitious traffic of this kind is a kind of deceit absolutely unlawful and heretical, and a grave scandal against morality.

In this light, such eminent spiritualists as Mde. Blavatsky, Daniel Dunglas Home, Andrew Jackson Davis, and a long list of mediums and defenders of mediumship (such as Sir Oliver Lodge, Sir Arthur Conan Doyle, and A. F. Schrenck von Notzing) are the agents or the dupes of The Devil. The Society for Psychical Research (founded in London in 1882) and other parapsychological research organizations, dedicated to separating paranormal and supernormal powers and experiences from superstition and Spiritualism, have attempted to see if there is anything but fraud in mediumship. (It also investigates veridical dreams, apparitions, psychokinesis, automatic writing, and extraordinary human powers and extrasensory perception—which is to say clairvoyance, prophecy, and telepathy—in general). That is science, or it will be when and if repeatable experimentation is achieved. At least it contributes to sciences such as psychology. But to participate willingly in attempts to communicate with the dead is either time-wasting or diabolical. No channeling!

To see or hear apparitions of the dead may be illusion, preferential treatment, or temptation of "the fiend that lies like truth." To call apparitions or voices of the dead, or to attempt to do so, is the work of The Devil. It is no better and no worse than calling up demons, which (Francis Barrett said in *The Perfection and Key of the Cabbala, or Ceremonial Magic*) can appear in the form of animals or birds (she-goats, magpies, owls) or people (a little boy, an old man with a beard, a crone leaning on a stick), as well as in the form of your dead friends and relatives.

Before leaving mention of mediumship, I must tell you my favorite séance story. A person attending a seance was invited to mention a relative. "May I speak with my grandfather?" he requested. The medium went into a deep trance and presently there was a moaning and a deep voice said, "I am your grandfather. You may ask me one question only." "Very well," the person said, "Grandfather, *what* are you doing here? You *aren't dead*!"

IN THE STILL OF THE NIGHT

Everyone tries to interpret dreams. Freud said that if you dream of going up or down stairs, you are thinking of sexual matters, that a smooth wall was male, that tables and boards were women, dreaming of flying was sexual emission, and playing with a small child was masturbation. If you do not dream of these things you may be repressing. You can't win.

Those emphases on sex remind me of the story of the young man who was sent to a Freudian psychoanalyst because (like Freud?) the young man was allegedly obsessed with sex. The psychoanalyst drew a circle and asked what that reminded the young man of. "Sex," was the reply. The doctor pondered this and had to agree that a hole, etc. "OK, what's this?" he asked, showing a straight line. "Sex," was the reply. Long and straight . . . all right. Then with a flourish the doctor drew a square. "Sex," said the young man. "Ah ha," said the doctor, "now that is impossible. You *are* obsessed with sex." "Me?" asked the young man. "Me? *You* are the one who's drawing all the dirty pictures!"

In Harlem, people read "gypsy" dream books and find in them much more than symbols of sex. Indeed, people have been reading dream books at least since Artemidorus' in the second century of our era and trying to see what's up with all that downtime.

The Navajo say that if you dream something black and round is pressing down on your chest, it's a ghost. Some people say they can dream up ghosts, see the future, or experience in their sleep events happening at that very moment but very far off. Dreaming may be indigestion, programming what the mind has taken in during the day, wishing, or many other things. Oneiromancy (divination by dreams) is not, however, dealing with devils and demons. It may be superstition but it's not Satanism.

If you dream of The Devil, they say, you are too prone to temptation or too susceptible to flattery.

PSYCHOLOGY AND PSYCHIC PHENOMENA

The rise of psychology as a science was paralleled by great interest in the pseudo-science of parapsychology, psychic research, mediumship, and Spiritualism. At first psychologists were wary of investigating psychic phenomena. This left psychic phenomena and extraordinary abilities of the mind, real or imagined, to be investigated by the Society for Psychical Research in both Britain and the US. This was true despite the fact that claims were being made that human minds had powers hitherto undreamed of and despite the fact that Sigmund Freud delivered himself of the opinion that if he had to do it all over, he would have investigated parapsychology, which was much more interesting, instead of psychoanalysis.

In time, however, writes Deborah J. Coon, in "Testing the Limits of Sense and Science" in *American Psychologist* for February 1992, the psychologists found a way to get involved without looking like "soft" scientists or pseudo-scientists. Just as the study of homosexuality was finally approached confidently from the angle of pyschopathology and later psychobiology and sociodynamics, so the occult was investigated with a certain hesitancy by psychologists who were able to say that they of course gave it no credence but it was, after all, a department of human behavior. How people loved to deceive themselves and others! How delusion was contagious! It was all rooted in William James, in fact, in the fascination of "the madness of crowds." What a great new field in which to test, measure, and pontificate! Away with the medieval and mystical! Hooray for the scientific and statistical! The modern science of the mind here to save mankind from the errors of the Dark Ages before Charcot, Breuer, Freud, Wilhelm Reich, and later *I'm OK, You're OK*, and human behavior as simple *Games People Play* and *Everything You Ever Wanted to Know about Sex (But were Afraid to Ask)*, not to mention *How to Be Your Own Best Friend* and keep from going nuts in your spare time, for fun and profit, and all in the privacy of your own home or office for pennies a day.

Ms. Coon persuasively argues that psychology, the new religion, was able to offer the layman expert advice on how to detect and avoid the occasions of mental unhealth. Defending the credulous against the deceptions by the Spiritualists which the SPRs conveniently exposed, psychology became the champion of reason and science against the irrational and the superstitious. While the societies for psychical research dedicated themselves to exposing fraudulent mediums, psychology developed a new specialty: the psychology of deception and credulousness—and asked the public to applaud and believe explicitly in what psychology taught. To become well-adjusted (better, constantly-adjusting) to such daily inconveniences as the existence of evil and a world in which *Bad Things Happen to Good People*. Real bad things. . . .

HELL AT THE MOVIES

I don't mean sitting behind idiots who discuss the film as if they were watching TV at home. I mean Hollywood's portrayal of The Pit. The *New York Press* 8–12 December 1995 says that

> only a small handful of films have undertaken . . . a representation of Hell—and most are either comedies (*Heaven Can Wait*, *Hellazpoppin*) or cartoons (*The Simpsons*, *Animaniacs*, Bugs Bunny, and Betty Boop). In *Dante's Inferno*, Spencer Tracy stars as a carnival ride owner whose rides (because of shoddy construction) keep killing people . . . . he goes a little funny in the head and has a remarkable, ten-minute vision of Hell, full of writhing and screaming souls . . . (probably lifted from an Italian silent film). . . .

> In 1975's *The Devil's Rain*, the souls of at least a few of the damned are kept for a few centuries in an otherwise-empty bubble-shaped aquarium, in which it rains all the time. *The Sentinel*, just a few years later, puts the entrance to Hell (complete with one-third of the text of Dante's sign) in the basement of a Brooklyn Heights brownstone [and uses] real circus freaks to play damned souls . . . adding a few planks to Catholic Hell mythology. According to the film, the Vatican places a priest or nun (inevitably a failed suicide before turning to God) at the entrance to Hell, just to make sure that the demons and damned souls don't break out and run around . . . [as] when an angel was placed at the entrance to the Garden to prevent the Devil from sneaking in.

At the end of Alan Parker's *Angel Heart*, Mickey Rourke, after being duped by Robert De Niro's Satan, is put on a wheezing freight elevator heading straight down into the bowels of a smoky, industrial-age Hell positioned somewhere just beneath the streets of New Orleans.

In an episode of *The Twilight Zone*, a man thinks he's gone to Heaven when he finds himself in a plush apartment, replete with everything he could ever want—then he gets bored, and realizes he's actually in Hell.

With a take on that theme—the idea that Hell's a place full of cruel practical jokes—a contemporary television commercial shows a jackass yuppie gleefully firing an employee, then being hit by a bus. He finds himself in the afterlife, where he's presented with a giant cookie. Only when he discovers a refrigerator full of empty milk cartons does he realize that he's not in Heaven.

Which brings us to what is probably Hollywood's best recent portrayal of Hell, in *Jacob's Ladder*. Again, not the greatest movie ever made by a long shot, but it does contain one scene that stopped me dead cold when I first saw it. . . . Tim Robbins, a Brooklyn postal worker/Vietnam vet, finds himself in a hospital after being thrown out of a car. He's trapped to a gurney and wheeled down corridor after endless corridor, the walls smeared with blood, the floors littered with severed body parts, the orderlies all deformed in some way, until he's finally confronted with a cold and evil doctor, who wants to do terrible things to him.

Hell is not about pyrotechnics and expensive makeup and special effects anymore. . . . [or] eternal supernatural torment at the hands of winged monsters or caverns filled with smoke and fire. . . . [or] being punished for not believing the proper things about one religion or another. Not in a world where evil and corruption are givens, where daily life in Red Hook or North Philly or Flint, Michigan—or an afternoon in the welfare office or Bellevue's waiting room—can outdo anything Dante could have imagined. In a world in which everything is a matter of personal choice, Hell is simply a matter of answering the question, "What would you least want to do for the rest of your life?"—then doing it.

THE DOOM GENERATION

A trashy flick featuring ne'er-do-wells on the road and the rampage, and *Time* for 6 November 1995 comments: "And the magic number of everything (the price of a burger meal, the address of a motel, even Amy's cumulative SAT score) is 666, the mark of Satan in *Revelations*."

TODAY'S REBELLION AGAINST GOD

Some people are turning to The Devil because they have confused what God made with what we have made it. They sound like the two houseflies that my favorite modern philosopher (Garrison Keillor) says he found had expressed despair in "a note written in tiny strokes in the dust" on his windowsill. It read in full:

> *go ahead and kill us god what are you waiting for you bashed our friends so whats two more you dont care youre a lousy god anyway you put us here in this beautiful world and just when life starts to get good you kill us so go do it just dont expect us to admire you for it*

Imagine! Houseflies who think very much like—and write very much like—my former freshman students at Brooklyn College! I was deeply moved.

WITCHCRAFT AND FEMINISM

You may catch a whiff of what's in the air politically from titles such as these:

Ecstasies: Deciphering the Witches' Sabbath (1991)
Wives, Widows, Witches and Bitches: Women in Seventeenth-Century Devon Lewd (1994)
Women and Wicked Witches: A Study of the Dynamics of Male Domination (1993)
A Witch's Manifesto (Z. Budapest in *Whole Earth Review*, Spring 1992)
Sexual Tyranny in Wessex: [Thomas] Hardy's Witches and Demons of Folklore (1994)
Lesbian Witches, Socialist Sodomites, and Cultural War (*Humanist* January/February 1993)

POPULAR CULTURE

The late Vito Russo in *The Nation* (31 October 1987, 499):

> In *Teen Wolf*, Michael J. Fox confides to his best friend that he has a confession to make. "You're not gonna tell me you're a faggot, are you?" asks the friend nervously. "No," replies Fox, "I'm a werewolf." His friend is greatly relieved.

WICCA AND FEMINISM

Adler, Margot, *Drawing Down the Moon*
Barstow, Anne, *Witchcraze*
Beth, Rae, *The Wiccan Path*
Beyerl, Paul, *Wiccan Reader*
Brynes, Steve, *Wicca Course*
Budapest, Z., *The Goddess in the Bedroom*
Cunningham, S., *Living Wicca*
Dunwich, Geri, *Wicca Spellbook*
Farrar, Michael, *Wiccan Resources . . .*
Hawkins, Craig, *Goddess Worship,
    Witchcraft . . .*
Lasky, Kathryn, *Beyond the Burning Time*
Matas, Carol, *The Burning Time*
Meddaugh, Susan, *The Witches'
    Supermarket*
O'Gaea, Ashley, *The Family Wicca Book*
Ryall, Rhyann, *West Country Wicca*
Stark, M., *Women's Medicine Ways*
"Tarotstar," *Witch's Spellcraft*
Telesco, Patrick, *A Kitchen Witch's Cookbook*

DEMONOLOGY TODAY

"The only thing wrong with magic is that it doesn't work," wrote Julian Symonds. Maybe not. But people hope against hope. *Hopefully* ranks with *ironically* among America's favorite (if illiterately used) words today. Magic promises to do something, to solve problems. When problems get too great, man turns to the irrational. If we cannot solve the problems of earth, and if the Antichrist is not yet, the confused may hope that perhaps creatures from outer space will come to help us in some *Close Encounter of the Third Kind*, in UFOs. In moments of crisis, magic returns; in moments of despair, the belief in devils and demons returns.

Magic, writes Daniel Lawrence O'Keefe in *Stolen Lightning*, "discards less than science does, or it only seems to discard or forget, only to revive everything in the next occult upsurge." Everything old here, however horrendous, may be new again.

O'Keefe concludes his book with this:

Even when civilization reaches great heights of rationality, science and secular order, something like the Nazi movement can spring up in a few years and threaten to bring the Valkyries back. The magical heritage that man creates out of his daring and his weakness casts a threatening and possibly permanent shadow over all his other creations. As the burden of his maturity grows heavy, there is always a limited but real danger that his unshakeable occult heritage might overwhelm civilized cultures and change their nature.

I conclude mine with this: I happen to believe that the term a journalist used to describe the part of the pseudo-rebellion of the sixties, *The Occult Explosion*, will much more honestly be applicable to the end of this millennium and the beginning of the next one. I have written on superstition, magic, and witchcraft, and also on devils, demons, and the disciples of the Devil, and I sincerely believe these topics are becoming daily more related to civilization and its discontents as we enter an era not unlikely to be characterized by a dizzying rate of change, increased irrationality, and more desperate yearning for supernatural solutions when all else seems to fail us, than has been the case for centuries.

Welcome to the new era of demonizing, disruption, and destruction. I ended another book on another topic (Chinese military history) more than forty years ago with the statement that I declined to predict politics. I wrote that if one guesses right, no one remembers, and if one guesses wrong, no one forgets. I am bolder now. I predict new deals with The Devil, the evil spirit of envy, spoiling, malice, and malefaction on the personal and political levels. I fear also cruel witch hunts in the war between failing authority and restless rebellion, riotous revenge.

SHAM OR SHAMAN?

There must be about half a million lawyers in the US and most of them are ready to sue, so when it come to psychics and their sidekicks, or deciding whether (as the *New York Times* headed in article on 3 March 1996) it's "Shaman or Showman?" most publications sidestep a judgment even as they publicize a guru, psychic, witch doctor, voodoo priestess, and so on.

Typical is the *New York Times* article mentioned that reports *El Indio Amazonico* (Mirachura Chindoy Mutumbajoy, 70, a Colombian), who has offices in New York, Los Angeles, and Bogotá, and is reported to be planning to open one in Miami. He sells *Agua milagrossa* (Miracle Water) in various colors (red=love, yellow=luck, green=health, white=mystical powers, blue=positive energy) and herbal extracts (ruda and "marjorie" to repel evil spirits, "romero" for cleansing and azalea to bring love), and gives advice on matters of life and love. He reads palms. He offers consultations from forty dollars up. Jane H. Lii in the *Times*:

> Whatever the opinion of him, he is clearly a presence in communities with large Hispanic populations like Jackson Heights [Queens, New York], where financial hardships and language barriers keep many immigrants away from social workers, doctors and psychiatrists.

Of course the newspaper cannot be faulted for quoting observers such as Orlando Torbón, himself from Colombia:

> I don't believe in what he is doing. . . . When a person starts to talk about the special powers from God, he is stealing the money from the people. He is keeping poor people dependent on him. I hope the Government will control the situation and stop people like him from stealing the money from the community.

But the government, cutting back on medical and psychiatric services, is not likely to put out of business the gypsy "readers," the African-American "gifted" spiritual advisers, the Hispanic witch doctors, the Indian gurus, the Tarot interpreters, and the removers of hexes, bad luck, and the threats of devils, demons, disease, and distress.

WITCHCRAFT INFLICTING THE BODY OF THE VICTIM

Whether it involves human victims or their cattle, etc., in every culture there are beliefs that in one way or another dangerous, even fatal, things can be introduced by witchcraft into bodies, even at a distance. So, in addition to poisoning (which the original language condemning witchcraft in the Bible suggests was the essential element of witchcraft at least in the eyes of the ancient Jews to whom the revelation was given), the witch has available the means to stick pins in dolls and hurt the people whom the dolls represent, and to shoot magical arrows, flints, or other objects into people and cattle, to wound and even to kill. It is incredible that all over the world people, varying only in minute details, hold these beliefs. Claude Lévi-Strauss has asserted that there is an "astounding similarity between myths collected in widely different regions;" this one of is global.

Of course, this belief is more in evidence in some times and places than in others. I have sought in vain, for instance, for evidence of this in Canada. There are psychics, astrologers, a Wiccan Church of Canada, a neo-pagan *Trumpeter* newsletter in British Columbia, etc., but Shelley Rabinovitch's studies of witchcraft in Canada remain unpublished, French and Ukrainian superstition largely unresearched, etc. I investigated this one belief in various sources both European-Canadian and among the Inuit and First National cultures. My guess was that evidence of witchcraft beliefs, this one especially, would be common in Canada. It isn't. Nor are Canadians, apparently, as concerned with Satanism these days as are their neighbors to the south whose fear of Satanic child abuse is often seen. Perhaps the Canadian climate makes dancing naked, "sky clothed and under Canadian skies," in covens of witches and Satanists ill advised for a great part of the year. . . .

Still, there are witchcraft beliefs and practices to be found in Canada. And in Luxembourg, Guam, and other places that do not get a lot of international attention for sensational goings-on. Witchcraft is everywhere.

INSTANT ANSWERS TO LIFE'S QUESTIONS

Old-fashioned? Get with it. Among "Top 20 CD-Roms for 1995" (according to *ComputerLife*) is *The Alchemist*, which reads your cards according to the rather silly and derivative systems of Amy Zerner and Monte Farber but with spectacular graphics on your little PC. Next: a flash-frozen bat's blood and 600 Channels! Withcraft on Internet!.

The Chinese, even those in America, give gifts of money in "lucky" red and gold envelopes. They also use red firecrackers to scare off evil spirits.

THE AMAZING RANDI

James Randi has devoted decades to exposing the frauds of those with so-called paranormal powers. He offers a $10,000 prize to anyone who can demonstrate to him a convincing ESP, spoon-bending, or similar power. No one has ever collected. Nor have faith healers (such as the one who was aided by a wife broadcasting details about members of the audience, collected from prayer cards filled out, to the "minister" who was wearing a in-car, tiny receiver) he has exposed been very successful in suits against him for ruining their lucrative businesses. His campaign is posited on the simple premise that "nonsense is dangerous," but he admits that astrology and other deceptions are so attractive to fools that they will never be effectively eradicated.

MAGIC AT THE SUPERMARKET

Forget blood of newborn babe and eye of newt. Everything you need for magic, says the Supermarket Sorceress (on what authority? she works in a New York "magic" shop), is right there in Aisle 1 or 2.

Want to keep your loverman faithful? Give him a glass of orange juice for breakfast and put coriander seeds in his pocket as he goes off to work. (This assumes that your man has a job.) As soon as he is out of the house— this assumes you don't go out to work, too—light a match on the heel of your shoe, intone "Be true!" and blow it out.

Spinach, lettuce, parsley, and all other green vegetables naturally connect with what a tot I know used to call the "lorne green," dollar bills. Leeks give strength because they contain so much iron (for your blood and your aura). (Does balsamic vinegar on arugula do anything enchanting?) Is there, in fact, a lot of iron in leeks or would you be better off with chopped liver? *Who says*? *How does that work*? These are the questions you need to ask, if you want to be carping. Don't expect any convincing answers; we are dealing here with faith, belief in things unseen, the inexplicable, the occult, the mysterious, magic cheap. Prayer heals. So can vegetables.

Still, almost anything works if you believe in it. Sure, carrying bananas on the plane will overcome your fear of flying—if you believe that. A pineapple on your coffee table (I always say) will give you non-fail success in the stock market if you properly time all highs and lows and make trades with a cheap broker.

Forget other routes to success. Just start carrying *my* book on the subway (make sure passersby can see the complete title) and smile cheerfully, or read it with seven appreciative nods per page in coffeeshops. This will, if you believe strongly enough, banish negativity, make your personality more attractive, improve your outlook and your love life, and perhaps clear up your complexion. I guarantee it. Try it. It will very likely make you happier. It will make me happier. It will bring happiness to you if you rearrange copies of my book in the bookshop for greater prominence in display and also if you hand your copy for examination (with the right hand, the positive one, the conscious-mind one) to friends, but never lend your copy to them. Say the formula, "You have to buy your own copy of this great book. Read the others, too." Do this three times a day. I'll be very happy with that.

As you wait in line at the supermarket checkout counter, take a glimpse at a horoscope conveniently provided in the periodicals there displayed. For best results—always read a horoscope *other* than the one assigned to your sign of the Zodiac, *any* other. This introduces a charming element of chance! Really! Trust me.

FIFTEEN REFERENCE BOOKS; MOSTLY STILL IN PRINT

Baskin, Wade, *The Sorcerer's Handbook*
Bennett, David, *A Treasury of Witches and Witchcraft*
Bird, Malcolm, *The Witch's Handbook*
Buczyski, E., *Witchcraft Fact Book*
Ennemoser, J., *The History of Magic*
Evans, Arthur, *Witchcraft*
Fitch, E., *Magical Rites from the Crystal Well*
Fox, S., *Circle Guide to Wicca and Pagan Resources*
Guiley, Rosemary, *Encyclopedia of Witchcraft*
Gardner, G.B., *The Meaning of Witchcraft*
Kuykendall, R. E., *Liturgies of the Earth*
Leek, Sybil, *The Complete Art of Witchcraft*
Levack, Brian, *The Literature of Witchcraft*
Michelet, Jules, *The History of Magic*
Plaskow, Judith & Carol P. Christ, *Weaving the Visions*
Robbins, Rossel Hope, *Encyclopedia of Witchcraft*
Time/Life Books, *Witches and Witchcraft*
Valiente, D., *An ABC of Witchcraft*
Wedeck, Henry, *A Treasury of Witchcraft*

TWO DOZEN ASSORTED BOOKS ON
HISTORICAL WITCHCRAFT

Anglo, Sydney, *The Damned Art*

Bellairs, John, *The Vengeance of the Witches*

Brown, Ruth, *Destroying the Works of Witchcraft*

Buckland, Ray, *Ray Buckland's Magic Cauldron*

Campbell, John, *Witchcraft and Second Sight*

Magicians invented all sorts of weird alphabets, including those attributed to the magi and to angels. This item is from "Abbé Julio" (Julien Houssay)'s *Le Livre secret des grands exorcismes et bénédictions priéres antiques, formules occultes, recettes spéciales . . . .* a rare book of 1908 reprinted in a limited edition in 1950 for those ready to *"faire le BIEN et de combattre le MAL sous toutes ses formes."*

Ewen, Cecil H., *Witchcraft and Demonianism*

Farrar, Janet, *The Witches' God*

Frangipane, F., *Exposing Witchcraft*

Gawr, Rhuddlw, *Celtic Rites and Rituals*

Guinzberg, Carlo, *Ecstacies*

Harrison, Michael, *The Roots of Witchcraft*

Hill, Frances, *A Delusion of Satan*

Hoffer, Peter, *The Devil's Disciples*

Kelly, A.A., *Crafting the Art of Magic*

King, Francis, *Witchcraft and Demonology*

Klaits, Joseph, *Servants of Satan*

Lehmann, Arthur, *Magic, Witchcraft, and Religion*

Leland, Charles, *Aradia: The Gospel of the Witches*

Levack, Brian, *Possession and Exorcism*

Luhrmann, T.M., *Persuasions of the Witch's Craft*

Melton, J. G., *Magic, Witchcraft, and Paganism in America*

Murray, Margaret, *The God of the Witches*

Riva, Anna, *Modern Witchcraft Spellbook*

Roper, L., *Oedipus and the Devil*

Rosen, Barbara, *Witchcraft in England*

Sargeant, Philip, *Witches and Warlocks*

Scott, G. M. *Cult and Countercult*

Stewart, Ross, *Witches*

Telesco, Patrick, *A Witch's Brew*

SAMPLE DISSERTATIONS

Pastron, Allen Gerald, *Aspects of Witchcraft and Shamanism in a Tarahumara Indian Community of Northern Mexico* (1978)
Taylor, John C., *A Critical History of Miltonic Satanism* (1966)
Wolf, Jack C., *Hart Crane's Harp of Evil: A Study of Satanism in The Bridge* (1972)

GAIA

After the Greek goddess of the earth modern pantheists have created a religion of Gaia (or Gaea). J. E. Lovelock's "Gaia Hypothesis" stresses the interconnectedness of all creation and neatly pulls together such New Age movements as feminist politics, ecological concerns, rebellious radicalism in matters sexual and social, Greenpeace, The Goddess, and more. Forget traditional monotheism and its patriarchal god. Forget Jungian archetypes—fuzzy Powers are more fun. We are pagan, postmodern, postpatriarchal, and with raised and marshalled confidence we can work wonders—say the enthusiastic, bonded adherents of this rainbow, ecoreligious movement— in ourselves, in our biosphere, in our universe. This with the bravado of the young who are ready to say, because they wear the poltically-correct or simply most fashionable sneakers—"This is my planet!" Some references to this growing movement in which social justice, solipcism, redefining sex, and spiritual seeking are strikingly combined are:

Farrar, J. & S., *The Witch's Goddess*
Griffin, D. R., ed., *Spirituality and Society* (1988)
Lovelock, J. E., *Gaia: A New Look at Life on Earth*
Plant, J., ed., *Healing the Wounds: The Promise of Ecofeminism* (1987)
Sheldrake, S., *The Rebirth of Nature: The Greening of Science and God* (1990)

MORE BOOKS ON WITCHCRAFT TODAY

Amber, K., *True Magick . . .*
Anand, Margot, *The Art of Sexual Magic*
Clifton, Charles, *Witchcraft Today*
Devine, Mary, *Magic from Mexico*
Farber, M. D., *Modern Witchcraft and Psychology*
Kemp, Anthony, *Witchcraft and Paganism Today*
Martello, Leo, *Witchcraft : The Old Religion*

Needleman, Jacob, *The New Religions*
Pepper, Elizabeth, *The Witches' Almanac*
Riva, Anna, *Spellcraft, Hexcraft, and Witchcraft*
Scarboro, A., *Living Witchcraft*
Watson, C. W., *Understanding Witchcraft*

WITCHCRAFT AT PREHISTORIC SITES

This fascinating subject is addressed in books such as *The Druids* (Peter Beresford Ellis), articles in journals such as *Antiquity* (L. V. Grinsell), and articles in books (such as the 1973 *Festschrift* for Katharine M. Briggs, *The Witch Figure*). More in art? See Luther Link, *The Devil* (1996).

INDIGENOUS WITCHCRAFT OF THE AMERICAS

Kerr, Howard & Charles L. Crow (eds.), *The Occult in America . . .*
Langdon, E. & G. Baer (eds.), *Portals of Power: Shamanism in South America*
Madsen, William, *A Guide to Mexican Witchcraft*
Merkur, Daniel, *Witchcraft and Sorcery of the American Native Peoples*
Raven - Wolf, Silver, *Hex Craft: Dutch Country Pow-Wow Magic*
Trigger, Bruce G. in *Indians, Animals, and the Fur Trade* (ed. S. Krech)
Walker, Edward E. & David Carasco (eds.), *Witchcraft and Sorcery of the American Native Peoples*
Weigle, Marta (ed.), *Two Guadalupes: Hispanic Legends and Magic Tales from Northern New Mexico*

SANTERÍA

This Afro-Latin religion has been the object of numerous scholarly and journalistic articles, from the United States to Hungary (Maria Dornback in *Acta Ethnographica Academiæ Scientiarum Hungaricæ* 26, 1977, in English and elsewhere in Hungarian), and is discussed in the book: Migene Gonzalez-Wippler, *Santería: African Magic in Latin America* (1973).

THE NEW SCHOLARSHIP

As scholarship gives up the hard old tasks of rooting among dusty manuscripts and books, coping with foreign and antique languages and cultures, and knowing what has led up to the present instead of simply watching the world at work around us, subjects such as magic and witchcraft have appealed not only to the theologians (who must find them embarrassing), but to the new advocates of cultural, cross-cultural, and popular culture studies. In consequence, there has been a greater admixture of modern opinion than historical fact in judgments and a skewing of reality to fit both into convenient pigeonholes created by Marxists and feminists and other politically motivated scholars. We see a lot about power, the body, gender, and minorities. All to the good. These are useful approaches. Some modern scholarship does go into areas that have been neglected and talks about people who until recently were almost thought to have no history. But how do we avoid the glib, the ax-grinding, and the shallowness that many modern scholars exhibit?

Magic and witchcraft are subjects that have been too long in the hands of self-serving theologians, for instance. It will be just as bad if they now fall into the hands of those for whom texts are only pretexts for social engineering and the advancement of strident partisans of self-proclaimed political, sexual, and other "communities."

It will also be unfortunate if Anne Rice is studied to the exclusion of, not in tandem with, Mrs. Radcliffe, or if "the gothic spaces" in Toni Morrison's *Beloved* or Stephen King's highly popular novels or the less-known ones of Angela Carter and Ramsay Campbell are featured without the context of the Great Tradition.

It is all very well to have an interest in *I Was a Teenage Werewolf*, *Salem's Lot*, and *The Witches of Eastwick*, but it ought not to be indulged to the total exclusion of that which is neither postmodern nor American.

To those who claim that traditional scholarship is elitist and undemocratic, I would like to suggest that there be an interest in the majority of people on record. And that majority is *dead*. Moreover, time has a way of putting things in perspective. Too instant and exclusive a fascination with the pop products of Now distorts what the historical records tell us of the past at certain times, and about human nature of those and all times, our own included. May post-postmodernism not be too narrow!

GUIDE TO RESEARCH IN DEMONOLOGY AND WITCHCRAFT

Demon researchers (in both senses of the term) can check the subject catalogues of great libraries (Library of Congress, British Library, New York Public Library, etc.) and large collections of rare books, the special collections on witchcraft (Van Pelt Library of the University of Pennsylvania, etc.) and folklore, the motif indexes of folklore (Anti Aarne, Stith

Thompson, Gerald Bordman, etc.) for tales involving magic and counter-magic, and bibliographies of individual aspects of the supernatural and superstition, as well as of folklore and religion in general. Also, of course, see the bibliographies in encyclopedias of witchcraft and the occult. The standard bibliography of folklore is *International Folklore and Folklife Bibliography* (biennial since 1939), following up on the fourteen volumes of *Volkskundliche Bibliographie* (which covered publications 1917–1938). The subjects can take you into fields as far apart as anthropology and theology; demonology and superstition, in general, are part of every culture ever known. For connections with literature there are many references, most important of which is the *MLA International Bibliography* (annually from the Modern Language Association, on-line for recent decades).

I have cited many of my sources right in the text and provided mini-bibliographies sufficient for those who want more information to get started. I say in the preface to one my earlier works, *The Complete Book of Magic and Witchcraft*, that such research takes one "to some unattractive places, among 'wizards that peep and mutter,' among the petty and the potty, the diabolical and the desperate, the sacrilegious and the fanatical."

Nonetheless, the study of the disciples of The Devil, of the rejected lover of God Himself, and of the wonderful story of how The Goddess became the Abomination of the Jews and witches were persecuted and feared and the world of nature, the very body of The Goddess became a battleground of good and evil under the aegis of a fierce male deity—what could be more interesting?

WITCHCRAFT IN LITERATURE

There are a number of articles in learned journals and anthologies about British and American witchcraft in literature, folklore, and drama. A doctoral dissertation by Gerilyn G. Tandberg, *A Comparison-Contrast of Witchcraft and Sorcery in Selected English and American Plays . . .* (1975) is useful. Witchcraft studies in general 1959–1971 are covered in Donald Nugent's bibliographical survey in the *Journal of Popular Culture* 5 (1971). Megan Lynn Isaac's dissertation (1995) on *Stages of Witchcraft* documents and examines witchcraft beliefs exhibited in early modern English drama. Joseph H. Marshburn uses ephemera (broadsides, ballads, and pamphlets), as well as plays, to document *Murder and Witchcraft in England, 1550–1640* (1971) and in her UCLA doctoral dissertation (*Creating the "Known True Story,"* 1993), Kristin Jeanne Leuchner also uses sixteenth- and seventeenth-century pamphlets and plays.

Women—shown here suffering fire as witches while alive and (in the underworld shown through the arch at the right) dead—in a German woodcut of 1555 are centuries later still feared for their powers. As far back as Anglo-Saxon England, the English tradition has feared "the woman who has sexual relations with The Devil" and maybe just the female sex itself.

You may disagree with my critical judgment, but, for my money, the occult is a major factor in the poets whom I consider to be the very best of all in the English language in the modern period: William Butler Yeats among British (or Irish?) poets, and Ezra Pound among American (or English?) poets. It is also inextricably bound up with the search for identity and for power, the subjugation of women and the demonization of radical thinkers or simply unusual people, and other central, crucial concerns of all modern literature and life. Witchcraft testifies to some of the deepest spiritual longings of humankind from time immemorial and what is wrong with individuals and society as a whole here and now. Whatever you think of its answers, it grapples with the most important of questions.

The book you hold is my modest contribution to the literature or scholarship about a significant aspect of the occult: witchcraft. It hopes to bring some of the fascination with deep subjects to a popular readership. Go, little book.

Index